ASIA IN JAPAN'S EMBRACE

CAMBRIDGE ASIA-PACIFIC STUDIES

Cambridge Asia-Pacific Studies aims to provide a focus and forum for scholarly work on the Asia-Pacific region as a whole, and its component sub-regions, namely Northeast Asia, Southeast Asia and the Pacific Islands.

Editor: John Ravenhill

R. Gerard Ward and Elizabeth Kingdon (eds)   *Land, Custom and Practice in the South Pacific*

Stephanie Lawson   *Tradition Versus Democracy in the South Pacific*

ASIA IN JAPAN'S EMBRACE

Building a Regional Production Alliance

WALTER HATCH
and
KOZO YAMAMURA
Henry M. Jackson School of International Studies
University of Washington

PUBLISHED BY THE PRESS SYNDICATE OF THE UNIVERSITY OF CAMBRIDGE
The Pitt Building, Trumpington Street, Cambridge CB2 1RP, United Kingdom

CAMBRIDGE UNIVERSITY PRESS
The Edinburgh Building, Cambridge CB2 2RU, United Kingdom
40 West 20th Street, New York, NY 10011–4211, USA
10 Stamford Road, Oakleigh, Melbourne 3166, Australia

First published 1996
Reprinted 1997

Printed in Hong Kong by Colorcraft

Typeset in Baskerville 10/12 pt

National Library of Australia Cataloguing in Publication data

Hatch, Walter, 1954– .
Asia in Japan's embrace: building a regional
production alliance.
Bibliography.
Includes index.
1. Japan – Foreign economic relations – Asia. 2. Asia –
Foreign economic relations – Japan. 3. Japan – Economic
conditions – 1945– . 4. Asia – Economic conditions – 1945– .
5. Japan – Economic policy – 1945– . I. Yamamura, Kōzō.
II. Title. (Series: Cambridge Asia-Pacific studies).
337.5205

Library of Congress Cataloguing in Publication data

Hatch, Walter.
Asia in Japan's embrace: building a regional production
alliance/Walter Hatch and Kōzō Yamamura.
p.   cm. – (Cambridge Asia-Pacific Studies).
Includes bibliographical references and index.
1. Japan – Foreign economic relations – Asia. 2. Asia – Foreign
economic relations – Japan. 3. Strategic alliances (Business) –
Japan. 4. Strategic alliances (Business) – Asia. 5. Trading blocs –
Asia. I. Yamamura, Kōzō. II. Title. III. Series.
HF1602.15.A74H38 1996
37.5052–dc20   96–282

A catalogue record for this book is available from the British Library

ISBN 0 521 56176 0 Hardback
ISBN 0 521 56515 4 Paperback

Contents

List of Tables		vi
List of Figures		vii
Preface		viii

Part One: Co-Prosperity Again

1	Crossing Borders: The Japanese Difference	3
2	Flying Geese: An Unequal Alliance in Asia	20

Part Two: The Embracer and the Embraced

3	Cooperation between Unequals	43
4	The Political Economy of Japan	62
5	The Political Economy of Asia	77
6	Holding Technology	97

Part Three: A Japanese Alliance in Asia

7	The Visible Handshake	115
8	Vertical Veins of Humanity	130
9	The Labor Network	146
10	The Supply Network	158

Part Four: A Powerful Embrace

11	The Ties that Bind	175
12	Loosening the Knot	192

Notes	205
Select Bibliography	261
Index	275

Tables

1.1 Japan's Technology Exports to Asia   8
1.2 Japan's Manufacturing Technology Exports to Asia   8
5.1 Asia's Macro-indicators   79
5.2 Ethnic Chinese in ASEAN-4   82
6.1 Joining Forces: Japan's Major Semiconductor Partnerships
    in Asia   105
7.1 Regional Distribution of Japanese ODA   128
8.1 Asian Countries to which Japan is Leading Donor (1992)   131
10.1 Source of Procurements by Japanese Manufacturers
     Overseas (1992)   159
11.1 Destination of Japan's Manufactured Exports   179
11.2 Destination of Asia's Manufactured Exports   181
11.3 Intrafirm Trade by Japanese Firms in Asia as a Percentage
     of Their Total Trade within Asia   186

Figures

1.1 Japanese and US FDI in Asia   5
1.2 Japanese Manufacturing FDI in Asia   7
1.3 Share of Total FDI by Japanese SMEs Going to Asia   7
2.1 Evolution of Japanese Networks in Asia   24
2.2 Toyota Motor Network   26
2.3 Mitsubishi Motors Network   34
5.1 Scientists and Technicians Working in R&D   84
7.1 The "Asian Brain" Managing Economic Cooperation   120
9.1 Japanese Personnel in Manufacturing Affiliates in Asia   156
11.1 Asia's Trade Balance with the United States, European
     Community, and Japan   175

Preface

At the turn of the last century, the United States was planted firmly in the Asia-Pacific region. It had opened trade relations with China and Japan, explored a number of islands, and even laid claim to its own archipelago, the Philippines. Puffed up with patriotic pride, expansionists such as Chauncey Depew crowed that the Pacific Ocean had become an "American lake" dominated by US merchant vessels and warships.[1] Asia's fate, they believed, was America's.

As a new century unfolds, US aircraft carriers laden with sailors and fighter jets steam in and out of Tokyo Bay, serving as floating symbols of America's now unrivaled military clout in a post-Cold War world. US container ships cruise these waters as well. But they are vastly outnumbered by Japanese vessels carrying automobile parts, machine tools, and myriad electric and electronic products manufactured by Japanese-affiliated firms all over the region. We are exaggerating only a little in saying that, in terms of commerce, the "American lake" has all but dried up; a "Japanese lake" is rising in its place.

The ebb and flow of economic power in Asia, the growth center of the world economy, is critically important to everyone inside and outside this region. While the industrialized economies of the world limp along, hoping for a growth rate of 3 percent a year, the industrializing economies of Asia are expanding at phenomenal rates of up to 13 percent. Developing Asia, which does not include Japan, generated only 9 percent of the world's output in 1990, but is generating a larger share every year and could, according to one estimate, contribute more than 50 percent of global production by the middle of the next century, the so-called "Pacific Century."[2]

Sadly, much of the discussion about what is transpiring in this corner of the world revolves around a nonissue, namely, whether Japan is building a regional trading bloc, a commercially based, peacetime version of the Greater East Asia Co-Prosperity Sphere it established during World War II. Many Western journalists believe it is. For example, Paul Maidment, a reporter for *The Economist*, says Japan has developed a new and little-noticed policy to use public and private resources to "sustain a stable and capitalist region that can provide raw materials, factories and, increasingly, markets for its industries."[3]

Neoclassical economists disagree, saying Japan is not building an exclusive or trade-diverting yen bloc in Asia. For example, Jeffrey Frankel uses a gravity model (which, in the world of statistics, is a form of regression analysis) to show that rising levels of intraregional trade in Asia are "correlated" with the geographical proximity and economic size of trading partners in the region, not any policy-induced bias or preference.[4] And Gary Saxonhouse, using a more traditional model of trade based on comparative advantage, finds "little evidence of a regional bias in Japan's relations with the rest of East Asia that goes beyond the existing pattern of East Asian resource endowments."[5] Frankel and Saxonhouse are, of course, correct – as far as they go.[6] An inward-looking yen bloc is not in the offing. Most countries in Asia, including Japan, remain highly dependent on export markets in the West.

So if Japan is not building an exclusive trading zone, then exactly what *is* it doing in Asia? That is the central question addressed in this book.

Some Western and Japanese economists argue that Japanese foreign direct investment (FDI) is merely a smart, or "rational," entrepreneurial response to changing cost conditions in Japan. Urata Shujiro, for example, writes that Japanese FDI "appears to be more or less consistent with the pattern of comparative advantage." Being "rational," direct investment from Japan, like that from other nations, has "contributed to the economic development of host countries not only by promoting capital formation, production and employment, but also by upgrading technological capability through technology transfer."[7] It is all part of a chain of unintended benevolence in which Japanese production begets Japanese economic growth, which begets overseas production in Asia, which begets technology transfer, which begets local economic growth.

Some Asian (but non-Japanese) economists offer a competing argument that is guided more by empirical research and less by neoclassical suppositions, but that remains theoretically confused. According to this view, Japanese multinational corporations (MNCs) expanding into Asia behave quite differently from Western MNCs. They are, for example, far more reluctant to transfer technology. Advocates of this view are, unfortunately, hard pressed to explain why. Although she concedes that Japanese MNCs are "stingier" than their Western counterparts, Pasuk Phongpaichit, a Thai economist, cautiously attributes this to the fact that they have been in Asia for a relatively short period of time, and thus have not yet faced the same protracted pressure to "localize" operations that Western firms have faced. "Generosity is not a function of race," she told us.[8] Mingsarn Santikarn Kaosa-ard, another Thai economist, appears stumped by the apparent difference. "There is no good theoretical explanation why nationality ought to explain the effectiveness of transmitting technology," she says. "What reason is there to believe that Japanese TNCs [transnational corporations] would be more or less generous in transferring technologies than other nations' firms?"[9]

The reason they behave differently, of course, is that Japanese firms are in fact different. They are shaped not only by market forces, but – like all firms – also by the distinctive set of institutions, policies, and norms that have evolved over the history of their society. For instance, in Japan, there is an unusual amount of cooperation between firms (especially those belonging to the same *keiretsu*, or enterprise group), between industry and government, and between labor and management. This cooperation allows firms to capture maximum gains from technological innovation and make the most efficient use of resources over time. Without a clear understanding of Japan's political economy and, in particular, Japanese-style cooperation, we cannot begin to comprehend the actual impact of Japan's deepening economic presence in Asia. This is because Japanese MNCs are trying to replicate their domestic system of networking in the region as a whole.

In this book, we argue that Japanese capital and technology are stitching together the disparate economies of Asia, integrating them into a multilevel production alliance. Trade data reveal Japan's increasing presence in the region. In 1970, the nation's total trade with the rest of Asia was worth only about half its trade with the United States. By 1990, however, Japan was trading more with Asia than with America.[10] High-technology products, especially machinery components, have come to occupy an increasingly important share of that intraregional trade.

This production alliance, as we suggested earlier, is not an exclusive trading bloc. It is in fact made up of literally thousands of vertically structured and quasi-integrated networks built across Asia by Japanese high-technology manufacturers hoping to maintain and even bolster their international competitiveness. These networks, promoted and nurtured by the Japanese government, are based on a division of labor; the parent firm in Japan generally supplies the most technology-intensive components used in production, while affiliates in Asia contribute less sophisticated parts. Risks are contained. Costs are minimized.

Japanese elites in government and business are using this alliance to buy time. After building and maintaining a political economy based on the interests of export-oriented, high-technology producers, not on the interests of consumers, they now face demands at home and abroad for fundamental change. They hope to prolong the life of this embattled system by regionalizing it, by building a broader foundation for economic revitalization. But what about the other economies of Asia? Like subcontractors in a vertical *keiretsu*, they enjoy the benefits of quasi-integration, including access to capital and technology. To varying extents, all Asian economies have used this Japanese production alliance to expand their manufacturing exports. On the other hand, they have become embraced by, or dependent on, Japanese capital and technology. It is difficult to imagine how these countries would maintain such high rates of economic growth without Japan's support.

We do not suggest here that a nefarious plot is afoot. Japanese high-technology industry is building a production alliance in Asia with the help of its government because it views such a strategy as efficiency-enhancing, not because it wants to beggar the other regions of the world. The effect, however, may end up being the same. Unless US and European MNCs establish themselves more firmly in Asia, they may be gradually squeezed out by the increasingly tight and exclusive nature of this highly competitive Japanese production alliance.

This is our argument, which is spelled out much more clearly and comprehensively in the first two chapters. Chapter three is a theoretical discussion of the economic concept of cooperation that makes two central points: cooperation is far more efficiency-enhancing than most neoclassical scholars have allowed, and cooperation is, by definition, exclusionary. In chapters four and five, we examine the political economies first of Japan and then of the rest of Asia in light of this economic concept of cooperation. We conclude that Japan, a nation of networks, is organized in such a way as to rapidly adopt new technology, while the rest of Asia is – to varying degrees – less equipped to do so. Chapter six shows how Japanese MNCs use their networks to control the pace of technology transfer to the rest of Asia.

Chapters seven through ten examine different manifestations of networking in the region: cooperation between Japanese government and business officials in the development and implementation of Japan's foreign economic policy toward Asia; cooperation between Japanese elites and Asian elites in the development of a Japanese production alliance; cooperation between management and labor in Japan's manufacturing facilities in the region; and, finally, cooperation between

Japanese assemblers in Asia and their parts suppliers and distributors. Chapter eleven considers the impact of this emerging Japanese production alliance on regional and global trade. Chapter twelve, the conclusion, has two goals. One is to stress the need for a much better understanding of why Japanese firms behave differently, both at home and abroad, from the firms of other industrial nations. The other is to recommend policy initiatives that the United States, Europe, and Asia might wish to take to avoid regionalizing the economic conflict that has been simmering for so long between Japan and the West.

Although most terms used in this book are defined in the text, a few require immediate clarification. For example, when we refer to "Asia" we generally are referring to the sum of China, South Korea, Taiwan, Hong Kong, Singapore, Thailand, Malaysia, Indonesia, and the Philippines. Occasionally, when noted, we throw Vietnam into the mix. Using technological capacity as our yardstick, we frequently divide the larger Asian region into sub-regions: the "NICs" (the newly industrializing countries) or the "Four Dragons," which are South Korea (sometimes referred to simply as "Korea" in this book), Taiwan, Hong Kong, and Singapore;[11] and the ASEAN-4 (core members of the Association of Southeast Asian Nations), or the "Four Little Dragons," which are Thailand, Malaysia, Indonesia, and the Philippines.[12] On the basis of its technological level, China should be lumped together with the ASEAN-4.

We carefully define the term *keiretsu* (or enterprise group) in chapter four. But because it is such a central concept in this book, and because we somewhat casually invoke it in chapters one through three, we offer a working definition here. While the Japanese word, translated directly into English, means "lineage," it actually refers to the close-knit networks that link many firms in Japan. In most Western minds, the postwar *keiretsu* are vaguely associated with the prewar *zaibatsu*, the large financial cliques such as Mitsubishi, Mitsui, and Sumitomo. Indeed, Japan today has six horizontal or "financial" *keiretsu* that share the same main bank and engage in joint ventures of many types (production, sales, resource exploration, etc.). In addition, however, it has many vertical or industrial *keiretsu*, linking parts suppliers with large assemblers, as well as many distribution *keiretsu*, linking distribution outlets with a major manufacturer. Although they are legally independent, the members of a *keiretsu*, both horizontal and vertical, are bound together over time by a number of very real commitments. These may include cross-shareholding, interlocking directorates, and intragroup trade, as well as capital, technology, and personnel transfers.[13]

Two other terms warrant attention here. "Dynamic technological efficiency" (DTE) is used to describe a firm's ability to adopt successively more sophisticated technology, thus reducing the cost of production and increasing the firm's competitiveness both in domestic and international markets. As we argue in chapter four, Japanese firms have enjoyed unrivaled success in achieving this kind of efficiency.

The other term, "developmentalism," is closely related. It refers to a set of policies and practices that promote cooperation between government and business, between otherwise unrelated firms, and between management and labor. Developmentalism, which we discuss in chapter three, is an effective vehicle for achieving DTE.

This book is an unusual hybrid. Scholars may find it excessively relaxed, even a little too breezy, in places. They may ask: Why do you rely so heavily on interviews, on anecdotal evidence? Where are the rigorous, econometric studies to support your conclusions? On the other hand, lay readers may find the book excessively ponderous or overly analytical in spots. They may wonder what all this theory really contributes.

Our approach, while unconventional, is easily defended on both fronts. First, we believe the anecdotal evidence presented here allows us to paint a richer picture of what is happening in the real world, and why. To ignore or downgrade such evidence is to go on believing in an imaginary world, a world free of people and thus complexity. Those who fail to see or choose not to see the utility and significance of anecdotal evidence remind us of the targets of an old Japanese proverb: *Mekura hebi ni ojizu* – blind men do not fear snakes.

In conducting their econometric studies, for example, neoclassical economists typically must make many assumptions, some of which strain our imagination (such as: all markets are perfectly competitive; all economies use the same technology). That is, they must concoct a world free of slithering snakes, free of all the messy realities that anecdotes tell us exist. This, of course, does not mean that econometric studies have no value. In many instances, they can be very useful as tools for summarizing quantitative findings (see chapter six), provided their assumptions are made explicit and the results are used in specific, limited ways. All this means is that such studies cannot be relied on as the foundation for analyzing problems in human society.

Second, the theoretical framework constructed here allows us to accommodate, or make sense of, all the bits of reality we encountered during our research. We do, as we must, make some assumptions. But we hope readers will find that our assumptions are realistic, thus helpful in presenting an analysis that attempts to describe a world of people and snakes.

The approach taken in this book suits its authors nicely. One of us is a reformed economist, increasingly dissatisfied with the narrow field of vision afforded by neoclassical theory; the other is a former journalist who has begun to question the utility of ungrounded analysis and meandering musings. Out of both faith and necessity, then, we have followed an interdisciplinary approach that is guided by theory but not controlled by a mechanical model. We give equal weight to the statistics of disinterested scholars, the experiences of affected individuals, and our own observations. In most cases, this is the same lively, bubbly stew of human "evidence" from which any good social scientist must draw. We hope both scholars and lay people will find some merit in this approach.

Names of authors are presented as they appear in the publication cited. In the case of an interviewee, we follow the standard practice used in that person's country. Thus, the family name of the Japanese, Chinese, and Koreans we quote will in most cases appear first. In the case of Thai, Indonesian, Malay, and Filipino interviewees, the given name comes first.

In the course of writing this book, we incurred many debts. One of us, for example, spent five nights at the Bangkok area home of the Kasem Choangulia family, which not only graciously shared its space and time, but also helped set up interviews and give directions in Thai to local taxi and *tuk-tuk* drivers. Thank you! Others in Thailand who guided us were Prasert Chittiwatanapong of Thammasat University, and Chaiwat Khamchoo of Chulalongkorn University. In Kuala Lumpur, public affairs analyst Noraini Abdullah not only helped arrange interviews, but offered insights on Malaysian politics as well. In Singapore, the staff at the Institute of Southeast Asian Studies was exceedingly helpful. In Korea, we relied on the generous assistance of Lee Keum-hyun, a freelance journalist, as well as Lee Jung Bok of Seoul National University and Kim Yong Kyu of Korea University's Asiatic Research Center. Officials of the Japan External Trade Organization (JETRO) all over the Asia-Pacific region, but especially Kuzumi Masayuki in Bangkok, provided useful data.

Literally dozens of people in Japan came to our aid, but perhaps none so much as Kitamura Kayoko of the Institute of Developing Economies (Ajiken), Iyori Hiroshi and Takeishi Akira of the Mitsubishi Economic Research Institute, Tanaka Tatsuo of the Center for Global Communications at International University, Matsunaga Kengo of the *Mainichi shinbun*, Ishii Toru of the *Asahi shinbun*, and Inoguchi Takashi of the University of Tokyo. We are deeply grateful to the many people who gave valuable time being interviewed for this book. Since we did not offer anonymity, this was not always easy – especially for some company officials. Nonetheless, a few worked overtime on our behalf, contacting colleagues at overseas affiliates to encourage them to meet with us. For doing so, we wish to extend our appreciation to Nishina Akira of Mitsubishi Electric, Ozaki Tetsuo of Nissan, Miyagi Kenichi of Fujitsu, Ono Shuichi of Marubeni, Nagano Akira of Matsushita, and Koiso Shigeru of Sony.

Back in Seattle, friend and colleague Dan Lev of the University of Washington provided a useful critique of our discussion of the political economy of Asia. Martha L. Walsh of the Japan Studies Program, University of Washington, rendered invaluable administrative and editorial assistance. We cannot thank her enough for her exceptional efficiency and civility in everything she did for us. Dan Slater helped us by culling statistics from many sources. We benefited enormously from the encouragement, guidance, valuable comments, and detailed criticism provided by John Ravenhill, editor of the Cambridge Asia-Pacific Studies Series. In addition, we are most appreciative of a grant provided by the Tamaki Foundation that constituted the lion's share of funds enabling us to have time to write this book and to make necessary trips to Asia. In the end, though, we alone are responsible for the views expressed in this book.

PART ONE

Co-Prosperity Again

CHAPTER ONE

Crossing Borders:
The Japanese Difference

At corporate headquarters in Osaka, Shuzui Takeo, director of Asian operations for Matsushita, draws a series of little circles on a sheet of paper. Then, with a few quick strokes, he ties the circles together in a grid of criss-crossing lines.

Shuzui is trying to demonstrate how he and his colleagues at Matsushita, the mega-maker of electrical and electronic goods bearing names such as National, Panasonic, Technics, and Quasar, hope to meld the company's 60 manufacturing plants in East and Southeast Asia into a more tightly integrated network. The new approach coincides with a plan by members of ASEAN to gradually reduce duties on products imported by one country from another in Southeast Asia.

"Over the next five years," Shuzui says, "we must restructure our operations to achieve a kind of intraregional division of labor, or functional specialization. That means concentrating production of single products or parts in different factories in different countries, and exporting most of the output to other markets."[1]

Malaysia, according to this strategy, might serve as the company's regional production base for air conditioners and refrigerators, Thailand as headquarters for washing machines, Singapore as the center for color televisions, and so on. The ultimate decision on where to locate each production activity, Shuzui says, "would be based on each country's strengths." If successful, the Matsushita strategy would enable the company's Asian operations to achieve economies of scale, scope, and

3

networking, allowing it to manufacture and export products that could
compete more effectively in markets throughout the world.

In his Tokyo office, Nishina Akira, head of Southeast Asian operations
for Mitsubishi Electric, is stewing. He knows about Matsushita's plan,
which he regards as an all-out assault on his own company's less developed
network in Southeast Asia. Mitsubishi Electric manufactures air conditioners, refrigerators, televisions, video cassette recorders, and assorted
electronic components at factories in Thailand, Malaysia, and Singapore.
"We must position ourselves to meet that challenge," Nishina says.[2]

The Mitsubishi executive has been promoting a counterstrategy to
integrate the company's regional operations, to build an equally or even
more effective network that assumes the entire world as its marketplace.
His is a new idea, and new ideas are not always welcome. Especially not in
such a large organization.

"It's a big headache for me," Nishina confides. "The managers [of
Mitsubishi Electric affiliates in Southeast Asia] just want to hold onto the
local markets they already control and continue to earn the high profits
they have been earning. They must learn to see the bigger picture, the
global picture."

Matsushita and Mitsubishi are not the only Japanese multinational
corporations (MNCs) trying to outmaneuver one another in Asia. In fact,
the region is buzzing with a competitive energy that is more than a little
reminiscent of the *katō kyōsō*, or "excessive competition," that marked the
rapid growth period (1950–73) in Japan. Just as they did then, high-
volume, high-technology manufacturers are racing to invest in new or
expanded production facilities, increase output, reduce costs, boost
exports, and grab larger and larger shares of the global market. Each
manufacturer enters this regional rat race, just as it might have entered the
domestic investment chase of the 1950s and 1960s, backed by two mutually
reinforcing insurance policies. One is issued by the government, which
uses its extralegal powers of "administrative guidance" (*gyōsei shidō*) to
manage the competition. The other, even more basic, coverage comes
from the *keiretsu*, the firm's own network, which spreads out the cost and
risk of doing business in a highly competitive and uncertain environment.

In this book, we argue that Japan has embraced the Asia-Pacific region
in a *keiretsu*-like production alliance. Although the Japanese government,
as we shall demonstrate, has used its influence in Japan and in the region
to build such an alliance, Japanese MNCs such as Matsushita and
Mitsubishi have supplied the actual bonding agents – capital and technology. In fact, the alliance we refer to is nothing more than the complex
web of vertically integrated production networks spun across Asia by the
many different high-technology firms seeking to expand their market
power by capturing the returns on their investment in innovation. At the

same time, though, it is nothing less than a coordinated effort to lock up the productive resources of the world's most dynamic region.

Others before us have used similar terms and concepts to describe what Japan is doing in Asia. Impressed by a heavy flow of intraregional trade, the Ministry of International Trade and Industry (MITI) has, for example, identified something it calls a "soft cooperation network." Takeshi Aoki, an economist for Japan's Institute for International Trade and Investment, has referred to a "core strategic network"[3] created by the multidirectional flow of Japanese investment and trade.[4] And Hisahiko Okazaki, former ambassador to Thailand, has said Japan is setting up "an exclusive Japanese market in which Asia-Pacific nations are incorporated into the so-called *keiretsu* system." The relationship is cemented by the trade of "captive imports, such as products from plants in which Japanese companies have invested" for "captive exports, such as necessary equipment and materials."[5]

These descriptions, by themselves, do not add up to a comprehensive analysis. But they do deserve some consideration because they run counter to the prevailing view expressed by most neoclassical economists that Japan is really doing nothing extraordinary at all in Asia, except perhaps to plug into the region's economic energy.[6] We intend to demonstrate that Japan is doing much more than that.

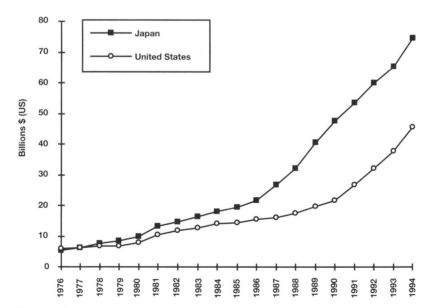

Figure 1.1 Japanese and US FDI in Asia
Source: U.S. data from Department of Commerce; Japanese data from Ministry of Finance.

Numbers

It is difficult to quantify the depth and breadth of a technology-based production alliance. Most studies of Japanese economic expansion into Asia have focused on the flow of capital, or foreign direct investment (FDI). As Figure 1.1 shows, in 1977 Japan's FDI stock in the region was roughly equivalent to that of the United States (at less than $6 billion). But 17 years later, in 1994, its cumulative FDI had grown more than twelvefold to $74.7 billion, while America's had increased to only $45.7 billion.[7] And despite the prolonged recession that began in Japan in 1990, Japanese investment in Asia has continued to increase rapidly. (Although Siemens [Germany], Thomson [France], and Philips [the Netherlands] are among the leading investors in Asia, European FDI as a whole has not been a force of late. In fact, Taiwanese, Korean, and even Singaporean investors outpaced the Europeans on FDI in Asia in the late 1980s and early 1990s.)

Japan's FDI in Asia, we concede, is only a fraction of its total overseas investment. As of 1994, Asia had received only 16.1 percent of cumulative Japanese FDI. North America, by comparison, had received 43.7 percent, while Europe had snared 19.4 percent.[8] Nonetheless, Japanese investment in East and Southeast Asia's relatively small host economies packs a disproportionately powerful punch. In Thailand, for example, Japanese affiliates accounted for about 40 percent of *total* (foreign and domestic) start-up investments in 1990 and 1991.[9] By 1994, about 7 percent of Thailand's production workers were employed by Japanese firms.[10] In Malaysia, one Japanese firm – Matsushita – accounts for nearly 4 percent of the entire country's GNP.[11]

We should also note that Japanese FDI in developing Asia has different characteristics from Japanese FDI in developed regions. For one thing, it is geared more to production. A 1995 survey found that manufacturers represented 53 percent of all Japanese-affiliated firms in Asia, but only 31.6 percent and 20.7 percent of the Japanese firms in the United States and Europe, respectively.[12] So we should not be surprised to learn that 36 percent of Japanese manufacturing investment (and nearly three-quarters of the projects) in 1994 went to the Asian NICs, the ASEAN-4, and China.[13] (Figure 1.2 documents the increasing flow of Japanese manufacturing FDI to Asia from 1985 through 1994, as well as the evolution of "favorite" destinations: first the NICs, then the ASEAN-4, and then China. The trend lines, however, do not reflect reinvestments, which have been robust all over Asia.) In addition, small and medium-sized firms from Japan are more active in the Asia-Pacific region than they are in other parts of the world. And as Figure 1.3 shows, they are increasingly active there. In 1994, 81.3 percent of small and medium-sized firms investing overseas opted to go to Asia.[14] As a result, by 1994

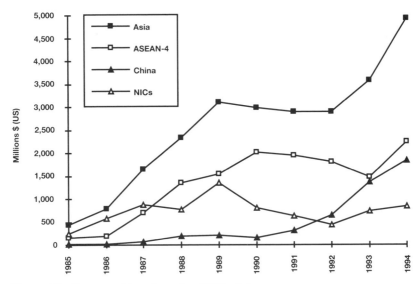

Figure 1.2   Japanese Manufacturing FDI in Asia
Note: These figures do not include reinvestments.
Source: Ministry of Finance.

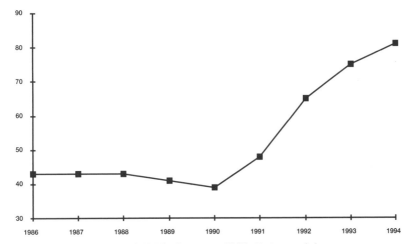

Figure 1.3   Share of Total FDI by Japanese SMEs Going to Asia
Source: MITI, *Chūshō kigyō hakusho,* various years.

there were almost as many Japanese affiliates in the Asia-Pacific region as there were in North America and Europe combined.[15] And in certain industries, especially high-tech industries such as electrical machine manufacturing, there were far more. As of 1994, there were 800 Japanese affiliates in Asia manufacturing electrical machinery. There were 413 in the United States and Europe combined.[16]

Table 1.1   Japan's Technology Exports to Asia

Year	Volume ($ billions)	Share of Japan's total exports (%)
1986	0.69	38
1987	0.69	40
1988	0.81	41
1989	1.03	39
1990	1.23	45
1991	1.36	46
1992	1.33	44
1993	1.49	47

Note: "Asia" includes India and Pakistan. Figures are based on a constant exchange rate of ¥125 = $1.
Source: Science and Technology Agency, *Kagaku gijutsu hakusho*, 1993, p. 348; and Management and Coordination Agency, *Kagaku gijutsu kenkyū chōsa hōkoku*, 1994, p. 168.

Table 1.2   Japan's Manufacturing Technology Exports to Asia (1993)

Types of machinery	Number of cases	Volume ($ millions)	Share of Japan's total exports (%)
General	561	67.9	57
Electrical	1,142	705.5	55
Transportation	565	378.5	45
Precision	74	6.1	45

Notes: "Asia" includes India and Pakistan. Based on 1993 exchange rate of ¥115 = $1. "Share" is percentage of all cases in that manufacturing industry.
Source: Management and Coordination Agency, *Kagaku gijutsu kenkyū chōsa hōkoku*, 1994, p. 168.

Japanese banks have moved aggressively into the region to support these manufacturing operations. Asia is now home to scores of Japanese branch banks.[17] With its liberal banking regulations, Hong Kong has emerged as the financial center of Japan's budding production alliance in Asia. Japanese banks extend 60.7 percent of all the loans issued there, many of them to Japanese affiliates in Asia but outside Hong Kong.[18]

For our purposes, we must also pay careful attention to technology license agreements, franchise arrangements, and other "intermediate" forms of overseas business activity. Table 1.1 shows the rapid increase of Japanese technology exports to Asia from 1986 through 1993, while Table 1.2 presents a breakdown of such exports in 1993 by four manufacturing sectors. Because they do not generate the capital flows that characterize FDI, these forms of business activity often go unnoticed despite their crucial importance, especially in the case of Japanese investment in Asia. As a result, the actual scale of Japan's regional expansion is substantially understated.

We tried to compensate by reviewing and recomputing statistics compiled by Tōru Nakakita from the *Nihon keizai* newspaper's electronic data system between September 1985 and June 1988.[19] We found that intermediate or nonequity forms of overseas business activity accounted for about 40 percent of Japan's total activity in Asia. Lacking the capital to build their own overseas production facilities, it seems that small-scale manufacturers such as parts suppliers have come to rely heavily on technology agreements to extend their reach into Asia. This has been especially true in places such as South Korea where FDI has not always been so welcome. In the five years from 1978 through 1982, Japanese automobile parts manufacturers entered into only four technology agreements with their Korean counterparts; however, in the same length of time, from 1983 through 1987, they entered into 40.[20]

Today, Japanese parts drive Asia's machine industries. Without them, the region could not produce the televisions, CD players, personal computers, fax machines, and air conditioners that it exports in such huge quantities each year to North America and Europe. It is no wonder, then, that Asia's trade deficit with Japan is growing even faster than its trade surplus with the West. The NICs, the ASEAN-4, and, increasingly, China's coastal economy have become embraced by Japanese technology. Rather than autonomous agents, these economies are functioning more and more like subcontractors, or junior partners, in an export-oriented, *keiretsu*-like alliance dominated by Japan.

Some may find our argument ahistorical, and thus difficult to swallow. After all, hasn't the Japanese government in recent years lost the political power and regulatory tools to guide private investment? Haven't employees, witnesses to or victims of layoffs in the post-"bubble" recession, become less loyal to their employers? And haven't *keiretsu* ties loosened somewhat in the past decade? We readily acknowledge that Japan's political economy has changed as it has matured and responded to international criticism. At the same time, however, we contend that it has not changed as much as others have suggested. The bureaucracy continues to carry considerable clout as it collaborates with business on the formulation and execution of public policy, including foreign economic policy. Production supervisors still count on factory workers at home and in Asia to help them achieve productivity goals. And high-technology firms, including those operating in places such as Taiwan and Malaysia, continue to maintain close ties with long-standing suppliers and distributors. Japan's political economy has become regionalized far more than it has been revolutionized.

In the early 1990s, the post-bubble recession accompanied by higher interest rates at home stanched the flow of capital to developed regions such as the United States and Europe. But Japanese manufacturers, particularly machine makers, continued to invest heavily in Asia. In 1994, an estimated 44 percent of the total overseas production of Japanese electrical and electronic machine makers came from their increasingly busy affiliates in the region.[21] Japanese firms in Asia now produce 27 percent more televisions, VCRs, stereos, and other audio-visual equipment than their parent firms in Japan do.[22]

To be sure, these affiliates do their part to feed growing local markets. At the same time, though, they have come to view the region as "a production base to service the global market," according to the Research Institute for Overseas Investment.[23] Hitachi, for example, shut down its Anaheim, California plant and moved its production of VCRs for the US market to Malaysia.[24] Other big Japanese investors in the United States, such as Fujitsu General, scaled back their American operations at the same time that they beefed up activities in Southeast Asia.[25]

Thai officials reported that Japanese FDI jumped sharply in that country in 1993 and again in 1994 as electronics manufacturers such as Casio and Sony, as well as automakers such as Toyota and Honda, spent huge sums of money to expand production capacity. In fact, Japanese firms accounted for nearly 40 percent of all foreign investment proposals in Thailand in the first half of 1994.[26] The fast pace continued into 1995, when Toshiba, for example, announced that it would invest $120 million over three years to expand production at its seven plants in Thailand.[27]

Thailand was not the only target of this new, post-bubble round of investment. In just one year, 1994, Japanese manufacturers expected to invest as much money in the Philippines as they did in the last five years of the 1980s. And in the three years from 1992 through 1994, they planned to invest nearly three times as much in Indonesia as they did in the three years from 1987 through 1989. Sanyo Electric Co. was one of the biggest investors, pumping $34 million into a plant to manufacture refrigerators.[28] And in Malaysia and Singapore, officials reported a similar although less dramatic burst of activity by Japanese firms. Aiwa and Yamaha, two major audio manufacturers, were planning to spend more to increase production in Malaysia, while Giken Sakata, a manufacturer of precision parts for consumer electronic products, and Yamazaki Mazak, which produces machine tools, were hoping to do the same in Singapore.[29]

But for all its power to attract Japanese capital, Southeast Asia's magnetism has appeared almost anemic next to China's. The Middle

CH INZ

Kingdom was the target of 636 cases of FDI in 1994, making it the most popular destination in the world for Japanese investors.[30] Although small, labor-intensive firms are behind most of this activity, large high-tech firms are playing an important part. Canon, for example, has opened a plant to manufacture fax machines in China.[31] NEC has established a joint venture to produce computer peripherals.[32] Sony has invested millions in a new facility to produce camcorders.[33] Toyota, a step or two behind Suzuki, says it will try to assemble 150,000 cars a year in China beginning in 1996.[34] And Matsushita is planning to build eight new factories there.[35]

This massive flow of Japanese capital into Asia is no flash-in-the-pan event. It is at least a medium-term phenomenon. "Japan's main target must be Asia," says Hosoya Yūji, deputy director of MITI's industrial policy bureau.[36] Based on its own survey, the government predicted that, from 1994 through 1996, more than half of all Japanese FDI would go to Asia.[37]

We do not expect the North American Free Trade Agreement (NAFTA) to upset expectations by drawing an increasingly large amount of Japanese FDI into Mexico. Investors have been put off by the agreement's strict rules of origin, which require assemblers to use a high percentage of North American inputs, as well as by the ongoing political and economic turmoil in Mexico.[38] For such investors, Asia continues to be the best bet – far better than Europe or the United States, the other relatively popular destinations. In 1993, for example, affiliates in Asia earned profits of $3.3 billion, while those in Europe lost $357 million and those in North America lost $772 million.[39] Although aggregate data are not available, statistics for individual corporations suggest that Japanese affiliates in Asia continue to perform well. Honda's five affiliates in Thailand, for example, earned about $50 billion – approximately 20 percent of Honda's total corporate earnings – in the first half of fiscal 1994.[40]

Many Japanese MNCs are using their Asian profits to boost the capacity of their production networks. Because the official data maintained by bureaucrats in Tokyo do not reflect the value of such reinvestments, they substantially understate the total amount of Japanese FDI in Asia. In fact, some believe they understate it by as much as 40 percent.[41]

Consider the case of Matsushita. It beefed up its facilities in Asia by reinvesting about $100 million of the profits it earned in the region between 1989 and 1991.[42] And, on a smaller scale, consider the case of Mitsubishi Electric. Faced with another year of losses at home, it too moved to restructure its global operations, pumping more money and manpower into Asia. Nishina says the company decided to follow the advice of the Japanese government, which had been prodding high-technology manufacturers to consolidate and integrate their Asian facilities. But Mitsubishi Electric, he adds, also chose to use its own common sense. "This recession is not just a news item. It's a reality, and we have to do something to pull ourselves up out of it. The countries of Asia, we believe, are our natural partners. They are the ones that can help us restore our profits."[43]

Keidanren, Japan's big-business federation, sounded a remarkably similar theme in a report recommending ways to rebuild the Japanese economy. Asian companies, it noted, are becoming "an indispensable part of the business and procurement activities of Japanese companies." Business ties linking Japan to the rest of Asia benefit both parties, it concluded, and thus should be strengthened. "Japanese companies will have to form a closer cooperative relationship in an effort to secure their international competitiveness."[44]

Theory

As a theoretical problem, foreign direct investment has bedeviled economists for a long time. Classical economic analysis, in fact, assumed that both capital and labor essentially were immobile due to what Ricardo called "the natural disinclination which every man has to quit the country of his birth and connections."[45] Early efforts to explain this unanticipated activity relied heavily, too heavily, on assumptions about differences in relative factor endowments between the home country and host countries. For example, Ohlin suggested that MNCs function as capital arbitragers, moving operations abroad in search of higher interest rates, and thus higher returns on capital.[46] This analysis helped explain portfolio investment, but did little to explain direct investment, which flows as heavily into relatively capital-rich countries. Studies also showed that foreign investors routinely tap local sources to finance part of their capital expenditures.

In other words, the approach based on factor endowments fell short. So in the 1960s, as veteran economists scratched their heads, a young graduate student came up with a new approach based on microeconomic theory. Stephen Hymer argued that MNCs, as oligopolists, enjoy "firm-specific" advantages including economies of scale, marketing skills, and – above all else – technical prowess. They exploit these advantages by investing abroad to *control* international operations and eliminate existing or potential competition from firms in the host nation.[47] Because it frontally challenged one of the most cherished assumptions of neoclassical theory (namely, that market forces inexorably bring about equilibria in factor markets), and because it appeared to condemn capitalism in general, Hymer's argument bothered many economists. Nonetheless, they had to acknowledge that it did seem to adequately explain the activities of American multinationals such as General Electric and General Motors, which at that time were setting up large production and distribution operations in Europe.

Grudgingly, then, scholars began to tinker with this new idea. One of the first to do so was Raymond Vernon, a professor at Harvard Business School who tried to integrate Hymer's theory of firm-specific advantages with neoclassical trade theory.[48] Vernon traced what he called "the product cycle," which evolves through three phases, ultimately leading to the transfer of technology across national borders. In the first stage, a firm in a relatively advanced country uses its innovative edge to manufacture a new product that it sells initially at home. In the second phase, the production technology becomes more standardized, rivals enter the market, demand for the product becomes more price sensitive, and firms begin competing to improve productivity and achieve economies of scale. Some even begin exporting the product. Finally, in the third phase, when the technology is fully standardized, firms begin searching for ways to trim costs. To hang onto markets, many are compelled to relocate production to developing countries with abundant supplies of cheap labor.

While Vernon's "product cycle" became a popular concept in business schools, it never really gained much currency among Western economists.[49] They wanted a broader, more inclusive theory of FDI. But to develop one, they found they had to return – again and again – to Hymer's original thesis that firms use FDI to exploit their own assets in imperfect markets. Economists such as Mark Casson began to focus on the ability of MNCs to reduce costs by "internalizing" transactions associated with research and development and the accumulation of know-how.[50]

Until the 1970s, the quest for a workable theory of FDI was dominated by Western scholars. But then, as a growing number of Japanese firms began to set up their own overseas operations, Japanese scholars began to consider the issue more carefully.

Of these scholars, the most controversial, as well as the most prolific, was undoubtedly Kojima Kiyoshi. He drew a sharp distinction between Japanese and American FDI. The latter, he wrote, is made by "oligopolistic enterprises [that] set up wholly owned subsidiaries or 'enclaves' ... [to manufacture] highly sophisticated and differentiated products in order to exploit their quasi-monopolistic advantages in Third World markets."[51] In other words, American-style FDI fits microeconomic theory. But Japanese FDI does not, Kojima argued. More often than not, it is carried out by small and medium-sized firms that are, unlike American MNCs, willing to serve as minority shareholders in joint ventures with local partners. And it is concentrated in labor-intensive industries. As a result, Kojima argued, we must use trade theory to understand Japanese FDI.

This he did.[52] In a comparison of Japanese and American FDI in Asia, Kojima found that Japanese direct investment tended to match a host nation's comparative advantage, and thus promoted trade. It was "more efficient in promoting the growth of host country output than American FDI," he concluded. "The reason for this is asserted to be the dynamic trade-oriented nature of Japanese FDI which promotes the development of industries in which the host country has an advantage."[53] And that's not all. Because of its smaller size, the composition of its factor endowments (high on labor, low on specialized knowledge), and its willingness to forgo majority ownership, Japanese FDI, Kojima argued, also makes possible a "more orderly" transfer of technology.

For good reason, many scholars have vigorously criticized Kojima's thesis. They demonstrated that Japanese FDI has been no more trade oriented, and perhaps even less, than any other country's FDI.[54] More importantly, however, they argued that the "unique" features of Japanese investment would not last, that they reflected nothing more than a transitional stage in Japan's industrial and technological development. For example, Mason argued that the greater willingness of Japanese investors to hold a minority interest in joint ventures was not a function of their altruism, but rather of their technological abilities, which in the 1970s were not as high as American or European investors, and thus did not require as much protection.[55]

This argument, a kind of "convergence theory" of investment, was stated most explicitly by Roemer, who predicted that "Japanese-style" FDI would come to resemble "American-style" FDI in the future.[56] And in many ways it has. Like the IBMs and Mercedes-Benzes of the West, Japan's largest companies now serve as the vanguard of their nation's overseas business activity. They represented almost 82 percent of the firms investing abroad in 1992, compared with 64 percent in 1976. In addition, Japanese firms setting up overseas plants have shifted their focus from labor- and capital-intensive industries to more technology-based, knowledge-intensive industries. In 1992, almost 41 percent of Japan's manufacturing FDI went into general machinery, electrical machinery, and transportation industries, while 30 percent did so in 1976. And finally, Japanese investors have acquired a taste for majority shareholding. Wholly owned subsidiaries accounted for almost 45 percent of Japan's overseas manufacturing operations in 1992, and only 18 percent in 1976.[57]

Despite these changes, however, we cannot conclude that Japanese FDI is the same as American or European FDI. In fact, Japanese overseas business activity is fundamentally different, although not at all in the manner Kojima suggested. Wisarn Pupphavesa, director of the Asia-Pacific Economic Relations Project at the Thailand Development

Research Institute (TDRI), a Bangkok-based think tank, comes much closer to capturing the distinction.

> The American way seems to me to be quite naive. The Japanese way, by contrast, is much more strategic. They study the [host nation's political and economic] environment, pool information and, through their many networks of communication, reach a consensus, a common strategy on how to proceed. Then, still working together, they go around and around until they get what they want.[58]

In a nutshell, we argue here that Japanese FDI is distinguished by the same characteristics of intranetwork cooperation that distinguish Japan's domestic political economy. These characteristics include the following.

Government–business cooperation. Unlike the US government, the Japanese government actively promotes and guides FDI. From 1990 through 1993, the Export-Import Bank of Japan financed about $27.8 billion of overseas investment, most of which was undertaken by small and medium-sized firms.[59] And MITI, eager now to promote overseas investment, insures against losses due to many of the commercial, as well as political, risks associated with overseas business activity.[60] In addition, the government uses its foreign aid to stimulate FDI by providing technical training to workers and by financing the construction of airports, roads, dams, and other infrastructure projects in developing countries. Through such agencies as the Japan External Trade Organization (JETRO), the Japan Overseas Development Corporation (JODC), and the Institute of Developing Economies (Ajia Keizai Kenkyūjo, or Ajiken), the government collects and disseminates information about economic and political conditions in different host countries. Most importantly, though, it collaborates with business at each step along the way. These issues are discussed in detail in chapters seven and eight.

Business–business cooperation. Despite the growing use of wholly owned subsidiaries, Japanese MNCs continue to engage in limited equity or nonequity forms of overseas production more frequently than American or European MNCs.[61] These business tie-ups with local entrepreneurs enhance the flexibility of a multinational network and can be accomplished without any significant loss of control over technology.[62] Take, for example, original equipment manufacturing (OEM), in which a foreign manufacturer is commissioned to produce a part or product under the original manufacturer's brand. Unlike US firms, Japanese firms often will enter into an OEM agreement for two or three years before taking the plunge and setting up their own overseas plant to produce that part or product.[63] As we will discuss in chapter ten, Japanese affiliates who do set up their own plants also try to assemble and control a team of reliable suppliers, many of which are really *keiretsu* sub-contractors transplanted from Japan. This has been the case in Asia, and was also the case in the United States in the 1980s.[64] And finally, Japanese MNCs in Asia, as elsewhere, have come to depend on the services of Japanese trading companies that have moved overseas to support the emerging production alliance.

Management–labor cooperation. Although they invariably must make adjustments, evidence shows that Japanese manufacturers expanding overseas bring with them some of the important components of their distinctive employment system. In particular, they try to guard their investment in human capital by paying competitive wages to shopfloor employees, often on the basis of seniority. Research by Yoshihara shows that Japanese MNCs achieve relatively high rates of productivity at overseas plants by encouraging teamwork, soliciting the opinions of employees on production matters, especially those relating to quality control, and offering stable if not lifetime employment.[65] At the same time, however, Japanese affiliates retain a relatively high percentage of expatriate managers.

In his analysis of Japanese investment, Panglaykim identified many of the same characteristics. "The uniqueness of Japanese MNCs lies in their management style, strong links with the government, sense of national mission, the key role of trading companies (*sogō shōsha*) and most importantly, the ability to combine and mobilize the various advantages into a formidable integrated system which undertakes direct investment."[66]

Japanese capital used to be timid. In fact, during the rapid growth period (1950–73) even the biggest firms were extremely reluctant to expand beyond the nation's borders. Producers prospered then by tying themselves securely into domestic networks or, as Imai prefers to call them, "micro-macro information loops," supervised and maintained in part by the government.[67] In the 1980s, however, these firms found they could no longer hold back. Japanese capital washed over the world. But as they expanded, Japanese MNCs found they could prosper just as much as before by building transnational networks. The trick, of course, was to secure the competitive advantages they had acquired in Japan's domestic political economy. In most cases, they did.

Japanese MNCs, then, are not really "multinational" in the same way as European or American MNCs. No matter how far they expand, they hold fast to their membership in a Japanese alliance structure. This fact, which should not surprise anyone acquainted with Japan's political economy, has been documented in numerous studies.

Comparing the purchasing practices of 20 Japanese, 20 European, and 22 American affiliates in Australia, Kreinin found that Japanese affiliates "are tightly controlled by the respective parent company, procure their equipment mainly in Japan and own and operate mainly Japanese machinery." In contrast, he found that American and European affiliates "have a great deal of autonomy to make purchase, sourcing and other decisions, procure most of their capital equipment by international competitive bids and own machinery made in three continents and six to eight countries without a preponderance of any particular source."[68]

Bartlett and Ghoshal took a slightly different tack, examining the management regimes at Japanese, American, and European MNCs. Their conclusions, however, were strikingly similar. In fact, they called American and European multinationals "decentralized federations," and dubbed the Japanese MNCs "centralized hubs." Bartlett and Ghoshal contrasted career systems at Philips, the Dutch firm, where "expatriate managers follow each other into assignments and build close relations among themselves," and Matsushita, where "there is very little interaction among the expatriate managers in the different subsidiaries."[69] Philips' overseas executives identify so strongly with the local organization that they form "a distinct subculture" within the MNC, while Matsushita's executives "tend to see themselves as part of the parent company temporarily on assignment in a foreign country."

> One result of these differences is that expatriate managers in Matsushita are far more likely to take a custodial approach which resists any local changes to standard products and policies. In contrast, expatriate managers at Philips, despite being just as socialized into the overall corporate culture of the company, are much more willing to be advocates of local views and to defend against the imposition of inappropriate corporate ideas on national organizations.[70]

Even MITI has produced evidence that Japanese MNCs are more Japanese than multinational. In a survey of foreign affiliates in Japan and Japanese affiliates abroad, it tried to determine just how much autonomy the affiliates had. On every subject, it turned out, the foreign affiliates had more. For example, nearly 30 percent of the foreign affiliates indicated they could decide on their own to raise additional capital; fewer than 10 percent of the Japanese affiliates could. "Thus, one can say that, compared to Japanese firms (investing overseas), foreign firms (investing in Japan) have achieved progress toward 'localization,'" MITI concluded.[71]

One could reasonably argue here, just as Kojima's critics did, that Japanese MNCs behave differently only because they are new to the game of foreign investment. Over the years, the argument might go, these affiliates will plant themselves more deeply into foreign soil and eventually begin to behave just like American and European MNCs. Indeed, there are hopeful signs that Japanese automakers who invested heavily in the United States in the early 1980s are now making progress toward "localization" by purchasing more of their parts from American suppliers.[72] But this change, we submit, did not occur naturally through the passing of time. It was forced on the Japanese by hard, steady pressure from US auto parts manufacturers and their allies in the US government. Given the relative bargaining strength of American interests, the only surprise is that change did not come sooner.

Japanese automakers have not achieved such progress in Asia, where they have been assembling cars since the 1960s. Nor have electronics firms, which began setting up plants in the region at about the same time.[73] They continue to import the most sophisticated auto parts and electronic components from Japan, or rely on Japanese-affiliated parts manufacturers who have followed them overseas.[74] And compared to US affiliates in the region, Japanese affiliates still employ a large number of expatriates in management positions.[75] Sure, technology is transferred, but only inside the narrow channels of a firm's vertically integrated network.[76]

A flagrant violation of the official doctrine that Japan is moving steadily and ineluctably toward *kokusaika*, or internationalization, this apparent lack of movement creates discomfort for Japanese business leaders in Asia and at home. In 1994, Nagamatsu Tōnan, general manager of Sumitomo Corp. in Kuala Lumpur, told a gathering of Japanese and Malaysian officials that, despite what Japanese firms describe as "steady efforts" to promote locals and transfer technology, "positive results are hardly emerging in a visible manner." For that reason, he concluded, "discontent is mounting considerably on the Malaysian side."[77] This reprimand came four years after Keizai Doyūkai, a respected group of corporate executives in Japan, announced a program of *genchika* (localization), pledging that Japanese affiliates in Asia would hire more local managers and purchase more local parts.[78]

Obviously, change is not such an easy thing to accomplish. At least that was what Japanese executives confided to Schon Beechler at the conclusion of her research on the methods used by Japanese MNCs to maintain almost complete control over their affiliates in Asia's consumer electronics industry.

> The respondents admitted that they felt under increasing pressure from both local governments and employees and from third parties, such as Japanese and Western academics, to transfer technology, localize management, decentralize control and "de-Japanize" authority. However, they also believed that this process would put their operations at risk and would therefore not be carried out until all other alternatives were exhausted.[79]

We heard similar "confessions" during our research. One particularly passionate one was made by Kōzuki Yasutsugu, president of the Japanese

Chamber of Commerce and Industry in Singapore. He told us that Japan would lose its status as an economic superpower if its global manufacturing firms relinquished too much control to local affiliates.

> In my personal opinion, we should keep the control in Japan. Once you lose that control, that power, it never comes back. It never returns. All you have to do is look at what happened to England in the late nineteenth century, or what is happening to the United States today.[80]

Kōzuki has a point. Western-style globalization does seem to generate its own self-destructive fallout, namely, an outbound flow of technology and a steady erosion (a "hollowing out") of domestic manufacturing capacity. This was anticipated by Vernon in his theory of the product cycle. And now a new school of international business theory is advising multinational firms not to spread their management resources too thinly. For example, Porter, the dean of this new school, urges firms to globalize "selectively," and only after consolidating their headquarters. "Unless the critical underpinnings of competitiveness are present at home, companies will not sustain competitive advantage in the long run," he writes. "The aim should be to upgrade home-base capabilities so that foreign activities are selective and supplemental only to overall competitive advantage."[81]

In Japan, the message is coming in loud and clear. So clear, in fact, that even those advocating stepped-up efforts to globalize the Japanese economy hasten to add the historically informed caveat. Globalization, according to an executive of the Sanwa Research Institute, "carries the risk of weakening our competitive ability. Thus, in shifting our production abroad, we must avoid making the mistake the United States made. We must achieve technological progress at home and retain the competitiveness of our high value-added domestic industries."[82]

This may prove, then, to be another advantage of "followership."[83] As a late developing nation, Japan has had the luxury of seeing the ill effects of Western-style globalization and of hearing the cautionary words of Western scholars like Porter. Now it has the opportunity to try to steer its own course, to devise its own model of globalization, a *strategic* model in which the various members of a high-technology production alliance (government officials and business executives, parent firms and subcontracting firms, management and labor) cooperate to reduce transaction costs and maximize the benefits of innovation.

That model is taking shape in Asia today.

CHAPTER TWO

Flying Geese:
An Unequal Alliance in Asia

In the late 1950s, Japanese investment in East and Southeast Asia was designed almost exclusively to extract raw materials for the home market. Firms in labor- and capital-intensive industries – textiles, chemicals, and steel – shifted some of their production to the region in the 1960s and 1970s, when wage rates, land prices, and environmental regulations in Japan began to pinch their domestic operations. These manufacturers had another motive, namely, to continue to supply markets that host governments in Asia had begun to protect.[1]

That was the "old wave" of Japanese FDI. Conventional wisdom suggests that, beginning in the mid 1980s, three factors conspired to create a "new wave" of export-oriented investment in Asia. The first was the deliberate effort by a number of Southeast Asian states to jump-start their sluggish economies by adopting policies to attract foreign investment and stimulate exports.[2] Firms from Japan, as well as the United States, Europe, and the Asian NICs, responded enthusiastically. The second factor was the equally deliberate effort by some of Japan's most important trading partners, principally the United States, to erect new barriers to Japanese exports. To circumvent those barriers, Japanese firms not only invested heavily in the United States and Europe, but also scurried to construct export platforms in Asia.[3] The third and most frequently cited factor was the Plaza Accord, which triggered a chain reaction that ultimately led to an eruption of Japanese capital.[4]

On 22 September 1985, US Treasury Secretary James Baker met with the finance ministers of Japan, West Germany, Great Britain, and France at the Plaza Hotel in New York City to sign a pact aimed at relieving America's nagging trade deficit via an "orderly appreciation of the main nondollar currencies against the dollar." Japan's currency responded, jumping in value from 250 yen to the dollar in the summer of 1985 to 150 by the summer of 1986.[4]

But *endaka*, the skyrocketing increase in the value of the yen, did not do what it was supposed to do. It did not curb Japanese exports, and thus reduce America's massive trade deficit.[5] *Endaka* did, however, undermine the profitability of Japanese exporters. (To appreciate the impact, imagine what would happen to American firms exporting to Europe if the value of the dollar suddenly doubled against the British pound, German mark, and French franc at the same time.) So the Japanese government, hoping to relieve the pain, reduced the official discount lending rate in stages to a historic low of 2.5 percent. The result was a dramatic increase in the money supply, creating a huge excess liquidity in the capital market. Banks competed to make loans to small and medium-sized firms, as well as individuals, who used the money to speculate in real estate and securities. Large firms raised money easily by issuing new shares of stock that rose rapidly in value. Not all of the capital raised in this way was channeled into new plant and equipment; a large amount was used for what came to be called *zaitech*, or financial engineering, which included the purchase of more real estate and securities offering higher and higher yields.

Thanks to the ongoing liberalization of Japan's capital markets, *zaitech* went global. Big banks and first-class firms faced few obstacles as they tapped into financial markets in London, Zurich, and New York. Foreigners, impressed by the sharp rise in the value of Japanese assets, lent money without hesitation.

In the end, Japan's economy became, in effect, a "bubble" puffed up by a speculative boom in asset prices. It was destined to pop (as it did in early 1990). But while the bubble lasted, Japan had more than enough money to invest in the developed markets of the West, as well as the developing markets of Asia.[6]

The preceding description of events is accurate, but woefully incomplete. What it omits is context. Japan's massive trade surplus, the appreciation of its currency, and the globalization of its industry are all symptoms of a larger phenomenon: Japan's transformation from an industrial economy to a high-technology economy, itself the product of a "developmentalist" system in which government and business, quasi-independent firms, and management and labor cooperate to achieve dynamic technological efficiency.

That system nearly came unhinged in the 1970s, when Japanese industry began to exhaust the global reservoir of existing technology.

This marked a new period of slower economic growth. But Japanese manufacturers soon responded by forging tighter ties with sub-contractors – a move that allowed them to streamline their operations, invest more in research and development, and begin producing an even richer menu of goods including luxury automobiles, semiconductors, numerically controlled machine tools, and communication satellites.

By the early 1980s, then, Japan had reached a new stage in its economic evolution. As a technological superpower, it was poised to globalize. The only thing holding it back was public debt, a legacy of the 1970s when the Japanese government bowed to public pressure and plowed money into social welfare programs. But this hurdle fell gradually as the government increasingly tightened its grip on the budget. By the end of the 1980s, it no longer issued the deficit bonds that had, in the 1970s, helped to soak up excess saving in Japan's private sector. Suddenly, the rest of the world became the sponge.[7]

About two-thirds of the capital that "bubbled up" out of Japan in the latter half of the 1980s went to the United States and Europe. A much smaller share went to Asia. But even this relatively small share represented a huge increase in the absolute amount of investment.

Asia, it seems, became an attractive outlet for some of Japan's manufacturing and exporting activity. But cheap labor was not the main attraction. In fact, it had not been for years. Before 1980, Japanese producers reported that 36.5 percent of their FDI in the Asian NICs and 22.5 percent in the ASEAN-4 was made chiefly to tap the region's abundant supply of low-cost labor. After 1980, however, survey respondents indicated that only 14.8 percent and 13.1 percent of the FDI they undertook in those sub-regions, respectively, was motivated by such a desire.[8] More recent surveys have confirmed the fact that cost considerations, by and large, are not driving Japanese FDI to Asia.[9] Japan, we argue, has become a "mature" economy, and an increasingly large share of its overseas manufacturing activity – in Asia and elsewhere – is undertaken by high-technology firms using highly automated production systems. Automation has dramatically reduced the need for low-cost production workers, while increasing the need for skilled workers.[10]

If cheap labor is not luring this FDI to East and Southeast Asia, then what is? We suggest that Japan's high-tech manufacturers are investing in Asia for a strategic purpose, namely, to achieve economies of scale, scope, and networking by capitalizing on the region's deepening division of labor. They come here, in the words of a Mitsui executive, to secure a "strategic distribution" of management resources and production activities.[11] This assertion requires some background. Machine production is, by definition, a multistage process with each stage requiring a different level of technological skill. Recognizing this, many Japanese

MNCs are breaking the manufacturing process into discrete pieces, retaining at home the R&D, design, and precision manufacturing work that adds the most value to the product, and parceling out the rest of the work to different host nations in Asia according to their technological levels.[12] Japan usually supplies the high-tech inputs; the Asian NICs supply the high- to medium-tech inputs; and the ASEAN-4 nations, as well as China, supply the medium- to low-tech inputs.

What we are suggesting, then, is that Japanese high-tech manufacturers view Asia as one integrated but technologically stratified economy, an extension of their own domestic production base.[13] In other words, as MITI itself has suggested, they view the region as "a single market from which to pursue a global corporate strategy."[14] This fact has become painfully obvious to those in East and Southeast Asia, like Soesastro, who are paying close attention to the manner in which Japan has embraced their economies: "Willing or not, the ASEAN economies have become an integral part of a production structure that is emerging in the Pacific region, with Japan as its core."[15]

There is ample evidence to support our contention. In a 1990 survey, JETRO found that 38 percent of Japanese manufacturing affiliates in Thailand, 39 percent in Malaysia, and 43 percent in Singapore considered themselves part of a production network based on a regional division of labor. Many others indicated in the survey that they actually belonged to a larger, more far-flung network based not merely on a regional, but an *international*, division of labor.[16] A 1992 survey of Japanese affiliates in Malaysia came up with similar findings. Ninety-seven respondents – or 53 percent of the surveyed firms – told JETRO they were or soon would be part of a cohesive unit coordinated by their parents.[17]

Electronics firms have led the drive to build such networks in Asia. Evidence (spelled out in chapter eleven) shows that they engage in a large volume of intraregional, intranetwork trade. Although automobile manufacturing affiliates still rely most heavily on local (host country) markets, they too are building regional production networks. Many began laying the foundation for such networks in the early 1980s.[18]

As they have evolved, the production networks built by Japanese MNCs in Asia have assumed at least three different forms, represented schematically in Figure 2.1. The earliest type, which we call the hub network, is a collection of regional affiliates that tie themselves closely to the parent firm in Japan but do not interact much, if at all, with one another. Many of these affiliates are joint ventures with well-connected business groups in the host nation, which a former Toyota executive in Thailand has appropriately labeled "local capital umbrellas."[19] Even in these cases, though, the Japanese partners usually control the day-to-day management of the regional affiliate. This is accomplished in different

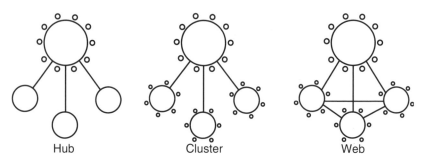

Figure 2.1 Evolution of Japanese Networks in Asia

ways. For example, the local capital umbrella may agree to function as a dummy shareholder, a partner only on paper. Or the two sides may sign a "basic agreement," turning over all but a few limited responsibilities (such as labor relations and local marketing) to the Japanese partner. Or, finally, the Japanese partner may win leverage by securing a loan to finance the local partner's equity interest.[20]

Sharp, a consumer electronics giant, did just that in the Philippines, where it holds a minority (40 percent) interest in a joint venture. The Japanese multinational gained the upper hand in the management of this electronics firm by arranging a loan to finance the local partner's investment. The loan came from the Rizal Commercial Banking Corp., owned in part by Sanwa Bank, the financial hub of the Japanese *keiretsu* to which Sharp belongs. Sharp's parent company in Japan guaranteed the loan, and Sanwa's director in Japan approved it. On paper, the Filipino partners had a majority (60 percent) interest in the firm; in fact they assumed a subordinate role.[21]

The typical joint venture in a hub network is a "screwdriver" operation, which does little more than assemble parts imported from Japan. But this fact is not always obvious. In a quiet, warehouse-like room at the FKL Donghwa plant in Sunghwan, South Korea, 80 women wearing pin-striped robes and floppy chef hats stare into microscopes as they coil wire for magnetic heads used in the hard disk drives that tap a computer's memory. Although it is manufacturing a product that embodies quite advanced technology, this joint venture contributes very little of the product's value. Ninety-nine percent of the essential parts and components used here come from Fujitsu Japan, which owns 50 percent of the joint venture. Only one part – a piece of stainless steel suspension – comes from a source other than the parent firm; it comes from a Japanese supplier in Thailand.[22]

As the 1980s wore on, *endaka* made it increasingly difficult for Japanese MNCs in Asia to continue to import parts from Japan. The price was simply too high. To remain competitive, they had to begin purchasing locally produced parts. They had, in effect, to build a new kind of network, a cluster network, based on a denser set of interfirm relationships. Most of the big assembly firms managed to persuade their Japanese subcontractors to pack up and move to Asia or sign technology license agreements with domestically owned suppliers in the region. But some, such as Mitsubishi Electric Co. (Melco), had to improvise.

In the late 1980s, Melco used its own capital to begin constructing a cluster network of local parts producers to supply its TV manufacturing operation in Thailand. It first set up a joint venture, Thai CRT, to produce cathode ray tubes based on Melco technology.[23] But this was not enough. Asahi Glass, a member of Mitsubishi's industrial *keiretsu* in Japan, soon announced plans to set up another joint venture to manufacture the glass valves used in those tubes.[24]

The Mitsui group is making a similar effort to help members advancing into China. Six Mitsui-related firms have agreed to pool resources and establish a plant near Shanghai to produce high-quality plastic resins for Japanese consumer electronics and appliance makers with factories in China.[25]

As they turn more and more to Asia as an alternative site for export-oriented manufacturing, Japanese MNCs in the 1990s are building a third and even more comprehensive type of network, which we call a web network. Spun together by intraregional and intragroup trade, this type of vertically integrated network serves to unite the scattered children of Japanese parents. Affiliates assemble high-tech parts imported from the parent in Japan and less sophisticated components from other affiliates in the region. Manufacturing activities are strategically placed in technologically appropriate sites according to a firm's own division of labor. Matsushita, as we have suggested, is setting up a web network in Asia. Many others are doing so as well.

As of April 1995, Sony had 15 manufacturing affiliates in Korea, Taiwan, Singapore, Malaysia, Thailand, Indonesia, and China employing about 30,000 people and producing billions of dollars worth of audio and video goods, semiconductors, and computer parts.[26] "Those plants in Asia are quite active, even more active, I think, than we are in Japan," says Koiso Shigeru, a manager of planning for Sony.[27] The company's success in the region is based, in no small part, on intranetwork cooperation. For example, to manufacture VCRs at its assembly plant in Bangi, Malaysia, Sony uses integrated circuits and other sophisticated components imported from Japan and printed circuit boards and other semifinished goods imported from Singapore. It purchases tape decks, as well as many other basic parts, from local suppliers in Malaysia, many of them Japanese.[28]

Hitachi is spread just as widely across Asia, producing televisions, VCRs, air conditioners, and semiconductors in many different locations. But company bosses in Japan are hoping to get a tighter grip on this vast network. They have announced plans to link all of Hitachi's Asian facilities, as well as its headquarters in Japan, via a computerized local area network (LAN). The purpose, they say, is to facilitate a steady, even flow of communication within the Hitachi group and to help company planners collect better production data.[29]

Japan's automakers are no less ambitious. Toyota, for example, is mass-producing gas engines in Thailand, diesel engines in Indonesia, steering parts in Malaysia, and transmissions in the Philippines (see Figure 2.2). It has established a regional trading center in Singapore, which co-ordinates the movement of automobile parts between Toyota affiliates throughout Asia. The affiliates are expected to assemble these standardized parts into finished cars and trucks.[30] Nissan, meanwhile, has announced plans to assemble "the first truly regional, strategic vehicle" in Asia. The new vehicle, "the NV," would include 180 parts from Nissan's Thai facility, 20 from its plant in Taiwan, 15 from its Malaysian affiliate, and 10 from its operation in the Philippines. Nissan in Japan would supply only the engine block.[31]

Until now, Suzuki, which has established manufacturing affiliates in nine different nations throughout Asia, has produced motorcycles on a country-by-country basis, trying to meet local government and local market requirements. Now, says Tani Masao, an overseas marketing

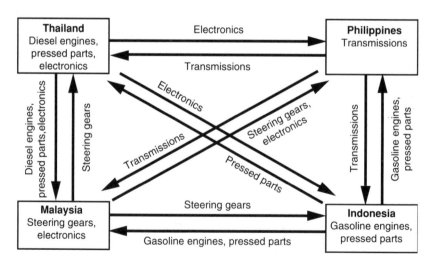

Figure 2.2 Toyota Motor Network
Source: Toyota Motor Corp.

manager for the firm, it too wants to try a regional approac.
realize a division of labor among our production bases in As.
each plant specialize in a certain type of motorcycle or compoi.
have these facilities supply each other with products, this would
more cost effective."[32] Using business networks that have becc
increasingly complex, evolving from hubs to clusters to webs, Japanes
MNCs have become agents of both regional economic integration and
developmentalism. We have referred to this process as the regionalization of Japan's domestic alliance structure. Tokunaga, using different
words but the same concept, has called it "the Asianization of the
Japanese economy."[33] Indeed, Japan, the Asian NICs, the ASEAN-4, and
China now function as partners in a regional production alliance. But
they are not equal partners, and are not likely to become so in the
foreseeable future.

Flying Geese

In the 1930s, Japanese economist Akamatsu Kaname developed what has
come to be called the "flying geese" theory of economic development.
Like Vernon's product cycle theory, it spelled out a protracted process,
driven by the gradual and international diffusion of technology, in which
a developing country upgrades its export and industrial structures.[34] In
the 1970s and 1980s, Japanese scholars used a modified version of the
flying geese theory to explain what they viewed as a synergistic pattern of
economic development and integration in Asia. Japan, of course, is the
"lead goose" in this regional pecking order, followed by the Asian NICS,
then the ASEAN-4, then China, and so on. As it flies forward, becoming
more and more technologically advanced, Japan pulls the entire V-
formation along with it. It does so by successively shedding industries in
which it no longer holds a comparative advantage. Through FDI, these
industries ultimately find a new home among the less developed
countries (the "follower geese") of Asia. Over time, these developing
countries master the new technology, upgrade their own industrial
structures, and themselves begin shedding outdated industries.[35]

Looking for anything that might justify the use of industrial policy,
Japanese government officials latched on tightly to the flying geese
theory. The Economic Planning Agency, for example, used it to exhort
Japan and Asia to "plan for adjustments in their industrial structures that
reflect shifts in comparative advantage."[36] Every now and then, a
bureaucrat will tinker with the metaphor, but the meaning does not
change much. In 1970, Ojimi Yoshihisa, then a MITI vice minister, told a
gathering of Western leaders that the development process in Asia was
one of "progressively giving away industries to other countries, much as

a big brother gives his out-grown clothes to his younger brother. In this way, a country's own industries become more sophisticated."[37]

At first glance, economic development in Asia does seem to follow a flying geese pattern of "hand-me-down" industrialization. After 1985, when *endaka* struck, Japanese FDI flowed first into the Asian NICs, then ASEAN, and then, more recently, China and even Vietnam, India, and Pakistan.[38] By the end of the 1980s, new multinationals from the NICs were rolling into Southeast Asia, setting up labor-intensive manufacturing facilities of their own. In 1991, for example, Taiwan was the leading foreign investor in Malaysia and Indonesia, and the second leading investor – behind Hong Kong – in China.[39] Not to be outdone, Thai, Malaysian and even Filipino companies began to invest in low-cost countries such as China, Vietnam, and Laos.[40]

According to the flying geese theory, however, the process does not stop there. First the Asian NICs, and then the ASEAN-4, are expected to catch up with the lead goose, turning the V-formation into a straight, horizontal line.[41] This catch-up process, we are told, is well underway. As Japan transfers more and more of its technology, and as it absorbs more and more of Asia's manufactured exports, the "old" division of labor (a vertical one) is giving way to a "new" division of labor (a horizontal one), based on intraindustry trade and other forms of "work sharing."[42]

Or so the story goes. We argue the contrary – that Japan is actually flying further and further ahead of the regional flock. The division of labor in Asia, based on the technological capacity of each nation, is becoming more – not less – vertical. In chapters six and twelve, we defend this position more thoroughly. For now we will try to illustrate our point simply by comparing the behavior of the region's leading capital exporters – Japan and Taiwan.

Like a good surfer, Japan has learned to ride the crest of the product cycle in Asia. Using vertically integrated production networks, Japanese MNCs have jealously guarded their technology, the source of their competitive advantage. Web networks, in particular, serve to minimize leaks. By locating discrete pieces of the production process at different sites throughout the region, high-tech manufacturers controlling such networks can thwart the ability of potential Asian competitors to master and appropriate the entire package of technology.

Global strategies, not cost considerations, are driving Japan to regionalize its economy. This is evident in the fact that high-tech manufacturers use the region in part as a platform for exports to developed markets in the United States and Europe, not merely as a source of "reverse imports" back to the home market.[43] The government has prodded these companies to constantly upgrade domestic operations.[44] And they have. Despite a massive outflow of investment in the late

1980s, Japanese MNCs never abandoned their home base. Far from it. Domestic spending on plant, equipment, research, and product development in that period equaled a quarter of Japan's GNP. Productivity rose so fast, in fact, that Japanese firms were able to overcome most of the competitive disadvantage they initially suffered under *endaka*.[45]

Even after the bubble burst and Japan's helium-filled currency soared to record levels of less than 100 yen to the dollar, Japanese electronics firms continued to invest heavily in domestic production. In 1994, for example, Fujitsu announced plans to expand production of 16-megabit dynamic random access memory chips at its plant in Iwate Prefecture, while Toshiba announced a plan for a new factory in Shiga Prefecture to produce liquid crystal display (LCD) panels. Capital investment rose sharply that year as high-tech firms sought to maintain their edge over rivals in the United States and South Korea.[46]

Japan's regional strategy, then, has yielded a technology-based division of labor between itself and Asia. Examples seem endless. When the Victor Company of Japan (JVC) expanded its production of compact color televisions in Thailand, it did not abandon its home base. Instead, it began to produce wide-screen, projection-type TVs and tuner-equipped big-screen TVs in Japan. After shifting its production of window-type air conditioners to Malaysia, Hitachi immediately retooled its Japanese assembly lines to begin manufacturing more sophisticated inverter-type units. When Canon boosted its production of relatively simple cameras in China, it opted to upgrade its domestic operations by focusing on high value-added models, such as the EOS 100. As Casio began producing more of its pocket calculators and other standard goods in China and Southeast Asia, it simultaneously began producing more cutting-edge goods, such as electronic organizers, at home. After Kumagaya Seimitsu established a plant in Indonesia to manufacture audio-visual equipment, it reserved its assembly line in Japan for the production of high-quality motors for high-speed printers. And Murata Manufacturing built new facilities in China and Malaysia to produce ceramic filters, an important component in cellular telephones, but nonetheless decided to retain at home the most technologically demanding task of making ceramic powder.[47]

Taiwan, in contrast, is following the flying geese pattern of development, using FDI merely to shed its labor-intensive industries. The experience of consumer electronics illustrates this point. In the early 1990s, according to Bernard and Ravenhill, Taiwanese firms virtually abandoned their home-based but export-oriented production of consumer electronics. Racing to beat rising labor costs, most opted for one of three alternatives: continuing to produce consumer electronics in Taiwan, but only for the domestic market; retooling plants at home for export-oriented manufacture of computer peripherals; or moving production offshore, particularly to low-cost plants in Southeast Asia.[48]

Unlike Japan's, then, Taiwan's FDI is not guided by any strategy other than cost reduction. Thus it is relatively footloose. In 1992, for example, Taiwanese investment in the ASEAN-4 fell precipitously as the country's multinationals abandoned places such as Thailand, which had experienced rapid wage inflation, and zeroed in on low-wage production bases such as Vietnam.[49] At home, Taiwanese firms have failed to make the capital investments needed to keep up with the Japanese pacesetters in this high-tech race. Wages have risen much faster than productivity, symptomatic of the fact that capital exports are not being accompanied by an upgrading of domestic industry.[50] And because the country's manufacturers have grown increasingly dependent on Japanese capital goods and high-tech components, Taiwan has run up a serious trade deficit with its powerful neighbor.

Taiwan, of course, is not alone. Most countries in the Asia-Pacific region – South Korea, Singapore, Hong Kong, Thailand, Malaysia, the Philippines – are running large and growing deficits with Japan.[51] This is a symptom of what we have called "embraced" development in Asia.[52]

Embraced development is not a bad thing. It certainly beats slow or no development – the fate of most Third World countries. Fueled by Japanese capital and technology, the Asian NICs, the ASEAN-4, and China are, in contrast, enjoying enviable rates of economic growth. In particular, they have made deep inroads into both the North American and European markets, supplying them with competitive, reasonably high-quality products.

Hasegawa Keitarō, who has written more than 60 books on Japanese business practices, uses a crude analogy to describe this pattern of embraced development. The economies of Asia, he says, are like cormorants, the diving birds used by some Japanese fishers to catch fish. Japan, which supplies the technology that runs Asia's export-oriented industrial machinery, is the patient fisher. It holds a line around the cormorant's neck, waiting for the hungry bird to take its next plunge into the water.[53]

We prefer a different analogy. The embraced economies of Asia are, we argue, like the small or medium-sized Japanese firms that belong to vertical *keiretsu* dominated by the large manufacturers to whom they supply parts. The subcontractors benefit enormously from membership in this corporate group, which provides a guaranteed market for their products, as well as ready access to the capital and technology needed to manufacture them. Through interfirm cooperation of this sort, these subcontractors – like the economies of Asia – become increasingly competitive.

Ultimately, however, embraced development could become "captive" development, a far less propitious model in which the benefits of cooperation are no longer shared so evenly. This is likely to occur as Japanese business and government elites penetrate host governments more and more deeply, securing policies that serve to strengthen Japan's control over its production alliance in Asia.[54] And it is likely to occur as Japanese MNCs use their tremendous advantages to capture more of the "advanced factors," such as skilled labor and supplier contracts, in those host countries.[55] Given those outcomes, Japanese firms could end up with an even tighter grip on their own technology, allowing them to earn monopolistic "rent" on its use. In addition, they might be able to enrich themselves further by engaging in such practices as transfer pricing.

But the Asian NICs, the ASEAN-4, and China may not actually feel the pinch of captive development until Japanese high-tech manufacturers stumble in their pursuit of dynamic technological efficiency (DTE). This is because the pace of technology transfer to Asia is largely determined by the pace of Japan's own technological innovation at home.[56] If Japanese high-tech firms are unable to achieve DTE (and thus Japan is unable to progressively upgrade its industrial structure), then we can expect these firms to take advantage of the built-in flexibility of their regional production networks. They will undoubtedly "squeeze" their junior partners in Asia, much like large manufacturers in Japan used to (and still do, albeit more subtly) squeeze their *keiretsu* suppliers in hard economic times. This could happen to local managers and technicians who dream of big opportunities in a Japanese company, as well as local entrepreneurs who dream of acquiring wealth and technological independence by joining forces with the Japanese.

In fact, evidence suggests that a limited form of *shiwayose*, or squeezing, occurred in the early 1990s, when economic growth suddenly slowed in Japan. That was when Japanese MNCs began requiring Asian affiliates to absorb some of their newly redundant managers in Japan.[57] "We have too many managers at Nissan Motors in Japan," explained an executive for the automaker. "Our overseas operations give us a convenient way to relieve this excess supply of management staff."[58] That was also when Japanese automobile and electronic assembly firms in Asia began squeezing local suppliers, insisting on paying less for parts and requiring stricter enforcement of quality standards.[59] And it was when some Japanese MNCs cited "market developments" as a reason to renegotiate their agreements to sell high-technology inputs to joint ventures. A Malaysian economist, for example, reported complaints that "once the company is locked into a particular product, the Japanese start squeezing the Malaysians on price."[60]

It would be, however, both untrue and unfair to characterize Japanese MNCs as economic predators, exploiting the ambitions and dreams of Asian workers and entrepreneurs. They are not. In many cases, they are doing exactly what local people want. Take the case of Wattana Choangulia. She used to be a middle-class homemaker in Tonburi, a busy, gritty community of tin and plywood buildings on the far side of Bangkok's Chao Phraya River. Now she is a partner in a joint venture to manufacture a high-tech device to test the integrated circuits used by Matsushita, Sony, Hitachi, and other Japanese electronics firms in Thailand.

Wattana's partner is Miyajima Yoshinori, the well-to-do, sophisticated son of a Matsushita subcontractor in Japan. The two became friends in 1984, when they attended the same college in California. Seven years later, Miyajima visited Wattana and her husband in Thailand. At the end of his stay, he floated a business proposition: the Choangulias would provide working space for a machine to punch little holes in a sheet of acrylic plastic, living space for two Japanese technicians to stay a few weeks a year, and their Thai citizenship to secure valuable tax savings for the business. He would provide the capital (including a loan for Wattana's 51 percent share), and the technology.

They shook hands, and Wattana suddenly was the director of P&F (Prosperity and Felicity) Choangulia, Bangkok. A very hands-off director, though. "This is his [Miyajima's] business. I'm going to leave everything up to him," she told us. "If we make a little money in the process, that's okay. But I really don't care that much."[61]

The moral of this story should be obvious: a business person who does not seek to acquire technology will not acquire it. Wattana is one of hundreds, perhaps thousands, of Asian entrepreneurs who are quite content to play the role of "technology-less" junior partner in a Japanese production alliance.[62]

But even those who do seek to acquire technology may not succeed. The outcome is subject to bargaining, and Japanese MNCs have enormous leverage. Among other things, they can withhold resources from local partners, suppliers, and employees they deem insufficiently cooperative, shifting those resources to others in their production network.

By forging an effective alliance with local capital, the state in a developing country can restore some balance to the bargaining process. Government policies and practices in South Korea, for example, have enhanced the capacity of that country's *chaebol*, or industrial conglomerates, to absorb imported technology.[63] And Chee argues strongly that the government of Malaysia, by setting up a special agency to review proposed technology licensing agreements, has aided local buyers who otherwise lack essential information about that technology.[64]

In general, though, the developing economies of Asia are becoming less able to resist Japan's embrace. They lose bargaining power just as steadily as Japanese MNCs build increasingly complex networks and deploy increasingly sophisticated technology that is, by definition, increasingly difficult to appropriate.[65]

Consider what happened in Malaysia, where Mitsubishi Motors Corp. (MMC) helped the government carry out its plan to build a national car, the Proton Saga. A cornerstone of Prime Minister Mahathir Mohamad's regime, the car project was supposed to push Malaysia into the major leagues of industrialized nations. Instead, it pushed MMC into the major leagues of production networks in Asia.

Mahathir personally authorized the state-owned Heavy Industries Corporation of Malaysia (HICOM) to negotiate a joint venture agreement with MMC. The automaker itself was reluctant at first to participate. But the Mitsubishi Corp., the general trading company for the Mitsubishi *keiretsu*, argued correctly that the project would benefit not only MMC, but also resource developers, parts makers, and others affiliated with the group. In the end, MMC agreed to provide the technology, and the *keiretsu* as a whole pledged the capital.[66]

From the beginning, MMC exercised enormous clout. When the government tried to increase the vehicle's local content, the automaker responded by using two of its built-in advantages. It raised the cost of the localization program by using a form of transfer pricing. Specifically, MMC did not fully discount the price of its imported CKD (completely knocked down) kit to reflect the cost of a deleted (locally produced) part. In addition, it monopolized the project's quality control program and thus was able to cite MMC-prepared test results to reject local parts produced by unaffiliated or unwelcome suppliers. This was perhaps unavoidable; the Malaysian government did not have a suitable testing facility of its own.[67]

In 1985, a development organization inside the United Nations studied the car project and concluded that "the probabilities of gain appear far more secure for Japan and Mitsubishi than for Malaysia."[68] Three years later, in 1988, few could disagree. With the plant running at less than a third of its capacity, losses began to mount. The actual culprit was a serious recession, which dramatically reduced domestic demand for automobiles and other expensive goods. But Mahathir was impatient; he blamed HICOM officials and turned to MMC for help in turning around the project. The automaker installed its own personnel in three top posts – managing director, business director, and corporate planning director. This new management scheme was supposed to last two years, until Proton was sufficiently turned around.[69] But as of 1993, MMC still controlled five of the 11 seats on Proton's management committee. And one of the company's Malay officials, Othman Bin Ismail, said Proton now needs the Japanese managers more than ever to steer the project toward new and more demanding markets because "in highly technical areas, we still have a lot to learn from the Japanese."[70]

Under its new management, Proton has become an integral part of MMC's sprawling, increasingly export-oriented production network in Asia (see Figure 2.3). It already supplies door panels to Mitsubishi's automobile manufacturing affiliate in Thailand. MMC's affiliate in the Philippines ships transmissions to that Thai affiliate, which in turn assembles and exports cars to Canada. Proton now exports cars to several countries in the British Commonwealth.[71]

In 1994, Mahathir began to realize how far he had allowed his pet project to become enmeshed in Mitsubishi's regionalization scheme. He took steps to ease Malaysia's dependence on Japan, forging agreements to purchase new technology from Citroen of France and Rover of England. But Mitsubishi continued to dominate almost all areas of design, production, financing, and marketing.[72]

Meanwhile, the *keiretsu* is casting its net even wider. Building on its experience in Malaysia, Mitsubishi Corp., the general trading company, has prepared what it calls a "master plan" for the development of a national automobile industry in Vietnam. Although it never mentions MMC by name, the plan seems clearly designed to persuade the

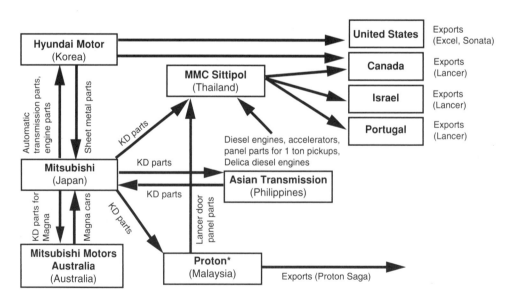

Figure 2.3   Mitsubishi Motors Network
Notes: KD parts = knocked-down parts, *Perusahaan Otomobil Nasional Bhd.
Source: Mitsubishi Motor Corp.

government of Vietnam to join the automaker's regional production network.[73]

If Vietnam did agree to go along, it would not be the first (and undoubtedly not the last) time that an Asian government has taken steps to foster regional economic integration and thereby consolidate Japan's emerging production alliance. As far back as the 1970s, in fact, ASEAN has pushed schemes such as ASEAN Industrial Projects (AIP) to reduce tariffs on goods traded between member countries. Predictably, the Japanese government promoted those schemes and even provided $1 billion in concessionary (below market rate) loans to finance AIP.[74]

In 1988, ASEAN authorized a brand-to-brand complementation (BBC) program by which member nations agreed to treat auto parts imported from other member nations almost like locally produced parts, thereby reducing import duties on those parts by 50 percent.[75] Mitsubishi Motors, Toyota, Nissan, and other Japanese automakers are using this program to expand their regional production networks and achieve economies of scale. "The benefits of this are substantial for the auto industry," contends Hayashi Nobumichi, industry research section chief of the Industrial Bank of Japan.[76]

In 1992, ASEAN moved beyond auto parts by approving a 15-year plan to reduce or eliminate tariffs on 15 products traded between member nations. Naturally, this plan to set up an ASEAN Free Trade Area (AFTA) was enthusiastically received by Japanese multinationals.[77] No surprise. AFTA was designed, after all, to attract an even stronger flow of FDI from Japan and elsewhere.

"It's a way of improving our competitiveness in the scramble for global investment capital," said Tan Kong Yam, director of the Research and Planning division at Singapore's Ministry of Trade and Industry.[78]

Japanese MNCs also benefit from the proliferation of sub-regional zones in Asia. In most cases, these zones are promoted by local, state, and sometimes even national governments that hope to achieve complementarities, or divisions of labor, between geographically proximate but economically disparate areas within their jurisdiction. The idea here is not unlike the Japanese government's flying geese model of regional integration and development. Both seek economic synergy. Lee Tsao Yuan, deputy director of the Institute of Policy Studies in Singapore, says these sub-regional zones are quite unlike customs unions or free trade areas; they are "investment-driven and export-oriented, inward-looking in terms of production networking, but outward-looking in terms of exports."[79] They are, in other words, perfect for Japanese MNCs.

Take the case of the Batamindo Industrial Park (BIP), the flagship project of the Singapore-Johore-Riau Growth Triangle.[80] A cooperative venture between the governments of Singapore and Indonesia, this project was designed to tap into Singapore's financial, planning, and marketing skills and Indonesia's surplus land and labor. Along the way, though, it also tapped into Japan's emerging production network.

Mitsui and Co., one of Japan's giant trading companies, was the only private equity partner allowed to participate in the development of the industrial park on Batam Island, one of Indonesia's Riau islands, located about 20 miles south of Singapore.[81] The huge park has its own water supply, new power generators (built by Kansai Electric Power), a microwave communications network, and a container shipping facility. Indonesian workers are brought there on two-year labor contracts and paid exactly the same – regardless of which company they work for. There are no import duties. And there are no restrictions on equity.[82] With such a generous package, the park has attracted multinationals from all over the world, but especially from Japan. Of the park's 37 tenants in 1993, 15 were Japanese. And half of the companies planning to move into the park were Japanese.[83]

Sumitomo Wiring Systems, which produces electrical parts for cars, was the park's first tenant. It has done quite well, thanks in part to its affiliation with Sumitomo Electric International, the Singapore-based headquarters for Sumitomo's regional operations. That company has coordinated all of the nonproduction activities at the $30 million Batam facility. It has purchased the plant's raw materials from Japan, exported its finished goods, handled its financing, and tried to develop new markets in Southeast Asia.[84] Batamindo Industrial Park has allowed Sumitomo to consolidate its Asian network.

An Alliance, not a Bloc

Far from building an exclusive trading regime, Japan is using its Asian production alliance in part as a platform from which to continue supplying high-technology products to Western markets. This, of course, serves a political as well as an economic purpose. Not only does it escape the potentially crushing impact of the high yen, but it reduces the size of the trade surplus attributable directly to Japan, and thus reduces some of the international pressure the nation otherwise might face.

While the United States and Europe continue to loom large as markets for Asian exports, high-technology manufacturers in the West are becoming increasingly marginal players in the region's emerging production alliance. It is Asia's supply structure, not its demand structure, that is turning inward.

The automobile industry is a case in point. Japanese affiliates account for 94 percent of production in Thailand and 90 percent in Indonesia.[85] Three Japanese firms – Toyota, Mitsubishi Motors, and Nissan – produce almost 80 percent of the locally manufactured vehicles in the Philippines.[86] European automakers, including Volvo, BMW, and Mercedes-Benz, have set up a few relatively small production facilities in Southeast Asia, while American firms are virtually invisible in that region. At first glance, Malaysia, where Ford-branded vehicles represent 8 percent of total production, might appear to be the exception. But it isn't. Those Fords you see in Kuala Lumpur are built according to a Mazda design.[87] The same is true in Taiwan, where 32 percent of locally manufactured automobiles are Mazdas sporting a Ford nameplate.[88]

South Korea, meanwhile, seems to have successfully nurtured its own automobile industry. But look again: Hyundai, Kia, Daewoo, and Sangyong all depend heavily on Japanese auto parts. And Samsung soon will, too. Korea's largest *chaebol*, which in 1994 received government approval to enter the automobile industry, has indicated it will import all of the advanced technology it needs from Nissan. To seal this cooperative deal in 1995, Nissan sent about 250 of its Japanese engineers and technicians to Korea and hosted about an equal number of Koreans in Japan.[89] Even before this deal was struck, Japan accounted for 60 percent of the technology licenses and more than 50 percent of the joint ventures in the Korean auto parts industry. US firms accounted for only 16 percent of the technology licenses and 31 percent of the joint ventures. European firms accounted for most of the remainder.[90]

China is really the only Asian country in which Western automakers have established a firm foothold. But now that Beijing has decided to lift its tight restrictions on entry, Japanese firms such as Toyota, Honda, and Mitsubishi Motors are vowing to jump in and give the market leaders – Volkswagen of Germany and Citroen of France – a serious run for their investment money.[91]

For Western automakers, then, the status quo is bleak and the future does not look any brighter. US firms, in particular, are extremely reluctant to enter a region that Japan appears to have sewed up. One source flatly states that there are "virtually no opportunities for new manufacturers because each market is already overcrowded."[92] In other words, the entrenched few will reap the bountiful spoils of rapid growth. Kenneth Courtis, chief economist for Deutsche Bank Capital Markets (Asia) Ltd in Tokyo, has predicted that by the end of this century Japanese manufacturers will build two-thirds of Asia's new automobile plants and grab as much as 60 percent of the region's fast-growing auto market.[93] In part, American automakers can blame themselves for this predicament. Stung by rising oil prices and communist victories in Vietnam, Cambodia, and Laos, General Motors, Ford, and Chrysler closed most of their assembly plants in Southeast Asia in the mid 1970s.[94]

In other manufacturing industries, especially electronics, Western MNCs maintain a far more solid presence – at least for now. Seagate, the Californian disk drive manufacturer, has plants in Singapore, Hong Kong, South Korea, Taiwan, and Thailand. Texas Instruments, a top US computer company, produces semiconductors in Singapore, Malaysia, and the Philippines. And it teamed up with Acer, an upstart Taiwanese firm, to build a $250 million memory chip plant in Taiwan.[95] Philips, the Dutch electronics giant, assembles audio goods in Malaysia and Indonesia, and manufactures semiconductors throughout the region. Thomson, a consumer electronics firm based in France, owns production facilities in Singapore, Indonesia, Malaysia, Taiwan, and South Korea.[96]

These firms, however, are not typical. American and European manufacturers generally have not kept pace with their Japanese counterparts. While Japanese firms have invested heavily in high-tech industries in Asia, US firms in particular have focused more on oil, gas, and other natural resources. Manufacturing accounts for only one-third of US FDI in the region.[97]

Here, too, American and European MNCs must shoulder some of the blame. They tend to be less patient, less willing to stay the course in a region that, at least in the past, was characterized by political instability and market uncertainty. More importantly, Western firms are uncomfortable in a business regime that runs so much on long-standing personal relationships, rather than on clearly established legal guidelines. At the same time, though, we have to acknowledge that a production alliance is, by definition, exclusionary. And the Japanese-dominated alliance in Asia is indeed difficult to penetrate.

Late arrivals, Japanese chipmakers have emerged almost overnight as the dominant semiconductor manufacturers in Penang, Malaysia's "Silicon Island." "They certainly keep us on our toes," says Yoon Chon Leong, manufacturing manager for Hewlett Packard, an American firm that produces semiconductors and components in one of Penang's sprawling free trade zones. "It's a big challenge to keep up with them."[98]

Yoon says the Japanese manufacturers – Hitachi, Toshiba, and Sharp – did so well so quickly in part because they had access to relatively large amounts of cheap capital. But they also succeeded, he says, because they leaned hard on a fixed group of subcontractors, many of them Japanese suppliers that followed their parent firms all the way to Penang. By contrast, Hewlett Packard buys its parts from a diverse and often changing cast of characters. Price is the key determinant. And unlike the Japanese assemblers, Yoon says his firm spends very little time up front hammering out a production process with its suppliers. "For us, it's a business relationship, not a marriage."

When we met him in Bangkok, Chirasak Sivarak was still a management trainee for Yamato Unyu (Thailand), a forwarding company that deals almost exclusively with other Japanese firms in the area. In just a few months, though, he had seen plenty of evidence of such marriages.

> One thing I've learned is that the Japanese are willing to trade with one another even though the price may be higher, even though they could save 15 or 20 percent by dealing instead with U.S. or European or even local firms. They hardly ever do that. The Japanese prefer to pay a little more for the sake of security.[99]

We saw this when we visited Melco Consumer Products (Thailand), a subsidiary of Mitsubishi Electric Co., that manufactures state-of-the-art air conditioners, as well as components for refrigerators and washing machines. The company's facility on the Bagna-Trad Highway outside Bangkok was designed and built by Takenaka International, a Japanese contractor, and is filled from floor to ceiling with Japanese machines: 13 plastic injection molding machines from Toshiba, 16 sets of metal presses from Komatsu, a robot from Ichiko, a computer from Onishi, forklifts from Mitsubishi and Toyota. In fact, the only non-Japanese machinery we could find in the plant was a metal bending device from Burr Oak, an American firm.

It is almost as difficult to find non-Japanese firms engaged in public works administered by Asian governments but funded by Japanese official development assistance (ODA). That, according to critics of Japan's ODA policies, is because Japanese architects and engineers, acting as consultants on such projects, write detailed specifications that only Japanese contractors and suppliers can meet. "You are beaten before you start," says a representative for Schlage Door Hardware International.[100]

Co-Prosperity Again

Although US President Clinton has focused more attention on Asia than his recent predecessors, he still has not developed a coherent policy toward the region as a whole. Instead, he has used his bully pulpit every now and again to rail against human rights violations, as well as mercantilist trade policies and practices in various countries within the region. To many Asians, the United States is caught up in its own domestic economic problems. It turns to this region only when it needs a scapegoat.

While leading members of the EU have won friends in Asia by pressing quietly and gently for human rights and free trade, they too have largely ignored the region. They have fixed their sights instead on the economic integration of Europe, a high-profile affair of statesmen and treaties.

Japan, on the other hand, is devoting more attention to Asia than at any time since World War II. The Foreign Ministry, for example, has created a position of ambassador for Asia-Pacific cooperation.[101] And the Ministry of Finance has helped to set up a think tank, the Foundation for Advanced Information and Research (FAIR), which promotes regional economic development and cooperation. Most importantly, the government is continuing to pump massive amounts of foreign aid into Asia – even though the region is faring much better, economically, than many other parts of the world such as Africa, Latin America, and Eastern Europe. In 1991–92, Japan spent about 35 percent ($4.453 billion) of its total foreign aid budget on six countries in the region we have identified as "Asia." The United States, by comparison, spent only about 2 percent ($342 million) of its total foreign aid budget on a pair of countries in that region.[102]

Upset by what they consider to be a cold shoulder from the United States and Europe, many Asian leaders are welcoming Japan's embrace. In fact, they are begging to be held closer. In 1988, Phisit Pakkasem, secretary general of Thailand's National Economic and Social Development Board, pushed the members of ASEAN, the Asian NICs, China, and Japan to set up a new organization, the Western Pacific Economic Cooperation, to represent Asia's interest in multilateral trade talks. In 1990, Malaysia's Mahathir called on the same countries (plus Vietnam) to form a consultative body, the East Asian Economic Caucus (EAEC), to encourage regional cooperation.

Both proposals define a region that is almost identical to the wartime Greater East Asia Co-Prosperity Sphere. And neither, of course, includes the United States, which has established its own North American Free Trade Agreement (NAFTA) with Canada and Mexico. Of the two, Malaysia's proposal has received by far the most attention, in part because of its tireless, outspoken architect. Mahathir is highly critical of the United States, which he says has turned protectionist at home and imperious abroad. "There is a tendency [in the US] to ride roughshod over the opinions of others," he said in one interview.[103]

Unless its political and business leaders begin to forge closer, more durable ties with their counterparts in Asia, the West may find itself on the outside looking in on the world's most dynamic region. Japan is quickly embracing Asia. Chung Moon Jong, a member of the South Korean National Assembly and the son of Hyundai's founder, put it bluntly, perhaps too bluntly: "It's not a matter of choice in Asia. That's a very hard fact to recognize. In terms of money and technology, the Japanese have already conquered Asia."[104]

PART TWO

The Embracer and the Embraced

CHAPTER THREE

Cooperation between Unequals

In 1993, a Nobel laureate in economics complained that the world envisioned in neoclassical theory exists "in the minds of economists but not on earth."[1] This may be a little harsh, but only a little. In this chapter, we argue that neoclassical theory cannot cope with the reality of Japan's embrace of Asia because it ignores or assumes away institutions (such as government, business alliances, and labor agreements) and fails to seriously consider the critical role of technological change in economic development.

We should concede at the outset that neoclassical theory has allowed many people, including us, to organize economic concepts more clearly and examine data more deliberately. But this analytical tool has proved to be blunt, even flawed – an unfortunate fact that too many neoclassical economists at colleges and think tanks all over the world refuse to recognize. Giddy with self-confidence, they continue to pound away, deluding themselves into thinking they are asking the right questions and getting the right answers. In doing so, they remind us of that old saying: if the only tool you have is a hammer, everything looks like a nail.

This chapter has three objectives. One is to summarize the shortcomings of neoclassical economic analysis, particularly the theory of the firm and the theory of international trade – the two theories relied on most often to analyze the motives, patterns, and significance of Japanese economic expansion into Asia. The second is to review efforts to perfect neoclassical theory and to present two alternative tools of analysis – neoinstitutional economic theory and developmentalist theory – that we believe are more faithful to reality and thus more useful. The third and

43

final objective is to present our own analytic perspective, based on the insights provided by those alternatives, which we believe allows us to better understand what Japan's government and high-technology firms are doing in Asia.

MIAs: Institutions and Technological Change

According to the microeconomic theory taught in most college classrooms and used, almost invariably, in "rigorous" economic analysis, the firm exists in a competitive market and requires a minimal amount of information to participate in that market.[2] It only needs to know from whom it will buy its inputs, to whom it will sell its output, and the price at which such trading occurs. The firm is assumed to be able to obtain this information instantaneously, without incurring costs, and to be able to fully comprehend and process it to maximize profit. All transactions are assumed to be based on spot prices, which in turn are assumed to "clear the market," or inspire a perfect equilibrium between supply and demand. Finally, the firm is assumed to make the best use of its resources (capital and labor) and to maximize its profit by responding to the market signals (prices) of today. All that matters is what the firm does today, in the short run, because it ostensibly faces a never-ending series of "todays" (meaning, in other words, no yesterday and no tomorrow).[3]

As almost anyone can see, this imagined world of neoclassical theory does not square with reality. Firms in the real world require much more information (for example, relating to product quality, delivery schedules, and the financial terms of a transaction). They incur costs in both time and money in obtaining the information necessary to do business. And even then, they sometimes make the wrong decisions, thereby failing to maximize profit. Prices do not always clear markets. Trading is often conducted over a long period, not on the spot, and the contracts used in such long-term transactions sometimes are not honored, necessitating the expenditure of time and money to enforce them. And finally, what firms do today (investing, hiring, and contracting to buy or sell) determines what they can or should do tomorrow.

In other words, there are transaction costs (the costs of doing business) in the real world that are assumed to be zero in the neoclassical world. This is no small matter. Transaction costs include the cost of locating a transaction partner (such as a buyer or seller of goods and services, or a lender or borrower of capital and property); the cost of obtaining all necessary information to engage in a transaction (price, quality of product, delivery schedules, output capacity, and many other factors upon which business decisions are based); and the cost of negotiating, writing, and enforcing contracts and agreements.

How, you might ask, can neoclassical economists erase all signs of transaction costs? Simple. They do so by ignoring or assuming away institutions – the social policies and practices that determine (reduce or increase) such costs.[4] In fact, they are *required* to do so in order to make their theory "universalistic." To the contrary, we argue in this book that different macrosocial units (such as nations) do in fact have different institutions that influence the behavior of economic agents (such as firms) and thus long-run economic performance.

Technological change is the other critically important piece missing from this puzzle. It is treated as an "exogenous" variable, something that (unlike labor and capital) operates outside the neoclassical model. For this reason, microeconomic theory tells us little or nothing about why firms engage in R&D, invest in on-the-job training, or make various long-range investment, employment, marketing, and other plans. In the neoclassical world, firms merely react to technological change.

This oversight (or premeditated neglect) becomes painfully evident in the well-known theory of international trade, also known as the theory of comparative advantage (the so-called Heckscher-Ohlin-Samuelson theory). The theory suggests that nations gain by trading with one another on the strength of a fixed endowment of resources that gives each a comparative advantage in producing some, but not other, goods. It assumes, among other things, that all firms in nations participating in international trade use the same technology to produce the same products. This is patently absurd.

So how did such an important variable as technological change end up where it did, on the outside looking in? One answer is that neoclassical economists had no choice but to place it there. If they had tried to account for technological change, they would have been hard-pressed to keep their price-driven model internally consistent. For example, by assuming that technology is fixed (and that all factor and product markets are competitive, all factors of production are fully employed, and all consumers in trading nations, regardless of income level or culture, share identical tastes), scholars of international trade are able to assert that the price of all productive factors will equalize across trading nations.[5] At the same time, we must be charitable and acknowledge the possibility that neoclassical economists didn't know any better. Their theory, after all, was assembled in the developed world to describe developed capitalist economies that already possessed advanced technology. It was not designed to analyze the process of industrialization or economic "catch-up." But as we should plainly understand by now, the ability of an economy to achieve industrialization depends on its ability to adopt or adapt new technology, which depends on its ability to build or rebuild suitable institutions.

Economists have had to improvise to explain the continuing increase in productivity they have seen in the real world. Alfred Marshall, a founder of neoclassical theory, attributed a reduction in production costs to the internal economies an especially large firm can realize in the use of resources, as well as external economies (created, for example, by improved infrastructure or a pool of skilled labor) that arise when an aggregation of firms begins producing the same product.[6] Another improvisation was introduced by Kenneth Arrow, a Nobel laureate who came up with the concept of "learning by doing." He argued that, as a firm acquires experience producing some product, its managers and employees become increasingly efficient and thus bring about a reduction in production costs.[7]

Although these and other improvisations have been used liberally by some economists, they remain ad hoc efforts that conflict with the underlying logic of microeconomic theory. This is why a large majority of economists, especially those making econometric studies of economic growth, continue to adhere to the assumption that technological change is an exogenous variable.[8]

Toward a New Theory of the Firm

In the 1970s, a growing number of economists began to acknowledge the presence and significance of transaction costs. Critics pecked away at the old (neoclassical) theory of the firm. Oliver Williamson, the leading critic, complained that:

> The neoclassical theory of markets regards the firm as a "rhetorical device adopted to facilitate discussion of the price system." Although the need to simplify the theory of the firm for this purpose is very real, the resulting gains come at a huge cost. What was an analytically *convenient* theory of the firm for the purpose of studying markets and equilibrium came to be treated as an *adequate* theory of the firm for purposes of understanding economic organization. The advantages of an all-purpose theory of the firm notwithstanding, the latter was a fateful mistake.[9]

Efforts to rectify this "fateful mistake" have yielded many scholarly works attempting to create a new transaction costs theory of the firm.[10] All zeroed in on the question: Why does a firm exist? In other words, why does an entrepreneur decide to produce some products rather than simply buy them in the market? A consensus soon emerged that a firm exists (to produce products) because its own internal market serves as a lower-cost locus for certain transactions. This implied that a firm grows in size (produces more) whenever the additional cost of internalizing a transaction is less than the additional cost of relying on the market.

Although it focused much needed attention on the problem of transaction costs, the answer provided by Williamson and others was, in a strict sense, tautological, and thus not terribly revealing. It did not, for example, tell us *why* the costs of organizing some transactions within a firm are lower than they would be in the market. Further work led to this hypothesis: A firm can reduce costs by internalizing some of its trans-actions rather than relying on the market because its management can summarily order or direct the use of resources (capital and labor) without having to recontract daily in response to changing market signals (interest rates, wage levels). This hypothesis, in turn, raised two sets of practical questions that greatly interest us.

One relates to what has been referred to as the "governance" of human resources within the firm.[11] Scholars examined the relative efficiency of different methods to organize and mobilize employees and concluded that efforts to specify detailed work rules are not only costly but pointless because no one can possibly devise rules to anticipate all possible permutations of circumstances. Furthermore, employees who know more about what is involved in day-to-day work can always find ways to circumvent the rules, or to "cheat."

Instead of detailed work rules, this sort of analysis seems to call for workplace incentive schemes. For example, firms could set up pro-duction teams and pay them bonuses based on their respective output. Or they could establish a salary schedule that rewards supervisors according to the efficiency of the teams they monitor. But many scholars have questioned the effectiveness of such incentive schemes. They have noted that it is difficult to measure, let alone assure, the quality of a team's ouput, and that it is virtually impossible to prevent "free-riding" by some team members.

The other practical question inspired by efforts to devise a new theory of the firm had to do with long-term trading relationships involving "asset specificity," the extent to which a transaction requires the buyer or seller to own a specific asset (such as a specifically tooled machine or a specifically trained employee) that would be of substantially less value if deployed elsewhere.[12] As asset specificity increases (as it does, for example, in the case of transactions between automobile assemblers and auto parts producers), the marketplace of prospective buyers and sellers grows smaller, collapsing in some cases to just one buyer and seller. Suffice it to say that it bears little resemblance to the wide-open free-for-all contemplated by neoclassical theory.

In such relationships, one party (usually the buyer) can demand better terms (such as a lower price) by threatening to stop trading or to trade a lesser amount. The effectiveness of this threat depends on the amount of the "hostage" (the specific capital and/or human assets dedicated to the specific trading relationship by the threatened party) and on the degree of difficulty involved in finding an alternative trading partner (who often must meet several necessary conditions to be a substitute). At the same time, however, the seller (supplier) in such a relationship may decide to make a suboptimal investment, hedging against the bet that its buyer will stop trading or purchase less because the buyer knows that the seller has a large sunk cost and is thus willing to take lower prices. A suboptimal investment, however, will not reduce production costs enough to allow the two parties to maximize profits.

One solution to this dilemma is long-term contracting between buyer and seller. But because they are usually quite complex, such contracts may impose high costs of writing, monitoring, and enforcement. On top of that, unforeseen situations may arise, requiring the parties to renegotiate their pact. Costs thus rise even higher. The other solution, often favored by Western firms, is integration of the seller into the buyer (via merger or acquisition). But this, too, falls far short of being a panacea. Integration means larger capital requirements and thus greater financial risk, as well as an increase in the cost of management and internal organization. In addition, it may not prove as efficient as the status quo. Even if savvy owners of acquired firms are retained as managers by the acquiring firm, they may no longer feel compelled to do their best. This is only natural. In their previous role as owner, they were able to capture all the benefits of ownership. And as we noted earlier, writing a contract to get the most out of a hired manager is no easy task. So the incentive structure facing the owner-turned-manager may not be ideal.

In short, the new theory of the firm yields valuable insights and thus represents a significant improvement over the old (neoclassical) theory, in which the firm appears to be little more than a "black box." But it still has some way to go. For one thing, it must become more dynamic, more able to analyze the behavior of firms over time.[13] Second, the theory must consider more carefully the role of knowledge, including technology, in determining the behavior of firms. Third, it must include a better analysis of *keiretsu* and other firm-like organizations that lie somewhere between long-term contractual relations and integration.[14] Fourth, it should evaluate the benefits and costs of firm-like organizations, long-term contracting relationships, and other exclusionary alliances. Who gains and who loses from such pacts and quasi-pacts? And finally, the theory should "endogenize" the variable of bargaining power. It must begin to ask: What effect does a difference in technology and managerial capacity, financial clout, and other assets have in determining the character of a trading relationship?[15] To satisfy us, in particular, a theory of the firm must be able to use the concept of bargaining power to distinguish the unequal relationship between a large multinational and a small, host-country firm from the more equal relationship between two large multinationals.[16]

If these and other nagging questions are tackled, the new theory of the firm can become a truly useful analysis. We are encouraged to learn that scholars working on this theory readily agree and have resolved to do much more.[17]

Neoinstitutional Analysis

If transaction costs, which are determined by institutions, create a structure of incentives that guides the behavior of a single firm, then perhaps they also operate on an aggregate level to guide the behavior of all firms and individuals in an economy. This is the intellectual spark that ignited neoinstitutional analysis, a kind of macroeconomic theory of transaction costs. It suggests that institutions, as the arbiters of transaction costs, hold the key to the long-run performance of any macroeconomy. No scholar has contributed more to this bold analysis than Douglass North, an economic historian who received the 1993 Nobel prize for his effort in the field.

North is motivated by a deep dissatisfaction with neoclassical theory, which he views as a short-run analysis. He writes that:

> We have paid a big price for the uncritical acceptance of neoclassical theory. Although the systematic application of price theory to economic history was a major contribution, neoclassical theory is concerned with the allocation of resources at a moment of time, a devastatingly limiting feature to historians whose central question is to account for change over time. Moreover, the allocation was assumed to occur in a frictionless world, that is, one in which institutions either did not exist or did not matter. These two conditions gave away what economic history is really all about: to attempt to explain the diverse patterns of growth, stagnation, and decay of societies over time, and to explore the way in which the frictions that are the consequences of human interaction produce widely divergent results.[18]

Institutions, according to North, encourage or discourage individuals and firms to save, take risks, and innovate – the three activities he believes are most crucial in determining the long-run performance of an economy. Although he defines institutions quite broadly to encompass not only formal structures but also social values, North focuses much of his attention on the role of government, which he calls the "definer" and "enforcer" of property rights – rights to use, earn, or transfer assets (defined broadly to include, for example, human capital).[19] The government, then, is the central institution that determines the costs of writing, monitoring, and enforcing contracts to ensure that an economic actor's (an individual or firm's) property rights are adequately protected, and thus that that actor can capture the maximum benefits of its assets (labor, capital, etc.). In other words, the government creates a structure of incentives or disincentives that determine whether individuals and firms will sufficiently save, take risks, and innovate.

We must bear in mind, however, that government may not always create an optimal structure of incentives for the entire economy. This is due to the fact that it is an economic actor in its own right, and not merely a faceless institution.[20] As such, the government may enact laws and engage in practices designed to retain power, or increase the wealth and/or privilege of favored constituents. For example, as we know all too well, public officials may act on behalf of "rent-seekers" who provide valued goods (from bribes to votes) in exchange for the political leverage that allows them to maximize their own income or wealth at the expense of society at large.[21]

In virtually every nation, a government will act in many different ways, sometimes reducing transaction costs and sometimes increasing them. What matters to the economy as a whole is the net effect of these actions. If the net effect is to reduce transaction costs, the economy will have a structure of incentives that boosts economic performance. But if the net effect is to increase those transaction costs, the economy will stagnate. Thus, to borrow North's terminology, the government is the pivotal institution that determines an economy's structural frontier (the structural limit of its economic performance), which he believes is even more decisive than its technological frontier (the limit of its economic performance as determined by its technological capacity).

North concedes, however, that institutions, including government, are "path-dependent" and thus difficult to change.[22] We can intuitively understand why. Those who are adversely affected by a change often have substantial influence, and use it to resist change. To overcome such odds, a sufficient number of persons who have a stake in changing that institution must pool their efforts to effect the desired change. History demonstrates just how difficult this task is.[23]

For our purposes, North's analysis is useful because it shows that institutions, particularly government, can act to help or hinder the performance of an economy over time.[24] Still, it is less than perfect.[25] As the intellectual sibling of the new "transaction costs" theory of the firm, it shares some of that theory's flaws. In particular, neoinstitutional analysis fails to shed much light on the powerful variable of technological change, and it does not spell out the operational conditions under which institutions (such as government and a high-technology industry, or two related high-tech firms, or management and labor within a high-tech firm) cooperate to reduce transaction costs. These tasks have fallen to others.

Toward a New Theory of Trade

A decade after they began to reexamine the neoclassical theory of the firm, economists began to rethink the neoclassical theory of international trade. This was long overdue. They could see plainly that trade no longer was driven by the fixed and underlying advantages of nations; instead, it appeared to flow according to the more fleeting advantages, particularly technological advantages, of large firms. The case for free trade was becoming harder and harder to make. Paul Krugman, for example, confided that he, among many others, was:

> forced to recognize that the industries that account for much of world trade are not at all well described by the supply and demand analysis that lies behind the assertion that markets are best left to themselves. As we have seen, much of trade appears to require an explanation in terms of economies of scale, learning curves and the dynamics of innovation – all phenomena incompatible with the kind of idealizations under which free trade is always the best policy. Economists refer to such phenomena as "market imperfections," a term that in itself conveys the presumption that these are marginal to a system that approaches ideal performance fairly closely. In reality, however, it may be that imperfections are the rule rather than the exception.[26]

Instead of mindlessly beating the drum for free trade in every possible case, Krugman and a handful of other economists cautiously suggested that perhaps a government could improve national welfare by pursuing activist or strategic trade policies (such as subsidizing or protecting targeted export industries) in two related but carefully circumscribed cases.[27]

The first case has to do with an oligopolistic industry that requires such large fixed costs of R&D, production capacity, and market development that it can accommodate only a very small number of mammoth competitors (say, a Boeing and an Airbus). Being so highly concentrated, such an industry generates unusually high returns (excess profits or "rent"). Potential rivals, unable to muster the required capital, will not enter the market and eat up this rent. In this case, government policies to protect or promote such an industry might help a domestic producer win a larger share of the global market, and thus a larger share of available rent. The second case, which has to do with spillovers, is more straightforward. Some industries may generate externalities, particularly knowledge from R&D activities, that benefit the domestic economy as a whole. This fact also seems to justify government intervention.

For us, the theory of strategic trade raises a fascinating question: If governments can pursue strategic *trade*, then why can't they also pursue strategic *investment*? We, of course, believe they can – and that the Japanese government, in fact, *is* pursuing strategic investment in Asia.

But the academic debate generated by this new theoretical approach has not yet come that far.[28] Instead, it has become bogged down in what can only be viewed as religion. Free traders attack the theory, saying it fails to consider the allocative inefficiencies that would be caused by favoring one domestic industry over others. They claim that a government, by subsidizing, say, domestic chipmakers, would end up raising the cost of capital for automakers, chemical and steel manufacturers, as well as other domestic producers. Free traders also argue strongly that governments would not react passively if their global counterparts adopted strategic policies. Instead, they would retaliate by adopting promotional or protectionist policies of their own, and a full-blown trade war could ensue.[29]

From the other side of the fence, proponents of "managed trade" attack the new theory for not going far enough. Like traditional trade theory, it is, according to Dosi, Tyson, and Zysman, "inherently static in orientation," concerned only with the possibility of achieving "once and for all" gains in national welfare.[30] Invoking the long-neglected wisdom of Joseph Schumpeter, the Austrian economist who argued that firms compete as much on the basis of new products and processes (in other words, on the basis of new technology) as they do on the basis of price, this trio advocates aggressive government intervention to capture the dynamic benefits of innovation and help launch a nation's economy on a long-term growth trajectory.

We welcome any debate that fixes attention on the cherished assumptions of neoclassical theory. This one, in particular, is significant in that it revolves around the presumed merits of studying economic growth without attempting to account for technological change. At the same time, however, the scholarly debate has not yielded much more than a contest of "clever" models, most of which cannot be empirically tested and others which cannot tell us anything of great consequence.[31] We include in this latter category the "gravity model" used by Jeffrey Frankel to examine trade flows between partners in Asia. This model, discussed briefly in the preface, is able to produce sheet after sheet of statistical data about the impact on trade of different variables. But in the end, it offers only this rather unsurprising and unrevealing conclusion: Countries that are geographically proximate and that have relatively large economies (measured in GNP) are likely to trade a lot with one another.[32]

Sifting through the results of Frankel's gravity model test reminds us of a remark made not too long ago by Krugman. In a moment of intellectual pique, he appealed to his colleagues to put down their calculators and put on their thinking caps. "The priority," he wrote, "is not to construct more clever models, but how to build a bridge to reality."[33]

Developmentalist Analysis

Murakami Yasusuke, a Japanese economist, has advanced an analytical framework that we believe can, with some structural reinforcement, serve as a bridge to reality.[34] The central premise of developmentalist analysis is that, contrary to neoclassical theory, firms in a developing economy that are able to adopt successively more advanced technology (firms that achieve what we have called "dynamic technological efficiency," or DTE) are thereby able to reduce their average production costs over the long run.[35] This begs the big question: How are firms able to achieve DTE?

Murakami's answer is that they can do so with the help of an effective government that uses indicative or guidance-based intervention, rather than heavy-handed regulation, to overcome market failures. For example, the government can promote saving and encourage financial institutions to allocate that additional capital to innovating industries. The government can also coordinate the pace of investment to avoid excessive competition, or what Murakami calls "domestic dumping." This controversial notion requires some elaboration.

Profit-maximizing firms that are adopting new technology will engage in market share maximizing competition because they face declining long-run costs, and thus can increase profits by increasing output and sales. Demand, however, is not likely to keep pace with increasing productive capacity. So firms will engage in domestic dumping, setting prices at a level equal to a normal rate of profit minus the amount saved by increasing output.

If it is allowed to run its course, this process of domestic dumping will breed chaos and inefficiency. Competitors will be bankrupted, leaving the market controlled by the (monopolistic) firm or (oligopolistic) firms that managed to increase output and market share most rapidly. Because capital and labor resources of bankrupted firms in the real world are not absorbed as tidily as neoclassical theory assumes, unemployment or underemployment of those resources is inevitable.

The government could take action to control such long-term economic and social costs. It could, for example, authorize a *temporary* cartel that would set prices at a level high enough to enable firms to remain in the industry and continue adopting new technology. With an incentive to maintain or increase their respective market shares, firms would continue to engage in all forms of nonprice competition (service, product quality, delivery schedule, etc.) over the life of the cartel. And as soon as demand caught up with supply, the government could terminate the cartel, enabling firms to begin competing again on price in the marketplace. Economic growth, unfettered by waste, would accelerate.[36]

Murakami acknowledges that, over the long run, such developmentalist policies will impose costs of their own. For one thing, they can create an entrenched bureaucratic-industrial infrastructure that outlives its usefulness, hanging on long after a developing nation has caught up and its firms have evolved to the level that they are operating at the frontier of global technology. This is because successful developmentalist policies and practices beget economic growth and economic growth begets complacency. But in a developed or industrialized country, he notes, such policies and practices can actually backfire, creating a corrupt political system that is "captured" by business interests, and a sclerotic economic system that stymies some of the cutting-edge innovation it needs to push itself forward. In addition, developmentalism is bound to be a source of trade friction when it is practiced by a country that already has achieved a substantial level of development or industrialization.

If for no other reason than that it helps explain Japan's rapid economic growth following World War II, as well as its more recent slow-down, Murakami's analysis is exceptionally useful. But we believe it loses some of its strength if we try to stretch it too far, to try to do what the author himself intended to do – that is, use developmentalism as a model for catch-up industrialization.

Murakami acknowledges that not all governments have what it takes to successfully carry out developmentalist policies and engage in developmentalist practices. He identifies two prerequisites: these governments must have a close working relationship with domestic industry, and they must have the legitimacy needed to mobilize citizens behind the goal of catching up and achieving economic growth.

We believe, however, that other fundamental conditions must be met. Not only must government and business cooperate to achieve DTE, but individual firms must be willing and able to work together (to pool technical knowledge, for example).[37] As Daniel Okimoto has argued, Japanese industrial policy has worked effectively because of the structural interdependence of firms in the Japanese economy. "It provides ready-made points of entry for selective government intervention."[38] In addition, labor and management must be willing to collaborate to achieve the goal of increasing productivity over time.

To really understand what Japan is doing in Asia, then, we must use both developmentalist analysis, which highlights institutional schemes to promote innovation, and neoinstitutional analysis, which explains how such schemes might actually work by raising or reducing transaction costs. Although neither states so explicitly, both approaches suggest clearly that cooperation can, in certain circumstances, overcome the risks associated with uncertainty (an inherent part of both innovation and globalization) and thus enhance efficiency.

Our Perspective

If, as we argue, neoclassical analysis in general and its theories of the firm and trade in particular are inadequate tools in thinking about the nature of Japan's economic expansion in Asia, what can we offer in their place?

We believe the following analytical perspective enables us to understand this ongoing phenomenon more accurately. We call it a perspective, not a theory, because it is not universalistic. But it does yield refutable hypotheses that neoclassical economists and others may wish to challenge. We hope our perspective will be useful in developing more adequate theories of the firm and trade.

To appreciate what Japan is doing in Asia, we must begin by recognizing that it is regionalizing the developmentalist policies and practices that generated rapid economic growth in Japan in the 1950s and 1960s – the same developmentalist policies and practices that put severe strains on the domestic political economy in the 1970s and 1980s, when Japan's leading manufacturers had achieved technological parity with their counterparts in the West. The most obvious strains have been bribery scandals, sky-high domestic consumer prices, and increasingly fractious relations with trading partners.[39]

As Saitō Seiichirō argues, Japan's developmentalism (which he calls a "production-first strategy") became "widely and deeply entrenched in the economic structure" of the nation. Although these policies and practices were quite effective during the catch-up phase of Japan's postwar economic development, they have "clearly become a source of distortion and imbalance now that Japan has become an economic superpower."[40] Japan could overcome this distortion and imbalance by dismantling its own developmentalist system. This option, which in Japan's popular press has become synonymous with deregulation, is favored by many Japanese academics and journalists. But it is vigorously opposed, for obvious reasons, by the business and government interests that benefit most from developmentalism. They prefer a different approach. They would rather export Japan's developmentalist system, putting it to work in a larger context, a region (Asia) that is still trying to achieve catch-up development.

Think of developmentalism as yeast. It has already done its job in Japan, producing a large glob of dough that now threatens to spill over the top of the mixing bowl. There are two ways to avoid a mess. One is to kill the leavening agent (by sticking the dough in the oven). The other is to find a larger bowl and let the yeast keep working, let the dough keep expanding. Japan's government–business network, the beneficiary as well as the architect of Japanese developmentalism (and an institution we examine more closely in chapter seven), is pursuing option two in Asia.

Asia is perhaps the most suitable site in the world for an expansion of Japanese developmentalism. Besides the fact that it is right next door to Japan, the region is still developing. Wage levels are rising quickly, but remain low compared to those in the developed world. Outside South Korea and Taiwan, technological levels also remain fairly low. At the same time, Asia is filled with developmentalist-minded governments that are eager to have their economies leavened not only by Japanese capital and technology, but also by Japanese guidance on government intervention and industrial organization.

Just what *is* this developmentalism that Japan now seeks to regionalize? We answer this question in some detail in chapter four. For now, however, it may be sufficient to say that Japanese developmentalism consists of a dense web of mutually reinforcing ties – between government and business, between business and business, and between management and labor. In a nutshell, cooperation is the principle that informs Japan's developmentalist policies and practices.

These days, many scholars have begun to examine what is called "international strategic cooperation" between high-technology firms in developed countries.[41] Firms facing uncertainty as they strive to adopt new technology are facing even greater uncertainty as they struggle to recoup their large fixed investments in R&D by competing in an expanded (global) market. Rather than relying on long-term contracting, which imposes high transaction costs, or resorting to vertical integration, which may reduce some but impose other costs, oligopolistic high-tech firms increasingly are turning to joint ventures, technology licensing agreements, production sharing agreements, and other forms of international cooperation. To use the language of game theory, cooperation in such cases is usually a form of coordination, an efficiency-promoting arrangement effected through "mutual forbearance."[42]

Most of this new research has focused on horizontal alliances between firms of similar size or technological capability. It has examined, for example, the cooperative relationship between Pratt and Whitney and Rolls Royce to produce a new aircraft engine, and the agreement between Motorola and Toshiba to share the complementary skills needed to develop a new generation of integrated circuits. But this research, while extremely valuable, too often ignores long-standing alliances between parties of unequal power, alliances that in Japan are called vertical *keiretsu* and that reflect what could be called "vertical quasi-integration" – a unique form of cooperation that lies somewhere between vertical integration of transactions within a single firm and long-term contracting between a stronger and a weaker firm.[43]

Japan is, we argue, regionalizing and thereby revitalizing its developmentalist system by exporting some of the *keiretsu* ties that already exist in

Japan and by forging new vertical ties between dominant Japanese firms and subordinate local firms. The terms "dominant Japanese firm" and "subordinate local firm," which suggest a difference in relative power, must be defined in context. Thus, in the relationship between a parent firm in Japan and its Japanese subsidiary or affiliate in Asia, the former is the dominant Japanese firm and the latter is the subordinate local firm. The same is true in the relationship between a Japanese affiliate that assembles manufacturing goods in Asia and a local supplier or distributor in the region, as well as between a Japan-based technology licensor and the Asian-based licensee of that technology. All of these vertical relationships are patterned after Japan's home-based vertical *keiretsu*, the firm-like relationships typically maintained between a large manufacturer and its suppliers, or between a large manufacturer and its distributors.

Using vertical quasi-integration, the firm with more bargaining power (with, in other words, greater technological and managerial capacity, as well as greater financial muscle) involves itself intensively and over a long period in the operation of the firm with less bargaining power. For example, the dominant Japanese firm will usually provide the subordinate local firm with one or more of the following: capital (either equity or loan financing), technology (either through a license, the export of machinery and parts, or the training of employees), managerial know-how (usually in the form of expatriate managers or advisers), and a market for the subordinate firm's goods (including perhaps the dominant firm itself and its own sales network). In almost all cases, however, the dominant firm will also assist, guide, or perhaps even direct the subordinate firm to use these resources in a particular way, and will play an active role in helping the subordinate firm devise plans for future investment, production, and marketing.

At first glance, Jinbao Electronics would not appear to fit the description of a subordinate local firm. It is one of Taiwan's leading exporters – big and bold enough to assume the risk of operating its own manufacturing plant in Thailand. But take a closer look. Jinbao is assembling calculators in Thailand for Sharp on the basis of an original equipment manufacturing (OEM) agreement. The Taiwanese producer runs the plant, but not much else. It manufactures calculators according to the Japanese firm's precise specifications and with parts imported from the dominant firm's suppliers in Japan. Jinbao stamps Sharp's name on every finished product, then turns them over to the Japanese firm for sale around the world.[44] It's a good arrangement for Jinbao, the subordinate firm, but an even better one for Sharp, the dominant firm.

Through vertical quasi-integration, the dominant firm maximizes the advantages of both integration and long-term contracting while minimizing the disadvantages of both. Because the owner of the subordinate firm is motivated by strong ownership incentives, the dominant firm can expect to receive the owner's maximum contribution (which is especially important when an overseas investor has much less knowledge of a local economy and society). At the same time, though, the dominant firm can nudge (or compel, if necessary) the local subordinate firm in Asia to invest a sufficient amount in resources, thus reducing the risk of ineffecent production due to underinvestment. And it is able to avoid both the financial burden of raising additional capital and the internal reorganization costs it would incur if it simply acquired the subordinate firm. Finally, the dominant firm has a substantial amount of flexibility (or discretion) to change output levels – more, in fact, than it would have under a long-term contract and nearly as much as it would have under full integration.[45]

Why is the subordinate firm willing to cooperate in allowing the dominant firm to realize all these advantages from the vertical *keiretsu* relationship? The answer is simple: it is attracted to the "carrot" and threatened by the "stick" wielded by the dominant firm.

The carrot includes not only the resources (capital, technology, managerial know-how, and a market) a dominant firm provides, but also the profits and wages earned over the life of the relationship. In addition, it includes the prospect of a more promising, or at least more certain, future than the available alternatives (such as operating independently or entering into a long-term contract with either a large local firm or a Western multinational). After all, the "typical" Japanese multinational operating in Asia has demonstrated a willingness and an ability to maintain such *keiretsu*-type relationships for long periods. And in the aggregate, these multinationals have been able to grab larger and larger market shares, and thus market power, by achieving significant economies of coordinated intranetwork investment, production, and marketing, and thus by becoming extraordinarily competitive producers. Finally, these local subordinate firms are fully aware that host governments in Asia, the recipients of enormous sums of foreign aid from the Japanese government, are predisposed to give favors and concessions to members of a Japanese-dominated production network (both dominant and subordinate firms). Under these circumstances, tying one's fortune to a dominant Japanese firm seems like the right thing to do.

Besides, the stick wielded by such a firm can appear quite menacing.[46] As in the case of vertical *keiretsu* in Japan, network ties in Asia are often cemented by hostages, which are assets (capital and human) dedicated to the relationship. This is what we previously referred to as "asset specificity." Although a few economists are just beginning to recognize its importance in determining the characteristics of interfirm relations, asset specificity in fact serves as a long-established operational norm in the case of vertical *keiretsu*. For instance, to meet the demands of their major manufacturing customers, Japanese suppliers often must invest in highly specific job training for their employees and use precisely calibrated tools and dies for production. These are dedicated assets that have virtually no value outside the particular *keiretsu* relationship. In one study, Japanese suppliers reported that 22 percent of their capital investments were so highly dedicated to their primary customer that "these customized physical assets could not be redeployed if the customer walked away." US suppliers, in contrast, indicated that only 15 percent of their investments could not be redeployed.[47]

Under these terms, a subordinate firm in Asia can ill afford to shirk or do anything but exert its maximum effort to maintain the vertical quasi-integrated relationship. This is because it faces the very real threat that the dominant Japanese firm will terminate the relationship, causing a drastic reduction in the value of the assets dedicated to the relationship. An example may be useful. Suppose that a Thai firm supplies auto parts to a Nissan affiliate in Bangkok. The parts are produced according to Nissan's detailed specifications using Nissan-supplied machinery and Nissan-trained employees. If it loses its tie-up with the Japanese assembler, the Thai supplier understands full well that it will have a very difficult time securing an alternative buyer. So it will do what it can to avoid that fate – a fate that would include having a large amount of its assets unutilized or underutilized for a long time.

Up to now, we have focused exclusively on the vertical business ties between Japanese and Asian firms. But we should not ignore the vertical *political* ties between the Japanese government and host regimes in Asia. These ties, which we discuss in chapter eight, are maintained and strengthened through a similar process of unbalanced bargaining. In exchange for large amounts of Japanese ODA (official development assistance, or foreign aid), host regimes in Asia grant Japanese government and business officials an opportunity to influence – and, in some cases, even write – the industrial policies of the recipient countries. Thus, it is no wonder that host countries are adopting policies that tend to solidify the production networks being built by Japanese MNCs throughout the region.

If the perspective we have outlined here is correct, the regionalization of Japan's *keiretsu*-based developmentalist system will have far-reaching consequences for local Asian firms and nations trying to develop their own technological capabilities, for the global trade regime in general, and for non-Japanese multinationals trying to set up operations in Asia. We examine these anticipated outcomes one at a time.

Using vertical quasi-integration, Japanese multinationals embrace their subordinate local firms in Asia just as the big Japanese assemblers embrace their parts suppliers in Japan.[48] They do so by carefully coordinating the deployment of the specific resources, particularly technology and management know-how, they bring to the relationship. This allows them to control the pace (and thus the level) at which they transfer technology, and in turn allows them to capture more firmly the gains from the technology they possess.[49]

For subordinate local firms in the host country in Asia, vertical quasi-integration serves to restrict the development of indigenous technical skills. Contrary to the sanguine assumptions of the flying geese theory, the Asian NICs, the new NICs, and the non-NICs (such as China and Vietnam) are not likely to achieve technology parity with Japan any time in the near future.[50]

In terms of trade, our analysis indicates that Japanese multinationals themselves determine the volume and composition of much of the trade between Japan and Asia. This is not to say that exchange rates and local business conditions don't matter. They do. But Japanese dominant firms, striving to increase the international competitiveness of their vertical networks, matter even more. This is because they dictate the flow of high-tech, high value-added goods (primarily capital goods and intermediate products) from Japan, through intranetwork channels, to appropriate processing sites in Asia. Thus, it is not difficult to see why Japan enjoys a large trade surplus with so many of its neighbors in the region.

But why do so many Asian nations export so much to the United States and Europe? One important reason is that the Japanese multinationals controlling regional production networks must seek new markets whenever their productive capacities in Asia exceed regional demand. They even resort to "forward pricing" (dumping) to export goods to Western countries, which have the incomes necessary to import the goods manufactured in these networks. This, of course, is reminiscent of the behavior of large *keiretsu* firms during the rapid-growth era in Japan. At that time, too, they sought to maintain high production levels, no matter what social cost might be incurred.

Finally, we must note that the vertical quasi-integration maintained by Japanese multinationals in Asia cannot help but be exclusionary. Just as foreign firms have had a hard time trying to enter Japanese markets dominated by *keiretsu* relationships, American or European multinationals will have a very hard time breaking into Asian markets dominated by Japan's vertical production networks. The degree of difficulty will increase proportionately as the market share and power of such networks increase.[51]

We believe that Western manufacturers of automobiles and electronics will experience the greatest difficulty. It is in these industries that Japanese multinationals, fully supported by the Japanese government, have established the most extensive vertical *keiretsu* networks in Asia. They have used these many networks to exploit their own technological advantages and expand their already considerable claim to world markets. Western high-tech firms, in contrast, generally use long-term contracts with suppliers and do not organize their operations on principles of vertical quasi-integration. This puts them at a disadvantage.

Let us conclude this chapter with a few caveats. First, ours is a medium-term analysis that cannot and does not attempt to predict what might happen in the relatively distant future. By 2050, for example, Japan may lose its technological edge; some Asian nations, weary of being squeezed, may manage to extricate themselves from Japan's embrace; and the region's cohesive alliance may unravel. In the medium term, however, this is not likely to happen. As we will show in subsequent chapters, the Japanese government is moving aggressively to secure the nation's innovative capacity. More importantly, Japan is consolidating (and regionalizing) its developmentalist system of cooperation, a system that promotes dynamic technological efficiency. Japanese firms suffer far less from the internal compartmentalization of planning, R&D, production, and other activities that stymies innovation in other countries, according to Wada Akihiro, vice president in charge of technology at Toyota. "This is Japan's strength and is not going to change."[52] At least not in the medium term.

Second, we do not pretend that our perspective is equally valid for all Asian economies, nor for all industries. As we have just suggested, our perspective applies best to manufacturing industries, especially high-tech industries such as automobiles and electronics. These industries, however, can function as an engine, transforming a low-wage, labor-intensive, and developing economy into a higher-wage, technology-intensive, and developed economy. Such was the case in Japan's developmentalist experience.

Finally, we fully acknowledge that we have made some bold, sweeping statements that, even in the medium term, may be contradicted here and there by facts. For example, there are cases in which integration, due to scale economies, will prove more efficient than quasi-integration; an Asian government will successfully intervene to restrict the behavior of a Japanese multinational; competition from an American or European rival will force a Japanese multinational to modify or even abandon a preferred course of action in Asia; a sudden, unexpected increase in production costs will cause a Japanese assembler to choose a low-cost but unrelated supplier. These are all possible scenarios. All we claim is that our perspective provides a more valid and useful analytic framework than neoclassical theory for organizing the evidence we observe in the real world in Asia.

CHAPTER FOUR

The Political Economy of Japan

To really understand how Japanese developmentalism is weaving together the economies of Asia, we must first know how the system works at home. This is a heavily tilled but thinly harvested field.

Some neoclassical economists argue that Japan operates just like any other capitalist economy, and thus can be analyzed adequately with the standard tools of neoclassical theory. A few even go so far as to suggest that Japan is closer to the neoclassical model – with more competition and less government intervention – than the United States or other industrial economies. There is little need for us to spend time on such a preposterous claim.[1]

We must, though, take seriously those neoclassical economists who recognize that Japan has used a distinctive set of institutions to promote economic development, but who nonetheless insist that it began dismantling those institutions in the prolonged, post-bubble recession of the early 1990s. Bergsten and Noland, for example, foresee a coming convergence between the capitalist systems of the world's two economic superpowers, Japan and the United States.

> Japanese business ... will in this view ease off at least a bit as employees and suppliers demand better treatment, and as the imperative of globalization induces Japanese firms to harmonize their practices with the rest of the world. Globalization of financial markets will meanwhile weaken the financial *keiretsu* and equalize the cost of capital across countries.... Japan is beginning to apply antitrust policy more aggressively and has started to liberalize its distribution system; both of these institutions can also erode the *keiretsu* system over time.

The bureaucracy will steadily lose its ability to guide the economy as a result of globalization and the inexorable increase in the economy's complexity and market orientation.[2]

Sound familiar? Similar views were expressed in the mid 1970s, when Japan's rapid growth was abruptly derailed by the big oil "shock," and in the mid 1980s, when Japan's exports suddenly had to swim against the rip tide of *endaka*. The country pulled through both these crises by retooling its distinctive set of institutions, not by dismantling them. And it is pulling through this one, too, in large part by regionalizing its developmentalist system.

This does not mean that today's Japan is the same as yesterday's. Nauseated by a long and polluted stream of corruption scandals, voters have become more volatile, less willing to automatically support the Liberal Democratic Party.[3] Employers, even some of the largest and most successful firms, have restructured operations, laying off employees that in the past might have been treated as "permanent." Japan's Fair Trade Commission, once a paper tiger, now takes its trust-busting respon-sibilities more seriously. And nearly everyone, it seems, is promoting some plan to curb the bureaucracy's power.

Unlike the so-called revisionists, who argue that Japan is a unique creature that resists change, we acknowledge that Japan has changed and is changing a great deal.[4] But we believe the changes now taking place are neither as sweeping nor as profound as some optimists such as Bergsten and Noland have suggested. Despite all the talk about deregulation, Japan's bureaucrats continue to wield far more influence than their counterparts in Washington, London, Bonn, or even Paris.[5] They do so by collaborating with business elites on everything from regulatory policy to monetary policy, from investment incentives to foreign aid levels. Japanese firms, including those not bound together by explicit *keiretsu* ties, continue to support one another in ways that would be unthinkable in a more traditional system of market capitalism, such as America's, where interfirm loyalty is, according to the former president of Bethlehem Steel, "only $2/ton deep."[6] And labor–management relations remain far more peaceful in Japan than in the United States or Europe.

Cooperation, we argue, is alive and well – not only in Japan's domestic political economy, but also in its regional production alliance. In fact, as an operating principle, cooperation serves to set Japan apart from the West and, as we hope to demonstrate in the following chapter, from its less cohesively organized neighbors in Asia as well. Thus, one American scholar has referred to Japan's model of political economy as one of "alliance capitalism," while a prominent economist in Japan has called it "network capitalism."[7]

Furthermore, we argue that the logic of cooperation will transcend this particular moment, driving Japan's developmentalist political economy well into the future. This is due not only to the path-dependent nature of institutions, which for many years have pushed and pulled individuals in Japan to subjugate their own narrow interests to the broader interests of clan, company, and nation. It is also due to a set of economic and political incentives, deeply rooted in Japanese institutions, that encourage such joint efforts. In other words, cooperation reflects rational expectations. As we attempted to show in chapter three, cooperation can, under certain conditions, reduce a firm's transaction costs and thus, in the aggregate, enhance a nation's long-term developmental prospects. It is particularly useful for firms that face uncertainty and risk as they try to adopt successively more advanced technology. That is to say, cooperation offers stability to those who plunge headlong into the hunt for dynamic technological efficiency (DTE), the goal of developmentalism.

Since a substantial amount of literature is already available, here we briefly sketch the evolution of cooperation inside three overlapping nexuses in Japan's political economy.

Government and Business

Using all the carrots and sticks at their disposal, government officials played a central role in the rapid growth of the Japanese economy between 1950 and 1973.[8] Perhaps most importantly, they took steps to increase the supply of loanable funds that fueled Japan's growth. Tax incentives were enacted to promote saving; money was printed at a swift, steady clip; and credit was steered through the financial system to large manufacturers adopting new technology.

Credit rationing served as an exceptionally powerful tool of industrial policy. By insulating Japan's capital market from the outside world and by setting interest rates at an artificially low level, the Ministry of Finance (MOF) created excess demand for credit. As a result, it was able to use what became known as "window guidance" to prod banks to loan funds to targeted industries and even favored firms. Most of the money went to Japan's biggest commercial or "city" banks, which emerged as the financial centers of the horizontal *keiretsu*, or enterprise groups. These banks in turn loaned much of this low-cost capital to large, *keiretsu*-affiliated firms. Over time, the targets of MOF's credit-rationing program evolved – from shipbuilders and steel producers to chemical and machinery manufacturers.[9]

MOF had more direct control over another source of capital, the Fiscal Investment and Loan Program (FILP), which Noguchi has referred to as the "second budget."[10] This program tapped into the postal savings accounts maintained by households all over Japan and supplied capital to government-controlled institutions such as the Export-Import Bank and the Japan Development Bank, which in turn pumped investment capital into infrastructure and industrial projects. Even as late as the 1970s, the FILP supplied nearly a third of all bank loans made in Japan.[11] But MOF was not, of course, the only patron of developmentalism. The Ministry of International Trade and Industry (MITI) also began providing subsidies, particularly tax breaks, to strategic manufacturing interests.[12]

The flow of cheap capital and government subsidies soon ignited an "investment race" as firms sought to adopt successively more sophisticated technology, increase output, reduce production costs, increase market share, and win larger profits. As we discussed in the previous chapter, this kind of race can wreak as much economic havoc as a tornado in a trailer park. Without intervention, it is almost certain to lead to chronic excess capacity, domestic dumping, widespread bankruptcy, and – in the end – uncompetitive markets dominated by a "winning" monopolist or a few "victorious" oligopolists.

To avoid these outcomes, MITI stepped in to supervise the investment race. It "guided" each oligopolist to invest an amount proportionate to its current market share, and thereby maintain the stability of that market. In many cases, especially those in which firms adopted new technology that provided economies of scale in production, MITI authorized the use of cartels to reduce or eliminate excess capacity.[13]

Without question, the government's power to guide private investment has waned over the past two decades. The liberalization of financial markets that began in the early 1970s gradually stripped MOF of its ability to allocate capital resources.[14] Politicization of the budget-writing process has reduced MITI's power and influence, forcing it to compete with vested interests, such as environmental and social welfare groups, for tax revenues.[15]

Turf battles have come to preoccupy bureaucrats, undermining their overall cohesiveness.[16] And foreign pressure (*gaiatsu*), especially from the U.S. administration and Congress, has pushed the Japanese government to use more transparent means of communicating with industry, rather than what is commonly known as "administrative guidance" (*gyōsei shidō*).[17] A new law that took effect in late 1994 reflects these developments. Although vague in places and filled with loopholes, the law does require bureaucrats, upon request, to put guidance in writing and to explain why a license or permit application was held up or not approved.

It would be naive, however, to expect bureaucrats to abandon such a flexible tool of industrial policy. Indeed, a review of news stories over the past decade indicates they have not. For example, MITI stirred up controversy by using administrative guidance to block the import of gasoline refined abroad by Lion's Petroleum, and MOF was criticized for guiding Japanese securities firms to collude and thereby earn exorbitant profits, which were used to compensate corporate clients for stock losses after the bubble popped.[18] In addition, the Japan Sewerage Corp. (JSC), a public corporation under the jurisdiction of the Ministry of Construction, was assailed for encouraging nine electric machine manufacturers to form a cartel that fixed prices on the sale of equipment to JSC.[19]

In short, bureaucrats in Tokyo no longer have the financial tools and political autonomy to "govern" the nation, but they still have considerable clout.[20] The hard measures (both carrots and sticks) undertaken in the name of industrial policy during the rapid growth period appear to have given way to soft measures that promote carefully cultivated teamwork. A group of government and business officials from America's Washington State recently visited the city of Kobe, Japan and marveled at the cooperation between the public and private sectors. This was, according to the Japanese hosts, a function of Japan's "Third Sector," a combined effort by business as well as national and local governments.[21]

Above all else, Japanese bureaucrats use soft measures to bring otherwise rival firms together to pursue joint R&D efforts and expand high-technology production.[22] This is neither a small nor insignificant chore. Innovating firms require both a free hand to move quickly in and out of markets and a helping hand in tying up with other firms to reduce fixed costs. And because the products of high technology almost always cross industrial boundaries, they also need a respected third party such as the government to help them organize new coalitions.

This is not altogether new. In the early 1960s, MITI helped set up the Japan Electronic Computer Company (JECC), which was jointly owned by the country's leading, but still fledgling, computer manufacturers – Hitachi, Fujitsu, NEC, Mitsubishi, Toshiba, and Oki. Over the following two decades, the government funneled about $2 billion in low-interest loans to JECC, which in turn used the money to buy computers from its member firms and rent them to users (primarily corporations) for low monthly fees. JECC was, in effect, the industry's vehicle to build a domestic computer market, and the government's vehicle to guide the industry.[23]

In the early 1970s, when IBM introduced its new 370-series computer, MITI responded by organizing a national research project. Fujitsu and Hitachi agreed to collaborate on the development of large IBM-compatible computers; NEC and Toshiba worked together to build medium-sized Honeywell-compatible computers; and Oki and Mitsubishi pooled resources to build a set of small, specialized computers.

Thanks to the "New Series" project (1972–76), Japanese computer manufacturers were able to vault over their own informational deficiencies and enter the global high-tech sweepstakes in a serious way. But it was the next big project (1976–79) that allowed them to pull even with their American counterparts, and perhaps even pull ahead, by achieving very large scale integration (VLSI) of semiconductor circuits. This time, MITI organized reluctant firms into two groups. Fujitsu, Hitachi, and Mitsubishi maintained one lab, NEC and Toshiba another. In the end, the cooperating firms were able to produce 64K RAMs and ultimately the 1 megabit chip. Under MITI's gentle "guidance," they also began producing computers that matched or exceeded IBM's top-of-the-line machines in performance and beat them in price.[24]

The government has not abandoned such efforts to promote joint R&D. In fact, as Tyson notes, "there has been no dramatic change in Japan's industrial policy objectives." Bureaucrats still strive to "encourage competitiveness in targeted industries because of special economic benefits they are expected to generate for the entire economy."[25]

Indeed, during the 1980s and into the 1990s, MITI was directly or indirectly (via its Agency for Industrial Science and Technology) continuing to support nine high-tech projects receiving at least ¥10 billion in public funds. The projects included high-speed computers, advanced robot technology, interoperable data bases, advanced material processing, and advanced chemical products.[26]

Business and Business

Perhaps no other institution in Japan's political economy has received more scrutiny than the *keiretsu*, or business network. It seems odd, then, that so much misunderstanding persists about this form of interfirm cooperation.

Some scholars have argued that Japan's *keiretsu* are not fundamentally different from corporate groups in any other country. Komiya and Irie, for example, maintain that "long-standing (or fixed) business relationships characterized by the repetition of transactions between the same two (or more) enterprises are generally based on economic rationalities and are widely observed in any industrialized economy."[27] Evidence, however, suggests that interfirm relationships in Japan are maintained over a longer period of time, in a more intensive manner, and across more facets of corporate activity.[28] Unlike their Western counterparts, Japanese firms, according to one expert, tend to steer clear of the spot market.

One can hardly say that trading relationships among Japanese firms are based on the principle of free market trade. Once a trading relationship is begun, it usually becomes long-lasting, thus trading partners as a rule become fixed. In most cases, the number of trading partners is not increased. What Japanese firms attempt to do is to maintain intensive, cooperative, and long-term relationships with a small number of firms.[29]

Other scholars have argued that the *keiretsu*, as an economic institution, is disappearing. In a study of Japan's changing industrial structure, Imai describes "a process of gradually loosening intercorporate linkages and blurring corporate boundaries."[30] There is something to this. The nature of interfirm relations in Japan has indeed changed dramatically over the past two decades.

For starters, many *keiretsu* members no longer rely exclusively on debt financing by the main bank in their group. Toyota Motors, for example, has amassed such internal wealth that it acts as a Toyota "bank" for itself and affiliated suppliers. Even those *keiretsu* members that continue to rely heavily on bank loans are diversifying their sources, turning to banks outside the group.

In addition, *keiretsu* firms have become more demanding of their colleagues within the group. Although they continue to cooperate, they now expect one another to meet more exacting standards of product quality and timeliness, and to be competitive in price. In other words, the supplier–buyer relationship between *keiretsu* members has evolved to meet the increasing competitiveness of non-*keiretsu* firms, including foreign ones.

But while it is quite accurate to say that Japan's *keiretsu* are changing, it is not at all accurate to say they are disappearing. This misconception may have been created by a selective reading of data collected during the bubble years (1988–91), when Japan's Fair Trade Commission (JFTC) found a steadily declining rate of equity and other financial ties between members of the same *keiretsu*. But a recent JFTC study found that "the trend has been reversed."[31] The average ratio of cross-shareholding (the percentage of a firm's shares controlled by other members of the firm's group) was 18.5 percent in 1992, compared with 14.5 percent in 1989. And the average ratio of intra-*keiretsu* loans (the percentage of a firm's debt that was borrowed from the main bank of the firm's group) was 19.5 percent in 1992, the highest in years. The JFTC concluded that *keiretsu* ties in Japan "are not weakening."

In retrospect, of course, it should not have been a surprise to learn that group ties weakened during the bubble years. Firms then were able to raise huge sums of capital by issuing new shares, reducing the relative amount held by fellow *keiretsu* members. And the largest firms, flush with cash, needed to borrow very little from their group's main bank. In short, this was a highly unusual period.[32] By 1992, the bubble had popped, the recession had begun to deepen, and firms moved quickly to reestablish strong *keiretsu* ties.

We agree with Gerlach, a scholar who has conducted exhaustive research on Japan's *keiretsu*. "What we are likely to see," he writes, "is not the decline of the *keiretsu* so much as an ongoing evolution in specific patterns of relationships with an underlying continuity in the basic processes by which Japanese firms remain connected."[33] In fact, we suspect that firms will turn increasingly to cooperation as they face the enormous risks associated with innovation and overseas expansion.[34]

Although *keiretsu* come in different shapes and sizes, they do share some common characteristics. Member firms in the network are legally independent, but are bound together by a set of tangible and intangible commitments. These may include cross-shareholding, interlocking directorates, and intragroup trade, as well as capital, technology, and personnel transfers. *Keiretsu* in Japan are marked by a distinctive pattern of cooperation. They do not operate within the framework of a hierarchy directed by a central power (the "visible hand" of Alfred Chandler's ideal bureaucratic organization), nor as autonomously self-regulating and impersonal units (the "invisible hand" of Adam Smith's ideal market organization). Rather, they function as "hands interlocked in complex networks of formal and informal interfirm relationships."[35]

The horizontal or intermarket *keiretsu* have received by far the most attention. Some of these are offspring of the prewar *zaibatsu* (literally, "financial cliques") that emerged as early as the 1880s to capitalize on new opportunities created by Japan's frantic industrialization drive. After World War II, the US occupation force in Japan dissolved the family-owned holding companies that controlled each group. But as soon as Japan regained its sovereignty, economic bureaucrats pushed the country's largest, most strategic firms to cluster again – this time around a "city" bank that would serve as the principal conduit for the allocation of MOF's cheap or "below equilibrium rate" credit. Four of the six *keiretsu* are reconstituted *zaibatsu*: Mitsui (which recently renamed its bank "Sakura"), Mitsubishi, Sumitomo, and Fuyō (formerly the Yasuda Group, now clustered around the Fuji Bank). The two other groups, named after their main banks, are Daiichi Kangyō and Sanwa.

If the city bank is the heart of the horizontal *keiretsu*, pumping life-giving capital and life-saving management oversight to its many limbs, then the general trading company (GTC) serves as its eyes and ears. This fact was perhaps most evident in the 1960s, and again in the late 1980s, when the GTCs, each boasting its own worldwide network of branches and stations, supplied valuable information and personal contacts to Japanese firms trying to set up overseas.

Cooperation in this kind of *keiretsu* is maintained through various means, including membership in a presidents' club that meets each month to exchange information on employment, production, and marketing issues. According to Imai and Kaneko, these meetings serve to "reduce uncertainties, meet growing mutual demands and settle investment decisions."

> Moreover, as a result of such information exchange, affiliated firms feel confident in making joint investments; investment decisions are made easier; and risks are reduced in an environment that calls for interdependent development. Because of potential competitive relations within the same group in the sector of the new venture, information exchange has an accelerating effect on investment decisions.[36]

While horizontal *keiretsu* occupy center stage, vertical *keiretsu* – the interfirm relationships between large assembly-type firms and their suppliers – now play perhaps an even more critical role in the Japanese economy. As the era of slower growth unfolded following the oil crisis of 1973, manufacturers increasingly began to forge even tighter relationships with subcontractors as a way of coping with rising production costs.[37] For example, more and more of them implemented the so-called *kanban* system, which reduced inventories and required suppliers to deliver parts "just in time" to the factory. The new flexible production strategy worked beautifully. The average annual growth rate of labor productivity for Japanese manufacturers between 1974 and 1981 was 10.7 percent, far higher than for manufacturers in other industrialized nations.[38]

This supports an emerging consensus that the vertical *keiretsu* relationship between manufacturers and suppliers promotes efficiency.[39] Parent firms, the assemblers, provide capital and technology to their trusted suppliers, and collaborate with them on product development. The payoff is huge. One case study found that 63 percent of the parts purchased at a Toshiba factory were custom-made for the parent company.[40] And in the automobile industry, Japanese parts makers contribute an estimated 70 percent of the value-added in the final product, while American suppliers, most of whom are completely independent, contribute only 40 percent.[41]

But we should not assume, as many neoclassical economists have, that the relationship between the assembler and parts supplier is perfectly symmetrical and reciprocal. It is not. In the auto industry, for example, "only an elite corps of about a dozen first-tier suppliers enjoy full-blown partnership with their customers," according to Kamath and Liker.[42] There is in fact a hierarchy of suppliers, with the overwhelming majority serving as production footsoldiers who follow the customer's marching orders. They are subjected to rigidly enforced targets for price and performance, and nonnegotiable deadlines for delivery. In the early 1980s, Toyota is said to have levied a penalty of ¥300,000 per minute (about $1,500 per minute at the prevailing exchange rate) for any delay in the delivery of a needed part.[43]

Do large manufacturers still exercise such raw power? Friedman, for one, says they do not. As Japanese manufacturers in the postwar period began to adopt more flexible production techniques, he argues, they transferred not only more responsibilities, but also more authority to their suppliers. Liberated from the shackles of exploitative subcontracting relationships, these suppliers, he writes, blossomed into "independent specialists" with a rich endowment of technical skills.[44]

The evidence, however, doesn't support such a cheerful conclusion. For example, between 1975 and 1986, when Japan's economy was restructuring, small and medium-sized firms (those employing fewer than 300) went bankrupt three times more often than large firms (employing more than 300).[45] In addition, the wage differential between large and smaller firms in Japan has actually grown, not shrunk. In 1965, small and medium-sized firms paid wages about 18–22 percent lower than large firms; by 1992, the last year for which we have data, the gap had widened to 31 percent.[46]

This is not to say that Japanese assemblers alone gain from vertical *keiretsu* ties. Clearly, both they and their subcontractors obtain benefits. But these benefits are not distributed evenly. This imbalance, a function of asymmetrical dependence, is especially apparent during hard economic times, when negotiations between assemblers and their subcontractors invariably lead to price reductions for parts. For example, assemblers put the squeeze on their suppliers in the first year following the Plaza Accord of 1985, when the value of the yen shot up dramatically, threatening the competitiveness of Japanese exports.[47] And they did so again in the post-bubble recession of the early 1990s.[48] The case of Hidaka Seiki Co., a small auto parts manufacturer in Tokyo, was by no means unique. The firm was forced by its automaking customers to cut prices by 30 percent during that period.[49]

Not only do Japanese manufacturers cooperate upstream with suppliers, they also cooperate downstream with wholesalers and retailers through distribution *keiretsu*. These sales networks are more cohesive than those in other industrialized countries.[50] In the steel industry, for example, manufacturers typically sell their products through exclusive outlets (*tokuyakuten*) they have maintained over many years. In fact, 80 percent of the steel traded in Japan in 1994 was called *himotsuki*, which literally means "strings attached," because the connection between producer and buyer was so tight.[51] Distribution *keiretsu* are also common in the consumer electronic, automobile, cosmetic, pharmaceutical, and newspaper industries. In the electrical appliance industry alone, a Japanese newspaper has identified some 70,000 wholesalers and retailers that are tied exclusively to a single manufacturer.[52]

The distribution *keiretsu* is a legacy of the 1950s and 1960s, when the rapid growth of Japan's industrial sector overwhelmed its badly fragmented and woefully undercapitalized marketing system. Manufacturers responded to this bottleneck by setting up and maintaining their own networks. Each carved out a complete marketing channel, providing capital and technical support to selected wholesalers and retailers. Each secured almost total control over that channel.

Manufacturers no longer enjoy such control. For one thing, consumers have become more savvy, even using mail order catalogues to circumvent domestic sales networks and secure access to cheaper foreign goods. For another, wholesalers and retailers – struggling to survive with lower margins – have become more uppity, less willing to go along with the restrictive practices used in the past by producers.[53] And finally, they have begun to win a few court cases challenging those practices. For example, the Tokyo District Court ruled in 1994 that Kao Cosmetic Sales Co., the marketing arm of one of Japan's largest producers of cosmetic and medical products, had violated the law by punishing distributors who refused to go along with the manufacturer's "suggested" retail prices.[54]

We should note, however, that Kao has appealed the court ruling, and that a policy group created by the prime minister found that Kao and other major producers "still use their power to maintain the price of lip sticks and other cosmetic products at twice to five times the comparable price in Western cities."[55] While Japan's distribution *keiretsu* do appear to be evolving into looser networks with less coercive authority in the hands of producers, this trend, too, may not be as robust as many observers believe.

In this section, we have focused on formal business groupings (horizontal, vertical, and distribution *keiretsu*). But Gerlach reminds us that Japan's economy also has scores of more loosely organized alliances. Even "independent" or non-*keiretsu* firms in Japan engage in cross-shareholding and other cooperative practices more often than their counterparts in the United States.[56] The *keiretsu*, Gerlach argues, should be seen as a metaphor for a general pattern of interfirm cooperation in Japan.[57]

Labor and Management

As we saw in chapter three, neoclassical theory presents the firm as little more than a "black box" reflecting the profit-maximizing interests of its owners, the stockholders or "entrepreneurs". But Aoki has argued – persuasively, we think – that the Japanese firm (that is, the large and innovating Japanese firm) is different. It is "a coalition of the body of stockholders and the body of employees, integrated and mediated by management which acts to strike a balance between the interests of both sides."[58] The Japanese firm is, in other words, dually controlled by stockholders and employees. Management, he argues, serves as an arbiter, carefully balancing the interests of the two parties. Unlike management in the Western firm, an agent that pursues short-run share-price maximization for its principals (the stockholders), management in the Japanese firm pursues a long-run market-share maximizing strategy (or "growth").[59] In doing so, it delivers a package of extra benefits to employees: quasi-permanent employment (*shūshin koyō*) and a related system of seniority-based pay (*nenkō joretsu*).

Sociologists have used similar concepts to describe the Japanese firm. Dore, for example, writes about "hierarchical corporatism," and suggests that Japanese managers act as "the benevolent guardians of the interests of the company as a whole (including the interests of the workers as well as the shareholders)."[60]

To understand the relatively cooperative relationship between management and labor in the large and innovating Japanese firm, we cannot completely ignore the variable of culture, or (more accurately) ideology wrapped in culturally rooted mythology. At the same time, however, we should recognize that this cooperation, like all "games" of cooperation, has evolved over a finite stretch of time. It is a legacy of industrialization.

In the 1920s, Japan's economy split into two pieces – one made up of hundreds of thousands of relatively small and unsophisticated firms, the other dominated by a handful of large, *zaibatsu*-controlled firms trying to adopt Western technology. Seeking to protect their growing investment in human capital, these large oligopolistic firms at the top of the dual structure of the economy began rewarding employees who stayed with them for many years. They offered job security, routine promotions, and wages that grew with tenure. In other words, these firms offered a structure of incentives designed to cultivate hard work and commitment to the firm.

But despite its obvious strengths, the prewar system fell short on one test. It did not bring about labor peace. Strikes erupted frequently, particularly in the social chaos and hard economic times following World War II. The enterprise union – the vehicle through which labor collaborates with management – did not catch hold in Japan until the 1950s, after US occupation forces ordered the old *zaibatsu* to liquidate their family stockholdings. *Keiretsu* emerged to fill the void, and quickly began engaging in cross-shareholding to reestablish group solidarity. In the process, management acquired more autonomy to act on behalf of employees by pursuing long-term growth.[61] It began to consult routinely with the leaders of the newly formed enterprise union, which represented and still represents all nonmanagement employees. This, of course, makes the enterprise union quite different from the Western-style industrial union, which represents workers who perform the same function – autoworkers, coal miners, secretaries, etc. – across an entire industry.

There is, then, an economic rationale that helps explain the distinctive features of what has been called the "Japanese employment system."[62] To secure benefits for employees, management pursues long-term growth. This in turn requires an unusually large investment in human capital (training). Workers gladly agree to work hard to boost the firm's productivity because they have a stake in its future. Through on-the-job training, they acquire firm-specific skills that have value – but only in the specific context of a successfully expanding firm.[63]

Using this analysis, it is easy to get carried away and begin viewing the relationship between labor and management in Japan as a happy-go-lucky affair, a process of bargaining between equals. But it isn't. Like Japanese subcontractors and their giant manufacturing customers, Japanese employees and their business-minded bosses bargain in an unbalanced relationship. Management provides a package of incentives designed to instill a sense of belonging, a desire to stay and contribute to the firm's success. But it never relinquishes its ultimate authority. Through quality control circles, factory workers do get a chance to suggest ways to improve the production process. In return, however, they are expected to do just about anything that is asked of them, from sweeping the factory floor to working late to meet a production deadline.

Robert Cole captures the essence of this unequal bargain in his book on Japanese labor, which he wrote after working at a diecast plant and an auto parts factory in Japan. Among other things, he documents a complex web of *giri* (obligation-bound) relationships that link workers and bosses but that are *nonetheless* "strongly weighted in favor of management as the superior party."[64]

Once hired, a Japanese employee in a large, innovating firm becomes a member of an extended family, a child who might be praised one minute and scolded the next, but who is always embraced. This is the essence of "familism," an ideology that uses preindustrial values such as *giri* to motivate loyal members. In most Japanese factories, banners hang from the wall, cheering for some campaign to meet a new production goal. Colorful buttons adorn uniforms, announcing yet another "zero defect" campaign. Workers who identify with the company are mobilized through such efforts.

For years, neoclassical economists and others have forecast the imminent demise of Japan's distinctive employment system. Like government–business cooperation and business-to-business cooperation, the cooperation between labor and management was identified as a feature of late development that would disappear as Japan began to catch up with the industrialized West. But it has not disappeared.

Take the case of quasi-permanent employment, an element of the Japanese system that has survived, defying routine predictions of its death.[65] In the 1980s, when Sony established a major research institute, the company decided to offer employees a choice between quasi-permanent employment and contractual employment. The former meant greater job security, but the latter meant higher pay. "As it turned out," former Sony chairman Morita Akio recalls, "no one opted for a contract."[66]

Even during the post-bubble recession of the early 1990s, large manufacturing firms went to extraordinary lengths to hang onto quasi-permanent employees. One such firm was Mazda, which in 1993 faced losses of up to $300 million, in part due to an enormous surplus of professional and technical employees. Rather than dismiss those white-collar workers, the giant automaker reassigned 500 of them to the assembly line to take over temporary jobs that had been performed by contract workers.[67] It was able to do so, in part, because Mazda is a member of the Sumitomo *keiretsu*, and thus is shielded from dividend-demanding stockholders, and because the Japanese government subsidizes companies like Mazda to retain and retrain redundant (unnecessary) workers.

A Cooperation System

Like the three sides of a triangle, the three nexuses of cooperation support one another. None really stands alone.

Cooperation between government and business is enhanced by trade associations, which serve as reliable points of contact between bureaucrats and executives, and enterprise unions, which allow the state to avoid the political trap of choosing sides between management and labor. Cooperation between firms is sanctioned by government, which often tries to restrict entry into certain industries.[68] Likewise, firms that hold onto employees for most of their lives have a strong incentive to collaborate with one another to share technical know-how they otherwise could acquire freely through the labor market. Finally, cooperation between labor and management is possible because administrative guidance and cross-shareholding reduce the transaction costs associated with risk and uncertainty. This allows management to pursue long-run growth strategies designed to protect the interests of employees as well as stockholders.

What we are describing is an integrated *system* of cooperation, not a set of discrete cases of joint effort. It has been, for the most part, an efficient system, extraordinarily useful in overcoming hard economic times and exceptionally capable of absorbing and diffusing new technology within its matrix of alliances.[69] At the same time, however, it has been an exclusionary system, a closed system. "By its very nature," Okumura notes, reciprocal dealing "locks trading partners into set relationships, preventing the participation of new partners."[70] In addition, as we argued in chapter three, a developmentalist system, such as Japan's, that remains in place after the developing nation has achieved technological catch-up will eventually begin to impose heavy costs.[71]

In the 1990s, Japanese voters and consumers began to do quietly what Japan's most important trading partners have done loudly for years. They began to complain about political corruption, soaring retail prices, and other real costs of Japan's post-catch-up developmentalism.

In response, we argue, the nation's industrial and bureaucratic elites have moved to iron out the kinks by regionalizing Japan's developmentalist system of cooperation. Japanese MNCs are establishing *keiretsu*-like production networks that link technology centers in Japan with manufacturing bases in places like Masan and Manila. And the Japanese government in Tokyo is trying to build a political infrastructure to support them.

"Laissez faire can't be recommended," says an official in Japan's Ministry of Foreign Affairs. "Careful utilization of market forces is always ideal."[72]

CHAPTER FIVE

The Political Economy of Asia

It has become axiomatic: following Japan's flight path, the other capitalist nations of the Asia-Pacific region have achieved, or are about to achieve, economic "lift-off" – an upward trajectory that has allowed them, or soon will allow them, "to escape the mire of perpetual 'developing' status."[1] In almost perfect harmony, scholars and journalists say that the nations of Northeast Asia, particularly South Korea and Taiwan, have already accomplished this aerodynamic feat and now are soaring "somewhere over or near the threshold of advanced industrial development."[2] Consequently, they are hailed as NICs, "tigers," or "little dragons." The nations of Southeast Asia, particularly Thailand, Malaysia, and Indonesia, are said to be rolling down the runway and gearing up for take-off. They in turn are known as new NICs, "new tigers," or "new little dragons."

If there is any serious disagreement about the economic development of Asia, it has to do with why so many of the region's capitalist countries have managed to fare so well. Predictably, neoclassical economists say the NICs have succeeded, and ASEAN members are beginning to succeed, by relying more on the private sector, encouraging exports, eliminating government-induced price distortions, and adopting prudent macroeconomic policies. In other words, they are doing well by hewing to the free market.[3] Just as predictably, many political scientists attribute the region's success to authoritarian and technocratic regimes that have managed to defy special interests and impose rational, if sometimes painful, economic policies.[4] Following Max Weber's sociological approach, others have cited the region's group-oriented (and, in the case of Northeast Asia, Confucian) "ethic."[5]

As readers of preceding chapters will expect, we take a very different approach. We argue that the developing nations of Asia (at least the nine we focus on in this book) are, to borrow Paul Krugman's phrase, "paper tigers" whose rapid growth in output is due to increased inputs (capital and labor), not to increases in what mainstream economists call "total factor productivity" or what we have called "dynamic technological efficiency."[6] While they may have the necessary will (a strong, developmentalist vision), these nations lack the necessary way (a well-established infrastructure of cooperation) to achieve DTE. So they have opened themselves up to the warm embrace of Japanese developmentalism.

Asian nations, then, are not lifting off under their own power. Rather, they are being pulled forward in part by Japanese capital and technology or, in other words, by membership in a Japanese production alliance. We cannot deny that these nations are achieving economic development. At the same time, however, we must recognize that this is a peculiar kind of development – something we call *embraced* development.

We trust that readers will not confuse our approach with dependency theory, a highly ideological perspective that grew out of studies of economic development (or "underdevelopment") in Latin America. Unlike the *dependencistas*, we do not believe that international capital in general is an instrument of exploitation, nor that foreign direct investment is a zero-sum game that always enriches the stronger nation at the expense of the weaker one.[7] But we do believe that a relatively powerful nation can embrace a relatively weak nation, creating a syndrome of dependence. In this respect, our approach may resemble that of Hirschman, who demonstrated that larger, wealthier nations can gain influence over smaller, poorer nations by unilaterally improving the terms of trade.[8]

Asia's growing dependence on Japanese technology is not a fleeting phenomenon created by asset inflation in the 1980s or oversaving in the 1990s. It is a structural condition that arises out of the complementary relationship between Japanese developmentalism and Asian pseudo-developmentalism.

This chapter attempts to highlight the differences between these two systems. To summarize, we argue that the developmentalist-minded nations of Asia do not possess the triangle of cooperation that distinguishes the Japanese political economy.[9] Some Asian countries, practicing a kind of reverse social engineering, are trying to construct one. But none has managed thus far to succeed.

In Southeast Asia, in particular, government officials and business people often are divided along ethnic lines. This is not a problem in a

Table 5.1   Asia's Macro-indicators

Country	Population 1993 (millions)	Per capita GNP, 1992 ($)	Real GDP growth 1980–93 (%)	Savings/GDP, 1993 (%)
China	1,176.1	380	9.2	35.5
Hong Kong	5.9	15,380*	6.7	31.2
Indonesia	189.1	670	6.1	36.9
Korea	44.1	6,790	7.9	35.1
Malaysia	19.1	2,790	6.6	38.3
Philippines	65	770	1.8	14.8
Singapore	2.9	15,750	8.1	47.9
Taiwan	20.9	10,200	7.5	26.8
Thailand	58.6	1,840	7.7	37.1

Note: *GDP instead of GNP.
Source: Asian Development Bank, *Key Indicators of Asian and Pacific Developing Countries* (Manila: Oxford University Press, 1994).

place such as South Korea, a more homogeneous society, where government and business form a close-knit strategic coalition to pursue development.[10] But even Korea's political economy is missing the two other sides of the triangle of cooperation. Large manufacturers and small suppliers do not collaborate as they do in Japan. And management and labor in many firms distrust one another deeply, as evidenced by frequent and bitter strikes.

Just as Japanese developmentalism promotes DTE, Asia's pseudo-developmentalism inhibits it. We try to show how it does this by briefly touring the region (see Table 5.1) and examining the political economies of some of its nations.[11]

ASEAN

We are sipping tea in a 17th-floor waiting room at Siam Motors, which has built itself into one of Thailand's largest and most successful conglomerates by affiliating closely with Nissan Motors in Japan. The president and chief executive officer of this industrial group is willing to answer our questions, but only after we have viewed a company video. The video shows factory workers wearing the red, blue, and white colors of Nissan, smiling pleasantly as they assemble cars. And it shows happy employees crooning at several different occasions, including an annual singing contest sponsored by Nissan.

As the video drones on about the company's accomplishments (Siam Motors, for example, was the first company in Thailand to import Japanese cars), our eyes roam. The waiting room itself looks like a miniature museum of Japanese culture, complete with a samurai helmet and a doll dressed in kimono. All from Nissan. Even the tea we are sipping comes in Nissan cups on Nissan saucers.

We finally are escorted into a large, pink office where Khunying Phornthip, daughter of Thaworn Phornprapha, the founder of Siam Motors, greets us. Wearing a long dress and dangling earrings, Phornthip is as close to royalty as one can be in Thailand without being a member of the king's family.

Seated now, Phornthip tells us she cannot actually envision a Nissan-less future for her company. Siam Motors, according to its boss, will forever require the technical services of its Japanese partner.

> The Japanese are very good at technology. They make excellent, high quality products because they are such a determined people, such a determined nation. The whole nation is motivated to act as one ... I am not suggesting that they are gods. But I do not believe that any one nation can do everything. We need each other. That's the way the world works.[12]

The Phornprapha family is uncommon in Southeast Asia, where capitalists tend to steer clear of risk-taking ventures, investing instead in commercial or financial enterprises, or in relatively low-tech manufacturing sectors such as lumber or garments. The automobile industry, in fact, has produced the most notable exceptions to this rule: Thaworn Phornprapha in Thailand, William Soeryadjaya in Indonesia, Loh Boon Siew in Malaysia, Jose Yulo in the Philippines, and others. However, by relying so heavily on Japanese capital and technology to build their industrial empires, these capitalists have functioned more as compradors and thus have helped create what Yoshihara calls "ersatz capitalism" or "technologyless industrialization" in Southeast Asia. Just as Phornprapha is tied tightly to Nissan, so is Soeryadjaya tied to Toyota, Loh to Honda, and Yulo to Mitsubishi Motors.

> The Southeast Asian capitalists are essentially the distributors of Japanese cars, with the difference that they have assembling plants. Technologically, however, they are 100 percent dependent on their Japanese licensers, and, under the present set-up, it would be impossible for them to become technologically independent and start exporting their products. Their technological dependency is not temporary but, being structural, semi-permanent.[13]

The anemic condition of native, industrial capital in Southeast Asia is in part a legacy of the region's stubborn tradition of patrimonialism, which organizes society into a network of ruler–subordinate (patron–client) relationships.[14] This system discourages social mobility, solidifying a binary order of elites and nonelites. Entrepreneurs, merchants, and traders end up squeezed in the minimal middle.[15]

In the Philippines, patrimonialism continues to guide social relations because landed elites continue to dominate society. Powerful plantation owners sit atop the political structure, handing out meager benefits – jobs, housing, health care – to followers who dutifully bless their bene-factor's political agenda. Landed elites control the National Assembly and thus are able to thwart reasonable efforts at land reform. In the mid 1980s, one analyst suggested that the economy of the Philippines was controlled by just 81 families.[16] More recently, a scholar has estimated that a fragmented middle class makes up only about 10 percent of the total population.[17]

Even in a place such as Indonesia, where land ownership is not nearly so concentrated, the rural economy operates according to an informal network of patron–client ties, not according to a formal set of property rights and regulations. This is, as neoinstitutionalist theory would suggest, a serious drag on development. Only 7 percent of the land on the Indonesian archipelago is said to have a clear owner; the other 93 percent is held communally or on the basis of hereditary claims.[18] Without a proper title, farmers in Indonesia cannot use land as collateral to secure financing to raise agricultural productivity. So they rely heavily on government irrigation and fertilization projects, which often are administered in an arbitrary, top-down, and archetypally patrimonial manner.[19]

The durability of patron–client relationships in Southeast Asia reflects the region's cultural diversity. As Brown argues, patrimonialism often holds together an otherwise unstable community that lacks "effective in-stitutional links between center and periphery" and a broader "cultural consensus."[20] Such a consensus is missing in much of Southeast Asia, where the economic giants – the ethnic Chinese – historically have been the political Lilliputians.

For centuries, this region has attracted Chinese immigrants, many of whom used kinship ties and other resources to establish themselves as the leading merchants in major port cities. Some prospered during the colonial era by supplying coolies for Western-owned plantations. Others functioned as intermediaries, selling local agricultural goods and buying goods processed in the West. Even in Thailand, which was never colo-nized, ethnic Chinese dominated the rice-trading and -milling sectors.

After World War II, the new states in the region nationalized plantations and banks that had been owned by Westerners, while almost all of them imposed strict limits on the role of foreign capital in local banking and manufacturing. Chinese entrepreneurs seized this opportunity, forging alliances this time with powerful patrons in the fledgling governments. And in the 1960s, when Thailand, Indonesia, Malaysia, and the Philippines began to open their doors to foreign

Table 5.2   Ethnic Chinese in ASEAN-4

Country	Share of population (%)	Share of private capital (%)
Malaysia	35	65
Philippines	5	40
Thailand	10	80
Indonesia	3	80

Source: USITC, *East Asia: Regional Economic Integration and Implications for the United States*, p. 51.

investors, these Chinese entrepreneurs extended their hands again – this time to hook up with small, labor-intensive manufacturers from Japan.[21]

As Table 5.2 demonstrates, ethnic Chinese continue to control a disproportionate share of business in Southeast Asia. This is especially pronounced in the cases of Indonesia and Thailand, where Chinese transplants hold an estimated 80 percent of private, local capital, even though they make up only 3 percent and 10 percent, respectively, of the local population.

Despite their relative wealth, the ethnic Chinese in Southeast Asia have been shut out of the halls of political power. In fact, they frequently have been subjected to ethnic discrimination, including public policies restricting Chinese immigration, education, and investment. This was the case under the regimes of Thailand's Phibun Songkhram (1938–44 and 1948–57) and Indonesia's Sukarno (1949–65). And it was the case, more recently, under Malaysia's New Economic Policy (NEP), which used state capital to promote *bumiputra* (indigenous Malay) enterprises. To cope with such discrimination, many ethnic Chinese entrepreneurs bought protection from their allies in government. Typically, this was done by making one-time bribes and long-term payoffs, such as a fixed percentage of corporate profits, in exchange for special favors – licenses, government contracts, government-sanctioned monopolies, and the like. In this way, captive Chinese capitalists became "rent seekers." They joined that costly, efficiency-bleeding chase not for profit, but for economic rent from government favors.[22]

It is too facile to blame the overseas Chinese for seeking and exploiting personal connections with government power-brokers in Southeast Asia; political elites, especially military officers and high-ranking bureaucrats, just as eagerly courted the private sector. Under Malaysia's NEP, for example, government officials granted business licenses to *bumiputra* entrepreneurs, who often then sold them to Chinese entrepreneurs. In many cases, the licensing officials accepted payments to ignore the shenanigans that led to such "Ali Baba" ventures.[23]

Mutual back-scratching is a daily routine in Indonesia, where *korupsi* (corruption) is estimated to absorb up to a third of the nation's GNP, or more than $30 billion a year.[24] By the mid 1980s, in fact, the problem became so acute that President Suharto opted to turn the nation's customs operations over to a Swiss company.[25] Chafing under criticism that he has allowed Chinese capitalists to monopolize the nation's economy, Suharto points to the growing number of *pribumi* (non-Chinese) business groups in Indonesia. He neglects to mention, however, that the two biggest groups of this kind are run by his sons.[26]

The Indonesian state, Crouch argues, has become nothing less than "a giant patronage machine with a network extending from Jakarta to the provinces." Senior military officers and high-ranking bureaucrats supervise this machine, trading commissions and bribes for special favors. In the 1960s, when they began to invest in Indonesia, foreign firms adjusted quickly to this system by establishing tripartite joint ventures with Indonesian-Chinese businesspeople and their patrons, according to Crouch. "No major enterprise could grow without a military patron who normally contributed neither capital nor managerial skills but performed the vital service of dealing with the bureaucracy in order to get licenses, credit, contracts, monopoly concessions and exemptions from the full application of onerous regulations."[27]

A "patronage machine" like this not only distorts the market; it also inhibits risk-taking. Instead of acquiring and developing new technologies, entrepreneurs focus their efforts on nailing down restrictive licenses. "If the returns from rent-seeking are so attractive, why care about developing your own capabilities?" asks Indonesian economist Djisman Simandjuntak.[28]

Anxious to preserve their privileged status, political elites in Southeast Asia have failed to cultivate sufficient capital or human resources. The Thai government, in particular, has done little to promote private saving – a fact that, to its credit, it now recognizes. In its current economic plan (the Seventh Plan, 1992–96), the government bemoans the fact that savings are woefully insufficient to meet investment requirements.[29]

Likewise, none of the governments in the region, save Singapore, has done enough to promote education. Only 0.6 percent of Indonesian youth graduate from college, and only 45 percent even enroll in a junior high school. Malaysia does only a bit better: 1.4 percent of its youth graduate from college, and 56 percent enter a junior high school.[30] This education deficit translates directly into a deficit of more than 15,000 skilled workers in Malaysian parts manufacturing industries, according to a Japanese scholar. A shortfall of such magnitude "could prove fatal for the country's economic development," Aoki writes. "In most advanced nations, the proportion of skilled employees was about 6–8 percent during their respective take-off stages. In 1985, this figure in Malaysia was only 2.4 percent."[31]

Although Thailand scores a little higher in terms of producing college graduates, it scores even lower in terms of producing technically skilled workers. Only 0.1 percent of the Thai population has a job as a scientist or technician, while 2.3 percent of the Singapore population and 4.6 percent of South Korea's population does.[32] As Figure 5.1 shows, the number of scientists and technicians engaged in R&D is relatively low in all the ASEAN-4 nations, including Thailand.

Prayoon Shiowattana, general manager of the Technological Promotion Association in Bangkok, says the Thai government doesn't really understand the need for technology training. As a result, he says, the nation is experiencing a worsening labor shortage – one that already "has gone from a crisis to a critical emergency." "We came face to face with this human resource crisis in the late 1980s. The supply of new engineers was equivalent to only half of the demand. We produced about 3,000 new engineers a year, and we needed about 5,000 to 6,000 a year. So our association approached the government, encouraging it to take action. But we got no response at all."[33]

As the human resource crisis has deepened, Thailand has become increasingly dependent on Japanese technology. Like Prayoon, Thai economist Wilaiwan Wannitikul blames the government. "Our country," she says, "should be embarrassed by the fact that it has become a leading exporter of textiles, and yet it still must import the weaving machines to manufacture those textiles."[34]

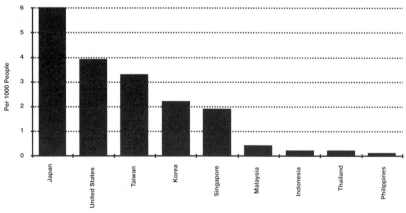

Figure 5.1   Scientists and Technicians Working in R&D
Note: Figure for Indonesia includes only scientists, not technicians, in R&D.
Source: UN Statistical Yearbook, 1993, Table 5-4.

Singapore

Although it is a member of ASEAN, Singapore is viewed more often as an NIC along with South Korea, Taiwan, and Hong Kong. On its face, this taxonomy makes sense. Singapore has an authoritarian regime in which some of the region's most talented and least corrupted technocrats determine economic policy with little interference from domestic interest groups. It is, then, a relatively "hard state" that is not trapped in the web of patron–client relationships that have bogged down other Southeast Asian nations.[35] As such, it has successfully pursued rational economic policies that allowed it to move up the technological ladder as it industrialized.

While all of this is true, it misses a fundamental point: Singapore's economy is driven by outsiders. In the mid 1980s, foreign capital accounted for 70 percent of the nation's gross output in manufacturing, over 50 percent of employment, and 82 percent of direct exports.[36] Even in the early 1990s, foreign firms accounted for 85 percent of total investment in Singapore.[37]

In retrospect, of course, we can see clearly how all this came to pass. In 1965, when Singapore withdrew from the Federation of Malaysia, Prime Minister Lee Kwan-Yew abandoned his strategy of industrializing through import substitution and began pursuing a new strategy of export-oriented industrialization. Because local capital was concentrated in real estate, services, and domestic trade, and thus unprepared to lead the charge, an impatient Lee established state enterprises in steel, chemical, shipbuilding, and other strategic industries, and tried to lure multi-national corporations.

He sponsored a series of measures to eviscerate the bargaining power of workers, and then used the government-controlled National Trades Union Congress (NTUC) to thoroughly coopt the labor movement.[38] Foreign investors welcomed these efforts to preserve relatively cheap labor. And they hungrily gobbled up other incentives – unlimited equity ownership of affiliates, full repatriation of profits, financial and technical services, and generous tax breaks. In many cases, these incentives were biased against domestic firms.

Domestic capital, hobbled by its own government, soon found itself competing against Japanese, American, and European multinationals for land, labor, and even local markets. It really was no contest. The MNCs squeezed out local manufacturers, using what a small business group in Singapore called "predatory pricing launched from protected home bases."[39]

Despite local capital's complaints, Lee's decision to tie Singapore's economic destiny to the trade and investment strategies of MNCs seemed to pay off in the 1970s. As a haven for foreign investment in labor-intensive manufacturing, the economy of this former entrepot grew fast. So fast, in fact, that it began to attract thousands of foreign workers, especially from Malaysia. Wary of anything that might disrupt his highly engineered society, Lee ordered his technocrats to steer a new course. In 1979, Singapore embarked on a carrot and stick program that its prime minister grandly called "The Second Industrial Revolution." It included new incentives and higher wages to shift foreign investment out of labor-intensive sectors and into higher-technology, higher value-added industries.

But Japanese firms did not respond as hoped. Not initially, anyway. Instead of upgrading their business activities, they scaled them back. New investment commitments, which hovered at $319 million in 1979, plummeted to $74 million in 1982 as Japanese MNCs looking for labor-intensive production sites snubbed Singapore in favor of Hong Kong.[40] And then, as if the evaporation of Japanese capital was not bad enough, a global recession reduced demand for Singapore's manufactured exports in North America and Europe. The effect of these misfortunes hit home in 1985, when GDP actually *declined* by nearly 2 percent. The government, forced to acknowledge how dependent the tiny, resource-poor island had become, abandoned its policy of trying to attract only high-technology investment and returned to its familiar propaganda extolling the virtues of hard work and long hours.[41]

In the late 1980s Singapore recovered and once again began to enjoy rapid growth. It did so largely on the strength of a new wave of Japanese investment that was pulled by the increasing technical capacity of Singapore's labor force, but also pushed by the high value of the yen and the excess liquidity in Japan's bubble economy. No longer seeking only cheap labor, both large and small Japanese firms have established a number of new manufacturing plants, many of which incorporate advanced technology. In addition, electronics giants such as Sony, Matsushita, and NEC have set up distribution and purchasing head-quarters for their expanding regional production networks. Because it occupies a central location in the Asia-Pacific region, and because it possesses a relatively large number of competent engineers and technicians, Singapore is prospering as an intermediary or broker in the regional division of labor created by Japanese MNCs.

With some justification, then, scholars have used Singapore's experience as evidence that a developing nation need not be a passive player in this process, that it can in fact use government policy to help determine its place in an international or regional division of labor.[42] Under Lee, they note, the government of Singapore successfully targeted high-tech industries by upgrading the technical skills of local workers.

But one can carry this argument too far. Local capital remains woefully weak in Singapore. Multinationals engaged in manufacturing production, especially the Japanese, have forged few linkages with domestic firms. In one survey, only four of 44 Japanese manufacturers indicated they obtained any inputs *at all* from domestically owned suppliers in Singapore.[13]

Despite all the government's brave talk about building a local manufacturing base, Singapore today functions primarily as an "industrial service center," according to Wong Chin Yeow, research director for the Singapore Manufacturers Association. "We provide service, back-up, to the multinationals."[14] Nigel Holloway, former Singapore bureau chief for the *Far Eastern Economic Review*, says much the same thing, only in blunter fashion. The city-state, he says, is "little more than a subcontractor of the rich countries."[15]

South Korea

Thirty limousines form a shiny black border in front of a heavily guarded, block-shaped office building. A handful are tickled gently by black-suited, white-gloved chauffeurs wielding feather dusters. But most just sit idly, waiting for their VIP cargo. From even a short distance, these sleek machines are dead ringers for the ones that carry high-ranking government officials and business executives in Japan. In fact they are Hyundai Grandeurs, not Toyota Presidents or Nissan Centuries; and this is Kwa'chon, a Seoul suburb and the sprawling headquarters of the Korean bureaucracy, not Kasumigaseki, the government office district in downtown Tokyo.

To the casual observer, the political economies of Korea and Japan seem remarkably similar. This is no accident. For all its Japanophobia, the former colony has tried hard to replicate a system that allowed Japan to subjugate Korea for 35 years. Like Japan, Korea has an elite corps of bureaucrats who guide the nation's economic development. It too has a handful of big corporate groups that exercise oligopolistic power over strategic industries. Korea even has a supreme political party (the Democratic Liberal Party) that, like Japan's Liberal Democratic Party, was conceived as a stable power center, a "grand conservative alliance" between parties that once had divided the nation's ruling elite.

But appearances can be deceiving. Although South Korea's political economy, unlike that of the new little dragons of Southeast Asia, is built on a solid foundation of cooperation between government and big business, it is missing some other critical pieces of the Japanese model. In particular, it lacks an efficient subcontracting network. The Korean *chaebol* (giant manufacturing combines) have never enjoyed the close, long-lasting relationships with local suppliers that Japanese manufacturers have. Instead, they have come to rely on Japan, importing intermediate goods such as highly engineered automobile parts and electronic components.

The bond between Korean and Japanese business is the chummy sum of personal relationships formed during the colonial period and political deals arranged during the negotiations that ultimately led to rapprochement. The Japanese themselves describe this cozy cabal as a form of *yūchaku*, a gooey glue of politics and business.[46] Park Chung Hee, a former lieutenant in Japan's Kwantung Army who seized power in Korea in 1961, functioned as a kind of broker, using $800 million in aid from the Japanese government and millions more in payoffs from Japanese corporations to finance pet projects – public and private – at home.[47] For example, Japanese capital funneled through Park's military regime nurtured a handful of fledgling conglomerates known in Korea as "the gang of five": Sonkyong Textiles, Shinjin Motors, Yonhap Iron and Steel, Korea Explosives, and Kukdong Construction.[48]

Besides all these personal and political alliances, a cold, hard reality propelled many manufacturers to look for industrial parts on the other side of the Sea of Japan: they had to. At home, the government was starving small business by allocating most of its low-cost loans to huge firms in strategic, export-oriented industries.[49] And despite a critical need for domestic suppliers, the government also clung fiercely to regulations that made it difficult, if not impossible, for new firms to satisfy that demand. One analyst estimates that a Korean entrepreneur had to obtain 312 signatures from government agencies before getting the go-ahead to start a business.[50] The result was predictable: although the number of employees in Korean manufacturing industries tripled between 1966 and 1976, the number of small manufacturers (with fewer than 100 employees) actually declined a bit.[51] Like a plump but spindly-legged turkey, Korean industry had become top heavy.

Beginning in the mid 1980s, the government tried to make up for past mistakes by promoting small business. But the effort came too late; the *chaebol* had become addicted to Japanese imports, and could not be weaned so easily. In chapters six and eleven, we take a closer look at Korea's deep dependence on Japanese technology. For now, we are satisfied to cite the results of just one study indicating that, in the late 1980s, more than 90 percent of the parts imported by Korea's electrical manufacturers came from Japan.[52] Local manufacturers apparently have come to depend on the quality of those imported parts, as well as the superior follow-up service.

In his office in Kwa'chon, Kim Kyo-shik, a policy analyst for the Ministry of Finance, shakes his head as he describes the deliberate, ongoing efforts by Korea's big domestic conglomerates to scuttle government programs to promote smaller domestic firms that could act as subcontractors. "For example," he says, "they routinely delay payments for parts ordered from local suppliers. We have adopted legislation to try to stop such unfair trade practices, but I don't think we've been very successful so far."[53]

On most issues, of course, Korean bureaucrats can still count on the *chaebol* to cooperate; big business, in turn, leans heavily on the government. This traditional alliance has produced obvious benefits – rapid industrialization, export-led growth, and an expanded technological capacity. But it has also contributed to a crisis – the serious rift between management and labor that jeopardizes the Korean economy.

Unlike Singapore, for example, South Korea has not followed Japan in building an employment system based on cooperation, rather than conflict, between management and labor. To be sure, Korea's employment system is far more like Japan's than America's; it emphasizes loyalty and discipline, not contractually defined rights and responsibilities. At the same time, though, it is not so thoroughly imbued with the ideology of teamwork, consensus, and harmony. Compared with Japanese employers, Koreans do not provide their workers with a great deal of nonwage benefits, such as housing. More significantly, they do not offer as many nonmonetary rewards – the titles that instill pride, the meetings that create a feeling of belonging, the honors that motivate hard work. Korea's top-down employment system may reflect the influence of its strongly hierarchical family system. But more fundamentally, it reflects the influence of the military in this society.[54]

Since at least the 1960s, domestic and foreign employers in Korea have relied on authoritarian regimes to quell labor. They have relied on this police state so much, in fact, that big business and big government have become indistinguishable to many Koreans. This was evident in 1987, when the student-led prodemocracy movement quickly evolved into a blue-collar campaign for greater bargaining rights, higher pay, and better working conditions.

The campaign represented an explosive release of pent-up demands. Given Korea's rapid economic growth, "one could no longer expect workers to be contained as a docile group," says Choi Jang Jip, a political scientist at Korea University. "It was simply unrealistic."[55] Between 1987 and 1990, more than 7,000 strikes paralyzed automakers, shipbuilders, textile manufacturers, and other big employers. During that same period, wages rose by nearly 70 percent.[56] Ultimately, of course, the ally of big business – big government – was able to mount a strong counteroffensive. It banned Chonnohyop, a radical union federation, and attacked even moderate unions in one court case after another. The government has also used extraordinary force to crush strikes and end union demonstrations. A dramatic example was the 1989 invasion of a

Hyundai shipyard in which 10,000 riot police descended from helicopters, floated in on boats, and rolled in on armored vehicles to rout striking workers.[57]

The backlash against labor did manage to slow the rapid pace of wage increases, but it also aggravated tensions within the society. Korea today is a country divided by age, income, and even region. The business and bureaucratic elite – represented heavily by older Koreans, many of whom were raised in Cholla, a politically blessed province in the southeast – blame radical union activists for reducing the international competitiveness of Korean exports. In turn, labor leaders – most of whom are young, and many of whom hail from Kyongsang, a politically disenfranchised province in the southwest – complain about the greed of industry and the brutality of government.

Despite this internal conflict, South Korea has managed to prosper, lending at least superficial credibility to Amsden's prediction that it soon will become "Asia's next giant."[58] Some firms here have emerged as formidable, global competitors. Samsung Electronics, for example, is now a leading producer of semiconductors. In 1994, it announced that it had, with the help of Japan's NEC, become the first to develop a 256-megabit dynamic random access memory (DRAM) chip.[59]

But Samsung is an exception. Most Korean firms are not investing in new technology at such an impressive rate. Instead, they are doing what they did in the late 1980s – taking advantage of a sharp jump in the value of the yen to price their rival products more cheaply.[60] Growth built on such a shaky foundation is not sustainable.

Many Koreans recognize this. In interviews, they talk about a widening technology gap between Japan and Korea, a deteriorating balance of trade. And they openly express doubts about the future. Have the *chaebol* spread themselves too thin?[61] Have Koreans got what it takes to compete over the long run?

On the 17th floor of the Kyobo Building, Seoul's largest office tower, Kim Chan-Jin sucks on a cigarette one minute, then chews on a breath mint the next. Once, he served as Park Chung Hee's leading economic adviser; today he is a prominent lawyer and, increasingly, a social critic. Although he is perhaps a bit too dramatic, he expresses a common concern when he says "the can-do spirit that drove Koreans to work hard, save money, and invest wisely has just dissipated. In recent years, our people have lost the motivation they once had. Morale is low."[62] Kim, we believe, is right to worry about Korea's economic future. Despite its rapid growth in the mid-1990s, this economy remains highly vulnerable. Unlike Kim, however, we attribute this not to a lack of discipline or "spirit," but rather to a lack of linkage between large and small manufacturers and between management and labor.

Taiwan

When discussing the Asia-Pacific economy, analysts often lump Taiwan together with South Korea, and for good reason. Both were colonized by Japan in the first half of the 20th century; received massive doses of US aid, especially in the 1950s and 1960s; followed industrial policies designed by government technocrats; and built an economy based on manufacturing and exports. In addition, both used highly authoritarian regimes to smother labor, keeping it quiet and cheap. Until recently.

Although Taiwanese workers were less dramatic, they nonetheless did what their counterparts in Korea did – they launched a labor movement by riding a wave of antiauthoritarianism. In 1987, when the Kuomintang (KMT) government yielded to public pressure and lifted martial law, labor leaders began calling for higher wages, bigger bonuses, more independent unions, and greater workplace democracy. Since most strikes remained illegal, they used other means, such as "sick outs" and "mass vacations," to push their demands. Nearly 3,000 labor disputes were reported in 1987 and 1988.[63]

The net result of all this agitation in Taiwan was as unsurprising as it was in Korea. Wages shot up. Manufacturing wages, for example, rose by 60 percent between 1986 and 1989.[64] And they still are climbing fast – faster than, or as fast as, productivity.[65] This trend does not bode well for an economy that relies so heavily on exports, especially labor-intensive exports. But the island's ruling elite, which whines routinely about labor's new militance, has only itself to blame. By repressing labor so harshly for so long, it undermined its own ideology of familism and spawned both resentment and mistrust among workers. Like Korea, Taiwan was unwilling or unable to follow Japan's model of controlled cooperation between management and labor. And it, too, will end up paying a high price.

One other critical component of Japan's political economy – the mutually reinforcing link between large domestic manufacturers and small domestic suppliers – is missing in Taiwan, just as it was in South Korea. The fact that these two countries share such a characteristic seems counterintuitive. South Korea, as discussed earlier, suffers because it has failed to support a sufficient number of efficient suppliers. But what about Taiwan, where 98 percent of an estimated 260,000 business enterprises are considered small?[66]

Small enterprises have survived, and often thrived, in Taiwan by forging alliances with foreign capital, not by serving as subcontractors for large domestic firms. This discontinuity in relations between big and small business in Taiwan reflects a longstanding rift between mainlanders and islanders – a rift that was documented by a US government consultant in a 1952 report on local business attitudes and practices. The consultant quoted a group of Taiwanese manufacturers who "stated emphatically that they employed no mainlanders in their plants and had no intention of doing so, and added that no Taiwanese hold responsible positions in government factories."[67]

To understand this mutual animosity, we must recall the events that followed the end of World War II. The allies had freed Taiwan, a Japanese colony for a half a century, only to turn it over to Chiang Kai-shek's Nationalist government in China. The KMT continued to treat Taiwan as a colony, plundering its relatively prosperous economy to help pay for a civil war against communists on the mainland. The Taiwanese, of course, grew hostile. In 1947, in response to swelling protests, Chiang all but declared war on the island, dispatching 10,000 KMT troops who went on a rampage, killing as many as 20,000 Taiwanese. It should come as no surprise, then, that two years later, when Chiang fled the Red Army on the mainland and established a rival government in Taipei, local residents staged no rallies, no parades.

Under US pressure, the KMT immediately went to work to rehabilitate its image by, for example, carrying out a massive redistribution of agricultural land, a reform that helped unleash productive energies on the island.[68] But Chiang's regime could never bring itself to really trust Taiwan's business community, a potential source of political opposition. This remains one of those marvelous paradoxes of history: the KMT, a party devoted in principle to anticommunism, functioned in reality as a highly centralized, Leninist-style party that tolerated no dissent.[69]

The government itself dominated steel, petroleum, telecommunications, and other strategic industries. As recently as 1994, it still owned three of the five largest corporations (in terms of sales) in Taiwan.[70] True, the KMT did undertake measures to protect and promote private capital in infant industries, particularly textiles, geared for the domestic market. But government aid was provided, first and foremost, to mainlanders who had followed the KMT from Shanghai and Shandong, and only later to those wealthy Taiwanese interests who were willing to pledge loyalty by aligning themselves with the party.[71] In a manner that resembles the Southeast Asian model of political economy, the KMT acted as a powerful patron, going so far as to reserve seats in its own Central Standing Committee for big business allies – mainlanders and Taiwanese.[72] Those corporate allies, in turn, set aside management posts for party leaders.[73]

Small business was not so lucky. The island's banking system, monopolized by the KMT, withheld cheap credit from all but state-owned enterprises and a favored few private corporations that had sufficient assets to use as collateral.[74] The less fortunate (meaning small) Taiwanese entrepreneurs coped with this discrimination initially by drawing on family savings and tapping an underground "kerb" market, both of which proved inefficient. Taiwan's financial system, we should note, remains rather primitive, and continues to discriminate against small and medium-sized businesses. In fact, Western analysts have noted that state-controlled banks still lend generously to close political allies, but not to promising innovators. This, of course, encourages the kind of rent-seeking that has plagued many Southeast Asian nations.[75]

Foreign capital has been the balm of small business. In the 1960s, when the Taiwanese government began to pursue a strategy of export-oriented industrialization, many small-scale producers on the island joined forces with MNCs, especially Japanese manufacturers, serving as subcontractors in a regional or global division of labor. Before wage inflation began to eat into Taiwan's comparative advantage in labor-intensive manufacturing, Japanese affiliates on the island produced about 12 percent of the components manufactured by Japanese firms around the world.[76]

In trying to secure ties to Taiwanese subcontractors, these Japanese manufacturers had several advantages over their competitors, primarily US multinationals. In addition to being physically closer, they had a history of close personal relationships with Taiwanese business interests. Most important, though, they usually provided an entree to a financial and marketing network that small-scale manufacturers in Taiwan could only dream about.

Admission, however, was not free. There were strings attached. Before long, Taiwanese subcontractors became ensnared in what Gold has called a "web of contractual agreements" that required them to import parts from the Japanese parent firm and to use a designated trading company based in Japan to market their products.[77] In time, these general trading companies managed to acquire control of 50–70 percent of Taiwan's trade.[78] This domination was so complete that, until the 1990s, almost no Taiwanese firms managed to sell their products under their own brands. Even as recently as 1991, four out of five pocket calculators bearing the Casio label were made by Cal-Comp, a Taiwanese firm.[79]

Today's Taiwan, we concede, is quite different from yesterday's. A new generation of leaders has come to power, creating a more open government and a more professional, more ambitious business community. Mainlanders and islanders have found ways to bury old grievances and cooperate more effectively.

But with the exception of fast-growing firms such as Acer and Mitac, small business in general still cannot afford to conduct its own R&D. The KMT bureaucracy has tried to compensate by creating public R&D facilities and by sponsoring technical training programs for workers. But Taiwan, like Korea, remains hooked on Japanese technology because it lacks a network of cooperation between small and large domestic firms. For the foreseeable future, both NICs will play a medium-tech role in Japan's regional production alliance.

China

Because of its fantastic growth in the early 1990s, China has emerged as the new prodigy in Asia, the economic debutante whose maturation as a manufacturing giant is widely anticipated. Indeed, the People's Republic enjoyed two straight years of 13 percent growth in 1992 and 1993, before inflation began to slow this locomotive.

But for all its much-ballyhooed economic reforms, we believe China still has a long way to go before it can be a real industrial power in the world. This is primarily because the muscle-bound Chinese bureaucracy has not yet learned to nurture – rather than command – local capital.

The problem is most acute in China's state-owned manufacturing sector, which accounts for about half the nation's industrial output. Although Beijing has loosened its grip over this sector, turning over more regulatory authority to local governments, and although it has introduced the *cheng-bao* system of separating ownership and management, nearly half of China's 100,000 state-owned firms continue to lose money each year.[80] Direct subsidies to these enterprises cost the state $8.3 billion in 1993, or 16 percent of the government's total revenue.[81] And in 1994, the state-owned People's Bank of China blamed these inefficient enterprises for pushing the nation's foreign debt above $100 billion.[82]

Ultimately, however, the blame must fall on the government itself. Not only has it refused to let inefficient enterprises go bankrupt, it has refused to let potentially efficient enterprises operate independently. Beijing continues to control prices for some strategic, bottleneck industries, such as energy and basic materials.[83] And while it has created a more diffuse system of regulation, it has not created a more simple and rational one. An American scholar who has examined purchasing practices at many of the big enterprises says Chinese executives must travel through a mind-bogglingly complex maze of national and government agencies just to negotiate a single transaction. "While multiple points of access and control have increased the tools and strategies available to the individual Chinese unit manager, the amount of time spent looking for a path through the Chinese organizational 'mazeway' has also increased correspondingly."[84]

This view is suppported by a well-respected journal, which concludes that China is "stuck halfway between the command economy and the market economy." The result, it says, "is a painful neither-nor existence that combines the worst of both worlds."[85]

It is perhaps no coincidence, then, that China's economic growth has been concentrated in the special economic zones where Beijing's heavy hand is less visible. Guangdong Province, home of the first such zone, Shenzen, accounts for only 6 percent of China's population but 21 percent of its exports.[86] Local officials there often follow their own lead. For example, when Beijing clamped down on government spending in 1988 to control inflation, officials of Dongguan, a thriving metropolis in Guangdong, invested local money in roads and other forms of infrastructure to attract foreign firms and accommodate economic growth.[87]

Likewise, then, it should come as no surprise that some of the most successful local firms in China are so-called "contract enterprises," which pay the government a fee for the right to operate free of routine interference. One such firm, Stone Office Technology and Equipment Co., a Beijing-based computer manufacturer, had sales in excess of $425 million in 1991. Even Stone, however, has been unable to keep the bureaucrats at bay. "Our ownership is murky now," says Duan Yongji, an engineer and cofounder of the business. "Even though we borrowed the money and built the company ourselves, the government says Stone belongs to the people – in other words, the state. But we have always wanted the company to be owned by private shareholders." The government refuses to allow Stone to expand by selling shares to the public.[88]

Beijing also tightly regulates its financial system, requiring banks to channel savings into inefficient state enterprises. And with the exception of low-yielding savings deposits and bonds, the country has few legal financial instruments that can hold capital for reinvestment.[89] As a result, capital all too often just flies away. Local governments and state companies "have stashed their loot in real estate or siphoned it offshore into shadowy Hong Kong companies."[90]

Corruption may be as severe today in China as it is in Indonesia. There were 60,000 reported cases of fraud, embezzlement, and other economic crimes in 1994 – a statistic that prompted the government to promise a new crackdown on corruption. But most citizens are not holding their breath.[91] They know that Communist Party officials, many of them engaged in private business, are the ones driving fancy cars and drinking imported liquor. Bribery, according to one Hong Kong businessman, has become "part of the cost of doing business in China."[92]

While the nouveau riche get richer in China's capital and its coastal cities, the poor in the countryside fall further behind. In the mid 1980s, the average city dweller in China earned about twice as much as the average rural resident; in the mid 1990s, that urbanite earned three times as much.[93] This income gap is even wider in a place like Guizhou province in China's rugged southwest, where a farmer earns only $70 a year – about a quarter of what the average urbanite earns. Many here have left their homes to join what is called the "floating population" of some 50 million poor people who roam the Chinese countryside looking for work. Others have participated in violent protests. In 1993 alone, about 100 people were killed and another 2,000 were injured in some 600 rebellions staged by disgruntled farmers all over China.[94]

The government is aware of this growing rural unrest. "Economic development in the central and western regions is lagging behind other places, and the gap between those regions and China's eastern region is becoming wider and wider," said state councilor Chen Jun-sheng.[95] To cope with this unrest, Beijing may decide in the end to increase its control over the nation's economy.

Conclusion

There has been a great deal of talk lately in the press, and even in some academic circles, about a "Greater China" or a "Chinese Common-wealth" in Asia.[96] The idea behind all this talk is that Hong Kong, Taiwanese, and Chinese capitalists are teaming up with one another, and with ethnic Chinese in Southeast Asia, to build a regionwide manu-facturing and financial network that will power local economies.

This is idle chatter. Unlike the well-oiled Japanese production alliance we describe in this book, the Chinese business "network" does not operate as a network at all. "It has no head, no organization, no politics, no boundaries," says Peter Kwong-ching Woo, chairman of Hong Kong-based Wharf (Holdings) Ltd.[97] Yes, deals are struck – but on an entirely ad hoc basis. For the most part, the ethnic Chinese multinationals now operating throughout Asia are "sprawling conglomerates between whose parts there is no attempt at synergy."[98] They are managed by family patriarchs who, as former merchants, often pursue a strategy of turning quick profits, rather than investing for the long run and thereby acquiring what we call dynamic technological efficiency. More often than not, they become embroiled in rent-seeking.[99]

It is *Japanese* business, not ethnic Chinese business, that is embracing Asia, drawing together the different economies of the region. In this chapter, we have tried to demonstrate that developing countries as diverse as Taiwan and Thailand have been unable to recreate Japan's developmentalism. Handicapped in their ability to adopt new tech-nology, they have felt compelled to open wide their arms.

In the following chapter, we describe how Japanese MNCs are squeezing tighter and tighter. After all, like the tango, it takes two to embrace.

CHAPTER SIX

Holding Technology

No one can deny that Japan has become a world leader in technology or that, in many areas, its technological prowess even surpasses that of the United States. Scholars attending a 1991 conference on the topic came up with "a unanimous, unambiguous conclusion": "Japan's technological capability across a wide spectrum of commercially significant fields is formidable and growing relative to that of the United States.... Over the past several decades, Japanese companies have captured growing shares of the global market for numerous high-technology products and have accelerated the pace of innovation in mature industries."[1] This conclusion is supported by studies in both the United States and Japan.

According to the US National Science Board, Japanese firms received 44 percent of all the patents issued around the world for robot technology from 1986 through 1990. US firms, by comparison, received 24 percent. The competition for patents for optical fiber technology was dead even (33 percent each) during this period. But Japanese firms showed remarkable improvement since the 1976–80 period, when they garnered only 23 percent of those patents.[2]

MITI, meanwhile, routinely assesses the technological competence of Japanese and American firms in a number of fields. It has found that Japan is now leading the United States in the reliability and performance of such products as VCRs, high-tensile strength steel, and semiconductor lasers.[3]

Japan is doing all it can to remain a technological leader. During the 1980s, when the Japanese economy was booming, public and private spending on R&D increased sharply. Such expenditures, a solid 1.7 percent of GNP in the mid 1970s, came to represent 3 percent by 1991. Measured in this way, the country now spends more than the United States does on R&D, and far more on R&D that is unrelated to defense.[4] In the early 1990s, of course, this technological edge seemed precarious – for a while. Private firms, which conduct most of the R&D in Japan, had trimmed their expenditures to cope with the post-bubble recession. So the Science and Technology Agency, anxious to fill the gap, called on the Japanese government to double its R&D spending "to help Japan compete with other nations."[5]

The question we ask here, though, is not whether Japan has acquired a large endowment of technology. We already know it has. Rather, the question is this: as Japan expands into Asia, will it transfer increasingly advanced technology quickly enough to allow its neighbors to become more equal partners in the region's emerging production alliance? In other words, will Asia's vertical division of labor, the V-shaped flying geese formation, be transformed, as Okita, Kojima, and others have predicted, into a horizontal division of labor, a straight line pattern?[6]

For the moment, the answer seems to be no. Evidence suggests that Japan is, as we argued in chapter three, continuing to pursue developmentalism – only now in an expanded (a regional rather than merely a national) context. Japanese high-technology manufacturers are using quasi-integration to forge vertical ties with Asian firms and thus carefully control the process of technology transfer. As they shed their old (relatively low-level) technology at a deliberate (relatively slow) pace, Japan flies further and further ahead of the flock in Asia and the V-formation grows steeper and steeper.[7]

Many observers seem to agree. A research group examining the transfer of technology from Japan to Thailand concludes, for example, that Japanese electronics manufacturers are achieving such a rapid rate of technical progress that, even though they constantly transfer old technology to Thailand, "new technology piles up" in Japan. "Thus, year after year, the technological gap between Japan and Thailand widens."[8] Even South Korea, which is the second most technologically advanced nation in Asia, cannot keep pace with the lead goose, according to Song Byung-nak, an internationally respected economist at Seoul National University. "In the case of televisions, an industry in which Korea has done quite well, one can easily see this trend emerging. Japan is moving way ahead in the new field of high-definition television. But it is happening across the board. And if this trend continues, the Japanese economy will become even more dominant in this region."[9]

These observations are confirmed in three very useful quantitative analyses. One, carried out by Chow and Kellman, begins with the presumption that, if the Asian NICs had indeed begun to catch up with Japan and reduce the technology gap, they would have displaced Japan in some of the global markets for technology-intensive goods. Between 1965 and 1990, however, they did no such thing.

> During this period, the NICs systematically switched their export patterns to more closely approximate past patterns of Japan's export vector.... Since Japan itself was rapidly shifting the basis of its comparative advantage from a labor-intensive to a physical and human-capital intensive basis during this period, the NICs managed to chase after Japan and yet complement, rather than directly compete with, Japan in the OECD market.[10]

Chow and Kellman keep track of this "chase" with the aid of a similarity index, a statistical tool that measures, at any given time, the similarity of two countries' exports to a third market. Because they are interested in dynamic changes in comparative advantage, they take several "snapshots" of the composition of exports from the NICs and Japan at different moments in recent history.[11]

In 1970, for example, Hong Kong's export pattern appeared quite similar to Japan's of 1965. This suggests that Hong Kong was at that time catching up with Japan. Instead it staggered and, by 1980, was still only beginning to approach Japan's pattern of 1970. The island did not manage to approximate that pattern until 1990. "This would suggest that systematic transformations in its export patterns, following Japan's leadership, slowed down after the early 1970s," according to Chow and Kellman.[12]

Like Hong Kong, South Korea has chased Japan without ever really catching up. Chow and Kellman show that, despite the rapid growth of its economy and the increasing competitiveness of its manufacturing industries, Korea remains far behind. In 1990, its degree of similarity with Japan was still only 51.4 percent. This means that Korea's exports competed with Japan's in only about half of the markets to which Japan exported.[13]

The second study, carried out by Tatsuo Tanaka, seeks to identify the forces creating the observed patterns of trade between Korea and Japan from 1973 to 1989. He finds that, after 1980, differences in labor productivity (which are, in practical terms, differences in technological level), rather than differences in factor endowments, largely determined these bilateral trade patterns. What happened around 1980 was that the relative capital–labor ratio of Japanese and Korean exports stabilized, or became "stuck," at 2:1, reflecting a technology gap between the two countries. In other words, Korea at that time stopped catching up with Japan.

Although he states it more broadly, Tanaka's conclusion is reminiscent of Chow and Kellman's.

> In most [high-technology] industries, innovation will continue.... When developing countries reached the technology level of the advanced countries five years ago, the advanced countries had moved to a more advanced technology level. The target is a moving one. Like the race of Achilles and the turtle, the developing countries can never catch up.[14]

Based on his review of the trade data, Tanaka is able to offer one other finding that is, for us, extremely significant. He notes that higher-priced Japanese exports have continued to flow heavily into Korea over the past two decades, and attributes this to the fact that those exports are not perfect substitutes for lower-priced Korean products. This is true even in the case of the semiconductor industry, which is often cited as evidence that Korea is closing its technology gap with Japan. The Japanese exports tend to be high value-added goods (such as more lucrative ASICs), not standard goods (such as the mass-produced DRAMs Korea is now exporting in increasing quantities). This supports our contention that manufacturing production in these two countries has become vertically integrated.[15]

The third and final study, an ambitious econometric effort, was carried out by Kim and Lau. They attribute the rapid economic growth of Korea, Taiwan, Singapore, and Hong Kong to the accumulation of capital and the increased input of higher quality labor, but not to home-grown innovation. The study demonstrates that indigenously generated improvements in technology have been "quite scarce" in the Asian NICs, leading to "a significant decline in productive efficiency," meaning technological progress, relative to both the United States and Japan.[16]

This widening technology gap, Kim and Lau suggest, is "not inconsistent with the fact that economic growth in the East Asian NICs, unlike the economic growth in the G-5 nations, is due mostly to increases in inputs, especially capital inputs, rather than to technological progress or increases in efficiency."[17]

On top of these quantitative studies, there are at least three good analytical reasons to believe that Japan will not only maintain but actually *increase* its technological lead in Asia over the next two decades. One has to do with the external environment. In the 1950s and 1960s, when it mobilized its national campaign to catch up with the West by adopting new technology, Japan was extraordinarily lucky. The US government, then guided by a geopolitical strategy of containing communism in Asia, prodded American companies to license new technologies to Japanese firms. It wanted to do all it could to help revitalize and strengthen the Japanese economy. Today, however, the developing countries of Asia are not so lucky. The United States no longer is able or willing to sacrifice its economic interests for political ones, and Japan has precious few political interests for which it would sacrifice its economic ones.[18]

Not only the political environment but the business environment today is less hospitable for challengers. Innovating firms have slashed the product cycle, the time between the discovery of a new technology and the development of a commercial application. In doing so, they have made it increasingly difficult for less sophisticated firms in developing countries to catch up.[19]

Finally, the current "technological paradigm," based on micro-electronics, is still evolving. By technological paradigm, we mean the uniquely grounded system of technical know-how that defines a given period. In this case, we refer to a paradigm that began in the 1970s, replacing the earlier paradigm of the 1870–1970 period that was based on electricity.[20] As long as the current paradigm continues to evolve, Japanese firms should benefit. After all, as Cantwell notes, they have developed effective organizational routines designed to capitalize on this paradigm. "The changes that will occur in the composition of tech-nological opportunities are likely to be mainly of an incremental kind, moving from the fast growth fields of the 1980s into related areas. Japanese firms are likely to lead such incremental shifts."[21]

The second reason to expect an even wider technology gap in Asia has to do with the relative strength of Japan's political economy, or what Freeman calls its "national system of innovation."[22] Cooperation between government and business creates a foundation for reasonably accurate technological forecasting, which in turn allows the two parties to "visualize a vast web of industrial objectives," as Brown and Daneke have suggested, and thus devise policies to encourage investment in targeted areas.[23] Interfirm cooperation makes it possible for companies to share information and thereby reduce the risk of innovation.[24] And coopera-tion between management and labor allows a firm to adopt a long-term perspective, which in turn allows it to accept the risk of investing in new technologies.[25] These effective methods of cooperation, which Japanese firms are using in their overseas operations in Asia, are either missing or are not as well developed in the political economies of the Asian NICs and the ASEAN-4. With a diminished capacity to assimilate new technology, these countries are handicapped in their efforts to catch up with Japan.

The preceding explains why Japan is able to develop and adopt new technologies more quickly than its neighbors. But it does not tell us how Japanese MNCs, as they expand into Asia, manage to secure that know-how so it does not spill into the laps of potential rivals. This is the third reason to expect Japan to increase its technological lead and fly further ahead of the regional pack. By building *keiretsu*-like production networks that embrace and even smother local entrepreneurs, technicians, and workers in Asia, Japanese MNCs carefully control the pace of technology transfer. In effect, they lock it up in the vertical, quasi-integrated networks they control. In doing so, they are able to extract an unusually large share of the rent on the use of their know-how.

This, we acknowledge, may sound implausible. High-tech firms that cooperate with other, unrelated firms always run the risk of spilling technology. How exactly do Japanese companies manage to minimize that risk?

Borrus contends that Japan's large, oligopolistic firms enjoy what he calls "relative asymmetries of access" to trade and investment opportunities in their own and their partners' countries. This asymmetry, created by government policy and business practice, makes Japanese know-how relatively difficult to appropriate.[26]

Other scholars go further, suggesting that Japanese firms have an edge in cross-border alliances because their own knowledge base is "context dependent," or embedded in an established social system and thus relatively difficult to penetrate. For example, Imai, a leading authority on Japanese business practices and technological change, says Japanese firms use an overlapping method of product design and development, a method in which linkages are made and information is shared between parties and processes over a long period. This method of implicit contracting speeds up product design and development in Japan. But in a partnership between a Japanese and a non-Japanese firm, it also "creates an asymmetry of learning and a conflict in the management of the alliance."[27]

This argument is seconded by Hamel, who has written extensively on strategic alliances. "Context-dependent knowledge (for example, principles of industrial relations in Japan) is inherently less transparent than context-free knowledge (e.g., the principles of a transistor)," he writes.[28] In addition, Hamel argues that Japanese MNCs are "averse to the very notion of symmetrical dependency between partners" and that they prefer to hold power – an attribute that, he notes correctly, derives from knowledge.[29]

Technology transfer is difficult to measure, in part because the term itself is vexingly vague. We define technology here to mean the method, knowledge, or skill used to realize or improve the production and distribution of goods and services. It can be embodied in different forms: the machinery used in production or distribution; the manuals detailing business procedures; or the minds of technicians, engineers, and managers who design and execute those procedures. Some might argue, then, that technology transfer is nothing more than the movement of such a method, knowledge, or skill from one country to another. But Lindsey makes a critical and, we think, appropriate distinction between the *transport* of technology, which only suggests movement, and the *transfer* of technology, which implies a degree of localization.[30] For effective technology transfer to occur, we argue that local firms and personnel must be able not only to operate the imported technology, but to adapt and perfect it to suit local conditions. This requires an understanding of the underlying nature of the imported technology, and thus a mastery of it.

An abundance of anecdotal evidence suggests that Japan is extraordinarily eager to acquire technology, but loath to part with it. Park Woo-hee, president of the Korea Academy of Industrial Technology, has called Japan the "black hole" of the innovating universe, forever sucking technology in but never spitting it out.[31] This does, we concede, sound extreme. But in interview after interview, government officials throughout Asia expressed profound frustration with their own inability to pry technical know-how from Japanese multinationals. One of these officials, Tan Kim Chong of the Malaysian Industrial Development Authority, told us that Japanese firms in general do not transfer technology as freely as American and European firms. He ticked off a long list of possible explanations: from language (many Japanese managers do not speak English, and even fewer speak Malay or Chinese) to geography (Japanese managers and technicians can fly to Kuala Lumpur in six hours); from business organization (Japanese affiliates in Malaysia are branches of a global enterprise strictly controlled by the parent firm in Japan) to corporate philosophy (Japanese MNCs adopt a long-range perspective). Tan said he didn't know exactly why; he only knew that, for Japanese firms, "the process of technology transfer is very, very slow. We've talked and talked and talked to them about this problem, but nothing ever seems to really change."[32]

Local elites sometimes vent this frustration openly. In fact, Malaysia's *Business Times* published a particularly grumpy editorial, criticizing Japanese companies for business practices that block the effective transfer of technology. "Those companies," the editors snapped, "need a change in attitude."[33]

In her research on Japanese FDI in Asia, Chia Siow Yue heard all of these complaints. Asians told her that "compared to American and European companies, Japanese companies are slower in the localization of managerial and technical personnel, slower in promoting them, and slower in training. Japanese firms also appear more reluctant to set up design and R&D units in the host countries."[34]

A team of Singaporean economists concluded in a 1986 study that Japanese MNCs, compared to MNCs from other countries, are "less willing to transfer technology" to Singapore. They did not attribute this fact to any innate defect such as stinginess or greed. Rather, they chalked it up to the fact that Japanese firms traditionally use a lifetime employment system that diminishes staff turnover, and to the fact that they rely heavily on Japanese suppliers that tend to follow them overseas.[35]

For their part, Japanese business executives have become – naturally – a bit defensive. They argue, with some justification, that the fate of any effort to transfer technology depends as much on the technological capacity of the recipient as it does on the behavior of the provider. If Asians are looking for a culprit, these executives grumble, they should look in the mirror. There they will find technicians who change jobs too often and managers who don't appreciate the importance of product quality.

In more relaxed and less confrontational settings, Japanese business executives will often concede they fear losing control of their accumulated know-how. It is, after all, the fundamental source of their competitive edge. "For us," confides the executive of a large Japanese semiconductor manufacturer, "production in Asia is an integrated operation. That means we must preserve our factories in Japan as the ultimate base for high-tech production. The result is that we have technology that cannot be transferred."[36] He is not alone. An equally possessive attitude was reflected in a 1987 survey of multinational firms in China. Only 61 percent of the Japanese, compared with 72 percent of the Americans, agreed that a key factor for the success of a joint venture in that country "is to offer your latest technology."[37]

Japanese MNCs, like all MNCs, transfer technology in one of two ways. They carry it with them when they invest abroad in new production facilities, or they license it to overseas firms. The technology transferred through licensing is often referred to as "unbundled" technology because it, unlike technology transferred via FDI, does not come with a bundle of management resources that continues to exert control. Asian countries, particularly the NICs, have exhibited an increasingly strong interest in such unbundled technology. And in the early 1990s, Japanese high-tech firms began to reciprocate. (See Table 6.1, which lists some of the technology agreements between Japanese and NIC firms in the semiconductor industry.)

Do these tie-ups signify that Japan has become more willing to share its technology? Not necessarily. In fact, we believe they reflect a strategic maneuver by Japanese manufacturers to "tame" otherwise uppity Asian competitors. With agreements to jointly design and/or produce, say, semiconductors, "it's easier to control the total chip supply coming into the market," says Inui Makio, an analyst with Kleinwort Benson International Inc. A spokesperson for Hitachi, which shares its memory chip technology with Goldstar Electron of South Korea, expresses this sentiment bluntly: "You don't have to make all DRAMs (dynamic random access memory chips) in order to sell all DRAMs."[38]

Table 6.1 Joining Forces: Japan's Major Semiconductor Partnerships in Asia

Japanese company	Asian partner (location)	Date formed	Type of partnership
Toshiba	Chartered Semiconductor Pte. (Singapore)	Nov. 1994	Toshiba licenses chip-building technology to CSM and buys a 0.6% equity stake
Oki Electric	Mosel Vitelic (Taiwan)	Oct. 1994	Oki shares 16 megabit memory-chip technology for production in Taiwan
NEC	Taiwan Semiconductor Manufacturing (Taiwan)	Aug. 1994	NEC shares chip designs for manufacture in Taiwan
Oki Electric	Nanya Plastics (Taiwan)	May 1994	Oki shares 16 megabit memory-chip technology for production in Taiwan
Fujitsu	Hyundai Electronics Industries (South Korea)	Oct. 1993	Cooperative memory-chip development
NEC	Samsung Electronics (Korea)	Mid 1993	"Exchange of information" on 256 megabit memory-chip development
Oki Electric	Samsung Electronics (Korea)	Dec. 1992	Cooperative 16 megabit memory-chip development
Toshiba	Samsung Electronics (Korea)	Dec. 1992	Toshiba shares flash memory-chip technology for joint development
Hitachi	Goldstar Electron (Korea)	1989	Hitachi provides memory-chip design for manufacture in Korea

Source: Wall Street Journal, 7 November 1994. Reprinted by permission of *Wall Street Journal* © 1994 Dow Jones & Company, Inc. All Rights Reserved Worldwide.

Even when they share unbundled technology, Japanese firms appear to be extraordinarily cautious. In many cases, they share only mature (older) or standardized technology. This was the conclusion of the Korea–Japan Economic Cooperation Association, a nongovernmental organization that conducted a survey of Korean firms that collaborate with the Japanese. Fifty-five percent of the respondents, impatient with Japan's reluctance to transfer its most sophisticated core technology, said they hoped to increase technology imports from the West. "Technology transferred from the United States tends to be at an earlier stage of the product life cycle, allowing Koreans to use it over time to increase exports," the authors conclude. "But technology transferred from Japan, especially in the electronics industry, is labor intensive and at a later stage in the product cycle."[39]

Here are two examples. In the late 1980s, Hyundai, the Korean conglomerate, made a bid for laser printer technology that Canon had developed. The Japanese manufacturer refused, agreeing only to license the low-end, low-margin technology for the dot matrix printer, which it no longer could produce competitively anyway.[40] About the same time, Korea's Kia Motors was seeking to upgrade the engine on the old Mazda models it was selling at home. But Mazda balked. In the end, Kia had to go to Germany to secure a new engine design.[41]

One way Japanese firms control the pace of technology transfer is by imposing stiff fees on the know-how they license to Asian firms. Using a multiple regression analysis, Lee and Kim found that, although Korean firms pay a higher price (per agreement) for technology from the United States, they actually end up receiving a better deal from American, not Japanese, firms. This is because US technology comes with fewer collateral charges (such as service and "guidance" fees) and because – being more advanced – it can be used longer. Adjusting for these facts, Lee and Kim concluded that Japanese firms receive a larger monopoly rent on the use of their technology.[42]

One scholar alleges that, in Malaysia, Japanese firms are exploiting smaller local companies, charging them royalties on expired patents.[43] But even some of the largest Malaysian firms are feeling pinched. David Wong, general manager of Tan Chong Motors, Nissan's local partner in that country, complains that his firm pays an "abnormally high" price for Japanese technology. "The cost for us to host a Nissan engineer for just one day is equivalent to paying a [local] foreman on the shopfloor for an entire month," he says.[44] And Proton, Malaysia's state-owned automaker, is said to have paid excessively high royalties to Mitsubishi Motors for its technology.[45]

A growing number of Japanese high-tech firms are using licensing fees as part of a deliberate strategy to undermine foreign competitors, especially the hard-charging Koreans. "Paying large royalties will boost South Korean makers' production costs, making it hard for them to pursue their low-cost, low-price business strategy," says a business executive in Japan.[46] In some cases, technology buyers are so eager to enter a field that they are willing to pay almost any price. Samsung, Lucky Goldstar, and Daewoo, all of which went to JVC, a Matsushita subsidiary, to acquire the technology for the VCR, are said to be paying almost $13 in royalties for every VCR they produce.[47] Samsung, meanwhile, is paying an estimated $40 million – a quarter of its pretax profits in 1991 – for access to Fujitsu's microchip technology.[48] At the same time, though, the Korean giant was unwilling to pay the steep price set by the Sony Corp.

for access to the Japanese firm's technology for video cameras used in television broadcasting.[49]

Another way Japanese firms control the pace of technology transfer is by restricting others' use of their know-how. Several studies show that the Japanese, compared to Americans and Europeans, place more restrictions on the technology they license to Southeast Asia.[50] For example, they often require licensees to purchase certain machinery or raw materials, or insist that they sell their products through specified agents or distributors.[51] And they often prohibit licensees from exporting their products to certain markets. This is a sore subject not only in Southeast Asia, but in Northeast Asia as well.[52] A study of Japan's technology transfer to Korea found that Japanese technology suppliers insist on conditions "restricting export markets and requiring the use of machinery and component parts produced by Japanese firms."[53] The case of Heung Yang, a Korean electronics manufacturer, illustrates this point. Heung Yang used Sony technology to produce a color TV with a built-in VCR. But according to the terms of its technology licensing agreement, it was unable to export the video unit to any markets in Europe.[54]

Although licensing agreements have become a popular mode of technology transfer throughout Asia, a closer look reveals that many of them are in fact "sweetheart deals" between parents of MNCs and their local subsidiaries or affiliates.[55] This is particularly true in Southeast Asia, where local capital remains by and large "technology-less," and where foreign capital thus serves as the most important source of new manufacturing know-how.[56]

For years, scholars have argued that FDI serves as a particularly effective mode of technology transfer.[57] Tran, for example, suggests that foreign investment is likely to "bring about a more effective transfer than other channels since it involves a sustained relationship between the transferer and transferee."[58] This assertion, though, is based on the assumption that technology naturally diffuses through the training of local suppliers, who may be expected to meet higher standards of quality control, reliability, and speed of delivery, and through the training of local managers and technicians, who eventually might move from foreign to local firms, transferring human capital with them.[59] But Japanese MNCs, we argue, are often able to block or at least constrict these traditional avenues of technology diffusion. Ernst agrees. He concludes that "the closed nature of Japanese regional production networks has constrained the opportunities for host country firms to develop their own technological and organizational capabilities that are necessary for a continuous upgrading of their production efficiency and product mix."[60]

As we discuss more fully in chapter nine, Japanese affiliates in Asia use a modified version of their home-grown employment system that tends to discourage employee turnover.[61] They also retain an unusually large number of Japanese expatriates in top management positions.[62] Finally, they emphasize "software" (on-the-job training, which produces company-specific knowledge that is not as easily transferable as general knowledge) rather than "hardware" (blueprints and manuals).[63] Written material explaining how to operate machinery or conduct management procedures is extraordinarily rare in Japanese factories in Asia.[64]

All these factors combine to stymie the diffusion of technology through local personnel. P. Arunasalam can attest to that. Although he spent 17 years manufacturing electric and telephone cable for Furukawa Electric Co. in Malaysia, he says he "can't tell you how a cable is made from start to finish."[65] Furukawa, he says, tried hard to keep local personnel in the dark. In 1980, when he was visiting the parent company in Japan, Arunasalam says he was barred from entering one of its plants. "The plant was working on optic fibers, and I was told that it was top secret, even for someone like me who had been with the company for so many years."

Subcontracting, the other possible avenue of technology diffusion, does not seem to offer much promise either. As we demonstrate in chapter ten, Japanese high-technology firms in Asia tend to import parts from Japan or purchase them locally from Japanese suppliers who have set up their own factories in the region. They do very little to promote the development of local suppliers. This is confirmed in study after study, including a Japanese government study that examined direct investment in Asia by Japan's television and camera manufacturers. It found little or no evidence of technology transfer to local firms. "Parts procurement networks are formed by Japanese companies, and there is a wall that prevents technology from being transferred outside this network."[66]

As if these facts of life were not enough, another factor frustrates the potential for technology transfer through FDI: Japanese MNCs, with the help of the government, are building production networks in Asia based on a regional division of labor. The production process is thus broken into pieces, which are parceled out to each country according to its technical ability. In this way, Japanese manufacturers achieve economies of scale and scope, as well as what we call "economies of networking" (efficiencies gained through the reduced transaction costs of quasi-integration), that give them a powerful edge against international competitors. But in the same way, local firms integrated into the lower strata of these coordinated networks are denied the opportunity to understand the overall production process or the underlying technology. They serve only as cogs in the wheel, stamping out standardized parts and exporting them to other production bases across the region.[67]

"It's like *ikebana* [Japanese flower arrangement]," says Kawasaki Masahiro, former head of Japan's National Institute of Science and Technology Policy and now senior vice president of the Research Development Corp. of Japan. "After it's all done, you can't see how it was really done."[68]

There is some evidence to suggest that these export-oriented networks actually stifle the innovative capacity of host nations in Asia. In Thailand, a research institute found that the ability to adapt or fine-tune imported technology was 10–14 percent lower in export-oriented firms, such as electronics manufacturers, than in domestic-oriented firms.[69] And in Malaysia, Anuwar says Japanese multinationals producing for domestic markets "have tried to diversify their R&D activities in terms of process alteration, raw materials substitution, marketing research and product design."[70] But these firms, which may in fact contribute to the host nation's reservoir of technical knowledge and skills, represent a slowly dying breed. The new breed, which consists of Japanese multinationals that simply swap standardized parts in an export-oriented network, appears to be solidifying Malaysia's technological dependence on Japan.

The new multinationals controlling these production networks in Asia are careful to retain at home those activities creating the most value. As a result, Japan is much better able to minimize the phenomenon of "hollowing out" – the massive export of a nation's manufacturing and innovating capacity – than can other advanced industrial nations.[71] Two cases illustrate our point. American firms such as Intel and National Semiconductor have established plants that carry out not only the labor-intensive work of wiring together wafers, but also the capital- and technology-intensive work of imprinting integrated circuits onto a silicon substrate. Japanese chipmakers, in contrast, have been slow to transfer wafer fabrication activities to the rest of Asia.[72]

The other case is R&D. Unlike their American and European counterparts, Japanese MNCs carry out very little R&D at overseas facilities in Asia. There are important exceptions to this rule, of course. The Matsushita air conditioning group in Malaysia has a new R&D facility in Shah Alam, a suburb of Kuala Lumpur, where it adapts Japanese technology for local market conditions and hopes to eventually design entirely new models.[73] In general, though, parent companies in Japan hang onto such work, thereby avoiding any chance of spilling secrets.[74] We are backed up here by two studies. In a survey conducted by the Japan Machinery Exporters Association, only 12 percent of 144 high-tech firms with manufacturing plants in Asia indicated they use parts designed and produced in the region. Far more said they import parts from Japan (79 percent) and/or purchase parts produced in Asia with blueprints prepared in Japan (41 percent).[75] The other study, carried out by Ernst, examined 45 R&D projects set up in Asia by Japanese firms. It found that only one of those projects was engaged in what Ernst calls "generic technology development," or basic and significant innovation that goes well beyond adaptive engineering, circuit design, or software redesign.[76]

Japanese firms have a minimal presence at Science Park, Taiwan's new R&D and high-technology manufacturing center in Hsinchu. "It's almost impossible to get technology from Japan," sighs H. Steve Hsieh, director general of the park, which was modeled after Japan's Tsukuba Science City. For dramatic contrast, he points to the substantial Japanese investment in three special zones in southern Taiwan, reserved exclusively for export-oriented assembly work. "That," says Hsieh, "is a good illustration of the mentality of Japan."[77]

Whether the vehicle is direct investment or technology licensing, Japanese MNCs usually transfer only those skills needed to operate machinery and equipment.[78] Imano calls this "how" technology, "the superficial technology that can be learned in a short period of time." He distinguishes it from "why" technology, which is usually retained in Japan and never really mastered by local technicians and engineers in Asia. "This is, of course, why local firms remain dependent on Japanese engineers ... and why Japanese *keiretsu* firms remain the primary conduit for technology transfer."[79]

Several studies have come to the same conclusion. In a survey of 133 firms in Asia, the Nikkei Research Institute of Industry and Markets found that 70 percent had transferred such "how" technology, but only 25 percent had transferred the technology to develop new products.[80] In a survey of Japanese firms in Southeast Asia, a Hiroshima University research team found that 74 percent had transferred operation technology, but only a fraction of the respondents indicated they had passed on skills related to production management (28 percent) and technology improvement (11 percent). Almost none had transferred design or product development technology.[81]

For local firms that have supplied parts to Japanese electronics and automobile manufacturers in Thailand, technology transfer may not have progressed even that far. In a survey, more than 30 percent indicated they had received operation technology, but fewer said they had acquired skills for production management (19.2 percent) and quality control (15.4 percent).[82]

These studies highlight the fact that Japanese MNCs have managed to embrace Asia, encouraging nations such as Thailand to grow – but chiefly in concert with Japanese technology. In the words of Prayoon Shiowattana, general manager of the Technological Promotion Association in Bangkok, "they have integrated Thai industry and labor into their own strategic networks."[83]

How did this come about? One could argue that Thailand and other Asian countries failed to take the necessary steps to secure technological autonomy and nurture innovation. Prayoon makes just this point. "By default," he says sadly, "we have become enmeshed" in a Japanese production alliance.

But one could also argue, as we do here, that Japan has deliberately pursued a strategy of regionalized developmentalism, a strategy of promoting its own technological growth by tightly embracing Asia. Karatsu Hajime, a former bureaucrat and business executive who now is a professor of technology development, has advocated nothing less. "What Japan should do in investing abroad is obvious: Keep production know-how firmly in its own hands and manufacture at whichever location offers the most advantage. As long as we do this, the Japanese economy will not be affected negatively in the least."[84]

PART THREE

A Japanese Alliance in Asia

CHAPTER SEVEN

The Visible Handshake

Japan's reputation in Asia has improved dramatically since 1974, when students in Bangkok and Jakarta greeted a visiting Japanese prime minister by burning him in effigy.[1] Who in those days could have imagined that:

- in 1989, virtually all of Asia's heads of state would converge on Tokyo to attend the funeral of the late Showa emperor, the human symbol of Japan's brutal occupation during World War II?
- a year later, Prime Minister Mahathir of Malaysia would call for a Japan-centered trading bloc that looked to some like a peaceful ghost of the Greater East Asia Co-Prosperity Sphere?
- in 1992, Thailand would prod its neighbors in Southeast Asia to support legislation in the Japanese Diet to allow Japan to dispatch soldiers to foreign lands for the first time since the war?

Indeed, the country that once generated hostility and suspicion today inspires respect and admiration in many parts of the region. One Thai official went so far as to describe his country's relationship with Japan as "a happy marriage."[2]

Viewed against the long backdrop of history, this rapid rise in Japan's standing in Asia seems miraculous. It is not. It is the product of a deliberate, largely successful strategy to embrace the region in a complex web of personal, governmental, and corporate ties – all united under the ubiquitous banner of *keizai kyōryoku*, or economic cooperation.

This statement, we readily admit, begs a big question: Who designed and carried out this Japanese strategy of economic cooperation? In other words, who really governs the nation? We are reluctant to join a debate that has consumed the attention of so many academics for so many years, a debate that has swung wildly between two extremes.[3] But we must, even if only briefly.

Until recently, scholars in the postwar era routinely characterized the Japanese state as a well-oiled machine piloted by an elite bureaucracy, particularly the Ministry of International Trade and Industry (MITI). In so doing, they ignored or dismissed the rising influence of free-standing interest groups in Japanese society, as well as the *zoku* (policy tribes) – the groups of Liberal Democratic Party (LDP) members of the Diet that emerged as independent power centers to address the concerns of those competing interest groups.[4]

For good reason, the traditional view of the Japanese state as a unitary body, a "Japan Inc." dominated by bureaucrats, has become passé. Even Johnson, a forceful advocate of the old orthodoxy, all but recanted in a brilliant analysis of the bloody turf battle over high-technology policy.[5] Today, he and other observers describe a fragmented, paralyzed, and rudderless polity that relies all too often on *gaiatsu*, or foreign pressure, to break new political ground.[6]

This picture of a Hydra-like, semifeudal, "stateless" system does seem all too often to reflect the reality of Japan's international diplomacy – especially with the United States. A case in point was the Japanese government's badly bungled and belated move to help bankroll the allied forces in Operation Desert Storm against Saddam Hussein's troops in Kuwait. The rest of the world alternately giggled and groaned as it watched the spectacle of a solicitous foreign minister promising financial assistance, an outraged finance minister challenging the amount of that commitment, and a nervous prime minister scurrying between the two ministries to try to resolve the impasse.[7]

But Japan, we argue, is in fact led by a coalition of political and economic elites. Membership in this coalition is somewhat fluid, changing minimally from year to year and from issue to issue. For example, farmers, represented by the *nōkyō*, or agricultural cooperatives, increasingly find themselves on the outside looking in.[8] Even at its core, the conservative coalition begins to unravel whenever it strays too far from its centripetal cause – national security, which it invariably defines as economic security. Nonetheless, we assert that, in most instances, the captains of industry and government in Japan collaborate closely on the design and execution of both foreign and domestic economic policy.

In making this assertion, we are flatly rejecting the false dichotomy posed by both the old and new orthodoxies. Japan has neither a bureaucratic authoritarian nor a centerless state. It is ruled instead by a government–business network.[9] Government has penetrated business, and business has penetrated government through a process Richard Samuels calls "reciprocal consent."

> In exchange for the use of public resources, private industry grants the state some jurisdiction over industrial structure in the "national interest." Business enjoys privilege, systematic inclusion in the policy process, access to public goods, and rights of self-regulation. It reciprocates by agreeing to state jurisdiction in the definition of market structure and by participating in the distribution of benefits.[10]

In other words, Japan's government–business network is a mutually reinforcing alliance or partnership that is capable of strong, decisive action so long as it hews to the established, conservative policy line.

Like a bloodhound, Japan's government–business network has followed that line carefully in Asia, particularly in Southeast Asia, which has long been identified as critical to Japan's national security. Thus, it has tried to cultivate close relations with elites in the region, hoping to secure the political and social stability, as well as the liberal trade and investment policies, vital to Japanese capital.

In the late 1960s, as Japan began for the first time to accumulate a steady and increasing trade surplus, it became not just a private investor in Asia, but also a public donor through rising volumes of official development assistance (ODA). Pushed by business interests, the government agreed at that time to revive the old Taigai Keizai Kyōryoku Shingikai (the deliberation council on overseas economic cooperation), an unofficial group that had recommended aid policies to the government. Of course, "economic cooperation" in Japan has never referred solely to aid, but rather to a "trinity" (*sanmi-ittai*) including ODA, FDI, and trade. (Even today, the government routinely uses this phrase, which once was reserved to describe Christianity's trinity of Father, Son, and Holy Ghost, in its discussion of "comprehensive economic cooperation" with Southeast Asia.)[11] So if we understand that economic cooperation is a holistic system including private and public capital flows, as well as merchandise trade, then we also can understand why the president of the Japan Chamber of Commerce and Industry replaced the Japanese prime minister as chairman of this newly revamped and revitalized deliberation council.[12]

Guided by a common but still somewhat vague notion, Japan's government–business network did not clearly articulate the purpose of economic cooperation – at least not until the early 1970s, when Arab states in the Mideast slapped an embargo on oil shipments, communists claimed control of Indochina, and students in the rest of Southeast Asia demonstrated against Japan's "economic imperialism." Back home, those events combined to reactivate a dormant but deep-seated sense of national insecurity. Japanese elites responded by devising a new policy of "comprehensive national security" that measured the nation's vulnerability in economic – not purely strategic – terms, and envisioned the use of nonmilitary weapons, such as government aid and private investment, to defend and promote Japanese interests around the world.[13] Japan's national security was premised on the security and stability of Southeast Asia, then a primary source of Japanese imports of petroleum, rubber, tin, and other critical natural resources, and now a junior partner in Japan's regional production alliance.

In 1977, prime minister Fukuda Takeo visited the region and pledged that Japan would "take actions reflecting its increasing responsibilities toward Southeast Asia." Sounding themes of regional hegemony and noblesse oblige, the Fukuda Doctrine, as it came to be called, had a familiar ring. "It is the duty of Japan as an advanced country in Asia to stabilize the area and establish a constructive order," explained the foreign minister.[14]

Japan's economic cooperation policy in Southeast Asia was, at that time, based on the need to secure a steady supply of raw materials and a low-cost production base for textiles, electronics, and other labor-intensive industries. Indeed, Japanese aid and investment helped secure both. But in the mid 1980s, the ground beneath that policy shifted. As we noted in chapter two, *endaka*, the dramatic appreciation of the yen, undermined the international competitiveness of virtually all manufacturing enterprises that export from Japan. In this harsh new environment, Japanese industry, particularly exporting industry, began to see the region as an extension of its home base.

In one report after another, the government–business network promoted this new vision of East and Southeast Asia as integral parts of a Greater Japan, critically important links in an expanded Japanese production and exporting alliance. MITI, for example, set up an advisory group that called for public and private efforts to more thoroughly integrate the economies of the Asia-Pacific region. "The globalization of economic activity has made it impossible to push ahead with economic development within the limited framework of a country defined by strict national boundaries," it concluded.[15] Likewise, the Ministry of Finance (MOF) created its own think tank to examine regional trade and investment policies. In the preface to its interim report, the think tank saluted the rise of the Asia-Pacific region as "one large economic zone and center of growth."[16]

These reports, and many others, demonstrate that Japan's government–business network was quite mindful of the political and economic liabilities posed by the massive, helter-skelter export of capital. Once again, the United States, a victim of its own deindustrialization, served as an object lesson. The Japanese coined a term, *kūdōka*, or hollowing out, to describe the dreaded process by which MNCs establish cheap production facilities in the Third World and export manufactured goods back to their home country. To avoid that fate, the government–business network began promoting a new division of labor within the region, a division based on each nation's technological level, rather than on its resource endowments. By serving as the region's innovative leader, a powerful R&D machine that will "push forward the frontiers of world demand by actively promoting the development of new products and new technologies that differ from existing types of commodities," Japan will be able to ride the crest of Vernon's product cycle.[17] In other words, it will be able to maintain its position as the lead goose in a regionwide V-formation of dynamic technological growth.[18]

In public pronouncements, members of the government–business network made it clear that Japan would not be the sole beneficiary of this new division of labor. All of Asia would prosper. "For the expansion and maintenance of Asian growth," says Kitamura Kayoko, senior researcher at the Institute of Developing Economies, "the international division of labor should be advanced ... with Japanese businesses at the helm. Each region and nation has to cooperate to solve internal problems and compete without friction."[19]

The most detailed description of this new division of labor is embodied in a report commissioned by the Economic Planning Agency (EPA), which, like MITI and MOF, plays a pivotal role in Japan's government–business network. The report, "Promoting Comprehensive Economic Cooperation in an International Economic Environment Undergoing Dramatic Change: Toward the Construction of an Asian Network," identifies Japan, the NICs, and ASEAN as upper-, middle-, and lower-grade economies. It calls for a regional organization, the "Asian Brain," to coordinate aid, investment, and trade policies so that these three layers can function together as one organic unit. (Figure 7.1 is a schematic representation, included in the original report, of this three-layered unit.) The report states that:

> A smoother movement of production and technology from upper-grade states to middle-grade states, and from middle-grade to lower-grade states is expected, and along with this, industrial adjustment efforts by each country will be required.... Japan has overwhelming comparative advantage in machine tools, textile machinery, food-processing machinery, other machinery parts, automobiles, and motorcycle sectors, and at present these sectors will not require intraregional production restructuring. But it is desirable to carry out a smooth production restructuring in office equipment, electronic musical instruments, and semiconductors [i.e. from Japan to the Asian NICs]. In addition, in personal sundry goods, veneer boards, and wood products, production restructuring is required between the Asian NICs and ASEAN. Knit, spun, and woven goods, and plastics will have to be reallocated among the Asian NICs.[20]

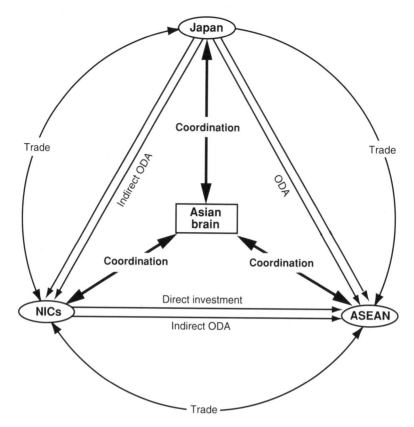

Figure 7.1   The "Asian Brain" Managing Economic Cooperation
Source: "Japanese Foreign Aid," David Arase, p. 479.

In case there was any doubt, the report identifies the source of all this Asian brainpower: "With a view toward setting up this gigantic economic cooperation with an appropriate role in international society, Japan's exhibition of leadership in creating this 'Asian Brain' would be a great contribution with respect not only to the Asian region, but also to international society as a whole."[21]

As bold (or bizarre) as it sounds, the EPA report is a reflection of Japanese economic cooperation policy in the Asia-Pacific region. Consider MITI's New Asian Industries Development (New AID) plan, which we will discuss in much more detail in the next chapter. It too explicitly embraces the concept of *sanmi-ittai*, the holy trinity of aid, investment, and trade that forms the "one body" of economic cooperation with Asia.

Like so many other policy documents, the New AID plan contemplates that the Japanese government will work in tandem with Japanese industry to promote the national interest, or, as its authors suggest, to "expand economic cooperation to improve the environment for investment in developing countries."[22]

The New AID plan is designed to "maximize the effect of FDI, to generate the most beneficial impact – one that does not conflict with the host country's economic policies or the policies of other nations in the region," according to Munakata Naoko, who is helping to administer MITI's economic cooperation program in Asia. "We have found that it's best to plan these things."[23]

We can easily recognize that Japan's government–business network is defending its own interests, as much as it is serving the national interest, by promoting such policies. For MITI, MOF, and EPA, Japan's three arms of economic policy, going regional means holding and even expanding bureaucratic turf, rather than squabbling over limited, highly contested pieces at home. And for large, export-oriented, innovating manufacturers, going regional means consolidating a developmentalist system that puts their interests (the producer's interests) ahead of the consumer's. Without an aggressive, coordinated program of economic cooperation, the government–business network might unravel.

Many scholars disagree with the analysis we have just set forth. They say the market, not the state, is driving the regionalization of Asia. Yamakage Susumu is one of these scholars.

> A blueprint for the turn of the century is now being realized even before the government launched a timetable for construction. Initiatives are taken by the private sector before the government sets up a new policy in giving incentives to invest abroad in accordance with the planned direction of structural transformation. A so-called horizontal division of labor is now taking shape.[24]

But this argument, we believe, founders on the unsupportable premise that public policy and private initiative are two distinct zones of activity in Japan. As we have shown here and in chapter four, they are in fact interpenetrated.

In a comparative study of foreign investment in Thailand, a leading economist agrees with us. She concludes that Japanese MNCs receive far more support from their government in Tokyo than other MNCs receive from theirs. "Japanese conglomerates tend to compete as a system of enterprises-cum-government more than other TNCs [transnational corporations]."[25]

A good example of this Japanese-style, "enterprises-cum-government" FDI can be found in Dalian, China, which in the 1930s was the southern terminus of the South Manchurian Railway operated by Japanese interests. In 1990, Japan's yen loan agency, the Overseas Economic Cooperation Fund (OECF), teamed up with 25 Japanese firms (primarily trading companies and banks) to build a 540 acre industrial park. The Japanese side contributed 80 percent of the project's $62.5 million investment, while the remainder came from the Dalian city government. In addition, the Japanese government committed $800 million in ODA to finance infrastructure for the park. Theoretically, tenants of the industrial park could come from any part of the world. But one Japanese newspaper already has referred to the project as a "Japanese" industrial park.[26] And MITI itself says the project was designed to attract 70–80 firms, "mainly small and medium-sized Japanese companies."[27]

The Japanese government has a number of policy instruments to promote what it and private industry regard as the national interest in the Asia-Pacific region. These include:

- low-interest loans to overseas investors, especially subcontractors for large manufacturers with assembly-type operations. In the mid 1980s, when it still released such data, the government, through the Export-Import Bank, the Japan Overseas Development Corporation, and the Japan Finance Corporation for Small Business, financed as much as 55 percent of the FDI undertaken by small and medium-sized firms.[28] Large firms occasionally receive a piece of this action as well. For example, the Export-Import Bank used a $50 million loan to help underwrite the largest Japanese investment in the Philippines at that time – a joint venture led by Asahi Glass of Japan.[29] And the bank has smiled on Japanese firms of all sizes moving into Indonesia. Twenty-three percent (¥638 billion) of the total credit it has provided for projects in that country has been channeled through the headquarters of Japanese multinationals;[30]

- foreign investment insurance. Under policies adopted in the late 1980s and early 1990s, MITI now covers overseas business losses due to unforeseen commercial, as well as political, circumstances. The maximum compensation for such losses has been raised from 90 percent to 95 percent (and to 97.5 percent in special cases). MITI administers this program through the Japan Trade and Investment Insurance Organization, which operates its own research institute to assess the risks of investing in different countries;[31]

- administrative guidance prior to investment. The government routinely counsels nervous investors before they actually take the plunge and shift operations to Asia. In at least one instance, a 1987 seminar sponsored by JETRO (the Japan External Trade Organization), it offered instruction on the proper techniques for bribing foreign governments.[32] Usually, though, the government sticks to more mundane matters. For example, in the spring of 1992, MITI began meeting with representatives of the consumer electronics industry to try to reach agreement on which companies should invest how much money to manufacture what products in which countries in Asia.[33] And in 1994, the Ministry of Posts and Telecommunications began meeting with representatives of the computer software, telephone, and electronics industries to discuss its ambitious proposal to build an information network throughout Asia;[34]

- administrative guidance overseas. Japanese government officials stationed at embassies and overseas offices in Asia keep close tabs on the local affiliates of Japanese industry. In early 1994, JETRO had 30 representatives in China to "guide" incoming firms.[35] And in Kuala Lumpur, where it maintains a regional office, the Japan Finance Corporation for Small Business (JFS) assists clients investing in Southeast Asia. One of its most important responsibilities is matchmaking, introducing small Japanese parts manufacturers to larger Japanese assemblers in the region.[36] Other government agencies are becoming just as active. In 1990, MITI announced that it would set up public–private councils in places such as Bangkok and Kuala Lumpur to begin dispensing what it called "local guidance" to Japanese-affiliated firms.[37] The utility of such an organization became evident in 1991, when 100 Japanese firms doing business in Malaysia agreed to limit their competition for electrical engineers in that country's tight labor market. Sony Corp. triggered the initiative to create such a wage cartel by raising the salaries it offered to skilled technicians by as much as 30 percent;[38]

- a public–private training program for foreign workers. By 1989, the Association for Overseas Technical Scholarship (AOTS), created in 1959 by MITI, had trained 40,000 workers – many of them from Indonesia, Thailand, South Korea, and China. Training was most common in the machinery, chemical, metal, and textile industries. Japanese business, which invests heavily in those industries in those countries, finances a quarter of the AOTS budget.[39]

Although all these policy instruments promote cooperation between Japanese government and industry, none has bound them more tightly than ODA. Japan's aid program, initially a program to pay reparations to the Asian victims of wartime aggression, has three distinctive features that highlight this public–private partnership.

First, it emphasizes large infrastructure projects such as bridges, roads, and ports that, among other things, help spur exports and attract otherwise reluctant overseas investment. In 1992, 40.7 percent of Japan's bilateral ODA was used for economic infrastructure, while only 3.5 percent of US aid was used to fund such projects.[40] These figures reflect some degree of self-interest. Japanese government and business officials have complained for years that FDI from Japan is stymied by infrastructure bottlenecks in many parts of Asia.[41] So we find it quite easy to agree with Katzenstein and Rouse, who argue that Japanese ODA has been used largely to build "the types of infrastructures that will benefit Japanese multinationals and their partners."[42]

Mainly because of its emphasis on expensive capital projects, Japanese ODA also carries an unusually heavy load of credit. This is its second distinctive feature. Unlike other donor countries, which are moving to programs based largely, or even exclusively, on grants, Japan continues to give about half of its aid in the form of low-interest loans.[43] It has marginally improved the quality of its aid in recent years, but the nation "continues to lag in financial terms," complains the Development Assistance Committee (DAC) of the Organization for Economic Cooperation and Development (OECD), which monitors the ODA policies and practices of its member nations.[44] The committee notes that, among its members, Japan ranks last (20th out of 20 nations) in terms of the ratio of grants to total ODA and second to last (20th out of 21) in terms of average grant element, a more complicated measurement that considers not only the volume of grants, but also the "softness" (a function of interest rate, grace period, and maturity) of loans.[45] As if that isn't damning enough, we must note that Japan's soft loans became harder and harder in the late 1980s and early 1990s as *endaka* accelerated, increasing the value of the yen and thus the effective interest rate of existing loans.

But Japan vigorously defends its loan-centered program, saying it is trying to lay a foundation for economic development in recipient countries while also instilling fiscal discipline.[46] This argument is not unlike the American truism that "you have to pull yourself up by your own bootstraps." In fact, Watanabe Toshio, an economist at the Tokyo Institute of Technology, complains loudly that the Westerners who dominate DAC are guilty of a double standard – pushing domestic "welfare reform" measures to promote self-reliance by their poorest citizens while continuing to pursue global welfare policies that emphasize "rescue-type aid." "There is no nation that achieves economic development simply thanks to aid," he says.[47]

There is one other (structural) reason why Japan gives so much of its aid in the form of loans. This has to do with what Orr has called "the dual budget structure from which funds are appropriated."[48] Unlike grants, which are financed entirely out of the general account budget, only half of Japan's concessionary loans are financed through this budget. The other half comes from the Fiscal Investment and Loan Program (FILP), which consists largely of the postal savings of Japanese depositors whose borrowed funds must be repaid with interest. This is an intriguing fact because the FILP was an invaluable tool of industrial policy during Japan's rapid growth period. MOF had discretionary authority (free of the Diet's interference) to use those funds to finance low-interest loans or subsidies to targeted industries. Although the program today is used more often to finance infrastructure projects, it remains a tool of discretionary fiscal policy.

In the past, Japan's aid was tied directly to the purchase of Japanese goods and services. This proved to be useful – as well as enormously profitable – not only for Japanese engineering and construction firms, but also for many manufacturers seeking to expand into Asia. To cite one example, Fujitsu, the electronics giant, plunged into the region only after getting its feet wet on an ODA-financed project. It was awarded a contract to help build Thailand's new telecommunications system.[49]

These days, however, the government is moving aggressively to appease critics, particularly Americans, by untying its yen loans.[50] In 1991, 83.3 percent of Japan's soft loans were legally untied – a better record than other DAC members (including the United States), except New Zealand, Portugal, and Sweden. It is too easy for cynics to dismiss the significance of this untying trend. Japanese construction companies, which used to be among the biggest beneficiaries of Japan's ODA, saw their share of the work on aid-financed projects fall precipitously during the 1980s.[51] And in interviews, representatives of Japan's six leading trading companies indicated that they now must go to extraordinary lengths – such as hooking up with firms from other *keiretsu* or, more significantly yet, from other *countries* – to win untied aid contracts.[52]

Despite this trend, however, Japanese engineering firms, contractors, and other private investors continue to receive the lion's share of work financed by Japan's ODA loans.[53] Tan Siew Hoey, a fellow at the Institute of Strategic and International Studies in Kuala Lumpur, complains that the Japan International Cooperation Agency (JICA), which administers most of Japan's technical grants, uses Japanese consultants, not local consultants, on its projects in Malaysia. "When I pointed out to them that they never seemed to hire local firms, they told me that Japanese firms were the only ones that really knew how to work as a team," Tan recalls. "To me, that is just an excuse. The fact is, they just don't like outsiders to get too close to their work."[54] Data compiled by Ensign confirms this alleged pattern. She found that non-Japanese firms obtained a mere 1.6 percent of the public works financed by the government's "soft" loans in 1989 and less than 6.5 percent in 1990.[55]

These statistics are linked to the third, and perhaps most important, feature of Japan's aid program: it is hopelessly understaffed. Japan has one-third as many ODA personnel as the United States, which gives less aid.[56] Because of this, Japan's aid bureaucracy is forced to rely heavily on business interests. Through the common practice of *shukkō*, or second-ment, private firms lend management staff to the OECF, JICA, and other agencies that carry out aid projects. An OECF official explains that his agency receives a large number of young analysts and accountants from financial institutions and security houses, who help evaluate projects.[57] But David Arase, a political scientist who worked full-time at OECF while conducting research, says the seconded managers come from engineering firms and manufacturing companies, as well as from the financial world, and perform a much more important function. They "act as a bridge for communication and cooperation between [the] home and host organizations," he writes.

> Thus, the person on *shukkō* embodies a complex and ongoing inter-organizational relationship of mutual cooperation and influence. As a result of his or her experience, this person is expected to cultivate contacts and to learn to relate the interests of both organizations. As a result of this experience, he may have value as an intermediary between both organizations for the rest of his career.[58]

Indeed, Japanese MNCs, particularly the big trading companies, occupy center stage in Japan's request-based aid program by recommending projects to recipient governments and helping them draft proposals to the aid bureaucracy in Japan.[59] In Thailand, Potter says, these trading giants act as intermediaries between the Japanese and Thai governments.

> They understand Japanese aid procedures better than most Thai implementing agencies and can therefore advise the agencies about how to go about formulating fundable requests. They also operate in Thailand with a facility the Japanese aid bureaucracy lacks. They therefore have access to both worlds, which places them in a unique position of influence in relation to each government and to their private sector rivals.[60]

To the foreign media, Japanese officials routinely deny they are using aid to promote private Japanese business interests in the Asia-Pacific region. (Of course, every once in a while, a Japanese official will speak candidly to a foreign reporter. So it was that Chino Tadao, a MOF vice minister, told the *New York Times* in 1991 that "the purpose of recycling [plowing capital from Japan's trade surplus into foreign aid] is to stimulate and assist private capital flows."[61]) But in Japanese-language publications, they dedicate themselves to just that cause. Even the Foreign Ministry, the most "international" of the four agencies supervising Japan's aid program, has proclaimed that ODA should "prime the pump to ensure a smooth flow of private financing" to the Third World.[62] And in private, officials acknowledge current practice and defend it thoughtfully. "As a Japanese taxpayer, I have no problem with our agency aiding Japanese industry," an OECF administrator confides over coffee. "Why should my money benefit some other country's industry?"[63]

Japanese ODA often serves as a "trigger" unleashing private investment. It confirms that the government is committed to helping its industry develop another country's economic base. "The go-sign for Japanese corporations to invest in Vietnam will be the time when the Japanese government decides to give economic assistance," said Taya Teizo of the Daiwa Institute of Research.[64] In November 1992, Tokyo did in fact resume aid to Vietnam, a socialist state in the middle of its own economic *perestroika*, which it calls *doi moi* (renovation). And true to Taya's prediction, Japanese FDI immediately followed. In fact, Toyota is already hawking cars at a shiny new showroom in Hanoi.[65] We must note, though, that the Japanese government was simply responding to private demand when it opted to resume aid. Half of all the foreign visitors to Vietnam in 1991 were Japanese businessmen.[66]

We could cite numerous cases of such synergy. In 1988, for example, OECF agreed to donate $145 million to help build a dam in China's Liaoning Province. Private investment, including a $155 million cement plant, soon followed. A study by A. T. Kearney, management consultant, estimates that half of the FDI in Liaoning now comes from Japan.[67]

More recently, the Japanese government authorized a $1 billion program to turn five rural provinces in the Philippines into a sprawling industrial estate for export-oriented manufacturing. The Calbarzon project, designed in Tokyo, includes roads, railroads, ports, and utilities – infrastructure needed to attract investment. Japanese firms have demonstrated the greatest interest thus far.[68]

Japan has tried to address concerns that its ODA is commercially biased. In 1992, the Ministry of Foreign Affairs (MFA) pledged to use its aid program to promote environmentally sensitive, sustainable development and to reward countries showing progress in the areas of human rights, democratization, and the peaceful resolution of conflicts. But the MFA guidelines apparently serve little purpose other than public relations. In January 1994, then foreign minister Hata Tsutomu registered a protest against China for resuming nuclear tests and increasing military expenditure. He could also have mentioned the ongoing imprisonment of political dissidents. Although the foreign ministry alerted Beijing to its new guidelines, it took no action to cut off or even reduce Japan's aid.[69] In fact, China was the leading recipient of Japanese aid in 1993. Indonesia, the number two recipient, also has a spotty human rights record. It has attracted international criticism for repressing labor unions and massacring rebels in East Timor. But Hata and his colleagues in Tokyo didn't even bother to threaten the Suharto regime.

We perhaps could find hope in the proliferation of nongovernmental organizations (NGOs), which have become increasingly active participants in Japan's overall overseas relief and local development efforts. But the government, which has set up an NGO cooperation center, has managed to coopt many of these organizations. "We secretly pride ourselves on having pioneered in assisting NGOs, giving them a strong impetus," says Kimoto Hiroyuki, director of the MFA-controlled center. NGOs are heavily dependent on government funding via the FILP program.[70]

At the Institute for Strategic and International Studies in Kuala Lumpur, we ran into Nagai Raitaro, a representative of the Association for the Promotion of International Cooperation (APIC), a Japanese NGO. Through Nagai, APIC functions more or less as an agent of the Japanese government in Malaysia.

"We try to bring the Japanese government and host government interests together more closely," Nagai explains.[71] An example of his work is an economic development proposal for Malaysia that reads much like MITI's New AID plan. Entitled "Win Win Games," Nagai's proposal calls on Japanese manufacturers to invest strategically in Southeast Asia, building mutually reinforcing production networks. *Kyōsei* (coexistence) "is the key to sustainable economic growth," writes Nagai.[72]

In the 1980s, the government–business network bowed to international pressure and began pouring a much larger share of its total aid into truly impoverished parts of Africa and Latin America. Many viewed this as a signal that Japan was gradually abandoning its use of ODA as a tool of regional industrial policy. It wasn't. In the early 1990s, as Japan's economic woes began to intensify, the government reaffirmed its traditional commitment to the Asia-Pacific region. "I wish to state clearly," former prime minister Kaifu Toshiki said in Singapore in May 1991, "that ASEAN and the rest of Asia will continue to be the priority focus for Japanese official development assistance."[73]

As Table 7.1 shows, Japan donated 65.1 percent of its total bilateral aid to Asia (defined by the government to include more than our nine countries) in 1992 and 59.5 percent in 1993.[74] We find even more regional bias in Japan's soft loans – 84.2 percent of which went to Asia in 1992 and 80.1 percent in 1993.[75] The top five recipients of Japanese ODA in 1992 were, in order, Indonesia, China, the Philippines, India, and

Table 7.1   Regional Distribution of Japanese ODA (% of total)

	1987	1988	1989	1990	1991	1992	1993
Asia	65.1	62.8	62.5	59.3	51.0	65.1	59.5
Middle East	10.0	9.1	5.4	10.2	20.4	4.3	6.4
Africa	9.8	13.8	15.3	11.4	10.3	10.1	11.8
Latin America	8.0	6.2	8.3	8.1	9.5	9.1	9.0

Note: "Asia" includes South Asia, including India.
Source: MFA, *Wagakuni no seifu kaihatsu enjo no jissho jōkyō.*

Thailand. Malaysia was number nine. The top five recipients in 1993 were China, Indonesia, the Philippines, Thailand, and India.[76]

Japan has resisted efforts by DAC of the OECD to dramatically trim the list of eligible aid recipients. Some DAC members wanted to restrict ODA to countries whose per capita GDP is less than $2,500 – a level that would exclude some of Japan's favorite targets, such as Malaysia and Thailand.[77] In 1993, Mikanagi Kiyoshi, special assistant to Japan's foreign minister, told Malaysian officials that his government would continue to provide aid to Malaysia despite its apparent economic success. Japan, he said, viewed Malaysia as a critically important country in the region.[78]

Over the past decade, Japan's government–business network has moved on several fronts to carry out its vision of economic cooperation in this strategic region. For example, in 1987, former prime minister Takeshita Noboru launched the $2 billion ASEAN–Japan Development Fund as a first step toward carrying out the New AID plan. At almost the same time, private organizations launched two new initiatives that dovetailed perfectly – as usual – with the government's.

One was the Japan–Asia Investment Co. (JAIC), a $200 million project of the Keizai Dōyūkai, a business organization, in collaboration with the OECF, a government organization.[79] JAIC was set up to invest in small and medium-sized enterprises, especially joint ventures, in Southeast Asia. But its public and private funds have gone mainly to Japanese firms firmly established in the region, such as Minebea in Thailand and Uniden in the Philippines. As of 1995, it had invested in 335 enterprises in Thailand, 70 percent of which were affiliated with Japanese capital.[80]

The second group, the Japan International Development Organization (JAIDO), had a similar mission. It was charged with helping risk-averse firms invest in developing countries. Created in 1989 by Keidanren, the big-business organization in Tokyo, and funded in part by the government (one-third by OECF), JAIDO has also served as a valuable instrument of Japanese industrial policy in Asia. "Because Japan is now restructuring, it has a large amount of surplus capacity," notes Yufu Shinichi, president of JAIDO.[81] "Such excess capacity should be sent to Asia." The organization promotes FDI by smaller firms struggling to cope with *endaka*, as well as younger firms in so-called "sunrise" industries. For example, it invested $2 million in three joint ventures in China to develop Japanese-language computer software.[82]

Much like members of a horizontal *keiretsu*, Japanese bureaucrats and business leaders have worked closely together to promote Japan's national interest in the Asia-Pacific region. In the next chapter, we examine the vertical ties Japanese elites have forged with their counterparts in Asia.

CHAPTER EIGHT

Vertical Veins of Humanity

Having just completed an interview, we gathered our belongings, paid our respects, and stood up to leave the foreign ministry of Thailand. Just then, however, a young aide rushed breathlessly into the room, closed the door behind him, and asked us to wait a minute so that a "very important person" could traverse the hallway quietly, board the elevator quickly, and leave the building undisturbed. We glanced at one another with the same quizzical look. Who could it be? The king himself? No. The VIP, it turned out, was Japan's ambassador, making one of his many house calls to political clients in the Thai bureaucracy.

We should not have been so surprised. "Gone are the days when statements or interviews given by the Bangkok-based envoys of the U.S. or other Western countries would automatically make headlines. Now it is the Japanese envoy," observes a Thai journalist. "His remarks about Japan's financial assistance and future plans for Thailand make the news."[1]

Indeed, Japan now enjoys enormous political clout throughout Asia. Economic policy for Thailand, Malaysia, Indonesia, the Philippines, and other nations in the region is often reshaped, if not formed out of the void, in Tokyo.

This fact is more than marginally related to the amount of official development assistance (ODA) that Japan provides. In 1993, it contributed $4.9 billion to Asia – nearly three times more than it gave to countries in Africa and Latin America combined.[2] Much of that aid came in the form of concessionary loans. At the end of 1994, Japan's Overseas Economic Cooperation Fund (OECF) had $69.6 billion worth of loans

130

Table 8.1   Asian Countries to which Japan is Leading Donor (1992)

Country	ODA from Japanese ($ millions)	Share of total (%)
Indonesia	1,356.71	68.8
China	1,050.76	50.6
Philippines	1,030.67	67
Thailand	413.97	59.5
Malaysia	152.12	80.6
South Korea	17.62	n.a.
Hong Kong	6.42	n.a.

Note: Both South Korea and Hong Kong are net donors. South Korea received 76.8 percent of its total ODA from Japan in 1991.
Source: MFA, *Wagakuni no seifu kaihatsu enjo no jisshi jōkyō.*

outstanding in Asia. That represented 78 percent of OECF's total portfolio.[3]

As Table 8.1 shows, nearly every nation in the region depends heavily on Japanese aid. Malaysia, for example, gets more than 80 percent of its ODA from Japan. Even China, the most passionately courted country in the region, gets more than half of its ODA from Japan. Orr estimates that, in the late 1980s, Japanese aid equaled 15–20 percent of the budget expenditures of virtually every nation in Southeast Asia.[4] Consider the case of Indonesia, which received more than $4.4 billion (an average of $1.11 billion a year) in aid from 1990 through 1993.[5] In 1990, the Japanese government issued a press release boasting that it had already financed 31 percent of that country's power-generating capacity, 11 percent of its roads, 14 percent of its railways, and 46 percent of the water supply capacity of Jakarta, its capital and largest city.[6] The press release, however, omitted perhaps the most impressive fact: more than a third of Indonesia's $41 billion debt in 1990 was owed to Japan.[7]

Notwithstanding the huge impact of ODA, it would be incorrect to conclude that Japan has merely "purchased" influence in Asia. It has done much more. In large part, Japanese business and political elites have "schmoozed" their way to power. They have, in other words, mastered the fine art of networking in Asia, a region in which most countries do not have a modern legal framework for commerce. They have used social bonds to overcome what is, for Western business people, a source of confusion, uncertainty, and thus risk. "In developing countries," explains Oda Toshio, senior advisor to Nissho Iwai, one of Japan's six leading general trading companies (GTCs), "we can talk directly with government officials, in the case of legal problems, and it sometimes helps solve the problem. Or one can make an even better arrangement. So, in this sense, lack of complete legal systems can be considered even a business chance."[8]

Trading companies, acting as the eyes and ears of would-be investors, are the adroit agents of linkage. In Vietnam, for example, where the Japanese government–business network began laying a foundation for manufacturing investment in the early 1990s, GTC representatives work overtime to solidify personal ties with Vietnamese elites who function as both government regulators and business managers. Sumitomo's head man in Hanoi plays tennis regularly with high-ranking Vietnamese officials. "This makes for a very good working relationship," explains Yoshitake Yoshiaki, manager of the Asia team in Sumitomo Corp.'s overseas planning and coordination department.[9]

Culture is undeniably important. The ethnic Chinese, who for years have dominated local industry not only in China, Taiwan, and Hong Kong, but also in Southeast Asia, conduct business on the basis of *guanxi* – family or clan "connections." The Japanese, the new regional powerbrokers, understand this concept intimately. In their language, the two Chinese characters for *guanxi* are pronounced *kankei*, meaning "connections." The Japanese maintain *kankei* by building *jinmyaku*, networks of personal ties or, literally, "veins of humanity." These veins, once confined to the four islands of Japan, now extend all the way from Tokyo to Taipei, from Osaka to Singapore, from Nagoya to Bangkok.

Trace the origins of some of these *jinmyaku* and you'll suddenly find yourself in the middle of Japan's World War II-era Co-Prosperity Sphere. Nishihara, for example, documents how former Japanese military officers, such as Nishijima Shigetada, who had served in Southeast Asia during the war, and industrialists such as Kubota Yutaka, who had pursued business opportunities in the region during the war, teamed up to create an unofficial "Indonesia Lobby" in Japan between 1958 and 1965. They used their personal connections with Indonesian officials in Jakarta and Japanese officials in Tokyo to tie the knot on a $223 million reparations package. A model for Japanese ODA, it financed massive development projects that boosted the political prestige of Indonesian president Sukarno, but also fattened the wallets of Japanese contractors.[10]

Dig even deeper and you'll find yourself in Korea and Taiwan when they were still struggling to free themselves from Japanese colonial domination. Many members of the elite in those two countries, including President Lee Teng-hui of Taiwan, learned Japanese as young students in colonial schools. Lee Byung Chull, the founder of Samsung, Korea's largest *chaebol*, made good friends in Japan when he went there to study at Waseda University. In the 1970s, as Korea built up its heavy and chemical industries, he parlayed his *kankei* into business tie-ups with Ishikawa Harima Heavy Industries, NEC, Sanyo, Minolta, and other Japanese firms.[11]

As noted earlier, Japanese investors have been more willing than Americans or Europeans to form joint ventures with local interests – a characteristic that has allowed them to penetrate deeply into the economies of host nations throughout the region. And when they forge such alliances, they often choose partners with substantial clout, or at least ready access to it. Westerners are not oblivious of such matters, but still appear politically naive compared to their Asian counterparts who grew up in decidedly more *kankei*-based societies.

In the Philippines, for example, Matsushita formed a joint venture (Precision Electronics) with Jesus del Rosario, a member of a wealthy, politically influential family who served as ambassador to Japan in the late 1980s.[12] Nissan teamed up with Imelda Marcos through her family. After Imelda's husband, President Ferdinand Marcos, fell from power, the Aquino family purchased shares in Pilipinas Nissan and Columbia Motors, two of Nissan's operations in the Philippines.[13]

Tsuda estimates that the Philippines partners in 77 major Japanese–Filipino joint ventures in that host country in the late 1970s represented the top 46 families in the Philippines. "These interlinkages, in effect, make the Japanese and Filipino investors a closely knit and cohesive sub-society."[14]

In Indonesia, Nissan linked up with Sigit Harjojudanto, President Suharto's eldest son, and Bob Hasan, one of Suharto's cronies.[15] Suzuki and Mazda hooked up with Liem Sioe Liong, the well-connected head of the Salim Group. He was the quartermaster to General Suharto's division in Java in the mid 1960s.[16]

In Thailand, Citizen Watch Co. linked arms with Dilok Mahadum-rongkul, a prominent politician, to build a new plant near Ayutthaya.[17] And in Malaysia, Mitsui & Co. has served as a major subcontractor for United Engineers Malaysia, a business arm of United Malay Nationalist Organization (UMNO), the ruling party in that country.

When they do not take on local partners, Japanese MNCs are more exposed to political crosswinds. Thus, to anchor themselves more firmly in foreign soil, they try to forge political partnerships with host governments in the region. This has worked remarkably well in Southeast Asia, where authoritarian regimes are organized according to such patrimonial principles as loyalty and reciprocity. It generally does not work as well with liberal regimes, which are more "transparent" to the public. Transparency reduces the room in which Japan's government–business network can operate, limiting their ability to influence local elites and determine political outcomes.[18]

Take the case of Matsushita, which built its first factory in Malaysia in 1972 after company founder Matsushita Konosuke received a direct appeal from the Malaysian prime minister.[19] The company is proud of the fact that it has successfully maintained close ties with the host regime in Malaysia. "We have a very strong rapport with the government," says Shōtoku Yukio, who was managing director of Matsushita's air conditioning group in Malaysia when we met him in 1993. "Whenever we have a problem, we contact them and work it out. We feel as though we have married Malaysia. We love the government and love the people of Malaysia."[20]

Mitsui & Co. followed a similar path in Malaysia. Its success is evident in the fact that Suzuki Kazumasa, general manager of the company's local trading company and the past president of the Japanese Chamber of Commerce and Industry in Malaysia, was awarded the honorary title "datuk" (doctor), and is often referred to as "deputy finance minister" because of his cozy connections with economic planners in the Malaysian bureaucracy.[21]

Imai Hiroshi, senior managing director for Toyota Motor Thailand Co., says his company enjoys "a very close relationship" with the host regime in Bangkok. "At almost any moment, we can meet with any of the top ministers in the government to discuss a problem or share information."[22]

On top of corporate and political ties, Japan's government–business network has enthusiastically promoted academic, cultural, and technical ties with local elites in Asia. Japanese prime ministers have been no exception. In fact, each seems to have tried to outdo his predecessor as an advocate of closer ties – especially with Southeast Asia. Fukuda Takeo set up the ASEAN Cultural Fund. Ōhira Masayoshi created the ASEAN Youth Scholarship Program. Suzuki Zenkō established the Regional Studies Promotion Program. Nakasone Yasuhiro initiated the 21st Century Friendship Program. Takeshita Noboru, following suit, launched the Japan–ASEAN Comprehensive Exchange Program. And so on.[23]

Two Japanese organizations, both introduced briefly in chapter seven, sponsor training programs for Asians. In 1992, the Japan International Cooperation Agency (JICA), an ODA-implementing arm of the Ministry of Foreign Affairs, hosted nearly 3,000 trainees from Asia (49 percent of all JICA trainees in Japan). JICA also dispatched more than 800 of its own experts to the region (55 percent of the total) – a routine but vitally important practice that we discuss later in this chapter.[24] The other training organization is the Association for Overseas Technical Scholarship (AOTS), an arm of MITI. It is currently hosting engineers from Southeast Asia, providing them with (among other things) data on specifications for machined parts used by Japanese manufacturers.[25] In addition, a MITI think tank, the Ajia Keizai Kenkyūjo (Institute for Research on Asian Economies), has cultivated ties for many years with regional scholars outside Japan. (The institute, known in Japan as Ajiken, refers to itself in English as the "Institute of Developing Economies." This mistranslation effectively blurs its sharp focus on Asia.) Of the 333 visiting scholars Ajiken hosted between 1970 and 1992, 225 (68 percent) came from Asia.[26] Other Japanese think tanks, such as the National Institute for Research Advancement (NIRA) and the Tokyo Club Foundation for Global Studies, have begun to forge their own ties. In 1989, for example, Japanese and Chinese social scientists gathered at an NIRA conference on regional cooperation in the face of rising protectionism in the United States and Europe.[27] In 1990, the Tokyo Club Foundation organized a conference for scholars throughout the Asia-Pacific region.[28]

Japanese universities, facing a shortage of Japanese candidates for graduate-level programs, are accepting – and in some cases aggressively recruiting – a growing number of students from neighboring nations. Most of these 40,000 Asian students pay their own way. But of the total population of foreign students in Japan who are lucky enough to receive a scholarship from the Ministry of Education, 71 percent are Asian.[29]

Toyota and Matsushita, two companies with substantial investments in the Asia-Pacific region, have contributed to efforts to build and strengthen ties between elites in Japan and the rest of Asia. Both spend large amounts of money to support postgraduate research by students from Southeast Asia. In addition, the Matsushita Institute of Government and Management sponsors a program to teach Japanese workers about the history and culture of certain Asian countries. And through its "Know Our Neighbors" program, the Toyota Foundation translates and helps publish books written by Southeast Asian authors.

Although we cannot precisely measure the impact of these varied network-building efforts, we can find tangible evidence that they have yielded benefits. For example, a Matsushita official in Malaysia concedes that his company's ties with the host regime in Kuala Lumpur "probably" have allowed it to avoid paying some taxes on the buying and selling of components from related suppliers and customers all over the region.[30] In addition, we know that Japanese high-technology firms in an industrial estate near Bangkok were able to win the support of local government officials in their labor dispute with disgruntled factory workers. Local Thai officials pressured the employees union to cancel a threatened strike over wages and benefits.[31] Similarly, we know that Japanese MNCs throughout the Bangkok area were able to use their *jinmyaku* to call on the Thai Board of Industrialization for help in controlling mounting labor unrest following the prodemocracy rebellion in May 1992.[32]

For Japan's government–business network, *jinmyaku* are especially handy when "official" channels are closed or restricted. In such cases, private interests fill in as *kuromaku* (which literally means "black curtain" but refers here to "behind the scenes" persons of influence) quietly – if not surreptitiously – promote Japan's political and economic goals in the region. For example, in August 1989, just two months after Chinese tanks rolled over the prodemocracy movement in Tiananmen Square, a private organization, the Forum for a Liberal Society, visited Beijing to discuss the possibility of resuming Japanese aid to China.[33]

Likewise, in late 1991, when Japan was still paying lip service to an American-led embargo against Hanoi, the Mitsubishi Corp. presented to Vietnamese officials a "master plan for the automobile industry in the Socialist Republic of Vietnam." The hefty document reads more like a master plan for a Japanese-dominated automobile industry in Vietnam. Drawing on its own experience in Malaysia, the giant trading company recommended a series of policy initiatives: a tariff structure that would encourage import substitution by protecting local manufacturers, including Japanese-affiliated firms in Vietnam; a licensing system that would promote economies of scale by strictly limiting the number of authorized manufacturers; and a program encouraging joint ventures and technology licensing agreements between foreign and local parts suppliers. Mitsubishi even identified some possible foreign suppliers. Predictably, almost all of them are Japanese and most belong to the manufacturer's Kashiwakai, a parts supply club organized by Mitsubishi Motors Corp. (MMC) in Japan. For example, the company named Mitsubishi Electric (starter motors, audio equipment), Mitsubishi Wire (wire harnesses), Asahi Glass Co. (windshields), Nippon Paint Co. (paint), Bridgestone Co. (tires), Akebono Brake Kōgyō (brakes), and so on. Finally, Mitsubishi urged Vietnam to join a regional automobile production network and "consider the treatment of such parts as domestically produced parts."[34]

Although it was not formally adopted, the master plan was well received, according to an official of Vietnam's State Committee for Cooperation and Investment (SCCI). He indicated that SCCI was, as of late 1994, negotiating with JICA, one of Japan's aid-implementing agencies, over specific measures that could be taken to carry out parts of the master plan.[35]

At the same time, the Vietnamese government has authorized MMC to be the first foreign automaker to participate in a manufacturing joint venture in that country. Along with MMC, the other participants in this groundbreaking business are the Mitsubishi Corp., Proton (the Malaysian national car company that is controlled by MMC), and Vietranscimex, Vietnam's state-run shipping and trading company. Each will own 25 percent of the joint venture, Vina Star Motors Corp., in Ho Chi Minh City.[36]

Asao Katsuharu, general manager of the Mitsubishi Corporation division that prepared the master plan, argues vehemently that the decision to authorize MMC to build an auto plant in Vietnam was unrelated to the trading company's industrial policy recommendations. But he concedes that his work on the master plan allowed him to forge *tsunagari* (linkages) with important officials in the Vietnamese government. He expects to be able to build on those linkages by introducing other Japanese companies – Mitsubishi group members or clients that, for example, manufacture tires and batteries – to some of his new friends in Hanoi. "It is very useful to have this kind of cooperation," he explains.[37]

Mitsubishi's is a true success story. But building and maintaining *jinmyaku* ties in Asia is not always such a snap. In many instances, it is downright costly. Bribes must be doled out. Under-the-table payments must be made. Still, compared to their counterparts in the United States, Japanese business elites seem quite willing to pay the price for special favors or concessions.[38] In fact, Wimar Witoelar, the president of a business consulting firm in Jakarta, says "the Japanese have no inhibitions about these things."[39] Franklin Weinstein came to the same conclusion many years ago: Japanese MNCs in Indonesia, he wrote then, "bribe without hesitation" and in Thailand are "incredibly crude" in their methods.[40] Consider this item: six Japanese companies doing ODA-financed work in the Philippines in the late 1970s and early 1980s paid more than $50 million in kickbacks to Ferdinand Marcos and his associates, according to documents confiscated after Marcos was ousted from office in 1986.[41]

Why are the Japanese more willing to engage in such practices? For one thing, they are not bound by anything like the US Foreign Corrupt Political Practices Act of 1976. More important, though, they view such extralegal payments as a necessary cost of doing business, of greasing their *jinmyaku*.

"We always pay *ochadai* ["tea money," a Japanese term for an under-the-table payment] to move our cargo smoothly through customs," confides the executive of a Marubeni subsidiary in Bangkok. "It's lubrication. We have no choice but to pay. It works out to 100 baht [about $4] per container for each port authority official and inspector we deal with. It's just an expense we include in our budget."[42]

For the government–business network in general, there are other costs associated with the maintenance of such a messy web of ties. Because they extend from so many branches of the network, and because they are not coordinated by any single source, these ties tend to overlap. In the past, some local interests have been able to reduce their costs by pitting Japanese elites against one another.

Not only has the Japanese government failed to alleviate this problem, it actually has contributed to it. The government's foreign aid program, which relies heavily on Japanese business interests in the host nation to generate project proposals, tends to create a feeding frenzy, a frantic free-for-all as Japanese trading companies push local regimes to submit requests for schemes that often compete with one another. But the status quo may not hold. Just as it did in Japan's rapid growth period, MITI is trying to impose order on chaos.

In a 1987 visit to Bangkok, MITI minister Tamura Hajime announced a bold new initiative, the New Asian Industries Development (New AID) plan to coordinate Japan's aid, investment, and trade policies toward Asia. He said the plan would stimulate export-oriented manufacturing throughout the region. What he did not say, however, was that Japan's government–business network also hoped to use the plan to facilitate the technological upgrading of Japan's economic structure by prodding small and medium-sized companies to move their low to medium-technology production facilities into Asia and thereby fill holes in the emerging Japanese production alliance. In other words, Japan would give birth to and then dominate an integrated regional economy based on what MITI itself calls "a new division of labor."[43]

The agency is carrying out the New AID plan in three steps. First, Japanese bureaucrats work with their counterparts in a particular Asian country to devise what MITI calls a "master plan" for "comprehensive cooperation" (sōgō kyōryoku). The master plan identifies specific industries (ranging from fax machines and electrical machinery to ceramics and rubber footwear) that, with the help of Japanese direct investment, could become internationally competitive. As of 1992, MITI had helped draft plans for Thailand, Malaysia, Indonesia, and the Philippines.[44]

Second, Japanese planners (bureaucrats and private industry consultants) recommend programs to promote those targeted industries. More often than not, they come up with detailed plans for both "hard infrastructure," such as new industrial estates or free trade zones, and "soft infrastructure," such as new, Japanese-style organizations within the country to promote cooperation between government and business in the targeted industries, as well as new, less restrictive policies to encourage imports of necessary components and attract FDI. A good example of hard infrastructure is the Calbarzon project in the Philippines, which was described in chapter seven. Japanese bureaucrats designed the scheme to create a massive industrial estate with new roads, new railroad lines, a new telecommunications network, and two new ports – all financed by ODA. Examples of soft infrastructure are rife in a Japanese consultant's report on Malaysia's computer industry. Among other things, the ODA-funded report urged the government in Kuala Lumpur to increase funding to train skilled technicians and provide new incentives to attract investment by foreign parts suppliers. Not surprisingly, a feasibility analysis conducted as part of the report assumed that a Japanese electronics firm would set up the factories to manufacture personal computers, monitors, printers, and keyboards. It also assumed that new computer products manufactured in Malaysia would be exported to the United States and Europe, thus displacing some of the local (US and European) production for those markets.[46]

The third and final step in MITI's New AID plan is what the agency calls a "concentrated and comprehensive" effort to implement each of the industrial development programs.[47] Japanese experts are dispatched to work with government agencies and private organizations in the host country. Japanese ODA is used to build industrial estates, ports, airports, roads, rail lines, and telecommunication systems. And government and private funds are used to promote foreign investment as well as to arrange joint ventures and technology tie-ups.

Some observers view the New AID plan as a freelance power grab by MITI, a further splintering of Japan's polymorphic aid system.[48] This is partially correct. Floated during a time of creeping deregulation and liberalization of Japan's domestic economy, the New AID plan does afford MITI an opportunity to protect and even expand its bureaucratic turf, to justify its demand for a substantial piece of a shrinking budget pie. And other agencies have indeed resisted – a fact that MITI duly noted in its economic cooperation "white paper" in 1993, when it called for the "introduction of institutional arrangements" to coordinate the activities of all parties interested in the ministry's ambitious plan.[49]

But some bureaucrats outside MITI are willing, even eager, to operate under this new policy umbrella. For example, in 1992, we spoke with a representative of Japan's foreign ministry who had just returned from a mission to India. He told us he had used the New AID plan as a "tool" in his negotiations with government officials in New Delhi. "Japanese investors would like to do more in India, but are very cautious because of investment policies that have been, traditionally, quite restrictive. For the past few years, India has been changing those policies to promote FDI. Under the New AID plan, we are trying to encourage this trend by helping to build an industrial infrastructure."[50]

Viewed in this light, then, the New AID plan becomes a vehicle of administrative guidance on a regional level. Just as the Japanese bureaucracy used the carrot of cheap credit to lure firms to invest in strategic industries during the rapid growth period, the government-business network today is using the carrot of foreign aid and investment to entice Asian governments to adopt policies that boost the Japanese economy. "We'd like to see recipient countries adopt more open trade and investment policies, to move away from protectionism and toward an export-oriented, free trade-oriented system," says one MITI official.[51]

The New AID plan is not the only case of administrative guidance applied on a regionwide level. In 1990, MITI announced that it would guide Asian governments through the process of setting up "techno parks" that would attract investment – much of it from Japan – in high-technology industries.[52] More recently, MITI indicated it would hold regular meetings with officials in China to promote technology tie-ups and joint ventures between Japanese automakers and their Chinese counterparts.[53] In addition, the Japanese government has promised soft loans to Thailand if the Thai government will join its Sigma Project, a proposal to build a regionwide, automated software industry.[54] And it has set up an ODA-financed training program, hoping to persuade Asian governments to adopt Japan's own patent system for computer circuits, semiconductors, and other high-technology products.[55]

Unlike the relationship between business and government in Japan, a political alliance that resembles a horizontal *keiretsu*, the relationship between Japanese elites and their Asian counterparts more closely resembles a vertical *keiretsu* in which a large manufacturer hovers over a constellation of smaller suppliers. The New AID plan exemplifies this relationship. Because it administers the plan bilaterally, Japan's government–business network is the only entity that knows how all the different industrial development programs in Asia add up. In this way, Japan serves as the wise member of the family of Asian nations, the one who – like father – always knows best.

From her desk at the back of an open office on the 14th floor of MITI's complex in downtown Tokyo, Munakata Naoko barks orders at her young minions. Deputy director of Asia-Pacific affairs in the agency's economic cooperation office, she leaves little doubt about who is in charge. Later, sipping tea and explaining the rationale behind the New AID plan, Munakata again is blunt. "The problem we have found is that developing nations often don't have a clear vision of what their economic priorities should be," Munakata says. "So instead of just waiting around passively for [aid] requests, we act as consultants and give advice."[56]

These days, Japanese experts dispense advice in nearly every corner of the Asia-Pacific region. By means of international *shukkō*, a border-crossing version of seconding, aid-implementing agencies lend personnel to government agencies and private organizations in host countries. Although officially listed as an employee of the host organization, the expert continues to receive a paycheck from the Japanese employer. Both the host organization and the Japanese employer expect the seconded employee to provide valuable assistance to the host organization. But the Japanese employer has other expectations as well. It hopes the expert will retrieve useful information and promote the interests of the Japanese government–business network within the host organization.[57]

A number of Japanese institutions are engaged in this form of consulting. One is the Japan Overseas Development Corporation (JODC), a

MITI affiliate that, between 1979 and 1992, dispatched 1,582 experts to foreign countries seeking technical training and guidance. Of that total, 1,394 experts (88 percent) went to Asia.[58] JODC is currently rounding up retired Japanese engineers and loaning them to small and medium-sized firms in Asia as part of MITI's Asia Supporting Industry Action (ASIA) program, which is designed to boost the technological and managerial capacity of parts suppliers in the region. JODC covers three-fourths (and the benefiting companies cover the remaining one-fourth) of the salary of the engineers, who teach Japanese manufacturing practices, including the *kanban* or just-in-time system.[59] This movement of retired engineers from Japan to Asia is vaguely reminiscent of the movement of retired technocrats from Kasumigaseki (the bureaucracy's headquarters in Tokyo) to Ōtemachi (the business and financial community's head-quarters in Tokyo) – a practice known in Japanese as *amakudari,* or "descent from heaven," that was most common during the rapid growth period.

Another institution offering practical advice to elites in Asia is the Japan Finance Corporation for Small Business (JFS), which maintains an overseas office in Kuala Lumpur. Among other things, it sponsors seminars to explain the Japanese subcontracting system to government officials and business leaders in Malaysia.[60] However, not JFS, JODC, nor any other institution can come close to matching JICA's outreach efforts.

JICA experts come in two types: those assigned to government offices in the host country, and those assigned to training centers or institutes set up to help carry out an ODA-funded project. Between 1985 and 1989, JICA sent a steady stream of experts (1,421 altogether) to Indonesia.[61] One was seconded to the Capital Investment Coordination Board in Jakarta, where he performed twin duties. He was expected, on the one hand, to serve as an adviser to the host government, recommending policies to promote investment by foreign firms. On the other hand, he served informally as an adviser to Japanese firms operating, or trying to operate, in Indonesia. This created a potential conflict of interest, according to Thee Kian Wie, an Indonesian scholar. "Striking the proper balance" between the two duties "was not particularly easy, as the JICA expert had become quite important in encouraging and facilitating Japanese direct investment to Indonesia."[62]

As of late 1992, about 60 JICA experts were serving as advisers to government agencies and private groups in Malaysia.[63] They play "a very big role in developing policy in this country," according to Tan Siew Hoey, an economist at the Institute of Strategic and International Studies, a quasi-governmental think tank in Kuala Lumpur.[64] But JICA advisers, it seems, play an even bigger role in Thailand. "They're every-where," proclaims one government official.[65]

Each year, about 300 JICA experts are dispatched to Thailand, and many of them are seconded to government agencies, including the National Economic and Social Development Board (NESDB), the Ministry of Commerce and the Ministry of Finance, as well as to private or quasi-governmental organizations such as the Metalworking and Machinery Industries Development Institute and the Thailand Development Research Institute.[66] JETRO also dispatches experts to Thailand. One has served as a full-time adviser to the Board of Investment. Another has helped draft investment and trade policies for the trade ministry's Department of Industrial Promotion. Still another has worked closely with the Association of Thai Industries and the Federation of Thai Textile Industries.[67]

Japanese experts have "tremendous influence" in Thailand, says Sutin Leepiyachart, an NESDB economist who doubles as an adviser to the deputy prime minister. Because he lived in Japan for 15 years, receiving a PhD from Keio University, Sutin serves as a kind of liaison between Thai and Japanese technocrats. "With the experience they have gained all over the world, the Japanese have a great deal of knowledge about how development can and should take place in our country. They give us useful advice. So, naturally, we listen to them very carefully."[68]

Since the early 1980s, Japanese experts have helped write all Thailand's national development plans. In addition, they have prodded the Thai government to follow the Japanese model of economic development by creating public institutions that cooperate with business, such as the Thai Export-Import Bank, and private sector organizations that cooperate with the government, such as the Thai Dye and Mould Industrial Association.[69] Japanese experts have even encouraged Thai firms, at least those in the textile industry, to forge "vertical links with different industries ... to improve ... information gathering, product development, and adaptation to wide variety in small lot production."[70]

Thailand, the proud owner of the world's fastest growing economy in the late 1980s, has profited enormously from Japan's guidance. But so has Japan. Without even pausing, Sutin can tick off a list of policy initiatives made by the Thai government in the late 1980s and early 1990s at the behest of Japan:

- the creation of an ombudsman to handle complaints from foreign investors;
- relaxation of investment and local content requirements for the automobile manufacturing industry;
- new rules restricting strikes and other labor activities;
- a reduction in the time taken to rebate taxes paid on exported products;
- tax exemptions for direct investments made outside the already heavily congested Bangkok and Ayutthaya areas.

Not only in Thailand, but throughout the Asia-Pacific region, local policy initiatives continually mesh – as if by magic – with Japan's economic interests in the region.[71] In the mid 1980s, as Indonesia and Malaysia sank beneath the weight of falling prices for petroleum and other primary products, and as Thailand choked on its own trade and budget deficits, each nation took action to rescue its economy by promoting FDI and exports. For example, Malaysia's government authorized foreign firms to set up wholly owned subsidiaries, at least temporarily, as long as they exported at least 80 percent of their output and employed at least 350 Malaysian workers, including a reasonable share of *bumiputra* (indigenous Malays). Both Malaysia and Thailand offered tax breaks and other incentives to foreign firms engaged in high-technology export-oriented manufacturing. Such policy changes were made just as *endaka* pushed Japanese manufacturers to locate new and lower-cost bases in the region for export-oriented production.

Then, in the late 1980s and early 1990s, technocrats across the Asia-Pacific region began rallying behind beleaguered small and medium-sized firms, which harbored high hopes of supplying raw materials and parts to large manufacturers. In Thailand, for example, the government cut taxes on suppliers in 10 different product areas, including dies, electrical machinery, and auto parts. Indonesia authorized small but 100 percent foreign-owned firms to enter some markets for the first time.[72] And Malaysia created new tax incentives to lure foreign firms to invest in supporting industries.[73] These promotional policies and programs came just as Japanese affiliates in Asia, burdened by the high price of parts imported from Japan, began leaning on their home-based subcontractors to pack up and follow them overseas. The result was predictable: Japanese manufacturers often ended up as the primary beneficiaries of host-country policies and programs.

That fact, however, does not faze Omar Yusuf, deputy director of the Malaysian Ministry of International Trade and Industry's small business section. "We have to fully support our private sector – whether it's local or foreign," he told us.[74] "There is no conflict there. Japanese industry is very much a part of the Malaysian economy."

Since the new policies and programs to benefit "local" suppliers often end up benefiting Japanese firms, we should not be surprised to learn that Japan's government–business network had a hand in designing them.[75] Nor should we be surprised to learn that it helped finance some of them. As of mid 1994, the OECF had loaned $170 million to the Industrial Finance Corporation of Thailand, which in turn helped finance capital investments in plant and equipment by small and medium-sized firms in Thailand's export-oriented industries. To be eligible, firms must be registered in Thailand, which means that dozens of Japanese suppliers in that country are "theoretically eligible for sub-loans," according to an OECF official.[76]

We are not suggesting that local officials are selling out their countries. When the Malaysian government, for example, sides with Hitachi in a labor dispute with the national electrical workers union, it is not only helping a Japanese MNC.[77] It is also consolidating its authority over a potentially unruly force in domestic politics. And when the Thai government donates aid to Laos and promotes free trade with Vietnam, it is not only helping Japanese MNCs that want to invest in Indochina. It is also creating economic opportunities for domestic capital. As an official in Thailand's foreign ministry says, "Our motives are simple. We're trying to get Japan to use us as a fulcrum to move into Indochina. We hope to provide whatever raw materials, labor, and other resources they need."[78]

Although we must recognize that Japan shares a set of interests with its Asian neighbors, we should not thereby conclude that they are equal partners, or that they are mutually interdependent. Japan is the dominant party in virtually all its bilateral relationships in the region. "I think basically the Japanese are calling the shots in all of the Asia-Pacific," says K. S. Nathan, an international relations expert at the University of Malaya in Kuala Lumpur.[79]

Nonetheless, many observers suggest that the Asian recipients of Japanese advice are getting a superb deal. Schlossstein expresses this viewpoint most clearly.

> Given its own considerable shortcomings, Thailand ought not to fear Japanese dominance but embrace it. For Tokyo can engineer industrial policies for Bangkok that Thai technocrats themselves may be incapable of devising. That may be Thailand's best guarantee that it will develop the disciplined human resources, the indigenous technologies, and the better-educated, stronger middle class it needs to compete successfully in a global market.[80]

What this argument ignores is the political reality that Japan's interests do not always coincide with the rest of Asia's interests. For example, Japanese officials did not act on behalf of Thailand in 1990 when they urged the Thai government to reject a proposal by Guardian Industries Corp. of Northville, Michigan to build a $117 million glass plant in that country. They acted solely on behalf of Thai Asahi Glass Co., which enjoyed a monopoly on the production of glass in Thailand.[81] In the same way, Japanese officials did not act on behalf of Thailand in disputes over the Eastern Seaboard Development (ESD) program. They acted solely in Japan's interest.

The ESD program has been called the "monument" to Japanese aid in Thailand.[82] Financed largely with yen loans from Japan's OECF, the project includes two industrial estates, one at Laem Chabang for export-oriented manufacturing industries and another at Map Ta Phut for heavy and chemical industries, along with related social infrastructure (housing, schools, hospitals, and parks) and economic infrastructure (port terminals, roads, rail lines, water, electricity, and telecommunications). By encouraging development, and by locating it outside the crowded confines of Bangkok, the ESD program obviously benefited Thailand. And by paving the way for export-oriented investment, it also benefited Japan.

But Japanese and Thai interests in the project soon diverged. In 1984, Thailand's Ministry of Communications, which was supervising construction of the port, announced that it would suspend the yen loan for that phase of the project. OECF, it complained, was spending its money almost exclusively on Japanese engineering and construction firms.[83] The Japanese government responded immediately and firmly by threatening to cancel future loans to Thailand.[84] The Thai government buckled and overturned the ministry's action.[85] Later, in response to a World Bank recommendation, the government tried to rise above its own budget deficit by scaling back the size of the ESD program, particularly a massive fertilizer complex. The Japanese ambassador, acting on behalf of Japanese participants in the project (Chiyoda Chemical, Marubeni, Mitsui, and C. Itoh), pressured the Thai government to reverse its decision.[86]

These incidents clearly demonstrate the political liability incurred by Asian nations that depend too heavily on Japan as a regional hegemon. As Krasner has suggested, ODA can create "asymmetrical opportunity costs of change," allowing the donor nation to exercise economic power over the recipient country.[87] Just as there is no such thing as a free lunch, there is no such thing as free ODA or free advice. Strings are always attached. Says Paichit Uathavikul, president of the Thailand Development Research Institute, "It is not very smart to depend so much on one country."[88]

CHAPTER NINE

The Labor Network

It is 7:45 a.m. In Petaling Jaya, a suburb of Kuala Lumpur, 2,000 men and women wearing the light blue uniforms of Matsushita twist their torsos back and forth. Back and forth. After five minutes of calisthenics, they begin singing the company song and reciting – in Malay or English – the company creed. Then, before they finally knuckle down to the chore of assembling truckloads of air conditioners, the Matsushita workers break into small groups to discuss production issues with their supervisors.

While carefully choreographed in Japan, this daily ritual is performed with only minor variations on Matsushita shopfloors all over the world. Here in Petaling Jaya, for example, a revised version of the company song exhorts employees to not only "produce forever general appliances for the people," but also to "create a new Malaysia." And in the morning meetings, any mention of race, religion, or politics – all potentially volatile topics in this heterogeneous society – is strictly prohibited. Otherwise, a Matsushita employee's day in Malaysia proceeds like a Matsushita employee's day in Japan.

This is, of course, no accident. The company is firmly committed to a paternalistic employment system that has demonstrated its ability to increase productivity over time. And Matsushita is not alone. As they have expanded beyond Japan to set up plants all over the globe, other large manufacturers have tried to replicate a distinctively "Japanese" style of management. Karatsu Hajime, a Japanese professor of technology development, says Japan's overseas production facilities are "mini-Japans."

All employees wear uniforms provided by the company.... All are involved in *kaizen* [product improvement] because they know the problems that must be solved daily.... What is going on is the sharing of information to improve product quality – a unique feature of Japanese business. Unless you can transplant such a corporate culture, there is no reason to spend money going abroad where people don't speak Japanese.[1]

Case studies suggest that Japanese multinationals have managed to clone their system most successfully in Asia.

Kumon, for example, found that Toyota, after opening plants in Kentucky and California, had to retool some of its employment practices to better fit the US labor market. Taiwan presented a far more compatible environment. "Application of the Japanese-style work organization and labor relations [was] relatively easy."[2]

Yoshihara found that Japanese electronics firms used quality control (QC) circles in Singapore, but not in Australia or New Zealand. Employees in those two countries, it turned out, had limited experience with such group activities, and little desire to work overtime. In a similar vein, Yoshihara found that employees in the United States fiercely resisted pressure from Japanese managers to participate in campaigns to clean up their factories. "Cleaning is not our function!" the Americans responded. Malaysian workers, however, complied without hesitation. "They were obedient to the directive and cleaned the plant."[3]

These different outcomes may reflect different social norms in the respective host environments. Or they may reflect different stages of industrialization. Without conducting further research, we can only speculate on this question – one that is fascinating but, for us, largely beside the point. Our primary goal here is to document the painstaking efforts of Japanese MNCs to transplant in the wider soil of Asia a cooperative labor-management regime that pulls and pushes employees to tie themselves more securely to their employers. In the process, we also hope to demonstrate how such a system limits job mobility, thereby blocking a natural avenue for the transfer of technology from Japan to the rest of Asia, and increases the international competitiveness of Japan's most innovative manufacturers.

As we discussed more fully in chapter four, this distinctive labor-management regime consists of three elements: quasi-lifetime employment, seniority-based pay, and the enterprise union. One thread – the ideology of "familism" – runs through all these different elements to help form a coherent system or regime. By treating its employees as valued members of an extended family, management coaxes maximum effort and maximum commitment from them.

"They try to get you to love the company," says Rosita, a young Matsushita employee in Malaysia. "They give cash incentives to work harder. Everybody gets a birthday present. They have an annual dance, with a drawing where you might get a bicycle. And if you go four months without being late or absent, you get a Tupperware dish."[4]

This ideology is undoubtedly reinforced by Japanese culture. But it does not rise on its own like a geyser from the hoary depths of tradition. As we discussed in chapter four, Japan's employment system acquired its distinctive character during two historical periods: the 1920s, when large and innovating firms adopted new practices (quasi-lifetime employment and seniority-based pay) to retain the employees they had trained to handle increasingly technical tasks; and the 1950s and 1960s, when newly empowered managers began to forge cooperative ties with employees (represented by enterprise unions). Catching up with the industrial West in both the prewar and postwar periods required new and sophisticated technology, which in turn required a highly skilled labor force, which in turn required a heavy investment in training. Japanese employers began using the practices and institutions that make up the familist employment system to protect their substantial investment in human capital.[5]

In the rest of Asia, where they are now building a network of new production facilities and trying to manage a haphazard assortment of employees, Japanese firms are again investing heavily in training, particularly on-the-job training (OJT). This is done by verbal communication and modeling, rather than via written materials such as manuals.[6] The managers of Japanese affiliates we visited described marathon hours of detailed instruction given to employees. "We show them how to do everything – which hand to hold the part in, how to screw the bolt in, everything," says David Wong, general manager of Tan Chong Motor Assemblies, a Nissan affiliate in Kuala Lumpur.[7] Toyota Motor Thailand boasts that each year it sends 150–200 employees to Japan to work in the parent firm's factories and receive hands-on training.[8]

Of course, some government officials in Thailand and elsewhere are highly critical of such training missions. Japanese MNCs, they told us, were simply tapping their reserve labor pool in Asia to remedy a labor shortfall in Japan. "What the Japanese call 'OJT' is often nothing more than the exploitation of cheap Thai labor," says Cholchineepan Chiranond, a top official in Thailand's Ministry of Foreign Affairs.[9] In general, though, local officials and even scholars praise Japanese efforts to improve employee skills. For example, a leading Thai economist says Japanese MNCs "put more emphasis on training than other MNCs and possess a more effective in-house training system."[10]

It must be noted, however, that the skills acquired through such training tend to be either firm-specific, and thus useful only in that particular company, or wholly untechnical.[11] For instance, many Japanese firms in Asia offer so-called "total development programs" designed to instill positive work habits and nurture company loyalty.[12] Matsushita sends its employees in Malaysia to a program like this to learn about discipline, punctuality, safety, paying attention to details, and cleanliness. Trainees "return as new people applying the Japanese work ethic with enthusiasm and deriving greater job satisfaction from their work," says Shōtoku Yukio, former managing director of the company's air conditioner group.[13]

Just as they did at home, Japanese firms expanding into Asia have begun to adopt a series of employment practices designed largely to safeguard their investments in training and to retain skilled workers. Imaoka argues, for example, that Japanese affiliates in Asia, a region otherwise known for its fluid labor markets, enjoy remarkably high levels of employment stability. Many of those affiliates, he concludes, have transplanted their home-grown management regimes, recreating successful training programs that allow employees to boost their skill levels and move up to better jobs inside the firm. "There is an extreme similarity," he writes, "between Japanese corporations in Asia and Japan in wage decision, use or nonuse of personnel evaluations, methods of employing supplementary personnel, standards for promotion and personnel training programs."[14]

At the same time, though, Japanese affiliates have had to improvise in places, to adapt their familiar regimes to accommodate different labor conditions in different environments. Most, for example, do not appear to link wage levels and seniority as tightly as their parent firms do, choosing instead to incorporate performance (or merit) evaluations into the pay-setting process.[15] Imaoka highlights this in his survey findings. With the exception of those in South Korea, no more than 10 percent of the Japanese affiliates in any Asian country used seniority as the exclusive means of determining wages. Twenty-five percent of the parent firms surveyed in Japan, in contrast, used this as the sole determinant of pay.

Thus, in a typical Japanese affiliate in Singapore, an entry-level white-collar employee of a Japanese affiliate might have to work about five years at the firm before becoming a manager – a climb that would take twice as long in Japan.[16] In addition, some affiliates do not rotate workers in and out of jobs as much as their parent firms in Japan do.[17] And, finally, Japanese managers moving into Asia have left behind some of the ostensibly democratic routines, such as group decision-making, that have attracted so much favorable attention over the years from Western journalists.[18] As a Canon executive in Malaysia bluntly explains, "We don't have to worry about *nemawashi* [consensus-building] over here."[19] What is emerging is a hybrid, a modified version of the Japanese employment system.

The larger and more technology-intensive the affiliate is, the more "Japanese" it seems to be. Consider the case of Melco Consumer Products (Thailand), a subsidiary of Mitsubishi Electric Co., that manufactures air conditioners, as well as components for refrigerators, and washing machines. The Bangkok-area plant, filled from floor to ceiling with Japanese machinery, not only *looks* Japanese; it even *sounds* Japanese. Shift changes are announced by four notes ascending in a scale. It is the same hypnotic sound we hear in train stations, on buses, and in department stores throughout Japan.

In Thailand, as in Japan, Melco employees work in small groups. They wear their status on their heads. Literally. Most factory workers sport blue and white hats with Mitsubishi's familiar red, three-diamond logo. Some wear red hats to indicate they are part of a factory-wide quality control team. Those with one yellow line on the red hat are foremen. Those with two yellow lines are supervisors. And those with one red line are section managers.

On a wall inside the factory is a poster that says "Ho-Ren-So = Spinack" (sic). In Japanese, *hōrensō* is spinach. In Melco-ese, however, it is a concocted compound of three Japanese words used by management to encourage employees to *HŌkoku* (report), *RENraku* (communicate) and *SŌdan* (discuss). A long banner on another wall in this busy but spotless factory lists the "5 Ss" promoted endlessly by Japanese managers: *seiri* (tidiness), *seisō* (cleanliness), *seiketsu* (neatness), *seiton* (order), and *shitsuke* (discipline). Every day after lunch, employees spend 10 minutes cleaning up their small piece of the factory. And every month, the most conscientious section of the plant receives a "5 S" award.

Now, for contrast, consider the case of United Industries. It is, by Malaysian standards, a reasonably large and sophisticated enterprise, a group of five companies that produce everything from hand trucks to tail pipes on a 20 acre site near the port city of Klang. By Japanese standards, though, UI is about as raw and rumpled – or, in a word, un-Japanese – as a Japanese affiliate can be.[20] "We're trying to make the transition from a Chinese, family-style operation to a more professional, Japanese-style operation," says company controller Tony Ng Seng Kee.[21]

One of five Chinese Malaysian brothers who run UI, Ng describes himself alternately as the "bulldozer" and the "preacher" who is leading efforts to change a business that has remained pretty much as it was when his father founded it in 1968. Ng faces a huge challenge – a fact that quickly becomes evident in a tour of the poorly lit and somewhat cluttered factory, where workers still use their bare hands to bend metal tubing and glue together the pieces of an air filter.

Shaking his head, Ng says his brothers continue to resist his and a Japanese partner's recommendation to send UI employees to Japan for comprehensive OJT. "They worry about workers leaving the minute they come back." Stymied but not totally defeated, Ng set up a *kaizen* (improvement) committee to solicit suggestions from employees to boost productivity. "But it just turned into a big gripe session," he recalls. "Everyone wanted to talk about water pressure at the hydrant. No one had anything to say about our production lines, our manufacturing process, or anything else that was at all useful." Chastened, Ng lowered his expectations. Instead of the usual "5 S" campaign, he launched a "4 S" program to clean up the plant. *Shitsuke* (discipline) was scratched from the agenda. "I figured we'd have a tough enough time getting our workers to just follow the basic four."

Big or small, high-tech or low-tech, Japanese affiliates in Asia generally have managed to cultivate cooperative labor relations. Indeed, no other piece of Japan's distinctive employment system has been reproduced here so successfully. Most of the factories we visited in the region either had a Japanese-style enterprise union or no collective bargaining unit at all. "Our employees are so young," explains Nakajima Daisuke, manager of administration for Fujitsu Thailand Co. "They're not quite ready for a union."[22] At Teijin Polyester (Thailand) Ltd, a synthetic fiber manufacturer in Bangkok, Japanese executives used to feel the same way – that is, until they decided to help organize a union that represents nearly everyone in the company but them. Says one executive: "Our president, Mr Asami, selected a group of employees and sent them to Japan for training in union management. When they returned, these new leaders were more than willing to encourage their colleagues to cooperate with us on meeting our productivity goals. The union has been quite helpful in promoting our programs."[23]

To "educate" its Thai labor leaders, Teijin Polyester received assistance from enterprise union officials in Japan. This is not uncommon. Japanese unions are more than willing to spread the gospel of cooperation, especially since they and their Asian counterparts share one multinational corporate family. They "endeavor to ensure that the labor contacts do not come into conflict with, but rather complement the way management runs the company's international operations," writes Williamson. "Stress is also often placed on the value of bringing together people working for the same company in different countries on the basis of identifying with the 'brand name' of the company."[24]

A newly created organization, the Japan International Labor Foundation (JILAF) also preaches this gospel to union officials visiting from Asia. JILAF, a nongovernmental organization created by Rengo, the conservative national union, is financed in part by the Japanese government via ODA. After attending one of JILAF's "invitation programs" in Japan, a union official from Hong Kong complained of being "indoctrinated with the Japanese version of trade unionism."[25]

But the gospel of cooperation apparently did not reach South Korea, where deep and bitter opposition to an authoritarian regime helped spark a militant labor movement in the late 1980s. Unions sprouted all over the country, agitating for higher wages and better working conditions. It was like a flash flood, a volcanic eruption of repressed expectations that no one – not even Korean police with riot gear, armored helicopters, and machine guns – could put down. Oda Hiroyasu, president of FKL Donghwa, a Fujitsu affiliate that manufactures magnetic heads for hard disk drives in Sunghwan, about 50 miles south of Seoul, is still trying to assess the damage he attributes to Korea's "immature" (*mijuku*) unions.

> Under [former military leaders] Park [Chung Hee] and Chun [Doo Hwan], the government tightly controlled all union activity. But in 1987, everything changed. Now there are no rules for strikes. Or, if there are any rules, we don't understand them at all. For example, even when workers go on strike, even when they aren't working for the company, they expect us to pay them. So we pay.... As a foreign company, and especially a company from the [former] *teikoku* [empire; colonial master], we have no choice.[26]

Wages at the Fujitsu plant have risen sharply and steadily. They jumped 21 percent in 1987, 14 percent in 1988, 22 percent in 1989 and 1990, 26 percent in 1991, and 20 percent in 1992. Despite a government-supported backlash against labor, pressure for wage hikes has not abated.

While he expresses displeasure with his firm's rising labor costs, Oda seems oddly resigned. What really alarms him is what alarms almost all Japanese employers in Asia: a relatively high rate (by Japanese standards) of employee turnover. "In just one month, we had 3 percent turnover," he says. "That's awfully high when you consider how much we spend on training."[27]

In Korea and Taiwan, and now even in some of the rapidly growing economies of ASEAN, Japanese employers have begun to complain more bitterly about "job-hopping" than about than any other personnel matter. To them, it smacks of disloyalty. In response to a JETRO survey, almost two out of three Japanese affiliates in Malaysia indicated that recruiting and retaining skilled employees was their biggest headache.[28] This is especially true for small but expanding firms, which are often buffeted by a volatile labor market spawned by a shortage of skilled workers. Aoyama Thai, a Toyota subcontractor, reports that, four months after dispatching 50 employees to Japan for an extensive job-training program, all but one of the newly trained employees had landed jobs with other firms in Thailand.[29]

Large employers can always hire headhunting firms, conduct "walk in interviews," buy expensive ads, and – if necessary – offer better benefits and higher wages. Even a quick stroll through the classified pages in a Malaysian newspaper reveals just how far (or near) some firms will go. In a pitch for female factory workers "21 years and below," Matsushita announced that it would provide, among other things: "free uniforms," "National and Panasonic products at special prices," "a five day work week," and "an air conditioned factory."[30] The competition for skilled and semiskilled labor, especially technicians, has become so fierce that Japanese employers in some parts of Asia have even opted to set up cartels, conspiring to limit job-hopping by fixing wages.[31] Yeoh Oon Lee, an economist who has advised the Federation of Malaysian Manufacturers, is one of the few opinion leaders in the region to publicly condemn such collusive behavior. Job-hopping, he notes, allows workers to improve themselves.[32] But host government officials have tacitly sanctioned such pacts.

In Shah Alam, an industrial estate on the outskirts of Kuala Lumpur, Japanese electronics manufacturers meet once a month to share information about starting salaries and fringe benefits at their different plants. Takano Tatsuo, president of Nippon Electronics Malaysia, says the group does not make formal or binding decisions, but does seek "mutual understanding" among its members. In fact, the group meets so regularly that it calls itself *Tiga Air*, a Malay translation of the Chinese characters meaning "third" and "Wednesday."[33] About 60 Japanese firms in Navanakorn, an industrial estate outside Bangkok, also meet each month to monitor job-hopping. They have reached what a member of the informal group calls a "gentlemen's agreement not to raid one another's staff."[34]

Efforts such as these to control job-hopping may be achieving some limited success. One study found that Japanese firms in Asia experience substantially lower rates of turnover than American firms in the region.[35]

But, like water flowing downhill, ambitious or anxious employees are never easy to contain. Despite the best efforts of Japanese MNCs, such employees continue to engage in job-hopping. Ironically, this practice may be fueled by the very employment system that was created partly to combat it. Dissatisfaction with Japanese management routines runs deep among white-collar employees in Asia – particularly, according to some observers, among those in Singapore and Malaysia.[36] In 1989, for example, the Singapore Institute of Management asked local professionals to identify the 20 "best" employers on the island. Several American and European MNCs made the list; not a single Japanese firm did.[37] Likewise, a study by Kawabe found that local managers in Malaysia generally preferred working in Western rather than Japanese firms.[38]

Kawabe explains this preference in historical/cultural terms. Malaysia, Kawabe argues, is "a kind of 'qualification society,' much influenced by British tradition." A college graduate in that nation wants to be treated as a valuable professional, not just another member of a corporate family.[39] Yoon Chon Leong, head of manufacturing for Hewlett Packard, an

American electronics firm in Penang, says several of his Malaysian managers left HP over the previous two years to take what appeared to be promising jobs at Japanese firms in the area – only to return a few months later. "They found that the job was there. The title was there," he explains. "But there was no real sense of responsibility. The Japanese management would tell them, 'Turn right here. Turn left there. Build this. Build that.'"[40]

The problem, however, is not restricted to Malaysia and Singapore. We also encounter frustration with Japanese management in the Philippines, Indonesia, Taiwan, and Thailand, none of which is a former British colony. This is perhaps inevitable. Talented professionals and technicians, no matter where they live, are eager to work for firms that offer them a chance to rise as high as possible on the corporate ladder. But Japanese firms present a shorter ladder. With few exceptions, top management posts in these firms are held by Japanese, not local Asians.[41]

This is nothing new. In the 1960s and 1970s, scholars documented the fact that Japanese affiliates, compared with their Western counterparts, retained a greater number of expatriates in key positions.[42] More recent studies show they continue to do so.

In Malaysia, scholars concluded that Japanese-controlled firms reserved about half of their top management positions for expatriates – far more than American or European-controlled firms.[43] And in Hong Kong, a research team found a high number of home-country nationals occupying important administrative posts in the Japanese affiliate, but not the US affiliate it examined.[44] The pattern is repeated throughout the region. "There is little question that Japanese firms [in Asia] employ more expatriates and replace them more slowly than U.S. firms," argues Stewart.[45]

Over and over again, Asian elites have loudly condemned this practice. "No locals are occupying senior positions in Japanese enterprises which have operated in Malaysia for more than 10 years. If this situation persists, the brighter and more entrepreneurial Malaysian executives will shy away from Japanese firms," complained Mokhzani Abdul Rahman, vice president of the Malaysian–Japanese Economic Association (Majeca). He was speaking at a Majeca conference attended by a large number of Japanese business executives.[46] "After 15 to 20 years, many American and European multinational corporations (in Singapore) have Singaporeans in charge, but there is none in a Japanese company," grumbled former prime minister Lee Kwan Yew in one interview.[47] (Lee was not completely accurate. Even as he spoke, two Japanese affiliates in Singapore [NEC and Minebea] actually had local Singaporeans leading their respective management teams.[48] But notwithstanding his oversight, Lee's basic criticism was and still is well taken.) We even hear such a complaint from the director of Astra International, which has grown into one of Indonesia's biggest conglomerates by hooking up with Japanese firms such as Toyota, Honda, Daihatsu, Mitsubishi, Komatsu, and Fuji. "The Americans and Europeans are more open to transferring management skills," says Edwin Soeryadjaya.[49]

Embarrassed by this unflattering image, a few Japanese officials have goaded their compatriots in overseas business to do a better job. Hara Izumi, senior economist at the Industrial Bank of Japan, is one of these. "Japanese companies," he says, "need to break away from their traditional 'closed' management policy, namely 'management by the Japanese only' or 'management remote controlled by headquarters in Japan' and have to adopt a new corporate strategy to promote management by local staff."[50]

In defense, apologists say Japan's overseas factories are newer than the West's, and that the transfer of technology under Japanese management routines is a longer, but far more thorough, process of step-by-step training.[51] Patience, they seem to say. The "indigenization" of staff in Japan's Asian subsidiaries is progressing slowly but surely.

But is it really?

After more than two decades in Malaysia, the Matsushita Industrial Corp. in 1993 had entrusted local managers to run only two of its 14 divisions.[52] And while Mitsui & Co., the trading giant, has spent the better part of a century in Thailand, building an empire of more than 80 joint ventures, as of 1990 it still had "no visible Thais in upper management." Japanese nationals continue to manipulate its many arms.[53] Overall, Beechler, who examined the relationship between Japanese parent firms and their electronics operations throughout Asia, found remarkably little progress.

> Instead of training and socializing employees to take on greater responsibilities, the Japanese expatriates effectively held on to these responsibilities themselves, regardless of the age of the subsidiary, the presence of qualified locals, or the high costs involved in keeping expatriates overseas. This is because, although only a few respondents openly stated this fact, Japanese managers do not, in a fundamental sense, trust their local employees, no matter how qualified they may be and no matter how long they have been in the company. It is not cultural distance, but a sense of foreignness which limits the use of pure normative control in a majority of the firms in this sample.[54]

In fact, there is ample evidence that, as Japanese operations in Asia have grown more technology-intensive, expatriates have become more common (see Figure 9.1). Between 1983 and 1988, the percentage of Japanese managers and technicians stationed at Japanese manufacturing plants in Thailand actually increased, on average, from 4.7 percent to 6.3 percent. At plants producing electrical and electronic machinery, the percentage *doubled* from 4.5 to 9 percent.[55]

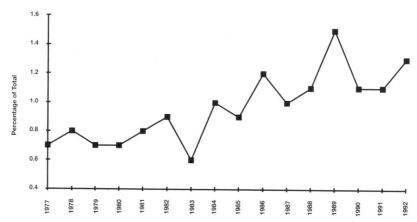

Figure 9.1   Japanese Personnel in Manufacturing Affiliates in Asia
Sources: Wagakuni kigyō no kaigai jigyō katsudō, Kaigai tōshi tōkei sōran.

In the early 1990s, as it raced to capture greater market share by introducing new models and new technologies, Toyota Motor Thailand borrowed even more managers and technicians from its parent company in Japan.⁵⁶ As of 1993, nine of its 13 senior managers were Japanese. During the same time, Fujitsu injected massive doses of Japanese capital, technology, and staff into its rapidly expanding operation in Thailand. Nakajima, chief of administration, gave an embarrassed chuckle as he related this statistic: 47 of the 57 managers at Fujitsu's Thai plant in 1993 were Japanese.

To be fair, there is evidence that indigenization is taking place in Japanese subsidiaries in Asia. But it is occurring in the factory, at the level of foreman and supervisor, not in the administrative offices.⁵⁷ MITI itself has noted this discrepancy. In surveys conducted in 1989 and 1992, it found that Japanese firms in Asia had not made significant progress toward entrusting local managers to oversee planning, purchasing, finance, and other critically important functions.⁵⁸

Since it began operating in 1970, Thai Polyester has halved (from 10 to five) the number of Japanese managers assigned to supervise production at its textile plant in Pathumthani, Thailand. At the same time, though, it has only marginally trimmed (from 10 to eight) the number of Japanese executives assigned to purchasing, marketing, finance, and other administrative duties at its downtown Bangkok office.⁵⁹

Conventional wisdom holds that progress toward the indigenization of senior staff is slowed by the parent firm's need to communicate with its affiliates in a common language (Japanese) and through a common corporate culture (the Japanese employment system, which is based on seniority).⁶⁰ This is quite true – but not terribly illuminating. It glosses over a new organizational logic: the Japanese parent firm no longer wishes merely to *communicate* with its regional affiliates; now it wants more than ever to *control* them, to utilize them as pivotal pieces in a strategy to build a high-technology production network in Asia.

"Investment means having some control when we invest," explains Oda Toshio, senior adviser at Nissho Iwai, a general trading company that oversees more than 70 joint ventures in Asia. The parent firm must be vigilant, he says. "Otherwise, it's just a giveaway of technology. The difficulty is when we can't control the management."[61]

This new organizational logic is manifested in different ways, with different results.

At a Sony electronics plant in Penang, Japanese executives serve as "big brothers" or advisers to the Malaysian managers who, on paper at least, run the firm's 12 divisions.[62] This arrangement doesn't seem to bother Lim Chin Ewe, the titular head of Sony's planning and control division. "We acknowledge that the Japanese are the bosses here and that we, the locals, are pretty much the assistant managers." On some issues, such as ethnic customs and government regulations, Lim says the Japanese solicit the advice of their junior partners.[63]

But at a Matsushita plant in Bangkok, Anchalee Sutthayakom cannot bring herself to be so philosophical. After 17 mostly good years as a personnel manager, she is distressed that the parent firm in Japan suddenly has sent a team of what she calls "nitpickers" to run National Thai. "Everything has changed – especially the way the Japanese managers view us. They look down on us now. They don't trust us to do anything. We aren't allowed to make even the smallest decisions. Instead, we are told to follow the Japanese management's orders on every little thing."[64]

CHAPTER TEN

The Supply Network

In the late 1980s, when Japanese firms shifted a record amount of production to foreign lands, pessimists warned that Japan's tightly integrated economy was likely to unravel. MITI's Small and Medium Enterprises Agency expressed an increasingly common concern that the globalization of Japanese industry would undermine the economic standing of Japanese suppliers, "irrevocably altering the ongoing relations between large parent firms and their smaller subcontractors."[1] Many foreign scholars agreed. "Increasing FDI," wrote Young-Kwan Yoon, a political scientist, "will negatively affect productivity growth through the destruction of the traditionally efficient domestic structure of production."[2] In other words, the globalization of the Japanese economy would erode one of the solid pillars of its developmentalism – the close ties between large manufacturers and their cozy coterie of domestic suppliers. But pessimists inside and outside Japan failed to anticipate that Japanese high-tech manufacturers would, by and large, manage to establish the same or similar ties as they moved into Asia.

This may surprise those familiar with the track record of Japanese MNCs in the West. Indeed, Krugman and Graham have found that Japanese firms in the United States import twice as much as other foreign firms in the United States.[3] But Japanese manufacturers in Asia, as Table 10.1 shows, actually rely less on imported parts and materials from Japan than their Japanese counterparts in North America and Europe, even though they are so much closer to their parents in Japan and thus conceivably able to import those intermediate goods more

158

Table 10.1   Source of Procurements by Japanese Manufacturers Overseas,
1989–93 (% of total)

	Local	Japan	Asia	North America	Europe	Other
Affiliates in:						
Asia	46.7	38.8	9.0	1.4	0.8	3.3
North America	47.4	47.2	3.0	1.2	0.5	0.7
Europe*	33.0	42.0	3.7	0.8	19.8	0.7
World	44.5	42.8	5.1	1.2	4.0	2.4

Source: MITI, *Wagakuni kigyō no kaigai jigyō katsudō;* MITI, *Kaigai jigyō katsudō kihon chōsa.*
*Note: Does not include 1993 data.

cheaply. This does *not* mean that Japanese firms in Asia are more "international," or that they enjoy more autonomy than their counterparts in North America, Europe, or elsewhere. Far from it. It means they are able to take advantage of an emerging production alliance that links Japan's large-scale, high-technology MNCs with smaller parts producers in host nations throughout Asia.[4]

We must be careful not to overstate our case. In many cases, Japanese affiliates in Asia continue to rely heavily on their parent firms in Japan for intermediate goods, especially high value-added components. For example, as of 1992, Tan Chong Motors, a Nissan affiliate in Malaysia, still imported 65 percent of its automotive parts from its Japanese parent.[5] In addition, Japanese affiliates in some parts of Asia have been slower than those in other parts of the region to build local supply networks. In Indonesia in the early 1990s, for example, electronics firms and automobile assemblers were still importing up to 90 percent of their parts and materials.[6]

Overall, though, the evidence suggests that Japanese manufacturers have begun – at least at the margin – to reduce their overwhelming reliance on the parent country. The electronics industry, for example, has achieved progress by securing an increasing share of its inputs from other Asian countries – a clear indication that a regional production alliance, or a web of individual networks, is emerging based on an intrafirm division of labor.[7] In 1989, Japanese electrical machine manufacturers in the region relied on imports from other Asian countries for 8.7 percent of their supplies. That share rose to 11 percent in 1990, 14.7 percent in 1991, 15.2 percent in 1992, and 19.1 percent in 1993.[8] And if we take a longer look at the transportation industry, we see that Japanese affiliates in the region, albeit under some duress, managed to raise the local content of their automobiles from about a third in the mid 1970s to almost a half in the early 1990s.[9]

These trends, we believe, are ongoing. In July 1994, 59 percent of Japanese assemblers in Malaysia who were surveyed by overseas representatives of the Japanese Chamber of Commerce and Industry reported they were buying more local parts than they had a year earlier.[10]

What these statistics don't show, however, is that a large and growing number of the "local" suppliers used by Japanese manufacturers in Asia are actually Japanese affiliates. We were able to uncover this fact by examining the purchasing patterns of individual firms. Toyota Motor Thailand, to cite one example, boasts that it gets 54 percent of its passenger car parts and 66 percent of its commercial vehicle parts from local suppliers. The fact is, however, that 75 percent of these "local" parts come from Japanese suppliers in Thailand.[11]

Sony is equally proud of its record of local procurement in Asia. It reports that affiliates spread across the region obtain about 90 percent of their audio parts and about 50 percent of their video parts from local suppliers. But a Sony official in Japan admits that "virtually all" of such locally supplied electronic (as opposed to mechanical) components come from affiliates of Sony and other Japanese MNCs in Asia.[12] Consider the specific case of Sony Mechatronics Products, which manufactures floppy disk drives in Penang, Malaysia. Although it purchases 40 percent of its parts and materials from firms in Malaysia, Singapore, and Thailand, Japanese affiliates in those three locations supply 95 percent of what Sony counts as its "local" inputs.[13] Matsushita Television in Shah Alam, Malaysia, relies on local suppliers for 55 percent of its inputs, but more than 94 percent of these "local" parts are produced by Japanese-affiliated firms in Malaysia.[14] Melco Consumer Products, a Mitsubishi Electric subsidiary in Thailand that manufactures air conditioners, gets 75 percent of its supplies from other companies in Thailand – almost all of them affiliated with Japanese capital. "Only packing materials and other not very important things come from Thai firms," says Fujii Noboru, former general manager of Melco Thailand.[15]

In general, then, we found that Japanese high-tech firms in Asia procured their most sophisticated components from Japanese suppliers based in the host country, in neighboring Asian countries, or in Japan. Local firms supplied few high value-added goods and services. This conclusion is supported by the findings of a 1990 business survey. Japan's Keizai Doyūkai (Association of Corporate Executives) found that Japanese manufacturers in Southeast Asia planned to increase their local content first by purchasing parts from other Japanese firms in the host country, then by securing them from non-Japanese suppliers in the host country, and finally by obtaining them from Japanese suppliers in other Asian countries.[16]

Most scholars have glossed over this fact, concluding in error that increased local procurement necessarily means increased business opportunity for domestically owned suppliers.[17] But a growing body of research suggests otherwise.

In Singapore, Sree Kumar and Ng Chee Yuen found that Japanese manufacturers routinely tap Japanese subcontractors in that city-state for high value-added inputs, turning to purely local suppliers only for such things as labels, packaging, and metal stamping.[18] The Export-Import Bank of Japan reached a similar conclusion, reporting that Japanese affiliates in Singapore produce 80 percent of the electronic components used by Japanese firms that manufacture audio equipment there.[19] The story is much the same in Malaysia, where Aoki Takeshi found that Japanese affiliates account for nearly 60 percent of the "local" parts and materials purchased by Japanese assemblers in Malaysia's transport industry.[20]

Even the Japanese government has begun to acknowledge these facts. In a study of Japanese investment in camera and color TV manufacturing in South Korea, Taiwan, Singapore, Hong Kong, Thailand, and Malaysia, Japan's National Institute of Science and Technology Policy found that "hardly any parts [for TVs] are procured from non-Japanese companies" and that parts for cameras "are procured almost entirely from Japanese companies."[21] The authors concluded that:

> There was an overwhelming tendency for parts to be procured from Japanese companies. The move towards procuring parts from the local area has progressed only in the form of Japanese parts manufacturers establishing local production bases. We believe this is due to the low technological levels of local companies, extremely stringent specifications covering the precision of parts and so on, and the strong ties with subcontract plants.[22]

In an interview with a Japanese newspaper, Tanaka Hiroshi, deputy director general of the Research Institute on Overseas Investment, an arm of Japan's Export-Import Bank, came to much the same conclusion: "Almost all components used to produce consumer electronics in Asian countries are either imported from Japan or produced locally by the subsidiaries of manufacturers or parts suppliers of Japanese origin."[23]

None of this should surprise us. Japanese MNCs in Asia traditionally have shown a clear preference for doing business with other Japanese firms. In the late 1970s, a researcher asked foreign firms to list in order of importance the factors they considered before investing in Singapore. Compared to their counterparts from the United States and Europe, Japanese MNCs attached greater significance to the fact that "other companies from the same country are here." In fact, they put almost twice as much weight on that factor as did German firms.[24]

Even so, Japanese subcontractors did not begin to invest heavily in Asia until the early 1970s, when host governments adopted "local content"

rules requiring foreign firms to use a minimum amount of locally produced parts and materials. Governments in Southeast Asia, in particular,
hoped such local content rules would benefit domestic parts producers.
In most cases, however, they did not.[25] Japanese car assemblers, for
example, simply responded by coaxing long-time suppliers in Japan to
follow them into Asia.[26]

This was bad news for local firms, who now faced stiff competition not
only from *keiretsu* suppliers in Japan, but also from *keiretsu* suppliers in
their own country. They had "little chance of penetrating this doubly
protected" market, according to the Thai Board of Investment.[27]

In the late 1980s, Japanese suppliers again rushed into Asia. This time,
though, the impetus to localize came not from host government policies,
but from the exigencies of the global marketplace. Japanese manufacturers in the region, particularly those in high-technology industries such
as automobiles and electronics, became edgy, even desperate, as they
watched the value of the yen climb higher and higher, dramatically
increasing the cost of the intermediate goods they imported from Japan.
So they began to lean on their trusted suppliers. When it moved into
Taiwan in 1988, Toyota, for example, simply insisted that its most
important parts makers come along.[28]

Most of the time, though, the pressure came in a more subtle form – a
gentle nudge, a firm handshake, an encouraging word. "I remember
giving a speech at a year-end party for our subcontractors," recalls Unoki
Hajime, president of Aiwa, one of Japan's leading consumer electronics
producers. "I said, 'Let's give a toast to leaving Japan.' They either had
no idea what I meant, or they were shocked. Today, most of them have
joined us in Southeast Asia."[29]

For Nippon Electronic, a producer of printed circuit boards for
Japanese mega-manufacturers such as Sony, Matsushita, and Sanyo, the
pressure from its customers was steady. Almost unrelenting. Takano
Tatsuo, managing director of the firm's new operation in Malaysia, says
Nippon Electric carefully examined the costs and benefits of moving
overseas, determined that short-run costs might exceed short-run
benefits, and still decided to go.

> For several years, our [Japanese] customers in Southeast Asia asked us to come
> and support them. They asked and asked, and finally we came. We had no
> choice really. Even though we thought we might lose money, at least at first, we
> had a responsibility [*sekinin*] to come. To survive in Japan, a supplier must
> serve his customers and make them happy. That's the Japanese way.[30]

Evidence suggests that many Japanese suppliers have felt obligated to
make the move into Asia. Sixty-five percent of the small companies responding to a Japanese government survey in 1989 said they either invested
in the region at the behest of their customers (25 percent), or had made a

decision to invest that happened to coincide with moves by their customers (40 percent). After examining these survey results, one Japanese scholar tentatively concluded that the latter answer was "a uniquely Japanese one in which the subcontractors hesitated to admit that their decision was dependent on, or more or less coerced by, their parent firms."[31]

For a Japanese supplier whose *keiretsu* customers are moving en masse into Asia, economic rationality – rather than just coercion or moral suasion – often compels a decision to tag along. One must, after all maintain one's market. "Subcontractors nowadays have no choice but to follow their parent companies," says Oku Koki, director of JETRO's office in Japan's Fukushima Prefecture, where many parts manufacturers operate.[32] To survive, these small firms must roam. Perhaps for this reason, a Thai writer refers to the hundreds of Japanese suppliers who flowed into Thailand in the late 1980s and early 1990s as "economic refugees," desperate vagabonds, not unlike the Vietnamese boat people who flooded Thailand in the 1970s.[33]

We may quibble about motivation, but no one can deny that small Japanese firms moved into Asia in record numbers during the *endaka* mania of the 1980s and early 1990s. In fact, as the yen climbed ever higher, not only parts makers but also suppliers of raw materials and semiprocessed goods such as plastics and metals began making the move. For example, Japan's trading companies set up a network of joint ventures all over Asia to import steel coil from Japan, cut it to order, and sell it to Japanese automobile or electronics manufacturers in the region.[34]

Many Japanese suppliers, either unable or unwilling to physically relocate their manufacturing operations, have moved into Asia without actually budging an inch. They have entered into technology tie-ups, lending their production or process know-how to local parts producers for a fee. In 1993, Japanese manufacturers (including but not limited to parts manufacturers) exported nearly $1.6 billion worth of technology to firms in Asia – about 40 percent more than they exported to firms in North America.[35]

The sum of all these investments and tie-ups is nothing less than the regionalization of Japan's vertical or supply *keiretsu*. In this way, Japanese high-technology, high-volume manufacturers have been able to replicate the core of their quasi-integrated production regimes. As we attempted to demonstrate in chapter three, quasi-integration reduces transaction costs and – if regionalized – may continue to generate efficiencies for many years.

In Thailand, for example, Toyota (Toyota Motor Thailand, or TMT) is able to purchase interior trim and springs from the local affiliate of NHK Springs, which has a plant next door to TMT's in Samutprakarn; spark plugs and other electrical parts from the local affiliate of Nippondenso; wire harnesses from the local affiliate of Yazaki; and so on. The affiliates of these parts makers, all members of Toyota's supply group in Japan (the Kyōhōkai), also belong to the Toyota Cooperation Club, a Thai version of the Kyōhōkai. Toyota set up the club in Thailand in 1982, providing its 45 members with an institutional means of exchanging technical information so they can help each other to better serve TMT.[36] Toyota, which revolutionized manufacturing in Japan with its *kanban* production system, is now installing a sophisticated computer system that it hopes will allow it to create a "recircular *kanban*" and thus improve the flow of automotive parts to its sprawling factory outside Bangkok. "For us to survive here, it is absolutely critical that we find a way, a creative way, to fully implement the Toyota Production System," says Imai Hiroshi, senior managing director of TMT.[37]

Nissan, which trails Toyota in sales in both Japan and Southeast Asia, is trying to build an equally cohesive network of suppliers in Thailand. All but one of the parts it assembles at its Bangkok plant come from members of Nissan's own supply club (the Takarakai). These Japanese subcontractors either have established joint ventures in Thailand or have agreed to license their technology to local suppliers. Thus, Ikeda Bussan's affiliate in Thailand supplies car seats, Tsuchiya's affiliate provides oil filters, Riken's affiliate sells piston rings, and so on. Without investing in Thailand, Calsonic has used a technology agreement to supervise the production of radiators for Nissan in that country, while Hitachi has supervised the production of alternators.

The one exception is a muffler-and-tail-pipe unit, manufactured without any Japanese help by Siam Parts and Engineering, a subsidiary of Siam Motors, the family-owned conglomerate that serves as Nissan's local partner in Thailand. Takase Saburo, a Nissan official who handles business planning for the automaker in Thailand, says the Thai supplier has failed to consistently deliver a high-quality product.

> This is one of our ongoing concerns. We are trying to devise a corrective program to improve the quality of the product. But we are not in any position to order the group to undertake any specific action plan. This [Siam Motors] is a family corporation, and it is not always possible to get everyone to act in a way we think is most efficient.... You know, sometimes I really envy the control Toyota has over its operations here in Thailand.[38]

In their quest for efficient supply networks, Japanese automakers in Asia are doing something that American manufacturers would never dream of doing. They are teaming up to form what could be considered super-*keiretsu*. Suzuki and Mitsubishi Motors, for example, have agreed to use some common components for the passenger trucks they assemble in Indonesia. Suzuki will produce the right-side doors, Mitsubishi will produce the left-side doors, and then they'll swap.[39] Likewise, in Thailand,

Toyota, Nissan and Isuzu have begun to collaborate on the production of cylinder blocks for diesel engines. This cooperation was designed partly to satisfy demands from the Thai government for higher levels of domestic content, and partly to maintain Japanese domination of the local market for small pick-up trucks. "To compete against American and European producers, we needed to find a way to reduce costs even further," says Tezuka Hiroyuki, the president of Siam Toyota Motors, which owns the casting factory that manufactures engine parts for the three Japanese firms.[40]

The automakers are not alone in trying to build *keiretsu*-like supply networks in Asia. In fact, a JETRO survey in 1991 found that 12 Japanese firms in Malaysia had set up subcontractor associations to promote technical cooperation and improve the quality of parts and raw materials they purchase from local suppliers. A year earlier, in 1990, only four companies had done so.[41]

Sony Electronics Malaysia, which manufactures audio equipment at a huge plant in Penang, calls on 251 vendors all over the region to supply everything from electronic components to cardboard boxes. "The audio market has been very flat, so we have to depend a lot on our vendors to help us control costs," says Lim Chin Ewe, manager of business planning. Like other Japanese manufacturers, Sony pushes its suppliers to deliver products "just in time" (JIT) so it can reduce its inventory and trim its expenses. "You hear it in meetings, in speeches, in training sessions. JIT is always emphasized around here."[42]

This obviously begs a question: How do you coordinate a JIT system that crosses national borders and even spans large bodies of water? Sony's answer was to hook up with Mitsui Soko, a logistics firm, which manages a regional distribution network that stores and sorts goods at several warehouses, pushes them through customs, and then, acting as a broker, purchases discount space on container ships heading to the desired port. A satellite system monitors the progress of the goods as they move through each step in the distribution process.

To plug into Mitsui's network, Sony first had to create a parallel structure of its own. In 1988, Sony International of Singapore (Sonis) became the company's operational headquarters in the region and immediately set up a subsidiary, Sony Logistics Singapore, to coordinate purchasing and sales activities for all Sony's manufacturing plants in Asia. As Tokunaga describes it, Sonis functions as the "heart" of a distribution system that includes "arteries," which carry parts to the company's Asian plants, and "veins," which collect manufactured products or semifinished goods for overseas distribution.[43] This system allows Sony's manufacturing plants in the region to focus their attention on producing high-quality, high-technology goods.

Assume that Sony Electronics Malaysia (SEM), a huge operation that manufactures more than half a million units of audio equipment every month, needs mechanical parts for its cassette recorders and optical pick-up components for its CD players. It uses Sony's on-line communications system to notify Sonis, which orders just enough mechanical parts from Mizuki, a Japanese firm in Thailand, and just enough optical pick-up components from Sony Precision Engineering Center, a Sony manufacturing affiliate in Singapore. Sonis then notifies Mitsui Soko, which pulls those products through its logistical network to arrive – just in time – at SEM in Penang.

Sony is not the only Japanese manufacturer trying to recreate an efficient parts delivery system in Asia, and Mitsui is not the only logistics firm providing such service. Indeed, all of Japan's general trading companies (GTCs) have gotten into the act, deploying their vast intelligence and transportation networks on behalf of overseas manufacturers. Using Singapore as their logistical headquarters, the GTCs have become the master merchants of Asia.[44]

Although a logistical tie-up with a GTC makes it more possible to establish a well-functioning JIT production system, it does not guarantee such an outcome. For Japanese manufacturers in Asia, the bottleneck continues to be the meager supply of top-notch suppliers. This is why they go to such great lengths to assist those they trust deeply. A Matsushita executive, for example, frequently visits the Malaysia Industrial Development Authority, prodding bureaucrats there to grant the licenses and incentives needed to lure its leading subcontractors from Japan to help it produce high-technology air conditioners.[45] In a similar vein, Honda rallied behind a Japanese joint venture in Malaysia, assuring the Joint Technical Committee for Local Content that it would purchase brake fluid and fuel tubing from the local supplier. The committee, representing both the government and private industry, was responsible for approving programs to substitute locally manufactured parts for imported ones.[46]

Japanese MNCs in Asia also introduce Japanese suppliers to prospective local partners, help them secure financing in the host nation, and share technical blueprints. Now and then, they even go out of their way to assist non-Japanese suppliers. Matsushita, for example, has been a steady customer, a caring parent, to Ngai Cheong Metal Industries, a Chinese family-owned firm that does up to 80 percent of its metal-stamping work for the Matsushita air conditioning group in Malaysia. Over the years, the small local supplier has borrowed most of its tools and dies from the Japanese giant. In 1987 it received an entire production line from Matsushita. "We have a very close relationship with them," says Chan Chun Kit, general manager of Ngai Cheong. "They have made a big effort, spent a lot of time, helping us grow along with them."[47]

But many other local suppliers have not been treated so well. In separate studies of subcontracting relationships in Singapore and Thailand, researchers found that Japanese MNCs controlled their own costs by squeezing parts makers on price, allowing them to operate only on razor-thin profit margins. "They give you enough to live on, but not too much to make a killing," local business people told researchers in Singapore.[48] Thai suppliers complained that Japanese manufacturers, who enjoy oligopolistic if not monopolistic power in many markets in host economies, unilaterally set prices for the parts they are willing to buy from locals.[49] In addition, they wield vague standards of quality that tend, predictably, to rise or fall according to market conditions. "When the economy is good, the Japanese subsidiaries tend to relax their inspections on quality in order to put the product on the market just in time to meet demand. But when demand slows down, Japanese assemblers will be strict on inspecting the products' quality."[50]

These are difficult, even vexing, problems. But hardly insurmountable. What truly stunts the growth of local suppliers is the fact that Japanese MNCs in the region are building a tight network of dedicated suppliers from Japan, but a far looser, or wider, network of domestically owned suppliers. In other words, they are employing what some call "market sharing agreements" and others call "multiple sourcing" – a practice in which large assembly firms purchase the same or a similar product from different suppliers at different times. Chuah Eng Hoe, manager of purchasing for the Matsushita air conditioning group in Malaysia, defended this practice, saying it promoted competition among local suppliers and – most importantly – increased his own firm's bargaining power with them.[51] But Sree and Ng say the practice creates vertical and segmented linkages that limit business opportunities, forcing local suppliers to scramble for new markets, thus restricting their ability to prepare long-range development plans.

> Market sharing agreements which MNCs thrust upon their suppliers and subcontractors act as deterrents to industrial upgrading. The quantities ordered from each supplier are enough for minimum production runs but insufficient for higher volumes where scale economies can be derived through the use of better technology, rationalised production lines and improved management techniques. Deliberate sourcing policies, such as the ones pursued by Japanese companies, provide no incentives for industrial deepening or upgrading by local SMEs.[52]

But a piece of the action is surely better than no action at all. And as more and more Japanese subcontractors respond to home and host government incentives by investing capital or licensing technology in Asia, native suppliers seem to get less and less action. They have finally begun to sound off, bending the ears of government officials throughout the region. "They are quite unhappy about this encroachment by Japanese subcontractors," says Tan Siew Hoey, an economist at the Institute of Strategic and International Studies in Malaysia.[53]

Protests, though, have not paid off. To get a piece of the action, local suppliers often must swallow hard and relinquish control to Japanese managers by entering into a joint venture or technical tie-up. This is precisely what the United Industries Group in Malaysia did. To produce fuel tanks for the Proton, Malaysia's national car and Mitsubishi Motors' regional care, it had to engage in a technical tie-up with Sankei Kōgyō, a supplier for Mitsubishi in Japan. And to produce fuel and brake tubing for Honda, Nissan, and Toyota, it had to enter into a joint venture with Sanoh Industrial, a subcontractor for those automakers in Japan. "My feeling is we can't beat them, so let's join them," says Tony Ng, company controller for United Industries.[54]

But try as they might, local business people cannot always convince Japanese business people to tie the knot. One hot night in Bangkok, Kosa Choangulia, brother-in-law of Wattana Choangulia (identified in chapter two), met for two hours with Miyajima Yoshinori, Wattana's partner, scouting opportunities, looking for cracks in what seems a thicker-than-ever coat of armor protecting the Japanese market. Choangulia, a former technician for Philips, the Dutch electronics firm, now manages his own business producing electronic components. "It has gotten harder rather than easier" to sell parts to Japanese manufacturers, he says. "Before they used a lot of Thai firms. But now that their technology has become so much more complicated, they tend to use only their own [Japanese] companies."[55]

In Malaysia, a local scholar has identified what he called a tendency for Japanese manufacturers "to switch from Malaysian subcontractors to the newly established Japanese concerns." Speaking to a largely Japanese audience, Imran Lim of the Institute of Strategic and International Studies in Kuala Lumpur tried to state the issue as diplomatically as possible: "If these become more than just isolated complaints, then the situation could become unhealthy."[56]

Japanese MNCs offer a variety of reasons to explain their strong preference for Japanese transplants rather than native suppliers. A Fujitsu official in Tokyo says, for example, that MNCs from the West moved into Asia ahead of Japan, locking up almost all of the reliable local suppliers. "We had to develop our own relationships, and often it was necessary to do that with Japanese companies," he says.[57] Others grumble that local suppliers cannot or will not keep up with their delivery schedules, causing them to shut down assembly lines as they wait for shipments of needed inputs. This is obviously no way to run a JIT production system.[58] Still others complain loudly that local suppliers, left on their own, too often fail to meet their minimum standards for quality. In recent surveys of Japanese manufacturers in Asia, this has become a leading gripe.

"In this part of the world, Japanese big businesses buy almost all of their parts and components from Japanese small businesses. They really have no choice because the quality of the work done by the local suppliers is still so low," says Isoyama Katsuhiko, a representative of the Japan Finance Corporation for Small Business in its Kuala Lumpur office.[59]

There is more truth in this assertion than some in Asia are willing to acknowledge. Local firms, particularly those run by family patriarchs who have acquired little or no technical knowledge and who never have devised a long-range business plan, often produce less reliable products than Japanese joint ventures in Asia, which themselves often produce less reliable products than wholly owned Japanese firms. This was illustrated by a chart posted on the wall at Melco Consumer Products. It tracks the defect rate for air conditioners produced each month at the plant outside Bangkok. The rate in April 1992 was by far the lowest – only 1.43 percent. "We did better that month," Melco's general manager explained matter-of-factly, "because we used a larger number of imported parts" from Japan.[60]

It is difficult, if not downright impossible, for local suppliers to keep pace with Japanese assemblers that are making what have been described as "day to day" innovations, or frequent changes in production or process technology originating in Japan. Doner uses the example of plastic bumpers, which Japanese automakers began using in Thailand even though local parts makers could only supply metal ones.[61]

Rather than just wringing their hands, several Japanese MNCs are trying to help local suppliers meet their high expectations. For example, Sony Electronics (Malaysia) visits each of its prospective vendors, offering recommendations on how to meet the company's quality standards. Later, if it passes an inspection, the vendor's product is stamped with a Sony brand – the AQCA, or Assured Quality Control Approval.[62] Sharp has a similar scheme, routinely dispatching quality control teams to 150 of its suppliers in Thailand.[63] Not to be outdone, Matsushita visits its vendors in Taiwan four times each year, training them to pay more attention to the quality of their products.[64]

Even the Japanese government has gotten into the act. MITI has held workshops in Southeast Asia, advising local firms to take specific measures to raise the quality of their manufactured exports and thereby meet new international standards (ISO 9000).[65] The Japan Overseas Development Corporation and Japan International Cooperation Agency have provided training to local managers and technicians.[66] Host governments in Asia, on the other hand, are following a different course. They are using matchmaking programs to bring together MNCs and local suppliers, hoping thereby to promote the transfer of technology and skills. Singapore, for example, has its Local Industry Upgrading Program. Thailand has its BOI Unit for Industrial Linkage Development. And Malaysia has its "vendor development program."[67]

But such government-supervised matchmaking programs have failed to bring many Japanese manufacturers to the altar. That is because they ignore microeconomic reality. Japanese firms "don't meet and immediately get married," notes Wisarn Pupphavesa, director of the Asia-Pacific Economic Relations Project at the Thailand Development Research Institute. "They just don't operate that way. They require a long, drawn out romance before they enter into any kind of relationship."[68]

Kodama and Kiba agree. Japanese MNCs, they say, are wary of linking up with non-Japanese manufacturers that "have not experienced for themselves the trial and error process" that led to the development of a particular technology. These MNCs, they say, "believe that the transfer of managerial responsibilities to non-Japanese companies can take place only gradually, as the required managerial skills and know-how are built through in-house, on-the-job training and work experience."[69]

Honda highlights this principle in a brochure it distributes to local firms that indicate an interest in selling parts and materials to the automaker's overseas plants.

> When a company becomes a supplier to Honda, we expect that company to become a supplier for the long term. This will require sincere effort and commitment resulting in recognition as a reliable supplier. Continuing efforts will be expected in areas such as short term parts development, commitment to zero defects, on time deliveries and the ability to respond quickly to solve quality and other problems.[70]

For non-Japanese firms, this principle – that time cements a relationship between a manufacturer and supplier – sets up a Catch-22. How can they prove themselves over time without first acquiring a track record of successfully supplying parts or materials to the Japanese? Honda's own activities in Thailand, where it planned to open a new auto plant in 1996, highlight this point. Anxious about the quality of local parts makers, the firm prevailed upon 10 of its Japanese suppliers to set up operations in that country.[71]

We recognize that small, local suppliers always face an uphill battle in trying to establish credibility, and thus a business relationship, with large, foreign manufacturers in their country. But they have an especially tough time with Japanese affiliates, whose purchasing policies are more often than not made by executives in corporate headquarters in Tokyo, Osaka, or Nagoya, not by overseas managers in Bangkok, Taipei, or Singapore.

Not too long ago, the manager of VCR production for Sanyo in Cimanggis, Indonesia was asked if a non-Japanese supplier could ever sell its products to the electronics plant. Maybe, but "you can't do it here," replied Arashima Masahiko. "The drawings and designs are all made in Japan. You have to sell to Sanyo in Japan."[72]

PART FOUR

A Powerful Embrace

CHAPTER ELEVEN

The Ties that Bind

The numbers are staggering. Between 1985 and 1993, Asia's trade deficit with Japan ballooned, rising from $9.3 billion to $54.2 billion. During the same period, Asia's trade surplus with the West (the United States and the EC) also grew rapidly, from $28 billion to nearly $70 billion (see Figure 11.1). Why is this happening?

Neoclassical economists say it is all quite predictable. Japan, they say, has been using FDI to shed industries in which it is losing comparative

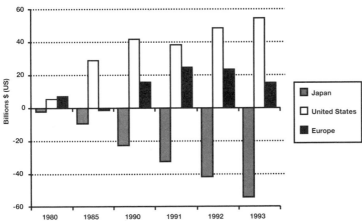

Figure 11.1 Asia's Trade Balance with the United States, European Community, and Japan

Sources: IMF Direction of Trade Statistics, various years, and Republic of China Statistical Yearbook, 1993, pp. 238-41.

advantage. This in turn has triggered a short-term surge in Japanese exports of capital goods to the region. But as Japanese FDI falls and local manufacturing firms become increasingly competitive, host countries in Asia will import less and less from Japan, and export more and more to Japan. With its wealthy neighbor acting as a giant sponge, soaking up the region's manufactured goods, Asia's trade deficit with Japan and trade surplus with the West will gradually but ineluctably vanish.

The neoclassical message is clear. Before too long, the V-shaped flying geese pattern in Asia will turn into a straight line, and the global trade regime will achieve a harmonious "equilibrium." Everyone will benefit in the end. Don't worry. Be happy.[1]

But we remain skeptical. To us, the trade data suggest that Japan is beginning to regionalize its developmentalist policies and practices – a strategic move that, if pursued with any success, will further widen the technology gap between Japan and Asia, and exacerbate the existing trade conflict between East and West. Our outlook for the future, then, is far less rosy.

This less-than-rosy view of the future is based on an unromantic review of the past. In a nutshell, we believe that Japan's pursuit of developmentalism at home, beginning in the 1950s, led to Japan's large and chronic trade surplus.

A central goal of home-based developmentalism was to transform Japan into the "factory to the world," the supplier of increasingly high value-added manufactured products.[2] To achieve this goal, Japan became a saver, a nation with enough resources to increase investment and thus increase productivity. But saving and investing more meant consuming less. And consuming less meant exporting more.

As we suggested in chapter four, the government pursued developmentalism by channeling savings into innovating and exporting firms that forged *keiretsu* ties with one another. Exports increased at an astonishing rate – about 100-fold between 1955 and 1985. Imports increased too, but far more slowly.[3] This was partly due to the fact that consumption rose slowly, but also due to the fact that a dense network of interfirm relationships sealed off strategic segments of the Japanese market. Because exports expanded rapidly while imports grew slowly, Japan racked up a massive trade surplus.

To be sure, interest rates, exchange rates, and other market forces helped determine the magnitude of exports and imports, and thus the tilt of Japan's trade balance. But the powerful, "nonmarket" force of developmentalism had the greatest influence over the longest period. This firmly established set of policies and practices kept Japan on its export-led path even after the United States unilaterally ended fixed exchange rates, major trading partners began to squawk, Tokyo agreed to "voluntarily" restrain exports, the value of the yen began to climb, and domestic critics, such as the Maekawa Commission, called on Japan to abandon "unfair or exclusive trading practices."[4] A developmentalist Japan could do nothing but stay the course.

There are still some neoclassical economists who argue that Japan's chronic trade surplus is due primarily to the excess consumption of its trading partners, not to any Japanese policies or practices encouraging exports and discouraging imports.[5] But as time goes on (and Japan's surplus remains), these "holdouts" become more and more rare. Today, a growing number of economists inside and outside Japan accept at least part of our argument.

If we are correct that Japan today is regionalizing its developmentalist system, we can expect several things to happen. First, Japan will export an increasing amount of high-technology products, particularly intermediate and capital goods, to Asia – a trend that will not decline in any significant way for several years. The reason is clear. Technology, embedded in Japanese machinery and parts, is the critical ingredient needed to sustain increasingly competitive production networks in Asia.

Even if the subordinate local firms in these networks manage to surprise us by steadily and significantly enhancing their own technical capabilities, they will continue to rely heavily on their dominant Japanese "partners" for such high-tech inputs. This is because they are quasi-integrated into an alliance structure that is coordinated by parent firms and *keiretsu* suppliers in Japan. As long as this is true, any increase in Asia's innovative capacity will be accompanied (and, more likely than not, driven) by a comparable increase in Japan's. Asia will simply end up importing ever more sophisticated technology from Japan.

Who will absorb the manufacturing output of these Japanese-dominated networks? If Japan's experience tells us anything, we can expect the networks themselves to eat up a large share of the intermediate goods (parts) they produce. Just as *keiretsu* suppliers in Kawasaki or Kobe manufacture parts for assemblers in Tokyo and Osaka, so do local suppliers in Singapore or Taipei produce parts for assemblers in Kuala Lumpur and Shanghai.

As Asia's per capita income continues to rise, the region will also consume a growing share of the final products manufactured in these networks. But in the short run, scale economies and the high value-added nature of these goods will force producers to target large, high-income markets as well. The options are limited: Japan, the United States, and Europe.

Japan, we believe, is not likely to be a significant absorber. Of course, it will import products on the lower rungs of the technology ladder that are produced by local firms in its Asian alliance. But these imports will, by and large, serve only the strategic needs of the dominant *keiretsu* members in Japan and will enter the country largely on their terms. Independent firms in Asia – that is, firms that have not been integrated into a production network – will find the Japanese market far tougher to crack. There is no reason to believe they will fare any better than independent firms in the United States and Europe that are backed by far more powerful governments (and threats of trade sanctions against Japan).

The United States and Europe, then, are likely to continue serving as the outside absorbers of the final goods produced in this Japanese-dominated production alliance in Asia. How much they absorb from year to year will depend on macroeconomic conditions and exchange rates. But other variables will almost certainly come into play. For example, the Japanese multinationals that dominate these Asian production networks are likely to engage in forward pricing (selling at below current cost in anticipation of a future reduction in cost) in order to increase global market share. And if Japan's regionalized developmentalism succeeds in boosting the international competitiveness of Japanese multinationals and their *keiretsu* allies, we can expect an ongoing flood of manufactured exports from both Japan and Asia to the developed nations of the West. The evidence suggests that our assumptions are valid.

It is widely acknowledged that Japan has become the world's leading supplier of high-tech parts and machinery, which by the mid 1990s made up about 60 percent of the nation's total exports. Fewer, however, recognize that a growing share of these made-in-Japan memory chips, wafer steppers, and fuel injection systems are destined for factories in Asia.[6] While Japan's manufactured exports to the United States and Europe combined doubled between 1985 and 1993, its manufactured exports to Asia *tripled* during that period (see Table 11.1). The nine nations in the region absorb 35 percent of all Japanese exports, and one analyst estimates that, by 1999, Asia will swallow 45 percent.[7]

Asia's appetite for Japanese products is not a fleeting fancy; it is imbedded in its economic structure. One study found a remarkably low elasticity of demand by the Asian NICs for Japanese imports. The author concluded that such imports were "indispensable" to Korea, Taiwan, Singapore, and Hong Kong.[8] This becomes evident when we consider that, in 1992, the value of parts imported from Japan represented 11 percent of Asia's manufacturing GNP; in contrast, parts imported from the *entire world* represented less than 2 percent of Japan's manufacturing GNP.[9] Hungry for the inputs required to feed its rapidly expanding manufacturing industries, Asia has become tightly embraced by Japanese technology. Both the NICs and the ASEAN-4 rely on Japan for 40 percent of their machinery imports.[10]

Table 11.1 Destination of Japan's Manufactured Exports ($ millions and % of Japan's Total)

	1993	1992	1991	1990	1985
Asia	121,561 (34.9)	113,359 (34.5)	95,776 (31.5)	80,249 (28.9)	40,288 (23.6)
United States	103,473 (29.7)	97,800 (29.8)	89,819 (29.5)	88,852 (32.0)	64,806 (37.9)
European Community	62,304 (17.9)	63,781 (19.4)	58,320 (19.2)	52,269 (18.8)	20,576 (12.0)
Japan's Total	348,556	328,332	304,189	277,302	170,779

Source: UN Commodity Trade Statistics, various years. OECD Trade by Commodity Statistics, various years.

South Korean officials aren't particularly proud of their country's trade dependence. "We're hooked on Japan, I'm afraid," says Lee San Yul, director general of the international trade bureau at the Korean Ministry of Trade and Industry. "When the Korean economy was just beginning to develop, we had to rely on Japan for technology and parts. Once we had their system, we kept buying them. So as our exports to the rest of the world increased, our imports from Japan had to grow."[11]

Japan's technological embrace of Korea is reflected in the numbers: Japanese high-technology parts and components have accounted for 20–30 percent of the value of Korean automobiles, 35–45 percent of the value of Korean machine tools, 60 percent of the value of Korean computers, 65 percent of the value of Korean printers, and 85 percent of the value of Korean televisions.[12] A pair of scholars, citing similar statistics, concluded that Korean industry is being integrated with Japan's "through formal alliances and deepening dependencies upon Japanese firms."[13]

Until the mid 1980s, South Korea imposed strict limits on foreign investment. It preferred instead to import Japanese technology in an unpackaged form, via technical licensing agreements. For years, Japan has accounted for about half of all the cases of technology transferred to Korea, and even more (61.5 percent) of all the cases of machine technology transfer.[14] In 1993, for example, Japanese firms agreed to export as much as $437 million in manufacturing technology to Korea. Only the United States received more unpackaged technology from Japan.[15]

Taiwan, which recorded a $13 billion trade deficit with Japan in 1994, is just as dependent. Two-thirds of its technology cooperation agreements have been with Japanese suppliers.[16] Although Taiwanese manufacturers have grabbed 20 percent of the world market for notebook computers, they have done so only by assembling Japanese components: the liquid crystal display screen, the nickel-cadmium battery, various semiconductors – in other words, virtually all of the high value-added parts.[17]

In 1994, Taiwan imported $14.3 billion worth of machinery and related components from Japan.[18] Chen Tain-jy, head of the international department at the government-funded Chung-hua Institution for Economic Research, says Taiwan is destined to continue to import an abundance of high-technology products from its powerful neighbor and former colonial master. "After so many years of working together with the Japanese and using their technology, or devising complementary products from their technology, we have benefited a great deal. You just can't change that overnight. If you do, Taiwan's competitiveness will be damaged, and we can't afford to do that."[19]

In the late 1980s, as they attracted larger and larger volumes of Japanese investment, Southeast Asian nations also found themselves wrapped tightly in the warm, potentially suffocating embrace of Japanese technology. Take Indonesia, for example. Thanks to its high volume of oil and gas exports, it is in the rare and enviable position of enjoying a trade surplus with Japan. But Indonesia is wholly dependent on Japanese capital goods to operate its fledgling industries. In 1994, it imported $5.3 billion of machinery and equipment from Japan, and exported only $289 million of such goods in the other direction.[20] This pattern is repeated in Thailand, Malaysia, and the Philippines. While Japanese machinery exports to the NICs quadrupled between 1985 and 1992, the same set of exports to the ASEAN-4 soared fivefold.[21]

Fueled by Japanese capital and technology, Asian factories have steadily increased their output of manufactured goods. For example, in the 1980s, the average annual growth rate of value added in Korean industry was 12.6 percent. And from 1990 through 1993, the rate was nearly 15 percent in China, about 11 percent in Malaysia and more than 12 percent in Thailand.[22]

Where does all this output go? The leading market is Asia itself – either the host nation or neighboring countries in the region. In 1993, Asia soaked up 37 percent of the manufactured exports from the NICs, 31 percent from ASEAN, and 42 percent from China.

Japan, it turns out, receives only a very limited share of Asia's manufactured exports. In 1993, it was on the receiving end of less than 10 percent of the region's total flow of such exports (see Table 11.2). Given the size of the Japanese market and its proximity to Asia, this seems a rather unimpressive amount. To appreciate this, we need only consider the fact that Hong Kong alone absorbed far more of the region's manufactured exports in 1993 (16.3 percent).[23]

Table 11.2 Destination of Asia's Manufactured Exports (Volume in $ millions: % of Total Exports)

	1980	1985	1990	1991	1992	1993
Asia	14,193	22,853	89,422	115,392	139,831	171,083
	(19.7)	(20.6)	(29.6)	(32.6)	(34.4)	(37.3)
Japan	6,125	8,896	30,686	35,272	37,790	44,242
	(8.5)	(8.0)	(10.2)	(10.0)	(9.3)	(9.7)
United States	20,145	43,162	86,878	94,278	108,923	121,109
	(27.9)	(39.0)	(28.8)	(26.6)	(26.8)	(26.4)
EEC-12	13,644	14,078	51,232	63,247	68,251	71,272
	(18.9)	(12.7)	(17.0)	(17.9)	(16.8)	(15.5)
World	72,194	110,785	301,660	354,341	406,145	458,601
	(100)	(100)	(100)	(100)	(100)	(100)

Source: International Economic Data Bank, Australian National University; United Nations, *Commodity Trade Statistics*, various years.

For the Asian NICs in particular, Japan has been a consistently important export market only for those manufactured goods "at the bottom of the production process such as chemicals, resource-based products, metal-based products and nonferrous metals," according to a study by Chow and Kellman. "For more sophisticated products, such as non-electrical machinery, Japan's market was notably smaller" than the United States'.[24] This trend is likely to become even more pronounced by the end of the century. Statistics compiled by Chow and Kellman indicate that the value of high-technology exports (general machinery, electrical machinery, transport machinery, and precision machinery) going from the NICs to Japan may actually fall by 13.6 percent between 1990 and 2000, while the value of those same exports to the United States may rise by 22 percent.[25]

In absolute terms, of course, Japan in the late 1980s dramatically increased the volume of manufactured goods it imported from Asia. Near the end of that decade, when Japan expanded in a bubble of asset appreciation, it turned to Asia for discount products, especially consumer electronics.[26] In those heady years, gutsy Japanese retailers opened new outlets featuring aisle upon aisle of radios, video cassette players, bicycles, and other cheap imports from South Korea, Taiwan, Hong Kong, and Singapore. Even Seibu and some of the other big department stores got into the act, setting up special sections dubbed "NICSONs" (son of NICs).[27]

It was a booming business, but short-lived. As early as 1989, the NIC Super Shops, the NICSONs, and similar outlets were ringing up fewer sales,[28] especially for products from South Korea and Taiwan. Japanese imports of audio-visual equipment and household electrical appliances from those two countries actually fell by one-third between 1989 and 1991.[29]

The NICs, it seemed, lost some of their competitive edge as their currencies appreciated and their production costs, especially wages, rose dramatically. As a result, they also lost some of their strongest exporters – the Japanese. We must recall that, in response to *endaka*, which was triggered by the Plaza Accord in 1985, Japanese manufacturers initially moved into the NICs, setting up or expanding production facilities and exporting ("reimporting") some of their output back to Japan. But in 1990 and 1991, in response to the same forces that battered local firms, Japanese manufacturers began to stanch the flow of capital into places such as South Korea and Taiwan, while maintaining a heavy volume of investment into less expensive sites such as Thailand, Malaysia, Indonesia, and, increasingly, China. It should come as no surprise, then, that the NICs reported slow or negative growth in manufactured exports to Japan, while countries in Southeast Asia (particularly Thailand and Malaysia) enjoyed continued strong growth in such exports.[30] Japan, it seems, is open to reverse imports from its own affiliates in Asia, but is far less receptive to high value-added imports from the region's non-Japanese manufacturers.[31]

Indeed, the evidence, which we must piece together from many different sources, clearly suggests that Japanese affiliates in Asia generate a sizeable share of the region's manufactured exports to Japan.[32] The "JapanNICs" – the whimsical label given to Japanese affiliates operating in South Korea, Taiwan, Hong Kong, and Singapore in the mid to late 1980s – accounted for 70 percent of the NICs' manufactured exports to Japan, according to one estimate made at that time.[33] Mitsubishi Bank went further, breaking it down by product. The JapanNICs, it estimated, produced 50 percent of the electric fans, 70 percent of the electronic calculators, and 90 percent of the televisions imported from the NICs.[34]

The story in Southeast Asia has been pretty much the same. The Japanese Chamber of Commerce and Industry in Bangkok, for example, has estimated that Japanese-related firms in Thailand generated almost 90 percent of that country's manufactured exports to Japan.[35] And the World Bank estimated that Japanese affiliates in Asia manufactured 97.5 percent of the region's electrical and electronic machinery exports to Japan.[36]

If the Japanese market absorbs only a relatively small share of Asia's output, and the Asian market absorbs a large and growing share of Japan's manufactured goods, the result should be pretty easy to anticipate. Japan enjoys a bilateral trade surplus with seven of the nine countries in Asia.

In most cases, Asian governments have done little more than grit their teeth as they endure ever higher bilateral trade shortfalls with the region's economic superpower. We encountered this stoic attitude in Pradup Pibulsonggram, economic adviser in Thailand's Ministry of Foreign Affairs. He appeared remarkably placid in the face of another round of unproductive trade negotiations with Japan. "Trade is not all that defines our relationship. One must also consider investment, technology agreements, and everything else that goes on between our two countries. The relationship is, overall, very much like a happy marriage. There are no demands. No deadlines. We just want to keep cooperating, keep getting along."[37]

There are, of course, exceptions to this rule.[38] Political grumbling, while usually quiet and generally diplomatic, appears to be gaining momentum. In a 1993 report to the ASEAN–Japan Economic Council, for example, a Southeast Asian delegation called the Japanese market "inscrutable and difficult to fathom."

"Such problems as excessive requirements for product quality and services frustrate genuine efforts by ASEAN to expand exports to Japan," the group complained. ASEAN, it said, "desires greater market access and would appreciate Japan's cooperation in helping to circumvent unnecessary obstacles."[39]

South Korea, unable to forget its tragic history and unable to forgive Japan for its brutal, dominating role in that history, is – naturally – the most consistent critic of Japanese trade policy. Korean officials keep pushing Japan to import more of their country's manufactured products. But as of 1994, Korea still had an $11 billion trade deficit with Japan.[40] "We talk and talk and talk and talk, but nothing ever seems to change," says a frustrated Shin Hee Suk, director general of the Asian and Pacific Studies program at the Korean government's Institute of Foreign Affairs and National Security.[41]

In general, though, Asians have tended to muffle their criticism. Despite the costs, they realize that capital goods and intermediate products imported from Japan have primed their own exporting machines. Indeed, the region has steadily increased its exports to the United States and Europe in recent years (see Table 11.2). While most Asian nations have fallen into deeper and deeper bilateral trade deficits with Japan, they have run increasingly large surpluses with the West.[42]

Outside the region, the United States remains by far the most popular destination for Asia's manufactured exports, and will become even more so – a fact that sober analysts in Japan readily acknowledge.

"Asia can't survive without the American market," says Miyamoto Kunio, chief economist at Sumitomo Life Research Institute.[43] Okita Saburo, a former foreign minister who was, until his death in 1993, perhaps the leading Japanese proponent of greater regional cooperation, used to caution against excessively high hopes about exporting to Japan. "In neither scale nor diversity is the Japanese market able to rival the American market," he told the Pacific Economic Cooperation Conference in 1985.[44] He argued that Japan's proper role in Asia was that of a supplier, not an absorber, of manufactured goods.

It has become fashionable to say that Japanese FDI has redesigned trade relations in Asia, creating a new division of labor.[45] According to this increasingly conventional wisdom, the old division of labor was vertical, hierarchical. Japan exported finished manufactured goods to Asia and imported only primary products, such as rubber, oil, and tin. The new division of labor, on the other hand, is horizontal, and is characterized by growing volumes of intraindustry trade. MITI, for example, cites the expansion of what it calls "work sharing." It notes that Japan is now a net importer of semifinished iron and steel products from Asia, but a net exporter of higher value steel products; a net importer of basic textile products from Asia, but a net exporter of synthetic filaments and other textile products requiring more sophisticated technology; a net importer of toys, furniture, musical instruments, sporting goods, and other miscellaneous manufactured goods from Asia, but a net exporter of more technology-intensive miscellaneous goods such as pianos and electronic games.[46]

As such examples subtly but unmistakably demonstrate, the "new" division of labor is not really so new. It remains highly vertical. We concede, of course, that Asian trading partners buy and sell a growing volume of manufactured goods within the same industry. But each contributes to the mix on the basis of its position in a stratified hierarchy of technological competence. Japan produces the highest technology goods; the NICs manufacture lower or medium-technology products; the ASEAN-4 nations, along with China, add even less value to the items they export.

In the electronics industry, for example, Japanese firms concentrate on the production of the most powerful semiconductors, the highest quality televisions, and the most sophisticated appliances, leaving other firms in Asia to manufacture more standardized products. The automobile industry is no different. In Taiwan, local automakers tied up with Japanese manufacturers have found themselves melded into a regional division of labor that, according to one Japanese analyst, "is not an equal division of labor as seen in the European Community countries, but a vertical one within the automobile industry as a whole." In this vertical division of labor, Taiwanese manufacturers specialize in "low-priced compact cars, which have fewer parts and a higher percentage of labor in the entire process."[47]

The simple fact that Japan engages in more intraindustry trade with the Asian NICs than with more industrialized trading partners, such as the United States, is by itself rather telling. It defies the theoretical principle that intra-industry trade occurs most often between countries with similar demand characteristics (chiefly, per capita income), and thus suggests that Japan's intraindustry trade with Asia is really more a function of supply-driven intrafirm (or, more broadly, intranetwork) trade between Japanese MNCs and related companies within the region. Urata, like us, concludes that such trade is rising due to the "pursuit of aggressive globalization strategies by Japanese multinationals."

> Intra-industry trade of this type differs substantially from the intra-industry trade that was analyzed extensively in the 1970s and 1980s because these previous studies focused on intra-industry trade in differentiated, finished manufactures, which is essentially demand driven. In contrast, the intra-firm trade analyzed here is supply or production driven.[48]

In 1992, Japanese manufacturing affiliates in Asia made 37.4 percent of their purchases from and 25.2 percent of their sales to other members of their multinational corporate family.[49] Although these figures reflect a large and growing amount of intrafirm trade, they do not even come close to reflecting what we justifiably assume are much larger amounts of intra*network* trade. This category would include not only transactions between parents and wholly owned subsidiaries, or between subsidiaries of an MNC, but also transactions between firms linked by minority equity holdings, long-term loans, technology licensing agreements, and marketing contracts.[50] As we argued in chapter one, Japanese multinationals in general – and particularly those in Asia – have shown a greater willingness than American or European MNCs to engage in such nonequity or limited-equity forms of overseas production.

High-technology products, in particular, have filled the intrafirm (and, to a far greater degree, we suspect, the intranetwork) pipelines of Japanese firms in Asia. In 1992, for example, 96.7 percent of the general machinery, 90 percent of the electrical machinery, and 96.5 percent of the precision machinery exported to Japan by Japanese manufacturers in the region actually went to parent companies. At the same time, 93.9 percent of the general machinery, 84.6 percent of the electrical machinery, and 85.6 percent of the precision machinery imported from Japan by Japanese manufacturers in Asia actually came from parent companies.[51] These two sets of figures are perhaps not so surprising because Japanese MNCs routinely farm out all or part of a production process to overseas affiliates who must then follow the parent firm's detailed design specifications.[52] More intriguing are statistics, presented in Table 11.3, showing that Japanese high-tech manufacturers in Asia use

Table 11.3   Intrafirm Trade by Japanese Firms in Asia as a Percentage of Their Total Trade within Asia

	General machinery	Electric machinery	Transportation machinery	Precision machinery
Exports (sales)				
1992	55.6	53.7	57.9	77.9
1989	25.1	45.5	1.0	33.5
1986	45.4	26.4	0	46.6
Imports (purchases)				
1992	84.8	59.8	34.6	100
1989	19.8	41.7	4.0	96.8
1986	0	65.1	0	94.6

Source: MITI, *Dai-go-kai, Kaigai jigyō katsudō kihon chōsa,* 1994.

intrafirm channels for a large and increasing share of their sales and purchases within the region.

What these machine makers are doing is turning macroeconomic necessity into microeconomic opportunity. As we suggested earlier, they are breaking down the manufacturing process into separate pieces, assigning each one to a different location according to its factor endowments, including "human capital," meaning here the skill level of the local labor force. The result is a vertically integrated production network, an intrafirm division of labor based on a technological pecking order, with Japan at the top.

By building such networks, and thus utilizing what one group calls the "organic teamwork of economies" in Asia, Japanese manufacturers have improved their ability to compete in international markets.[53] In 1993, manufacturing affiliates in Asia exported 45.5 percent of their total output – much higher than the ratio (33.1 percent) for Japanese affiliates throughout the world.[54] Because they can so easily divide the production process into its component pieces, the producers of electrical and precision machinery tend to be the most export-oriented. But to a much more limited extent, even Japanese manufacturing affiliates in Southeast Asia's heavily protected automobile industry are beginning to scour the earth for new markets.[55] They are anxious to modernize and expand inefficient, labor-intensive factories in the region.[56] And host regimes have encouraged this new approach by enacting policies (such as the ASEAN brand-to-brand complementation scheme, as well as AFTA) to reduce relatively high trade barriers, even if only for goods manufactured within the region.

To the dismay of union leaders, as well as a few economists in Japan, more than a third of these exports by Japanese manufacturing affiliates

in Asia find their way home in the form of reverse imports.[57] This has led
to fears that Japan's domestic industry is undergoing *kūdōka* (hollowing
out, or deindustrialization), the same whirlwind of forces that helped roll
back manufacturing employment in the United States in the 1970s and
1980s. *Ekonomisuto*, a well-respected weekly magazine of economic
analysis, devoted a special section to the issue in 1993.[58]

Concerns about *kūdōka* are not without foundation. In 1993, for the
first time ever, Japan became a net importer of TV sets, VCRs, and
refrigerators, most of which were produced by Japanese affiliates in
Asia.[59] This prompted a turf-conscious MITI in 1995 to introduce a trio of
bills to provide low-cost loans and special tax breaks to labor-intensive
industries facing cutbacks, as well as to small and medium-sized firms
trying to launch new high-tech ventures in Japan.[60]

In reality, though, the government does not expect *kūdōka* to pose any
significant, long-run threat. In its 1993–94 white paper on the economy,
the Economic Planning Agency (EPA) suggested that "economic
efficiency and expansion will be promoted if [Japan] can shift economic
resources freed by the increase in direct investment to more value-added
sectors. Therefore, it is important to deepen the interdependence with
Asian countries and to make the trade and industrial structure more
value-added."[61] *Kūdōka*, the agency contended, is manageable.

Thus far, the EPA appears to be right. Despite the explosion of FDI
that began in the mid 1980s, overseas activity still accounts for only 7.4
percent of Japan's total manufacturing output – a molehill, albeit a
growing one, compared to an American mountain of 25.1 percent.[62] And
the manufacturing investment that *has* flowed into Asia has not
jeopardized the scale merit of domestic industries, according to nearly
90 percent of the Japanese firms responding to a survey.[63] Capital stock in
Japan's domestic industries continued to expand even during the lean
years of the early 1990s – a sign that manufacturers planned to stay busy
at home, at least for a while, and not pack up all their plants and move
offshore.[64]

But even if Japanese manufacturers did dramatically step up the pace
of overseas investment, *kūdōka* would not necessarily follow. Japanese
FDI, as we have demonstrated, is not like American FDI. It does not
merely chase cheap labor for "outsourcing." Instead, it pursues a global
strategy to achieve economies of scope and scale by building or
maintaining an intrafirm or intraindustry division of labor, a strategy that
is, more often than not, tied tightly to the domestic interests of a very
Japan-centered MNC.

Rather than *kūdōka*, Japanese manufacturers in Asia actually are
promoting what some have called *kōdōka*, an upgrading of Japan's technological capacity and thus its industrial efficiency. Although they are

turning over less sophisticated production processes to related firms in Bangkok and Beijing, Japanese parent firms in Tokyo and Osaka are not following the lead of their American counterparts in places like New York and Pittsburgh. They are not, in other words, using freed-up resources to finance moves into real estate and retailing. Instead, they are using those resources to assume more sophisticated production duties at home.[65]

"Many American computer companies use circuit boards from Taiwan for their computers," says Aikawa Tadashi, executive managing director of Matsushita Electric Industrial Corp. "But we think they are the most important component, so of course we make them ourselves."[66]

For years, the Japanese government has encouraged labor and capital-intensive manufacturers to move all or part of their production to Asia "so that Japan can concentrate on high technology and knowledge intensive industries."[67] More recently, it has urged parent firms to spin off low and medium-tech production, but to hang on to the production of the highest value-added inputs.[68] Japanese MNCs have complied. In the hard economic times of the early 1990s, semiconductor manufacturers, for example, shifted production of less advanced 1 megabyte and 4 megabyte chips to overseas affiliates, allowing their domestic facilities to concentrate on the production of 16 megabyte chips, the next generation of dynamic random-access memory chips.[69] By pursuing such a strategy, Japanese high-tech manufacturers have benefited themselves and, in the process, have retooled and revitalized the Japanese economy as a whole.

To understand the difference between *kūdōka* and *kōdōka*, we need only compare the sales of US and Japanese affiliates in Asia's electric machine industries. Both are export-oriented, but while American affiliates sell as much as three-fifths of their output back to the United States, the Japanese affiliates sell less than a quarter of their output back to Japan.[70] And while US electronics firms in Asia export a negligible amount to Japan, the Japanese firms in Asia export a substantial amount to North America – an average of $1.47 billion a year, or 10 percent of total sales, from 1990 through 1993. Another 5 percent is exported to Europe.[71]

In other words, Japanese high-technology firms in Asia, unlike their American counterparts in the region, do not live and die on reverse imports to the home market. Instead, they mix things up, tapping more and more into the growing markets of East and Southeast Asia while continuing to penetrate deeply into the already developed markets of the West.[72]

Studies highlight the fact that Western consumers remain important targets for Japanese MNCs operating in Asia. In a 1993 survey conducted by the Research Institute on Overseas Investment, an arm of Japan's Export-Import Bank, respondents with production bases in Southeast Asia and China said they expected to dramatically increase their reliance on exports to the United States and Canada over the following decade.[73] And in a 1994 survey by the Japan Machinery Exporters Association, 52 percent of the respondents said they viewed their Asian factories as platforms from which to export manufactured goods to North America and Europe. Fifty-six percent projected that, by 1998, they would be operating with that strategy in mind.[74]

Our research confirmed that Japanese high-tech firms in the region are continuing to look West. Of the electronic machinery it produces in Asia, Sony ships two-thirds to North America and Europe.[75] Sixty percent of the copiers and bubble jet printers produced at Canon's expanded facility in Thailand are exported to North America.[76] Minebea, which enjoys a virtual monopoly on the production of precision ball bearings for computers, exports almost everything it manufactures at its huge plants in Singapore and Thailand. Eighty percent of the output goes to the United States and Europe.[77] Sanyo, which used to produce all its America-bound VCRs in Japan, now ships 700,000 VCRs a year to North America from its new factory in Cimanggis Borgor, Indonesia.[78] In the late 1980s, Sharp shipped 500,000 TV sets a year to North America and Europe from its facility in Malaysia – a practice that was attacked by some European governments as dumping.[79]

All told, Japanese capital and technology is transforming Asia into a powerful export center. In 1985, the four Asian NICs and the ASEAN-4 accounted for only 12 percent of world exports. By 1993, their share had climbed to 19 percent, and was still rising. It was estimated to reach as high as 23 percent in 1998. And that includes neither Japan's massive contribution, nor China's increasingly significant one.[80]

Even the Philippines, until now the wayward child in the family of rapidly expanding Asian economies, is beginning to join the club. The government announced that electronic exports in 1994 climbed 54 percent above the previous year's total, thanks largely to Japanese manufacturers operating in that country.[81] Thailand's case is perhaps the most dramatic. In 1986, it exported computers and other office machines valued at $60 million. Seven years later, in 1993, the value of such exports had increased about 47 times, to $2.82 billion. The value of its exports of televisions, washing machines, and other household appliances soared even higher (200-fold), from $11.8 million to $2.36 billion.[82]

But this is only half of the story. The other half, which is far more revealing, has to do with the structural change in the composition of Thai exports to the United States and Japan. In 1985, technology-intensive goods represented only a small share of total manufactured exports to both countries: 15.9 percent in the case of the United States, and 19.7 percent in the case of Japan. By 1989, however, the share of technology-intensive products in Thailand's total package of manufactured exports to the United States had doubled to 32.7 percent. In contrast, the share of such goods in the total package of exports to Japan had increased only marginally, to 23.5 percent.[83]

What we are describing, then, is a pattern of triangular trade in which Japanese firms export high-technology machinery and parts to Asian countries, where they are assembled into final products for reexport to relatively affluent markets in the West, especially the United States. The pattern serves to obscure the actual size of Japan's trade surplus with America. Here's how. Although billions of dollars in reexports sail across the ocean to the United States from Japanese-affiliated or Japanese-related factories in Asia each year, they never show up on the ledger of trade flows between the two countries. "It's fruitless to look at trade on a bilateral basis," argues Kenneth S. Courtis, senior economist at Deutsche Bank Capital Markets (Asia) Ltd. "You've got to look at how Japan has harnessed Asia."[84] Owing to the capital and technology it has invested in its regional production alliance since the mid 1980s, Courtis estimates that Japan has managed to slough off to Asia as much $15 billion of its annual trade surplus with the United States.[85]

Triangular trade has reinforced, perhaps even cemented, America's role as an absorber of Asia's exports. In 1980, the four dragons (or NICs) shipped 21.4 percent of their exports to the United States, and 15.5 percent to Japan. By 1994, they were exporting a larger share (23.3 percent) to the United States and a much smaller share (9.0 percent) to Japan. Both the ASEAN-4 and China experienced a similar flip-flop. The share of ASEAN-4 exports going to the United States rose from 17.5 percent in 1980 to 22.2 percent in 1993, while the share going to Japan fell from 37 percent to 18.6 percent. The share of China's exports going to the United States climbed sharply, from 5.4 percent to 17.7 percent, while the share going to Japan dropped from 22.2 percent to 17.8 percent.[86]

While Japan has enjoyed a bilateral trade surplus with almost all the countries of Asia, the United States has had to cope with a series of trade deficits. Added together, they came to more than $135 billion in 1994 – nearly six times the $18.1 billion deficit the United States had with Asia (including Japan) in 1980. The dire consequences of such a growing trade shortfall are obvious. Unless corrected, it could cost the American economy as many as 700,000 jobs by 2000.[87]

Some Japanese have begun to recognize this danger. For example, Miura Akihiko, editorial columnist for Japan's *Asahi shinbun*, says *endaka* actually has served to undermine the American – not the Japanese – economy "by making Asia a base from which to export to the United States." Such a trading pattern "cannot continue," he concludes. "The United States will not be able to bear the pressure of this development."[88]

How did this triangular pattern of trade come into being? Far from evolving on its own through market forces, some people believe it was carefully crafted by Japanese government and business leaders. John Stern, head of the American Electronics Association, is one such person. He says Japan is trying to appease the United States by disguising the fact that it is the actual source of an Asian *tsunami* of high-technology exports. It is playing what he calls "an export shell game."[89]

In 1986 and in 1992, MITI urged Japanese manufacturers to transfer some production activities to Asia as a way of trimming Japan's trade surplus with the West.[90] And Japanese officials have tried to promote the region's export-oriented manufacturing industries. As we mentioned in chapter ten, MITI has tried to help local manufacturers in Southeast Asia who are struggling to meet new quality standards for exports to Europe.[91] And as we mentioned in chapter eight, JETRO has studied the feasibility of enlisting Malaysia to replace Japan as the primary site for the production of standardized computer peripherals, such as keyboards and monitors, for the European and US markets.[92]

As Japan embraces Asia more and more tightly, using vertical quasi-integration to regionalize its developmentalism, the triangular pattern of trade we have described here will, we believe, become increasingly solidified. Thus far, the West seems unaware of or unconcerned about this possibility. But Japanese officials fear this state of ignorance and/or bliss will not last. "If East Asia becomes a quasi-Japan," says one MITI official, "the U.S. and Europe may confuse Asian products with Japanese products, causing unnecessary trade friction."[93]

CHAPTER TWELVE

Loosening the Knot

In November 1993, President Bill Clinton charged into Seattle like a hungry hunter who could smell his prey. As the host of the annual conference of Asia Pacific Economic Cooperation (APEC), a loosely organized forum representing 18 nations, he viewed this meeting – and APEC in general – as an unparalleled opportunity to plant the United States more deeply, more securely into the world's most economically fertile region.

No one can blame him for having such high expectations. The Asia-Pacific economy, including Japan, is growing so rapidly that, according to one estimate, it will be 15 percent larger than the American economy by the turn of the century.[1] Even such an optimistic forecast may prove to be an underestimate if the NICs and ASEAN-4 keep expanding as rapidly as they have over the past decade, and China continues to maintain its surprisingly high rate of economic growth. Toss in Vietnam and Laos, which are just beginning to open and build up their economies, and the region's future appears even more promising. One would have to be a fool to sit out this dance.

At the same time, though, one would have to be a fool to think APEC is America's ticket to the ball.[2] The economies of Asia are indeed becoming increasingly intertwined. But the thread that is sewing them together is not APEC, nor any other formal body or treaty. It is, to a large extent, Japanese developmentalism. Japan is regionalizing a dense web of mutually reinforcing ties – between government and business, between independent firms, and between management and labor.

Japanese bureaucrats use ODA (or, more generally, "economic cooperation"); Japanese manufacturers use FDI (including the intermediate
forms, such as technology licensing). And the two work together to vertically quasi-integrate the economies of Asia into a Japanese-dominated
high-technology production alliance.

This alliance poses an enormous challenge not only for outsiders, but
also for some insiders. The former, we suspect, have little or no idea what
they are up against. The latter, we fear, have only a vague idea what they
have gotten themselves into.

Outsiders, including American, European and even independent
Asian firms, face growing competition from integrated firms that are well
equipped with Japanese capital and Japanese technology. Lacking
sufficient knowledge, they run the risk of choosing inappropriate
business strategies, or of failing to muster the resolve needed to compete
effectively. Insiders, including Asian firms that supply low value-added
parts to Japanese multinationals in the region, may find themselves
squeezed on prices in the future, but unable to peddle their goods
anywhere else. They too lack knowledge.

Fortunately, useful information about the likely costs and benefits of
Japan's emerging production alliance in Asia is readily available. The
regional alliance is coordinated by the same government–business
network that has dominated Japanese society for half a century. And it is
based on the same set of developmentalist policies and practices that has
informed Japan's domestic political economy since World War II. In
other words, we already have a model to examine.

Japanese developmentalism (the home-based version) has generated
huge – but less and less evenly distributed – benefits. It was this system
that enabled Japan to realize its dream of becoming an *ittokoku*, or first-
class nation. Under developmentalism, innovating manufacturers rapidly
increased their productive capacities, turned to exports, and began
achieving dynamic technological efficiency. Government lent a very
visible hand by allocating low-cost capital to selected industries and firms,
offering subsidies, blocking manufactured imports, loosely enforcing the
antimonopoly law, and using "administrative guidance" to promote
saving, adopt new technology, and increase exports. Finally, the largest
firms created and maintained *keiretsu* networks – the quasi-integration of
subordinate firms by dominant firms – to rapidly increase the international competitiveness of Japanese high-tech industries.

But what about the costs of Japanese developmentalism? Cooperation
between government and business has, in recent years, turned collusive,
even corrosive. Newspapers in Tokyo now seem filled with stories about
ham-handed bureaucrats, corrupt politicians, and influence-peddling
business executives. More importantly, government policies to promote

dynamic technological efficiency have led to a dual economic structure, one characterized by technology-intensive, export-oriented firms at the top and a far greater number of labor-intensive, domestic-oriented firms at the bottom. In addition, cooperation between members of Japanese *keiretsu* has proved exclusionary, and thus highly controversial.

Foreign firms pay a stiff price whenever they try to export high-technology goods to Japan or set up local manufacturing plants. Statistics show that Japan is still an outlier in both of these areas.[3] But the Japanese themselves may bear the greatest cost. They are the ones who must endure high consumer prices, inadequate housing, and other anomalies of life in a country with such a high per capita GNP.

Despite nagging, even mounting complaints from sources both outside and inside Japan, developmentalism persists. This is because it is a system of policies and practices now deeply ingrained in the Japanese political economy. It has become a solid structure of incentives that resists change, even though it has outlived its usefulness.

Japan's government–business network hopes to revitalize this embattled, anachronistic system by expanding and exporting it to Asia. In the process, the same set of benefits and, alas, costs will follow.

For Asian firms, the benefits of developmentalism via quasi-integration are large, especially in the early stage of network formation. That is when these firms receive invaluable infusions of capital, technology, and managerial guidance. The contributions being made by the Japanese government, including ODA, also help increase these gains. Even though we have begun to see evidence of unequal cooperation, the production alliance now emerging in Asia is still in its early stages; the benefits it is producing for Asian economic growth still exceed the costs it is imposing. If we use only a short-run perspective, as neoclassical economists so often do, we are likely to be quite impressed by these benefits.

Eventually, however, we must expect that embraced firms in Asia will become captive ones – much like low-level subcontractors in a vertical *keiretsu* in Japan. In other words, what had been a beneficial alliance will prove increasingly costly as Asian firms and economies find themselves stuck in a subordinate role and as more and more of the gains of cooperation are captured by Japanese firms that, faced with the prospect of slower growth, become even less willing or able to transfer technology.

There are two mechanisms by which Asian firms may become stuck. The first has to do with asset specificity, which we discussed in chapter three. Since most of the physical and human capital of the subordinate firm is dedicated to maintaining its relationship with the dominant firm, the subordinate firm is exposed to constant demands regarding price, quality, and time. The dominant firm, in other words, is able to squeeze the subordinate firm as it strives to increase its profitability and international competitiveness. The subordinate firm often has little choice but to bow to the pressure if it wishes to maintain the value of its assets and continue benefiting from its ongoing relationship with the dominant partner. In the real world, as opposed to the land of make-believe in neoclassical theory, transactions quite often revolve around dedicated assets (or hostages), and more often than not take place between firms of unequal bargaining power.

In addition, Asian firms may find themselves stuck in a subordinate position if their own governments become captives of Tokyo. That is, they may find their own governments adopting policies that benefit Japanese capital more than local capital. We saw this in the case of Japanese-funded "economic cooperation" projects that promoted the interests of *keiretsu* suppliers moving from Japan into Asia.

The net result, we fear, is that Asian economies will become, like subordinate firms in the Japanese production alliance, so technologically dependent on Japan that they can only be called captive economies.

The other costs associated with this production alliance will be borne by outsiders. These include Western multinationals trying to set up operations in Asia, as well as Western nations that run up increasingly large trade deficits with members of the alliance.

What can be done to minimize these costs?

First of all, Western high-technology firms must find a way to penetrate this Japanese-dominated alliance. For the most part, they will have to do it the old-fashioned way – by being as efficient and as competitive as possible. We recommend two strategic moves. First, Western firms should enter into more alliances of their own with local (non-Japanese) firms in Asia. General Electric already has done this, linking arms with Korea's Samsung Group to produce medical imaging equipment in competition with Hitachi.[4] Combining their own technical skills with the marketing know-how and political savvy of well-established local firms, Western manufacturers can establish solid footholds in this region.[5] Second, these firms should form their own regionwide production networks, setting up facilities according to the different endowments of the host countries. Nestlé, the Swiss food giant, has shown that a Western firm (albeit one that does not produce cars or electronic goods) is capable of adopting such a strategic approach to investment. It sells breakfast cereals from its facility in the Philippines, where there is plenty of corn; chocolate drinks from its facility in Malaysia, where there is plenty of cocoa; and so on.

In forging their own alliances and building their own production networks, Western firms should avoid adopting the strategic policies and practices used by Japanese multinationals in the region. That is, they should resist the temptation to exert their power over subordinate firms in Asia, locking them into unequal relationships of quasi-integration.

Fortunately, American and European multinationals have done a comparatively good job of hiring local managers, using local suppliers, and transferring technology. Will they become less competitive by eschewing Japanese-style policies and practices in Asia? This depends upon whether local elites in the region acquire the political will to challenge those policies and practices, which in turn depends largely on whether local capital acquires enough technological competence and autonomy. Because we believe that, in the long run, Asia will manage to assert itself, we remain confident that Western MNCs will profit by pursuing what might be called "enlightened quasi-integration."

In the short run, though, the United States and European Union nations can help themselves, as well as Asia, by pushing the newly formed World Trade Organization (WTO) to adopt antitrust policies to regulate crossborder alliances.[6] Such policies are needed to combat anticompetitive behavior by multinationals, especially Japanese firms building *keiretsu*-like production networks in Asia. For example, the WTO should crack down on Japanese car makers that bar potential entrants by jointly manufacturing auto parts in Asia, as well as Japanese electronics firms that squeeze suppliers in the region by locking them into market-sharing agreements.

On a larger scale, Western governments could and should do much more to help their firms establish and maintain a presence in Asia. But sadly, members of the European Union seem preoccupied with their own regional affairs. Their investment in Asia has fallen far short of Japan's, and has not even kept pace with America's. Policymakers in Washington, meanwhile, have all but ignored this corner of the world. In fact, ever since the early 1970s, when it withdrew in humiliation from Vietnam, the United States has treated Asia almost like a leper, focusing instead on conflicts in the Middle East, Europe, and Latin America.

George Bush, a former ambassador to China, maintained this official attitude even though he had a historic opportunity to chart a new policy course in a post-Cold War world. Michael Oksensberg and Hong Ying Wang note that no one in any position of authority in that administration spoke Japanese, and that former Secretary of State James Baker spent more days in Mongolia on hunting expeditions than he spent in either Japan or China on official business. "Just as a business firm must invest in growth areas to protect its future, great powers secure their destiny not only by bringing peace and prosperity to problem areas but also by nurturing ties with regions of growing importance."[7]

We welcome the renewed interest in Asia expressed by the Clinton administration, but fear it is longer on rhetoric than substance. Even today, as a new century approaches, the United States seems to drift along without a coherent, well-thought-out policy toward Asia. This drift, we suspect, is due to the fact that the president has not assembled a team of advisers capable of understanding the political economies of Asia, and thus capable of devising a long-range strategy to promote American interests in the region. Ron Brown, the former Democratic Party chief turned commerce secretary, and Mickey Kantor, the Clinton campaign coordinator turned trade representative, are successful lawyers, skilled technocrats, competent problem-solvers. But they lack what Bush used to call "the vision thing."[8] The state department is filled with China experts, as well as security specialists, but has precious few policy aides who can decipher either a Japanese newspaper or a regression analysis.

The central focus of US foreign policy toward Asia should shift from China to Japan, and the central goal of that policy should be acquiring and maintaining economic security, not military power. Although more than a million US troops were stationed in Asia during the Vietnam War, nearly 100,000 remain there today.[9] Barring some regional conflict, this presence should prove sufficient. The United States must resist the temptation to always the play the role of regional policeman. One could even argue that the US military presence in Asia has propped up authoritarian regimes that are fundamentally more compatible with Japan's bureaucratic–industrial complex than with American business interests. In any case, the United States is losing its moral authority in the region because it is viewed increasingly as an economic weakling that blames other countries for its own shortcomings. It cannot afford to continue frittering away valuable fiscal and human resources.

The United States also runs the risk of diluting its influence in Asia by constantly demanding that other governments in the region behave according to its own ethical standards. We do not mean to imply here that human rights are unimportant, or that they must always be subjected to US commercial interests. Rather, we believe the United States must flex its muscles more effectively, more skillfully, and perhaps more selectively. In the spring of 1994, the Clinton administration was threatening to close American markets to Chinese goods unless Beijing improved its human rights record, was criticizing Singapore for caning an American teenager accused of vandalism, and was pushing Indonesia to grant more rights to workers in that country.

"A series of American measures, threatened or employed, risk corroding our positive image in the region, giving ammunition to those charging that we are an international nanny, if not bully," wrote Winston Lord, the top US official on East Asian affairs, in a confidential memo to the secretary of state.[10] Lord was right. And so was Clinton when he eased up on his threat against China. The United States can be much more effective as an engaged member of the region's political community than as a heckler standing on the sidelines.

The United States must, however, continue to push Japan to open up its markets, not only to American merchandise and capital exports but also to Asian exports. This, we acknowledge, is a high-risk strategy. The relationship between the United States and Japan is the most important bilateral relationship in the world today. If it splinters, a more exclusive, inward-looking regionalism becomes possible in Asia. On the other hand, if the United States and Asia continue to serve only as consumers of Japanese high-technology goods, neither stands much chance of really prospering.

The Clinton administration has adopted an aggressive trade policy toward Japan, a policy we generally have supported. At the same time, however, it has agreed in principle to an APEC plan under which the United States and other developed countries belonging to the group would remove barriers to intra-APEC trade by 2010, while developing countries in the organization would lower those barriers a decade later. This, we believe, is unwise. It shows again that Western policymakers – in this case, the Americans – do not understand the nature of Japan's developmentalism, which uses exclusionary relationships more often than explicit government policies to bar unwanted imports.[11] The APEC plan would do little if anything to open the Japanese market, but quite a lot to open the US market to high-tech exports from Japanese-dominated production networks in Asia. In the end, we believe it would exacerbate the triangular trade pattern we described in chapter eleven.

The United States has other, better alternatives. It could, for example, capitalize on the North American Free Trade Agreement, using Mexico as a production platform from which US multinationals could export to third countries, including Japan.[12] Japan, as we have shown, has used Asia in much the same way. As long as US parent firms supply the capital goods and high-tech parts to their affiliates in Mexico, skills and jobs in the United States should increase, not decrease.

In general, the US government must become more active in helping American firms, especially small and medium-sized manufacturers, export to Asia as well as set up and maintain overseas operations there. The Clinton administration has already taken some small steps in this direction. But trade missions are not enough. The public and private sectors must work more closely together to promote US economic interests in Asia. Dollars can help. The US Export-Import Bank could, for example, do more to help finance the sale of American high-technology products in Asia.[13]

As nebulous as it sounds, however, the greatest contribution the US government could make to promote America's economic interests in Asia would be to put its own fiscal house in order. The US budget deficit sucks up personal savings that could be used to finance long-term investments, including business ventures in Asia. And while they're at it, American policymakers should make a much more serious effort to coordinate US macroeconomic policy with Japan's. In the 1980s, Japan pursued a policy of easy money and fiscal retrenchment, while the United States indulged in a deficit-financed expansion. The legacies of that decade include a grotesquely swollen US debt and a prolonged recession in Japan. Such a calamity need never be repeated.

As for Japan, we hope – perhaps in vain – that its government–business network will unilaterally end its drive to regionalize the nation's developmentalist policies and practices. There are, of course, prominent voices in Tokyo arguing, as we do, that Japan would foster a more stable global economy by loosening government regulations and business ties that conspire to close its economy. The *Asahi* newspaper represents one such voice. On the eve of an APEC summit meeting, it editorialized that Japan, after contributing heavily to Asia's rapid economic growth by exporting so much capital and technology to the region, must now focus on "correcting the distortions that resulted from that growth." "If Japan becomes a larger, more open market for Asian economies, then those economies will earn enough to allow them to import more from the United States."[14]

But this voice of reason has been all but drowned out by a rising chorus of resentment toward the West. Perhaps for the first time since World War II, Japan is speaking out, charting a more independent policy course – at least in Asia.[15] This, by itself, should be welcomed, not condemned. What troubles us is that Japan's new nationalism is linked to a sentimental and patronizing notion of "Asianism" that appears to be defined only in contrast with an equally vague conception of "Western" values.[16]

A commission set up by the Japanese government made this East–West distinction in a report to the Economic Planning Agency.

> While Asian countries appreciate the role that the United States and the European countries have assigned to Asia, we fully recognize that Western values have negative aspects, and thus we strongly desire a role based on Asian values. For Japan, a member of Asia, to forfeit an Asian viewpoint and behave in a manner based on an American and European centered belief system, causes a variety of uneasy responses from other Asian countries.[17]

Speaking to Japanese and Korean scholars, Nukazawa Kazuo of Keidanren, the big-business federation in Japan, made a similar distinction, forecasting an ideological competition between Asian and Western styles of capitalism.

> In the years to come, we can expect to see a battle among alternate systems of capitalism. People will be asking, for instance, if the Japanese and Korean models can be applied to development in Asia and elsewhere, including the

former Soviet Union and Eastern Europe. At the same time, the kinds of efforts being made in Japan to humanize capitalism and make it a better system for international coexistence and co-prosperity will undoubtedly go forward in a variety of forms.[18]

We are not suggesting here that Japan is girding for war. Only a few right-wing extremists, such as Ishihara Shintaro, the coauthor of *The Japan that Can Say No* and (with Mahathir) *No to ieru Ajia* (*The Asia that Can Say "No"*), hold fast to the paranoid worldview that gripped Japan in the 1930s and 1940s.[19] Many others, though, have become extremely defensive, even combative in the face of mounting criticism. They say the West, especially the United States, is "bashing" Japan – as well as Asia – for refusing to conform to Western norms. Not surprisingly, newspapers and magazines have complained the loudest, publishing articles (such as one entitled "No More Japans! Japan and the US Policy of Beating Up on South Korea and Taiwan!") suggesting that the United States, unlike Japan, acts unfairly toward the region.[20]

Perched on a couch in his spacious office in the center of Tokyo, Sakakibara Eisuke, deputy director general of the international finance bureau of Japan's Ministry of Finance, expresses this new Asianism in a firm but dispassionate tone.

> The Asia-Pacific region has become increasingly important to us. That is why we are doing so much to promote economic development there. Without forcing our ideas on anyone, Japan has supplied much needed capital and technical assistance. The US, on the other hand, has become almost belligerent in its efforts to impose the laissez faire principle on others. These efforts are, I believe, quite counterproductive – as witnessed by the declining presence of the United States in Asia. But the US really should withdraw further – not only for its own sake, but also for the sake of Asia. Just look at the effects of US economic influence in the Philippines, where American firms have invested most heavily. It's a disaster.[21]

Sakakibara, a Harvard graduate, believes Japan is destined to replace the United States as the principal leader in Asia. This view is quite common in Japan.

Ishiyama Yoshihide, a former MOF official who later joined IBM Japan as economic research director, has written that Japan can do little to promote peace and stability in areas such as Eastern Europe and the Middle East. "It is only on the East Asian stage that Japan can seriously take part in the process of building a new international order." Ishiyama says Japan should "move toward the targeting of areas for the promotion of trade and investment, the formulation of procedures to eliminate trade barriers, and the formation of a council that would meet regularly to discuss such regional issues as trade, investment, macroeconomic policy and the settlement of disputes."[22] Even the mild-mannered economist Nakatani Iwao has asserted that Japan must step out of America's diplomatic shadow and begin serving as an economic "coordinator" in Asia by "making the basic groundrules and eliminating the fundamental conflicts of ideology."[23]

Japanese officials have already taken it upon themselves to represent the economic interests of the NICs and ASEAN at G-7 summit meetings. With both pride and scorn, they have frequently noted that Japan, unlike the United States, continues to classify NIC exports under the Generalized System of Preferences, which calls for lower duties on commodities from developing countries.[24] And as a payback, they called on Asian leaders to join them in fighting America's results-oriented trade policy, a radical approach that would have required Japan and others to commit to setting aside a fixed percentage of their markets for American products.[25]

Evidence of Japan's new assertiveness in Asia can be found in its growing support for Mahathir's proposal for an East Asian Economic Caucus. When it was first announced, the government feared the proposal would alienate the United States, and thus opposed it. More recently, though, it has warmed to the idea. FAIR, a think tank established by MOF, is even trying to mobilize NGOs (nongovernmental organizations) in the region to support it.[26] And some government officials, such as Sakakibara, have begun to question the apparent hypocrisy of US policy advocating a North American Free Trade Area that does not include any East or Southeast Asian nations, while opposing an East Asian Economic Caucus that does not include any North American nations. "There's absolutely nothing wrong with the concept of Asian countries banding together to help one another. Japan would never ask to be included in a US alliance with Latin America. So why should the US expect to be included in a Japanese alliance with Asia?"[27]

While uncommonly frank, Sakakibara is no crackpot. In fact, he is a leading representative of Japan's government–business network, which is embracing Asia in a conscious effort to rescue its embattled developmentalism. We cannot expect this network to change on its own.

But some scholars, notably Ernst, remain hopeful, arguing that a series of structural pressures will force Japanese multinationals to open up what have otherwise been closed production networks in Asia.[28] These pressures include the ongoing appreciation of the yen, reduced domestic demand, rising labor costs in Asia, and increased competition from rivals setting up their own production networks in the region. Having watched Japanese high-tech firms meet even tougher challenges at home in the 1970s and 1980s, we are convinced that Japanese MNCs will be able to overcome these challenges. In fact, we believe that vertical quasi-integration will allow these multinationals to cope more effectively than their rivals with difficult problems such as overcapacity and rising production costs.

We are much more inclined to agree with Ernst on another point he makes, one that seems to fundamentally contradict his generally sanguine assessment. He suggests that the process of opening up the Japanese production networks in Asia will be "painfully slow and difficult," and that Japanese MNCs themselves are likely to pursue "defensive rearguard strategies." For this reason, Ernst asserts, and we agree, that host country governments in Asia may end up having to pry open these networks by force.[29]

With this in mind, we humbly offer some recommendations to the governments of Asia. Our greatest concern here is to ensure that their economies do not become captive members of a Japanese production alliance. Avoiding that fate, we concede, also happens to be in the interest of the West.

First, Southeast Asian nations, in particular, must do more to increase their own technological capacities. This means investing wisely in education, and creating stronger links between public research facilities, particularly universities, and private industry.

Asian governments should also follow the example of Japan in the 1950s and 1960s by reviewing technology agreements before they are signed. Although this might discourage some foreign firms from proposing tie-ups in the first place, and thus might reduce overall opportunities for technology transfer, we are convinced that an effective review program would improve the bargaining position of local firms, allowing them to gain better agreements with fewer restrictive provisions.

Although Asian governments have adopted measures designed to promote supporting industries, they have often ended up providing assistance to foreign suppliers trying to establish domestic facilities, rather than domestically owned suppliers. Financial incentives should be reserved for the latter. Some countries, such as Thailand, Singapore, and Malaysia, are trying to broker tie-ups between foreign and local parts manufacturers. This is a worthy goal, but perhaps an overly ambitious one. These governments might do better to rewrite some of their own investment incentive policies that allow large foreign assemblers to import manufactured parts without paying full tariff rates. Policies such as these discriminate against local suppliers.[30]

In general, the incentives offered by competing countries in Asia have done little for their own economies except create a bidding war for FDI. In most of the cases they examined, Alburo, Bautista, and Gochoco found that foreign investment was neither directly nor indirectly related to the incentive package offered by the host government. They criticized Southeast Asian regimes for allowing redundancy to creep into their incentive systems.[31] Here, too, policy coordination would curb tax holidays and other unnecessary give-aways.

Some Western observers smugly contend that history is on their side. They note that Japan engendered local hostility by brutally occupying Korea for 35 years, bullying China for more than two decades, and incorporating most of Southeast Asia into its oppressive Greater East Asia Co-Prosperity Sphere during World War II. Asia, according to these observers, will resist any Japanese campaign to set up a production alliance that it dominates.

In the case of Northeast Asia, where officials have watched – sometimes in horror, sometimes in disgust – as their Japanese counterparts have tried to justify Japan's past misdeeds, the region's only economic superpower does seem to carry a heavy burden of history. Ding Xinghao of the Shanghai Institute of International Studies expresses a common sentiment in China. "Japan's view is always a flying geese formation with Japan as the head goose. Our memories are long, so we aren't about to fly in Japan's formation."[32]

Despite public criticism, however, Chinese, Korean, and Taiwanese elites continue to cooperate closely with their Japanese counterparts. And elites in Southeast Asia, where authoritarian regimes have openly tried to adopt features of Japanese developmentalism, tend to be even more positive.[33] Noordin Sopiee, director general of the Institute of Strategic and International Studies in Malaysia, says no nation in that part of the world wishes to halt the steady progress toward what he has called "Pax Nipponica," or an "East Asian mutual benefit zone" dominated by Japan. "All welcome it and lay out the red carpet."[34]

We must acknowledge, then, that Japan is moving quickly to stake its claim to Asia. But we should also recognize that the region has not yet fully complied. In fact, despite the lure of Japanese capital and technology, and despite the attractiveness of the Japanese model of economic development, there are a growing number of signs that Asians are not comfortable with their subordinate role in the production alliance now taking shape in the region. Steven Wong, the former head of the Center for Japan Studies at the Institute of Strategic and International Studies in Malaysia, conveyed these misgivings in an interview with an American reporter. "Japan was supposed to be the engine of growth," he complained. "But instead of making Malaysia richer, we're making Japan richer."[35]

Wong is not alone. Government officials and business executives all over the region fear that, before too long, their economies will be smothered in Japan's embrace. They hope that the United States, a potentially strong, countervailing influence, will remain economically engaged here.

In 1992, during an American president's rare visit to Asia, prime minister Goh Chok Tong of Singapore called on the United States to be "a partner in our economies to help balance the growing presence of Japan."[36] And in an interview with a US reporter, Thailand's former prime minister, Chatchai Choonhavan, was even more blunt: "You Americans don't compete enough with the Japanese. I don't want our children speaking only Japanese. I want them to speak English."[37]

Asia, then, is still open for business. At least for now. But if Western high-technology manufacturers wait too long to set up shop in this fast-growing corner of the world, they may miss an unparalleled opportunity. Japan's production alliance could leave them out in the cold.

Notes

Preface

1 Howard K. Beale, *Theodore Roosevelt and the Rise of America to World Power* (New York: Collier Books, 1962), p. 80. It is worth noting here that General Douglas MacArthur also invoked this metaphor during the Allied occupation of Japan, except that he cast it in racial rather than national terms. MacArthur called the Pacific "an Anglo-Saxon lake": see *New York Times*, 2 March 1949, quoted in Allen S. Whiting, *China Crosses the Yalu: The Decision to Enter the Korean War* (Stanford: Stanford University Press, 1968), p. 39.

2 The estimate by Gus Hooke, a former economist at the International Monetary Fund, puts Asia's share at 57 percent: *Asian Wall Street Journal*, 14 January 1993, p. 3. The concept of a "Pacific Century" (and, more specifically, why we should anticipate its arrival) is discussed in Mark Borthwick, *Pacific Century: The Emergence of Modern Pacific Asia* (Boulder: Westview Press, 1992), pp. 507–45, and Nihon Keizai Shinbun-sha (ed.), *Shin-Nihon keizai* (*New Japanese Economy*) (Tokyo: Nihon Keizai Shinbunsha, 1989), pp. 278–303.

3 Paul Maidment, "The Yen Block: A New Balance in Asia?", *The Economist*, 15 July 1989, pp. 5–6.

4 Frankel's gravity model is examined again in chapter three. Jeffrey Frankel, "Is Japan Creating a Yen Bloc in East Asia and the Pacific?" in Jeffrey Frankel and Miles Kahler (eds), *Regionalism and Rivalry: Japan and the U.S. in Pacific Asia* (Chicago: University of Chicago Press, 1993); Jeffrey Frankel, "Is a Yen Bloc Forming in Pacific Asia?" in Richard O'Brien (ed.), *Finance and the International Economy: The AMEX Bank Review Prize Essays* (Oxford: Oxford University Press, 1991).

5 Gary Saxonhouse, "Pricing Strategies and Trading Blocs in East Asia" in Frankel and Kahler (eds), *Regionalism and Rivalry*, p. 105.

205

6 A central theme of this book is that neoclassical economic theory, by ignoring institutions and exogenizing the variable of technological change, does not go far enough. The models used by Frankel and Saxonhouse, which we believe are ill-equipped to fully survey the extent of Japan's economic influence in Asia, exemplify this shortcoming. Others share our view. In a critique of Frankel's argument, Robert Z. Lawrence notes that "in a few sectors, particularly machinery and electronics, there is more evidence that *keiretsu* activities are particularly strong. In these industries, there appears to be an extensive and growing network associated with the activities of Japanese firms." Robert Z. Lawrence, "Comment," in ibid., p. 86. And Robert Gilpin complains that Saxonhouse has failed to address the most interesting question: "whose trade and what trade are benefiting from the increasing economic and institutional ties in the region that are created by Japanese investment and ODA flows." Gilpin already has a partial answer. "We know that Japanese firms control the production and trade in almost all high-tech industries such as automobiles and consumer electronics." This fact, he says, is "a datum point that is as important as Saxonhouse's gross trade figures." Gilpin, ibid., p. 121.

7 Urata Shujiro, "Changing Patterns of Direct Investment and Implications for Trade and Investment" in C. Fred Bergsten and Marcus Noland (eds), *Pacific Dynamism and the International Economic System* (Washington: Institute for International Economics, 1993), p. 295.

8 Interview, 13 July 1992, Bangkok.

9 Mingsarn Santikarn Kaosà-ard, "Comparative Analysis of Direct Foreign Investment in Thailand," a paper for a conference sponsored by the Hoover Institution, Stanford University, on Japan and the Regionalization of Asia, March 1993, p. 17.

10 International Monetary Fund, *Direction of Trade Statistics Yearbook, 1992* (Washington: IMF, 1992), pp. 240–1.

11 The term "NICs" is synonymous with the term "NIEs" (newly industrializing economies), a piece of linguistical diplomacy designed to appease China, which claims sovereignty over Taiwan as well as Hong Kong.

12 The two other members of ASEAN are Singapore, which we generally refer to as one of the NICs, and Brunei, a tiny oil-producing country that has very little manufacturing capacity.

13 Masahiko Aoki, *Information, Incentives and Bargaining in the Japanese Economy* (Cambridge: Cambridge University Press, 1988); Iwao Nakatani, "The Economic Role of Financial Corporate Groupings" in Masahiko Aoki (ed.), *The Economic Analysis of the Japanese Firm* (Amsterdam: North-Holland, 1984); Michael Gerlach, *Alliance Capitalism: The Social Organization of Japanese Business* (Berkeley: University of California Press, 1992).

1 Crossing Borders: The Japanese Difference

1 Interview, 9 April 1993, Osaka.

2 Interview, 21 July 1992, Tokyo.

3 *Far Eastern Economic Review* (hereafter *FEER*), 6 June 1989, p. 53.

4 Takeshi Aoki, "Integration in the Asia Pacific Rim: Formation of Networks by Japanese Foreign Direct Investment as the Driving Force to Integrate," a paper for the third joint research conference on Asia-Pacific Relations sponsored by the Foundation for Advanced Information and Research (hereafter FAIR), 5–7 July 1992, Kuala Lumpur, p. 261.

5 Hisahiko Okazaki, "New Strategies Toward a 'Super Asian Bloc,'" *This Is* (Tokyo), August 1992, pp. 42–90. Reproduced in *Foreign Broadcast Information Service Daily Report: East Asia Supplement*, 7 October 1992, p. 18.

6 Besides Frankel and Urata (cited in the preface), see Edward M. Graham and Naoko T. Anzai, "The Myth of a De Facto Asian Economic Bloc: Japan's Foreign Direct Investment in East Asia," *Columbia Journal of World Business*, Vol. 24, No. 3 (Autumn 1994), pp. 6–20.

7 Japanese data are from Ministry of Finance (MOF), *Taigai chokusetsu tōshi no kyoka todokede jisseki* (*Statistics on the Approval/Notification of Overseas Direct Investment*) (Tokyo: Ministry of Finance Printing Bureau, 1978); and MOF, *Heisei roku-nen ni okeru taigai oyobi tainai chokusetsu tōshi jōkyō* (*The Status of Outward and Inward Direct Investment in 1994*) (Tokyo: MOF, June 1995). US data are from US Department of Commerce, Bureau of Economic Analysis, *U.S. Direct Investment Abroad, 1977*, April 1981, p. 46; and US Department of Commerce, Economics Statistics Administration and Bureau of Economic Analysis, *Survey of Current Business*, August 1995. We must sound a note of caution about comparing statistics, such as these, that are compiled using different methodologies. In general, US figures, based on estimated capital flows, tend to be more conservative than Japanese figures, which are based on information supplied to the government by private firms planning to invest overseas.

8 MOF, *Heisei roku-nen ni okeru taigai oyobi tainai chokusetsu tōshi jōkyō*, p. 2.

9 Planning Division, Office of the Board of Investment, Thailand, May 1992.

10 *Economist*, 7 May 1994, p. 73.

11 Interviews with Matsushita and Malaysian government officials, April 1993, Kuala Lumpur.

12 Shūkan Tōyō Keizai, Tōyō Keizai Shinpōsha, *Kaigai shinshutsu kigyō sōran, 1995* (*A Comprehensive Survey of Firms Expanding Overseas*) (Tokyo: Tōyō Keizai Shinpōsha, 1995), pp. 34–44.

13 MOF, *Heisei roku-nen ni okeru taigai oyobi tainai chokusetsu tōshi jōkyō*. In 1994, Japanese manufacturers planned to invest $4.9 billion in Asia. That represented 53 percent of all Japanese FDI in that region. By comparison, planned manufacturing investment in the same year represented only 27 percent of all Japanese FDI in North America, and only 30 percent in Europe.

14 MITI, *Chūshō kigyō hakusho* (*White Paper on Small and Medium-sized Enterprises*) (Tokyo: MOF Printing Office, 1995), p. 416.

15 In 1994, there were 6,632 Japanese affiliates in Asia, 3,417 in Europe, and 3,751 in the United States. See Tōyō Keizai Shinpōsha, *Kaigai shinshutsu kigyō sōran, 1995*.

16 ibid.

17 These banks do most of their business with Japanese customers. In Taiwan, for example, Dai-Ichi Kangyo, the leading foreign bank, conducts about 80 percent of its business with Japanese firms in that country, or with Taiwanese firms engaged in trade with Japan. See Chi Schive, "Japanese Investment in Taiwan," a paper for a conference sponsored by the Hoover Institution, Stanford University, on Japan and the Regionalization of Asia, March 1993, p. 11.

18 Institute of Developing Economies, *Investment Risk in Post-Deng China* (Tokyo: IDE, 1995), p. 32. By contrast, Jameson notes that US banks provide only 5 percent of all loans issued in Hong Kong: Sam Jameson, Los Angeles Times Service, "Japanese Investment Booming in South China," in *Honolulu Advertiser*, 26 December 1991, p. A23.

19 Tōru Nakakita, "The Globalization of Japanese Firms and Its Influence on Japan's Trade with Developing Nations," *The Developing Economies*, Vol. 26, No. 4 (December 1988), p. 310.

20 Matsui Mikio, *Nikkei sangyō shiriizu: jidōsha buhin* (*Nikkei Industry Series: Automobile Parts*) (Tokyo: Nihon Keizai Shinbunsha, 1988).

21 Japan Machinery Exporters Association, "Wagakuni kikai sangyō no Ajia ni okeru seisan bungyō jittai ni tsuite" ("The Actual State of Production and Division of Labor by Japanese Machine Industries Operating in Asia"), a survey, June 1994, p. 5. One hundred and forty-four firms responded to the survey, indicating they expected to produce $45.6 billion worth of electrical machinery at their Asian plants in 1994 – 41 percent more than they produced in 1992.

22 ibid.

23 *FEER*, 16 January 1992, p. 40.

24 *Nikkei Weekly*, 25 April 1992, p. 27.

25 ibid., p. 1; *Straits Times* (Singapore), 19 May 1994.

26 Interviews with Thai government officials, April 1993, Bangkok; *Nikkei Weekly*, 10 May 1993, p. 1; *Nikkei Weekly*, 1 November 1993, p. 1; *Shipping and Trade News* (Tokyo), 17 February 1994; *Nikkei Weekly*, 15 August 1994, p. 18; JETRO Bangkok, Economic Survey Group, "Tai e no tōshi dōkō o dō kangaeru ka" ("How Should We Consider the Trend in Investment in Thailand?"), 29 March 1993.

27 *Japan Digest*, 2 February 1995.

28 *Nikkei Weekly*, 15 August 1994.

29 Interviews with Malaysian and Singaporean government officials, April 1993, Kuala Lumpur and Singapore; *Straits Times*, 12 May 1992, p. 40; *Straits Times*, 19 May 1994; *Business Week*, 23 May 1994, p. 52.

30 China accounted for almost $2.6 billion of Japanese FDI in 1993. Measured in this way (by total value, rather than number, of investments), the country actually was the second leading recipient of Japanese investment – behind the United States: see MOF, *Heisei roku-nen ni okeru taigai oyobi tainai chokusetsu tōshi jōkyō*. But small manufacturers appear to be focusing on China more than any other country. And perhaps increasingly so. The research arm of Japan's Export-Import Bank found that most of the 382 Japanese firms it surveyed in 1994 were planning to invest in China over the medium to long run. Of those firms, 265 listed China as a leading candidate for FDI. The also-rans in this popularity contest were Vietnam (114), Thailand (92), the United States (85), and Indonesia (83): see Research Institute for Overseas Investment, *Kaitōken repōto* (*Overseas Investment Research Report*), Report No. 7–9, Export-Import Bank of Japan, 15 May 1995.

31 *Asian Wall Street Journal*, 7 January 1993, p. 5.

32 *Japan Times*, 28 July 1994.

33 *FEER*, 9 June 1994, p. 44.

34 *Nikkei Weekly*, 20 June 1994, p. 1; *Economist*, 24 April 1993, p. 33.

35 *Japan Times*, 3 February 1994.

36 *Financial Times*, 21 December 1992, p. 23.

37 *Asian Wall Street Journal*, 18 October 1993, p. 10.

38 See Carlos J. Moneta, "Japan and the North American Free Trade Agreement" in Craig G. Garby and Mary Brown Bullock (eds), *Japan: A New Kind of Superpower?* (Washington: Woodrow Wilson Center Press, 1994), pp. 101–20. Japanese firms invested only $53 million in Mexico in 1993, the year NAFTA was enacted. They invested four times that amount in the Philippines, the Asian country receiving the smallest share of Japanese FDI.

39 MITI, *Wagakuni kigyō no kaigai jigyō katsudō* (*The Overseas Business Activities of Japanese Firms*), No. 24 (Tokyo: MITI, 1995), pp. 134–5. These figures, calculated based on the exchange rate of ¥115/$1 then in effect (1993), are similar to those for 1992. But in 1991, Japanese affiliates in Asia outperformed their counterparts in the West by larger amounts. They earned profits of $3.25 billion, while Japanese affiliates in Europe and North America lost $808 million and $2.79 billion, respectively. These figures were calculated based on the exchange rate of ¥133/$1 then in effect (1991): MITI, *Wagakuni kigyō no kaigai jigyō katsudō*, No. 22 (Tokyo: MITI, 1993), p. 33.

40 *Asahi shinbun*, 3 January 1995, p. 7.

41 *Business Week*, 23 May 1994, p. 52; JETRO Bangkok, Economic Survey Group, *Tai e no tōshi dōkō o dō kangaeru ka*. The Export-Import Bank of Japan estimates that, in 1992, the reinvestment ratio was 45 percent for Japanese affiliates in the ASEAN countries and 38 percent for those in the NICs, but only 18 percent for North America and 17 percent for Europe. See Shigeki Tejima et al., "The Recent Trends of Japanese Foreign Direct Investment and Prospects in the 1990s Based on the Japanese Ex-Im Bank's Survey Implemented in FY 1993," *EXIM Review*, Research Institute for Overseas Investment, 1994.

42 *Asahi shinbun*, 10 April 1993.

43 Interview, 6 April 1993, Tokyo.

44 *Keidanren Review*, special issue, 1993, p. 8.

45 Piero Sraffa (ed.), *The Works and Correspondence of David Ricardo* (Cambridge: Cambridge University Press, 1951), pp. 289–90.

46 Bertil Ohlin, *Interregional and International Trade* (Cambridge, Mass.: Harvard University Press, 1933).

47 Stephen Hymer, *The International Operations of National Firms: A Study of Direct Foreign Investment* (Cambridge, Mass.: MIT Press, 1976).

48 Raymond Vernon, "International Investment and International Trade in the Product Cycle," *Quarterly Journal of Economics*, Vol. 80 (May 1966).

49 We should note, however, that British economist John Dunning, like Vernon, refused to completely discard the theory of comparative advantage in his effort to explain FDI. He hypothesized that firms relocate production to capitalize not just on firm-specific advantages, but also location-specific advantages, such as cost savings achieved by overcoming trade barriers, as well as relatively low labor costs and relatively high levels of technical competence in the host country. Among his many works see, for example, John Dunning, "Toward an Eclectic Theory of International Production: Some Empirical Tests," *Journal of International Business Studies*, Vol. 11 (Spring/Summer 1980).

50 Mark Casson, *Firm and the Market* (Cambridge, Mass.: MIT Press, 1987).

51 Kiyoshi Kojima, "Transfer of Technology to Developing Countries – Japanese Type versus American Type," *Hitotsubashi Journal of Economics*, Vol. 17 (February 1977), p. 6.

52 Kojima was not the only Japanese economist using the theory of comparative advantage, rather than one of industrial organization and firm-specific advantages, to explain Japanese FDI. Others included Terutomo Ozawa, *Multinational, Japanese Style: The Political Economy of Outward Dependency* (Princeton: Princeton University Press, 1979); Kunio Yoshihara, *Japanese Investment in Southeast Asia* (Honolulu: University Press of Hawaii, 1978); Sueo Sekiguchi, *ASEAN-Japan Relations: Investment* (Singapore: Institute of Southeast Asian Studies, 1983).

53 Kiyoshi Kojima, "Japanese and American Direct Investment in Asia: A

Comparative Analysis," *Hitotsubashi Journal of Economics*, Vol. 26 (June 1985), p. 32.

54 See, for example, Tien-Chen Chou, "American and Japanese Direct Foreign Investment in Taiwan: A Comparative Study," *Hitotsubashi Journal of Economics*, Vol. 29 (1988); and Jung Taik Hyun and Katherine Whitmore, "Japanese Direct Foreign Investment: Patterns and Implications for Developing Countries," The World Bank, Industry and Energy Development Working Paper, Industry Series Paper 1 (February 1989).

55 R. Hal Mason, "A Comment on Professor Kojima's 'Japanese Type versus American Type of Technology Transfer,'" *Hitotsubashi Journal of Economics*, Vol. 20 (February 1980).

56 John E. Roemer, *U.S.–Japanese Competition in International Markets: A Study of the Trade-Investment Cycle in Modern Capitalism* (Berkeley: Institute of International Studies, University of California, 1975).

57 These data come from MITI, *Wagakuni kigyō no kaigai jigyō katsudō* (*The Overseas Business Activities of Japanese Firms*), No. 7 (1978); and MITI, *Dai-gokai, kaigai jigyō katsudō kihon chōsa*, 1994 (*Basic Survey on Overseas Business Activities*), 5th edn (Tokyo: MOF Printing Office, 1994).

58 Interview, 20 April 1993, Bangkok.

59 Research Institute on Overseas Investment, "Nihon yushutsunyū ginkō yūshi shōdaku jōkyō to tōkei shiryō" ("Statistics on Loans Approved by the Export-Import Bank"), *Kaigai tōshi kenkyūjōhō* (*Report of the Research Institute on Overseas Investment*), Vol. 19, No. 5 (May 1993), p. 107; and Vol. 20, No. 5 (May 1994), p. 75.

60 In November 1993, MITI adopted new policies making it easier for small and medium-sized firms to set up factories overseas. See *FEER*, 31 March 1994, p. 55.

61 This is hardly a new assertion. See, for example, P. J. Buckley and R. D. Pearce, "Overseas Production and Exporting by the World's Largest Enterprises," *Journal of International Business Studies*, Vol. 10 (1979); Chee Peng Lim and P.P. Lee, *Japanese Direct Investment in Malaysia* (Tokyo: Institute of Developing Economies, 1979); Thomas W. Allen, *The ASEAN Report*, Vol. 1 (Hong Kong: The Asian Wall Street Journal, 1979); Economist Intelligence Unit, *The ASEAN Motor Industry* (London: The Economist, 1985).

62 Even when they settle for a minority stake, Japanese partners in a joint venture often insist on holding the top management posts. And Japanese firms typically impose tight restrictions on the use of technology before they agree to license it.

63 US International Trade Commission, "East Asia: Regional Economic Integration and Implications for the United States," USITC Publication 2621, 1993, p. 120.

64 Ulrike Wassmann and Kozo Yamamura, "Do Japanese Firms Behave Differently? The Effects of *Keiretsu* in the United States" in Kozo Yamamura (ed.), *Japanese Investment in the United States: Should We Be Concerned?* (Seattle: Society for Japanese Studies, 1989).

65 Yoshihara Hideki, "Nihonteki seisan shisutemu no kaigai iten" ("The overseas transfer of the Japanese production system") in Yoshihara Hideki, Hayashi Kiichirō and Yasumuro Ken-ichi (eds), *Nihon kigyō no gurōbaru keizai* (*The Global Economy of Japanese Firms*) (Tokyo: Tōyō Keizai Shinpōsha, 1988).

66 J. Panglaykim, *Japanese Direct Investment in ASEAN: The Indonesian Experience* (Singapore: Maruzen Asia, 1983), p. 17.

67 Ken-ichi Imai, "The Japanese Pattern of Innovation and its Evolution" in

Nathan Rosenberg, Ralph Landau, and David Mowery (eds), *Technology and the Wealth of Nations* (Stanford: Stanford University Press, 1992), pp. 225–46.

68 Mordechai Kreinin, "How Closed is Japan's Market? Additional Evidence," *World Economy*, Vol. 11, No. 4 (1988), pp. 540–1.

69 Christopher A. Bartlett and Sumantra Ghoshal, "Organizing for Worldwide Effectiveness: The Transnational Solution," *California Management Review*, Vol. 31, No. 1 (Fall 1988), pp. 62–3. Copyright 1988 by The Regents of the University of California. Reprinted by permission of The Regents.

70 ibid.

71 MITI, *Tsūshō hakusho* (*White Paper on Trade*) (Tokyo: MOF Printing Bureau, 1991), p. 225.

72 Martin Kenney and Richard Florida, *Beyond Mass Production: The Japanese System and Its Transfer to the U.S.* (New York: Oxford University Press, 1993), p. 149.

73 Not everyone, of course, agrees with us. For example, Wong Chin Yeow, research director for the Singapore Manufacturers Association, believes Japanese MNCs are becoming truly multinational, truly global actors. The production alliance we describe in this book is, he told us, a thing of the past, "a Mafia system that is breaking down, an old boys network that is falling apart." At the same time, however, he agrees that Japanese MNCs are trying to avoid the mistakes of the Americans. "Rather than a simple cost-reduction strategy, they are pursuing a global business strategy." Interview, 27 April 1993, Singapore.

74 C.Y. Ng, R. Hirono, and Robert Y. Siy, *Technology and Skills in ASEAN: An Overview* (Singapore: Institute of Southeast Asian Studies, 1986), p. 42.

75 Charles T. Stewart, Jr, "Comparing Japanese and U.S. Technology Transfer to Less Developed Countries," *Journal of Northeast Asian Studies*, Vol. 4 (Spring 1985), pp. 13–15.

76 See Takao Kiba and Fumio Kodama, "Measurement and Analysis of the Progress of International Technology Transfer: Case Study of Direct Investment in East Asian Countries by Japanese Companies," NISTEP Report No. 18, the National Institute of Science and Technology Policy (NISTEP), Science and Technology Agency of Japan, April 1991.

77 *Asian Wall Street Journal*, 9 August 1994, pp. 1, 4.

78 "ASEAN shinshutsu jinzainan nado nayami" ("Concerns such as human capital difficulties in expanding into ASEAN"), *Nihon keizai shinbun*, 28 November 1990, p. 5.

79 Schon Beechler, "International Management Control in Multinational Corporations: The Case of Japanese Consumer Electronics Firms in Asia," *ASEAN Economic Bulletin*, November 1992, p. 163.

80 Interview, 27 April 1993, Singapore.

81 Cynthia A. Montgomery and Michael E. Porter (eds), *Strategy: Seeking and Securing Competitive Advantage* (Cambridge, Mass.: Harvard Business Review, 1991), p. 163.

82 Harada Kazuaki, "Ima attōteki ni tsuyoi endaka yōin" ("The Main Reasons Today for the Yen Appreciation"), *Ekonomisuto*, 11 May 1993, pp. 48–51.

83 Alexander Gerschenkron, *Economic Backwardness in Historical Perspective: A Book of Essays* (Cambridge, Mass.: Belknap Press of Harvard University Press, 1962).

2 Flying Geese: An Unequal Alliance in Asia

1 For more in-depth analysis of the "old wave" of Japanese FDI in Asia (1955–85), see Terutomo Ozawa, *Multinationalism, Japanese Style: The Political*

Economy of Outward Dependency (Princeton: Princeton University Press, 1979); Kunio Yoshihara, *Japanese Investment in Southeast Asia* (Honolulu: University Press of Hawaii, 1978); and Sueo Sekiguchi (ed.), *ASEAN-Japan Relations: Investment* (Singapore: Institute of Southeast Asian Studies, 1983).

2 See, for example, Seiji Naya and Eric Ramstetter, "Policy Interactions and Direct Foreign Investment in East and Southeast Asia," *Journal of World Trade*, Vol. 22, No. 2 (April 1988), pp. 61–5.

3 Stephen Guisinger, "Foreign Direct Investment Flows in East and Southeast Asia," *ASEAN Economic Bulletin*, Vol. 8, No. 1 (July 1991), p. 33.

4 Those seeking a solid but not technically demanding analysis of these exchange rate movements are referred to Yoichi Funabashi, *Managing the Dollar: From the Plaza to the Louvre* (Washington: Institute for International Economics, 1988), and Takatoshi Ito, *The Japanese Economy* (Cambridge, Mass.: MIT Press, 1992), pp. 313–62.

5 Japanese exports to the United States actually climbed from $66.7 billion in 1985 to $91.1 billion in 1990. See International Monetary Fund, *Direction of Trade Statistics* (Washington: IMF, 1992). At the turn of the decade, the US merchandise trade deficit was still $124 million, $44 million of which was with Japan. Why? The principal reason was the huge savings shortfall in the United States in 1985–90 (high "absorption" – consumption plus domestic investment – financed by a very large budget deficit). However, America's trade deficit with Japan was aggravated by the pricing behavior of Japanese firms. That is, in the face of *endaka*, these firms may have remained competitive in part by "pricing to market," or pricing their exports low enough to maintain market share. This practice is discussed in Richard C. Marston, "Price Behavior in Japanese and U.S. Manufacturing" in Paul Krugman (ed.), *Trade With Japan: Has the Door Opened Wider?* (Chicago: University of Chicago Press, 1991), pp. 121–41.

6 This is a highly abbreviated discussion of the causes and effects of Japan's bubble. Those wanting more should read Yukio Noguchi, "The 'Bubble' and Economic Policies in the 1980s," *Journal of Japanese Studies*, Vol. 20, No. 2 (Summer 1994), which offers a good summary in English of his book written in Japanese: *Baburu no keizaigaku* (*Economics of the Bubble*) (Tokyo: Nihon Keizai Shinbunsha, 1992).

7 We are simply restating here the macroeconomic accounting identity: $S - I = (G - T) + (X - M)$, where S is saving, I is investment, G is government expenditures, T is taxes, X is exports, and M is imports.

8 Tran Van Tho, "New Trends in Japan's Foreign Direct Investment and Implications for the Division of Labor in the Asian Pacific Region: A Preliminary Examination," JERC Discussion Paper No. 1, Japan Economic Research Center, Tokyo, Japan (June 1987), p. 22.

9 Asked to identify the principal reasons for setting up manufacturing plants overseas, about 30 percent of the firms investing in the NICs and about 20 percent of those investing in ASEAN omitted any mention of labor costs. The survey, reported by MITI in a 1991 white paper (MITI, *Tsūshō hakusho* [*White Paper on Trade*], 1991, p. 214), allowed multiple responses to each question.

10 In some high-technology industries, labor costs today represent as little as 10 percent of total production costs. See, for example, Hans Peters, "Trade and Industry Logistics in Developing Countries: A Strategy for Improving Competitiveness in Changing International Markets," a paper for the World Bank, February 1992, p. 5; and Ian Chalmers, "International and Regional Integration: The Political Economy of the Electronics Industry in ASEAN,"

ASEAN Economic Bulletin, November 1991, p. 204. While they may not require low-cost production workers, Chen argues that high-technology MNCs *are* attracted to some developing countries by the availability of relatively low-cost engineers and technicians. See Edward K. Y. Chen, "The Electronics Industry" in Hadi Soesastro and Mari Pangetsu (eds), *Technological Challenge in the Asia-Pacific Economy* (Sydney: Allen & Unwin, 1990), p. 68.

11 The quote is from a speech, "Asia's Development and Japan's Role in Asia," by Suzuki Kazumasa, managing director of Mitsui and Co.'s branch office in Kuala Lumpur. See FAIR, "Economic Cooperation in Asia," proceedings of the third joint research conference on Asia-Pacific relations in Kuala Lumpur, 5–7 July 1992, p. 373.

12 See Tran, "New Trends," p. 36.

13 Louise do Rosario has a similar perspective. "Japanese firms," she wrote in the *Far Eastern Economic Review* (20 December 1990, p. 48), "have come to view Asia as an extension of their industrial machine, producing goods for both their domestic and world markets."

14 MITI, *White Paper on International Trade, 1987*, as cited by the Japan Economic Institute in "Economic Regionalism," JEI Report #25A (Washington: JEI, 29 June 1990).

15 M. Hadi Soesastro, "Southeast Asia's Expectations of Japan with Respect to Investment" in the Institute of Strategic and International Studies, Malaysia, *JASA: A New Era of Cooperation*, proceedings of the first Japan-Southeast Asia (JASA) conference, Kuala Lumpur (24–27 November 1989), p. 7.

16 Takeshi Aoki, "Japanese FDI and the Forming of Networks in the Asia-Pacific Region: Experience in Malaysia and its Implications" in Shojiro Tokunaga (ed.), *Japan's Foreign Investment and Asian Economic Interdependence: Production, Trade and Financial Systems* (Tokyo: University of Tokyo Press, 1992), pp. 98–9.

17 JETRO Kuala Lumpur, "NIES, ASEAN ni okeru Nikkei seizōgyō no katsudō jōkyō (Mareishia)" ("Japanese Manufacturing Industry Activities in the NIEs and ASEAN [Malaysia]"), unpublished report, 1992.

18 Stephen Marvin of Jardine Fleming Securities Ltd in Tokyo was quoted to this effect in *Business Week*, 7 May 1990, p. 54.

19 Sato Ichiro, "Localization Policy for Automobile Production," Japanese Chamber of Commerce and Industry, Bangkok, 1982; cited by Richard Doner, *Driving a Bargain: Automobile Industrialization and Japanese Firms in Southeast Asia* (Berkeley: University of California Press, 1991), p. 80. The label Sato applied to local business partners is quite fitting because, in many cases, those partners provide little more than political cover for Japanese investors.

20 See Franklin Weinstein, "Multinational Corporations and the Third World: The Case of Japan and Southeast Asia," *International Organization*, Vol. 30 (1976); and Yoshitaka Okada, "The Dilemma of Indonesian Dependency on Foreign Direct Investments," *Development and Change*, Vol. 14 (1983), and "Indigenization Policies and Structural Cooptation by Multinational Corporations," *Development and Change*, Vol. 16 (1985).

21 *FEER*, 2 May 1991, p. 46.

22 Interview with Ōda Hiroyasu, president, FKL Donghwa, 28 July 1992, Sunghwan, South Korea.

23 Interviews with Melco officials, 21 July 1992 and 6 April 1993, Tokyo; and Preyaluk Donavanik, "Thai Electronics – Not Just a Production Base" in *Bangkok Bank Monthly Review*, Vol. 31 (October 1990), pp. 430–1.

24 *Kokusai keizai,* 20 August 1990, pp. 195–6.

25 *Japan Digest,* 20 September 1994.

26 Source: Sony Corporate Communications, "Sony's Manufacturing Operations in Asia," April 1995.

27 Interview, 9 July 1992, Tokyo.

28 *Straits Times,* 7 February 1990; Mari Pangetsu, Hadi Soesastro, and Mubariq Ahmad, "A New Look at Intra-ASEAN Economic Cooperation," *ASEAN Economic Bulletin,* March 1992, p. 343; interviews with Sony officials, July 1992, Tokyo.

29 *The Star,* 23 April 1993, Kuala Lumpur, Malaysia.

30 Interviews with Toyota executives, 21 April 1993, Bangkok; *FEER,* 15 February 1990; *Nikkei Weekly,* 22 February 1993; *Asahi shinbun,* 30 December 1994, p. 7.

31 Interview with Ozaki Tetsuo, manager of manufacturing and sales, Asia and Oceania operations division, Nissan, 10 July 1992, Tokyo; *Asahi shinbun,* 23 December 1992.

32 *Japan Times,* 6 January 1993.

33 Tokunaga (ed.), *Japan's Foreign Investment and Asian Interdependence,* p. 35.

34 Akamatsu's theory was designed to explain how Japan managed to industrialize between 1880 and 1930. He surmised that a less developed country is able to build up its own industrial capacity in stages by substituting domestic production for the import of successively more sophisticated goods. As it acquires its own manufacturing capability, the less-developed country exports these successively more sophisticated products to still less-developed countries, which then go through this same process of import substitution and industrial upgrading. The theory acquired its name because the wedge-shaped pattern of import substitution, plotted on a graph reflecting time, resembled a flying geese formation. See Akamatsu Kaname, "Shinkōku kōgyō no sangyō hatten" ("The Industrial Development of Newly Emerging Industrial Nations"), *Ueda Teijirō hakushi kinen ronbunshū,* Vol. 4 (July 1937). In English, see Akamatsu, "A Historical Pattern of Economic Growth in Developing Countries," *The Developing Economies,* No. 1 (March–August 1962).

35 Rather than flying geese, Watanabe has used the image of a "multilayered chase" to describe this development pattern. It functions in precisely the same manner. See Watanabe Toshio, *Seichō no Ajia, teitai no Ajia* (*Growth and Stagnation in Asia*) (Tokyo: Tōyō Keizai Shinpōsha, 1986).

36 Economic Planning Agency, *Ajia taiheiyō chiiki, han'ei no tetsugaku: sōgō kokuryoku no kanten kara mita Nihon no yakuwari* (*The Philosophy of Prosperity in the Asia-Pacific Region: Japan's Role as Viewed from the Perspective of its Comprehensive National Capability*) (Tokyo: Ministry of Finance Printing Bureau, 1989), p. 158.

37 Quoted in James C. Abegglen and George Stalk, Jr, *Kaisha: The Japanese Corporation: How Marketing, Money and Manpower Strategy, Not Management Style, Make the Japanese World Pace Setters* (New York: Basic Books, 1985), p. 260.

38 "Ajia tōshi ni dai-san no nami" ("The Third Wave of Asian Investment"), *Nihon keizai shinbun,* 7 July 1992, p. 1.

39 US International Trade Commission, "Economic Integration in East Asia: Implications for the United States," Investigation No. 332-26 (1993), pp. 5–42, 5–44; *Straits Times,* 9 January 1993, p. 47.

40 *Economist,* 8 May 1993, pp. 70–2.

41 "Because the geese that take off later are able to benefit from the

forerunners' experiences to shorten the time required to catch up, they gradually transform the pattern from a V-formation to eventual horizontal integration," wrote Okita Saburo, a former Japanese foreign minister, in a paper ("Asian-Pacific Prospects and Problems for the Further Development of the Asian-Pacific Cooperative Framework," p. 2) presented to a symposium in Santa Barbara, California, 1–3 February 1990, p. 2. Kojima had written earlier that Japanese FDI would enable the developing countries of Asia, in due time, to "raise their economies to the level and quality of Japan's." Kiyoshi Kojima, *Direct Foreign Investment: A Japanese Model of Multinational Business Operations* (London: Croom Helm, 1978), p. 168.

42 MITI, *Tsūshō hakusho*, 1992 (Tokyo: Ministry of Finance Printing Bureau, 1992), pp. 129–58.

43 In the 1990s, of course, the volume of reverse imports in some sectors, such as consumer electronics, grew almost as fast as the value of the yen. We discuss this trend in more detail in chapter twelve.

44 MITI, *Tsūshō hakusho*, 1989 (Tokyo: Ministry of Finance Printing Bureau, 1989), pp. 237–8.

45 Kozo Yamamura, "The Legacies of a Bargain: The Reagan Deficits and Japan's 'Bubble,'" a paper presented at a conference on the macroeconomic policies of the United States and Japan during the 1980s, July 1994.

46 *Nikkei Weekly*, 11 July 1994, p. 1.

47 JETRO, *White Paper on Foreign Direct Investment: A Summary* (Tokyo: Japan External Trade Organization, March 1993), p. 20; *Yomiuri Daily News*, 25 June 1994; *New York Times*, 23 October 1994, p. F3.

48 See Mitchell Bernard and John Ravenhill, "Beyond Product Cycles and Flying Geese: Regionalization, Hierarchy and the Industrialization of East Asia," *World Politics*, Vol. 47, No. 2 (January 1995), pp. 187–8.

49 *Economist*, 8 May 1993, p. 72.

50 "A Survey of Asia's Emerging Economies," *Economist*, 16 November 1991, pp. 12–13.

51 China and Indonesia have used petroleum and natural gas exports to maintain a trade surplus with Japan.

52 Translated into Japanese, the term "embraced" might become *marugakaeno* (wholly held in) or *kakaerareta* (held and taken care of). Both words convey an imbalance of power; the "embracing" party is clearly dominant. In addition, the two words imply that the relationship between the "embracing" and "embraced" parties is conditional. To be precise, it depends on the "embraced" party behaving in such a manner as to bestow benefit on the "embracing" party.

53 *FEER*, 8 June 1989, p. 90.

54 For all of their talk about "imperialism," neodependency scholars such as Evans fail to recognize the possibility that the foreign state, which after all has the most leverage over the multinational corporation, might have a part to play in bringing about dependence in a Third World or peripheral economy. This is a glaring omission, particularly in the case of Japan's growing economic presence in Asia. See Peter Evans, *Dependent Development: The Alliance of Multinational, State and Local Capital in Brazil* (Princeton: Princeton University Press, 1979).

55 See William Rapp, "Japanese Multinationals: An Evolutionary Theory" in Theodor Leuenberger and Martin E. Weinstein (eds), *Europe, Japan and America in the 1990s: Cooperation and Competition* (Berlin: Springer-Verlag, 1992), pp. 248–9.

56 Fumio Kodama and Takao Kiba, "The Emerging Trajectory of International Technology," Asia-Pacific Research Center, Stanford University, 1994, p. 21.

57 Fujitsu, for example, said it would use "attrition, transfers to subsidiaries and reduced hiring" to cut its 56,000-member workforce in Japan by about 10 percent. Associated Press, "Like IBM, Japanese Computer Makers Are Struggling," *Seattle Times*, 1 August 1993.

58 Interview, Takase Hiroyuki, 24 July 1992, Tokyo.

59 Samart Chiasakul and Prasert Silapipat, "The Case of Thailand," in Institute of Developing Economies (IDE), *The Role of Japanese Direct Investment in Developing Countries* (Tokyo: IDE, 1992), pp. 233–4.

60 *FEER*, 28 March 1991, p. 54.

61 Interview, 15 July 1992, Bangkok.

62 See Yoshihara Kunio, *The Rise of Ersatz Capitalism in Southeast Asia* (Singapore: Oxford University Press, 1988).

63 J. L. Enos and W. H. Park, *The Adoption and Diffusion of Imported Technology: The Case of Korea* (New York: Croom Helm, 1988), p. 248.

64 Chee Peng Lim, "Regulating the Transfer of Technology: An Analysis of Malaysia's Experience," *Contemporary Southeast Asia*, Vol. 7, No. 1 (June 1985).

65 Jung Taik Hyun and Katherine Whitmore, "Japanese Direct Foreign Investment: Patterns and Implications for Developing Countries," World Bank Industry and Energy Development Working Paper, Industry Series Paper 1, February 1989.

66 Mitsubishi Motors and Mitsubishi Corp., which together control 15 percent of Proton's stock, initially held 30 percent. But other members of the Mitsubishi *keiretsu* – led by Mitsubishi Bank and a lending company affiliated with the group – financed HICOM's 70 percent share. Guaranteed by the Malaysian treasury, this loan carried little risk for Mitsubishi interests. Kit Machado, "Japanese Transnational Corporations in Malaysia's State Sponsored Heavy Industrialization Drive: The HICOM Automobile and Steels Projects," *Pacific Affairs*, Vol. 62, No. 4 (Winter 1989–90), p. 516.

67 Doner, *Driving a Bargain*, pp. 114–15.

68 *FEER*, 14 February 1985, p. 82. The report, "Japan and Malaysia's Car Industry: Rising Sun or False Dawn of Economic Cooperation," was prepared by the United Nations Industrial Development Organization.

69 Machado, "Japanese Transnational Corporations," p. 521.

70 Interview, 23 April 1993, Kuala Lumpur.

71 Mitsubishi Motors Corp., "Kantaiheiyō chiiki no buhin sōgo hokan taisei" ("Pacific Rim Parts Complementation Scheme"), undated internal company document.

72 *Asahi shinbun*, 25 March 1995, p. 11.

73 Mitsubishi Corp., Motor Vehicle Department C, "Master Plan for the Automobile Industry in the Socialist Republic of Vietnam," June 1992. We discuss this proposal further in chapter eight.

74 See Pasuk Phongpaichit, *The New Wave of Japanese Investment in ASEAN* (Singapore: Institute of Southeast Asian Studies, 1990), p. 55; and Hafiz Mirza, *Multinationals and the Growth of the Singapore Economy* (London: Croom Helm, 1986), pp. 210–13.

75 U.S. International Trade Commission, *East Asia: Regional Economic Integration and Implications for the United States*, USITC publication 2621, 1993, pp. 109–10.

76 *Nihon keizai shinbun*, 13 May 1993, p. 27. The BBC program is described adequately in *Asahi shinbun*, 30 December 1994, p. 7.

77 *Straits Times*, 11 January 1993.

78 *Washington Post*, 17 November 1992.

79 *Business Times* (Kuala Lumpur), special supplement, "The Growth Triangle," 15 April 1992, p. 3.

80 BIP is one of eight industrial parks on Batam Island but, as of mid 1995, the only one living up to the expectations of the investors. See *Nikkei Weekly*, 3 April 1995, p. 19.

81 *Nihon keizai shinbun*, 30 August 1990, p. 13.

82 *Fortune*, 5 October 1992, p. 138; *Nikkei Weekly*, 8 March 1993, p. 27.

83 *Nikkei Weekly*, 8 November 1993, p. 24.

84 *Business Times*, 15 April 1992, p. 2.

85 USITC, "Regional Economic Integration," p. 104.

86 Economist Intelligence Unit, *EIU International Motor Business* (London: EIU, April 1992), pp. 158–60.

87 USITC, "Regional Economic Integration," p. 104.

88 ibid., p. 103.

89 *Asahi shinbun*, 8 December 1994, p. 12.

90 ibid., p. 102.

91 *Nikkei Weekly*, 20 June 1994, pp. 1, 23.

92 John Guy, *The Motor Industry of South East Asia* (London: Economist Intelligence Unit, 1991), p. 200.

93 *Japan Times*, 16 July 1992; *U.S. News and World Report*, 21 December 1992, p. 70.

94 In 1993, we should note, Chrysler opened a plant outside Kuala Lumpur to manufacture Jeep Cherokee utility vehicles. Along with General Motors, it also appears poised to move back into Vietnam now that the US trade embargo against that country has been lifted. *New York Times*, 13 September 1993; *Seattle Post-Intelligencer*, 5 February 1994. GM has also opened truck factories in China and Indonesia. *Asian Wall Street Journal*, 20 June 1994, p. 18.

95 *Fortune*, "Pacific Rim 1990," special section, p. 10.

96 Louis Kraar, "The Rising Power of the Pacific," *Fortune*, "Pacific Rim 1990," special section, Fall 1990, p. 10; Ian Chalmers, "International and Regional Integration: The Political Economy of the Electronics Industry in ASEAN," *ASEAN Economic Bulletin*, Vol 8, No. 2 (November 1991), pp. 200–1; Pangestu, Soesastro, and Ahmad, "A New Look at Intra-ASEAN Economic Cooperation," p. 343.

97 US Commerce Department, *Survey of Current Business*, Vol. 74, No. 6 (June 1994), p. 74.

98 Interview, 15 April 1993, Penang, Malaysia.

99 Interview, 16 July 1992, Bangkok.

100 *Business Week*, 10 April 1989, p. 44.

101 *New York Times*, 8 May 1990, p. A1.

102 By "total foreign aid budget" we refer not only to bilateral assistance but also to multilateral ODA and unallocated funds. The figures come from Alexander R. Love, chairman of the Development Assistance Committee, *Development Cooperation: Aid in Transition* (Paris: Organization for Economic Cooperation and Development, 1994), pp. 221, 227.

103 *Wall Street Journal*, 29 March 1983, p. A8.

104 *Washington Post National Weekly Edition*, 26 February–4 March 1990, p. 8.

3 Cooperation between Unequals

1 Ronald H. Coase, "1991 Nobel Lecture: The Institutional Structure of Production" in Oliver E. Williamson and Sidney G. Winter (eds), *The Nature of the Firm: Origins, Evolution and Development* (New York: Oxford University Press, 1993), p. 229.

2 We certainly could make the same points about macroeconomic theory, which is after all merely a policy-minded extension of microeconomic theory. But if we did, we would have to burden readers with a lengthy discussion of the many schools of macroeconomic theory. Besides, as we hope to make evident, we are keenly interested in a central concept of microeconomic theory – the theory of the firm.

3 Few would disagree with our observation that neoclassical theory is a short-run analysis. To deal with this, economists have devised what they call "comparative static" and "dynamic" analyses. But neither is really useful in analyzing how an economy changes over time in the real world, because of numerous bold assumptions.

4 For North, institutions are all "humanly devised constraints on human actions that determine the structure of incentives." This, then, would include not only laws and policies, but also language and customs. See Douglass C. North, *Institutions, Institutional Change and Economic Performance* (Cambridge: Cambridge University Press, 1990), p. 3.

5 This is the so-called factor price equalization theorem.

6 Alfred Marshall, *Principles of Economics*, 8th edn (London: Macmillan & Co., 1925), pp. 318–19. Marshall's improvisation ultimately created what become known as "Marshall's problem," the contradiction between his suggestion that some firms will become large enough to dominate a market and the fundamental assumption of neoclassical economics that markets are perfectly competitive.

7 Kenneth J. Arrow, "The Economic Implication of Learning by Doing," *Review of Economic Studies*, Vol. 29 (1969).

8 This observation is affirmed by a survey of analytic models of economic growth. See Kazushi Ohkawa and Katsuo Otsuka, *Technology Diffusion, Productivity, Employment and Phase Shifts in Developing Economies* (Tokyo: University of Tokyo Press, 1994), pp. 19–36. It is true, though, that a small number of economists have devised competitive, long-run equilibrium models that aim to incorporate technological change (i.e. increasing marginal productivity). However, all have been highly deductive, mathematical models relying on the usual numerous assumptions needed for competitive equilibrium analysis. The best known among such models is presented in Paul M. Romer, "Increasing Returns and Long-Run Growth," *Journal of Political Economy*, Vol. 94, No. 51 (1986), pp. 1002–37.

9 Oliver E. Williamson, "Introduction" in Williamson and Winter (eds), *The Nature of the Firm*, p. 10. His quote is from Harold Demsetz, "The Theory of the Firm Revisited" in ibid., p. 161. Williamson's seminal contribution to this intellectual effort was his book, *Markets and Hierarchies* (New York: Free Press, 1975).

10 Williamson and Winter (eds), *The Nature of the Firm*, offers an excellent, up-to-date survey of the literature.

11 The "new" theory of the firm also produced many works on the relationship between shareholders and management. See, for example, Masahiko Aoki, *The Cooperative Game Theory of the Firm* (London: Oxford University Press, 1984).

12 Richard Schmalensee, "Industrial Economics: An Overview," *Economic Journal*, Vol. 98 (September 1988), p. 656.

13 Proponents of an evolutionary theory of the firm are trying to achieve this objective by focusing attention on the path-dependent (or momentum-driven) characteristics of firm behavior. Although it has offered some useful concepts, this effort is still young and faces substantial difficulties. One of them is how to build a theory while endogenizing so many variables. The best work on the evolutionary theory of the firm to date is Richard Nelson and Sidney Winter, *An Evolutionary Theory of Economic Change* (Cambridge, Mass.: Harvard University Press, 1982).

14 As we spell out later in this chapter, the firm-like organization is the basic building-block of the Japanese production alliance in Asia. Demsetz offers this description: "Specialization, continuity of association, and reliance on direction are characteristics of firm-like coordination. They substitute for self-sufficiency and spot markets. These are frequently found characteristics of firm-like organization because they are productive in many circumstances. This productivity derives in part from transaction and monitoring cost considerations, but it also depends on other conditions. Particularly important are the conditions that underlie the acquisition and use of knowledge." See Demsetz, "The Theory of the Firm Revisited," p. 171.

15 For our purposes, technological and managerial capacity (the ability to acquire and process information) is the most important variable determining a firm's relative bargaining power.

16 The failure to consider this crucial variable of bargaining power is a fundamental failure of neoclassical studies analyzing the behavior of Japanese firms in general and Japanese firms in Asia in particular.

17 Kenneth J. Arrow, "Reflections on the Essays" in George Feiwel (ed.), *Arrow and the Foundations of the Theory of Economic Policy* (New York: New York University Press, 1987), p. 734.

18 North, *Institutions, Institutional Change, and Economic Performance*, pp. 131–2.

19 This definition of property rights actually comes from Thrainn Eggertsson, *Economic Behavior and Institutions* (Cambridge: Cambridge University Press, 1990), p. 34.

20 Government, by definition, has a monopoly on power. The problem comes when it behaves as a discriminating monopolist.

21 This concept is chronicled in Robert D. Tollison, "Rent-seeking: A Survey," *Kyklos*, Vol. 35, No. 4 (1982), pp. 575–602. See also Anne O. Krueger, "The Political Economy of the Rent-seeking Society," *American Economic Review*, Vol. 64, No. 3 (June 1974), pp. 291–303.

22 North was hardly the first nor the last scholar to grapple with this concept of path-dependence. See, for example, Paul David, "Clio and the Economics of QWERTY," *American Economic Review*, Vol. 75 (1985), pp. 332–7. (QWERTY refers to the arrangement of letters in the top row of the typewriter keyboard, set in the late nineteenth century. It has not changed, despite attempts to replace it with a more efficient arrangement.)

23 To explain why it is so difficult to change institutions, North relies on the theory of collective action that deals with free-riders, the "passionate minority," and related problems. See Mancur Olson, *The Logic of Collective Action* (Cambridge, Mass.: Harvard University Press, 1971).

24 Since our discussion of neoinstitutionalist analysis is so selective, those interested in a deeper understanding are referred to North's work cited above (and several of his earlier works cited therein) and Eggertsson, *Economic Behavior and Institutions*.

25 A thoughtful criticism of neoinstitutional analysis is found in K. Basu, E. Jones, and E. Schlicht, "The Growth and Decay of Custom: The Role of New Institutional Economics and Economic History," *Explorations in Economic History*, Vol. 24 (1987), pp. 1–21.

26 Paul Krugman, "Introduction: New Thinking About Trade Policy" in Krugman (ed.), *Strategic Trade Policy and the New International Economics* (Cambridge, Mass.: MIT Press, 1986), p. 12.

27 Examples of work on strategic trade theory include Barbara J. Spencer and James A. Brander, "International R&D Rivalry and Industrial Strategy," *Review of Economic Studies*, Vol. 50 (October 1983), pp. 707–22; Elhanen Helpman and Paul Krugman, *Market Structure and Foreign Trade: Increasing Returns, Imperfect Competition and International Economy* (Cambridge, Mass.: MIT Press, 1985); and Paul Krugman, "Is Free Trade Passe?", *Journal of Economic Perspectives*, Vol. 1 (Fall 1987), pp. 131–44.

28 There are at least two exceptions. Graham and Krugman have acknowledged that governments might be able to complement their own strategic trade policies with strategic investment policies. See Edward M. Graham and Paul R. Krugman, *Foreign Direct Investment in the United States* (Washington: Institute for International Economics, 1989), p. 54. And Encarnation has suggested that the high transaction costs and large economies of scope associated with FDI constitute additional market failures inducing governments to pursue such strategic investment policies. See Dennis Encarnation, *Rivals Beyond Trade: America Versus Japan in Global Competition* (Ithaca: Cornell University Press, 1992), pp. 31–2.

29 See, for example, Anne Krueger, "Free Trade is the Best Policy" in Robert Lawrence and Charles Schultze (eds), *An American Trade Strategy* (Washington: Brookings Institution, 1990), pp. 68–105; and Jagdish Bhagwati, "Aggressive Unilateralism: An Overview" in Jagdish Bhagwati and Hugh Patrick (eds), *Aggressive Unilateralism: America's 301 Trade Policy and the World Trading System* (Ann Arbor: University of Michigan Press, 1990), pp. 1–45.

30 Giovanni Dosi, Laura D'Andrea Tyson, and John Zysman, "Trade, Technologies and Development: A Framework for Discussing Japan" in Chalmers Johnson, Laura D'Andrea Tyson, and John Zysman, *Politics and Productivity: The Real Story of Why Japan Works* (Cambridge, Mass.: Ballinger, 1989), p. 11.

31 Paul Krugman, *Rethinking International Trade* (Cambridge, Mass.: MIT Press, 1990), p. 181.

32 See Jeffrey Frankel, "Is Japan Creating a Yen Bloc in East Asia and the Pacific?" in Jeffrey Frankel and Miles Kahler (eds), *Regionalism and Rivalry: Japan and the U.S. in Pacific Asia* (Chicago: University of Chicago Press, 1993), pp. 53–85; and Frankel, "Is a Yen Bloc Forming in Pacific Asia?" in Richard O'Brien (ed.), *Finance and the International Economy: The AMEX Bank Review Prize Essays* (Oxford: Oxford University Press, 1991).

33 Krugman, *Rethinking International Trade*, pp. 181–2.

34 This analysis is spelled out in great detail in Murakami Yasusuke, *Han-koten no seiji keizai-gaku* (*An Anticlassical Political-Economic Analysis*) (Tokyo: Chūō Kōron-sha, 1922). Murakami's developmentalist analysis of industrialization should not be confused with Chalmers Johnson's analysis of the capitalist development state in *MITI and the Japanese Miracle* (Stanford: Stanford University Press, 1982). The former is an economist's examination of the manner in which the state in a developing economy can help firms adopt new technology, reduce production costs, and maximize market share. The

latter is a political scientist's look at the way private economic behavior is coaxed, corralled, and guided by an elite, development-minded bureaucracy. They use concepts that are overlapping in meaning, but not isomorphic. Since we can offer only a very limited discussion of Murakami's analysis, interested readers are referred to the translation of his book which will be published by Stanford University Press in 1996 under the title *An Anticlassical Political-Economic Analysis: A Vision for the Next Century.*

35 Neoclassical theory assumes that long-run average costs increase, leading to a stable equilibrium in output and factor markets.

36 For a more comprehensive and technical discussion of this question, see Murakami Yasusuke and Kozo Yamamura, "A Technical Note on Japanese Firm Behavior" in Kozo Yamamura (ed.), *Policy and Trade Issues of the Japanese Economy* (Seattle: University of Washington Press, 1982).

37 Long-run interfirm cooperation is dependent, in turn, on intrafirm cooperation between stockholders and employees. We spell out why in the following chapter.

38 Daniel Okimoto, *Between MITI and the Market: Japanese Industrial Policy for High Technology* (Stanford: Stanford University Press, 1989), p. 236.

39 Former Sony chairman Morita Akio, who once encouraged his country to say "no" to the West, now attributes Japan's rocky trade relations with the West to its refusal to abandon a "maximum sales at low profit" policy. Morita Akio, "Nihon-gata keizai ga abunai" ("Japanese-type Management in Peril"), *Bungei shunjū*, February 1992, p. 102.

40 Saitō Seiichirō, "Nihon keizai no chū-chōki-teki chōsei" ("Medium- and Long-term Adjustments in the Japanese Economy") in Kano Yoshikazu, Noguchi Yukio, Saitō Seiichirō, and Shimada Haruo (eds), *Nihon keizai no kadai to tenbō* (*Problems and Prospects for the Japanese Economy*) (Tokyo: Foreign Press Center, 1993), p. 87.

41 In the expanding literature on international strategic cooperation, two books stand out: Lynn Krieger Mytelka (ed.), *Strategic Partnerships: States, Firms and International Cooperation* (Rutherford: Fairleigh Dickinson University Press, 1991); and Farok J. Contractor and Peter Lorange, *Cooperative Strategies in International Business* (Lexington, Mass.: D.C. Heath & Co., 1988).

42 Those who are interested in a general discussion of game theory should see Robert Axelrod, *The Evolution of Cooperation* (New York: Basic Books, 1984). Those interested in a more focused discussion of game theory's application to international strategic cooperation should see Peter J. Buckley and Mark Casson, "A Theory of Cooperation in International Business" in Contractor and Lorange, *Cooperative Strategies in International Business*, pp. 31–53.

43 Aoki uses the term "quasi-disintegration" to describe the process by which a Japanese manufacturing firm spins off production responsibilities to subcontracting firms as a way to keep its own workforce more homogeneous. See Masahiko Aoki, "The Japanese Firm in Transition" in Kozo Yamamura and Yasukichi Yasuba (eds), *The Political Economy of Japan, Volume 1: The Domestic Transformation* (Stanford: Stanford University Press, 1987).

44 Mitchell Bernard and John Ravenhill, "Beyond Product Cycles and Flying Geese: Regionalization, Hierarchy, and the Industrialization of East Asia," *World Politics*, Vol. 47, No. 2 (January 1995), pp. 186–7.

45 To understand why these advantages are truly "advantageous," we should recognize that the industrial world is undergoing a major shift in its technological paradigm. Until the 1970s, when electricity began to give way

to microelectronics, innovating firms used vertical integration to manage transaction costs. It was an appropriate strategy for an era of "Fordism," mass production with standardized technology. But this strategy no longer suffices. In an era of flexible production, in which economies of scope are as important as economies of scale in adjusting to consumer volatility and shortened product cycles, more and more high-tech firms – led by those in Japan – have turned to the hybrid corporate structure we have called vertical quasi-integration. For a general discussion of this issue, that does not focus narrowly on Japanese firms, see G. Jones and C. Hill, "Transaction Cost Analysis of Strategy-Structure Choice," *Strategic Management Journal*, Vol. 9 (1989).

46 Just as the carrot is equivalent to the subordinate firm's structure of incentives to fully cooperate, the stick equals its set of disincentives to shirk (either exert less than maximum effort or withdraw entirely from the vertical *keiretsu* relationship).

47 Jeffrey H. Dyer, "Dedicated Assets: Japan's Manufacturing Edge," *Harvard Business Review*, November–December 1994, p. 177. Dyer's study affirms earlier research by Clark and Fujimoto, who found that "off-the-shelf" or standardized parts made up 38 percent of the auto parts used by US automakers but only 18 percent of those used by Japanese automakers. See Kim B. Clark and Takahiro Fujimoto, *Product Development Performance* (Boston: Harvard Business School Press, 1991).

48 As we noted in chapter two, this embrace can quickly turn into a squeeze. During hard economic times, the bankruptcy rate among small subcontracting firms in Japan is about twice that of similar firms in the United States. See Kokuzeichō (National Tax Agency), *Kokuzeichō tōkei nenpō* (*National Tax Agency Statistical Yearbook*), published annually.

49 In economic terms, they are internalizing, and thus maximizing, their rent on the technology they own.

50 The same argument is made forcefully in Bernard and Ravenhill, "Beyond Product Cycles and Flying Geese."

51 See Robert Z. Lawrence, "Japan's Different Trade Regime: An Analysis with Particular Reference to *Keiretsu*," *Journal of Economic Perspectives*, Vol. 7, No. 3 (Summer 1993), pp. 3–19.

52 Special issue on Japanese technology, *Ekonomisuto*, 28 February 1995, p. 66.

4 The Political Economy of Japan

1 A good example of scholarly work that identifies Japan as exceptionally "market-oriented" is Iida Tsuneo, *Nihon-teki chikarazuyosa no saihakken* (*Rediscovering Japanese-type Strengths*) (Tokyo: Nihon Keizai Shinbunsha, 1979), pp. 80, 206.

2 C. Fred Bergsten and Marcus Noland, *Reconcilable Differences? The United States–Japan Economic Conflict* (Washington: Institute for International Economics, 1993), p. 9.

3 The LDP, which had reigned for 38 years, lost control of the government in 1993, but regained it a year later by forging an odd coalition with the Japan Socialist Party, the LDP's long-standing arch-rival.

4 In general, we believe Karel van Wolferen and other so-called "revisionists" including Chalmers Johnson, Clyde Prestowitz, and James Fallows overemphasize the role of political institutions in Japan's political economy almost as much as neoclassical economists overemphasize the role of market forces. For a sample of this sometimes polemical writing, see Chalmers

Johnson, "Trade, Revisionism, and the Future of Japanese-American Relations" in Kozo Yamamura (ed.), *Japan's Economic Structure: Should It Change?* (Seattle: Society for Japanese Studies, 1990), pp. 105–36.

5 As we finished writing, sources in Japan were noting that the Murayama administration's efforts to promote deregulation had run into strong opposition from special interests and bureaucrats, and thus stood a good chance of being substantially weakened or derailed altogether. See, for example, *Asahi shinbun*, 24 February 1995, p. 11; and *Inside U.S. Trade*, Vol. 13, No. 5 (2 February 1995).

6 This pithy remark was quoted in Alan Wolff, "U.S.–Japan Relations and the Rule of Law: The Nature of the Trade Conflict and the American Response" in Yamamura (ed.), *Japan's Economic Structure*, p. 144.

7 Michael Gerlach, *Alliance Capitalism: The Social Organization of Japanese Business* (Berkeley: University of California Press, 1992); Iwao Nakatani, "The Asymmetry of the Japanese-Style versus American-style Capitalism as the Fundamental Source of Japan–U.S. Imbalance Problems," National Bureau of Economic Research and Japan Center for Economic Research, a background paper for the US–Japan Economic Forum, February 1992.

8 At long last, it is no longer so controversial to suggest that the government was a driving force behind Japan's economic success in the early postwar period. English-language sources on this once heavily debated topic include Kozo Yamamura and Yasukichi Yasuba (eds), *The Political Economy of Japan, Volume 1: The Domestic Transformation* (Stanford: Stanford University Press, 1987); and Gary R. Saxonhouse and Kozo Yamamura (eds), *Law and Trade Issues of the Japanese Economy: American and Japanese Perspectives* (Seattle: University of Washington Press, 1986).

9 See G. Ackley and H. Ishi, "Fiscal, Monetary and Related Policies" in Hugh T. Patrick and Henry Rosovsky (eds), *Asia's New Giant: How the Japanese Economy Works* (Washington: Brookings Institution, 1976). Calder argues to the contrary, that the government "did not seek to impose a particular pattern of allocation:" Kent Calder, *Strategic Capitalism: Private Business and Public Purpose in Japanese Industrial Finance* (Princeton: Princeton University Press, 1993), p. 89. But when it allocated capital to particular banks, the Bank of Japan knew where its money was going.

10 Yukio Noguchi, "The Role of the Fiscal Investment and Loan Program in Postwar Japanese Economic Growth" in Hyung-Ki Kim et al. (eds), *The Japanese Civil Service and Economic Development* (Oxford: Oxford University Press, 1995).

11 Noguchi, "Role of Fiscal Investment."

12 George C. Eads and Kozo Yamamura, "The Future of Industrial Policy" in Yamamura and Yasuba (eds), *The Political Economy of Japan, Vol. 1*.

13 Kozo Yamamura, "Success that Soured: Administrative Guidance and Cartels in Japan" in Kozo Yamamura (ed.), *Policy and Trade Issues of the Japanese Economy: American and Japanese Perspectives* (Seattle: University of Washington Press, 1982).

14 See Eads and Yamamura, "The Future of Industrial Policy."

15 For a discussion of Japan's drift toward pluralism, see Inoguchi Takashi, *Gendai Nihon seiji keizai no kōzō* (*The Structure of the Contemporary Japanese Political Economy*) (Tokyo: Tōyō Keizai Shinpōsha, 1983); and T. J. Pempel (ed.), *Policymaking in Contemporary Japan* (Ithaca: Cornell University Press, 1977).

16 A classic example of such a turf battle is nicely documented in Chalmers

Johnson, "MITI, MPT and the Telecom Wars" in Chalmers Johnson, Laura D'Andrea Tyson and John Zysman, *Politics and Productivity: The Real Story of Why Japan Works* (Cambridge, Mass.: Ballinger, 1989).

17 Foreign "oversight" of Japanese policy is evident in the United States–Japan Advisory Commission's report, "Challenges and Opportunities in United States–Japan Relations," September 1984.

18 The gasoline controversy is covered by Johnson, "MITI, MPT and the Telecom Wars," p. 184.

19 *Asahi shinbun*, 7 March 1995, p. 10.

20 A specialist on Japanese administrative procedure has calculated that bureaucrats still regulate about 40 percent of the nation's economic activities, issuing nearly 11,000 permits and licenses every year. While acknowledging that some of these regulations are required to protect the public interest, he nonetheless argues that "a very large percentage" are designed only to protect the interests of regulating agencies and regulated industries. See Yoda Kaoru, *Nihon no kyoninka-seido no subete* (*All about Japan's Permit and Licensing System*) (Tokyo: Nihon Jitsugyo Shuppansha, 1993), p. 12.

21 *Seattle Times*, 7 August 1994, p. F1.

22 Masahiro Okuno-Fujiwara, "Industrial Policy in Japan: A Political Economy View" in Paul Krugman (ed.), *Trade With Japan: Has the Door Opened Wider?* (Chicago: University of Chicago Press, 1991).

23 Marie Anchordoguy, "Mastering the Market: Japanese Government Targeting of the Computer Industry," *International Organization*, Vol. 42, No. 3 (Summer 1988), pp. 517–22.

24 ibid., pp. 526–30.

25 Laura D'Andrea Tyson, "Comment" in Krugman (ed.), *Trade with Japan*, p. 297.

26 ibid, pp. 298–9.

27 Ryūtarō Komiya and Kazutomo Irie, "The U.S.–Japan Trade Problem: An Economic Analysis from a Japanese Viewpoint" in Yamamura (ed.), *Japan's Economic Structure*, p. 93.

28 Masahiko Aoki, *Information, Incentives and Bargaining in the Japanese Economy* (Cambridge: Cambridge University Press, 1988); Iwao Nakatani, "The Economic Role of Financial Corporate Groupings" in Masahiko Aoki (ed.), *The Economic Analysis of the Japanese Firm* (Amsterdam: North-Holland, 1984).

29 Itami Takayuki, "Nihon kigyō no jinponshugi shisutemu" ("The Employee-first-ism of the Japanese Enterprise System") in Komiya Ryūtarō and Imai Ken-ichi (eds), *Nihon no kigyō* (*Japanese Business*) (Tokyo: University of Tokyo Press, 1989), p. 57.

30 Ken-ichi Imai, "Japanese Business Groups and the Structural Impediments Initiative" in Yamamura (ed.), *Japan's Economic Structure*, pp. 169–70.

31 The study was reported by *Asahi shinbun*, 27 July 1994, p. 12, in an article entitled "Keiretsu shihai, futatabi takamaru" ("Keiretsu Control Strengthened Again"). According to the newspaper, the JFTC study examined the records of 189 firms belonging to Japan's six major horizontal *keiretsu*.

32 Our assertion that this period was an aberration is borne out by JFTC statistics for 1981–87, before inflated asset prices turned Japan's economy into a bubble. The cross-shareholding ratio rose steadily during that period, according to a JFTC study released in 1989. "It is not justified to conclude that the *keiretsu* presence in our economy is declining," the study asserted. "Their collective power continues to be great, and cannot be ignored." See

Japan Fair Trade Commission, "Kigyō shūdan no jittai ni tsuite" ("A Study of Enterprise Groups"), 23 May 1989, p. 45.

33 Michael Gerlach, "Twilight of the *Keiretsu*? A Critical Assessment," *Journal of Japanese Studies*, Vol. 18, No. 1 (Winter 1992), p. 94.

34 While we attribute the durability of *keiretsu* ties to the structure of incentives facing Japanese firms, others – such as Murakami and Rohlen – attribute it to culture. The "tightly knit world of relational transacting is changing, and yet it is important to point out that it is certain to change slowly, for it is indeed a cultural underlying feature of the Japanese political economy." Yasusuke Murakami and Thomas P. Rohlen, "Social Exchange Aspects of the Japanese Political Economy: Culture, Efficiency and Change" in Shumpei Kumon and Henry Rosovsky (eds), *The Political Economy of Japan, Volume 3: Cultural and Social Dynamics* (Stanford: Stanford University Press, 1992), p. 101.

35 Gerlach, *Alliance Capitalism*, p. 3.

36 Imai Ken-ichi and Kaneko Ikuyo, *Nettowāku soshiki ron* (*Theory of the Network System*) (Tokyo: Iwanami Shoten, 1988), pp. 40–1.

37 Surveys by the Small and Medium Enterprise Agency show that the ratio of subcontractors to the total number of small and medium-sized firms in Japan's manufacturing sector climbed steadily between 1966 and 1981. See SMEA, *Report of the Basic Survey of the Industrial Situation* (Tokyo: MITI, 1966–81).

38 Economic Planning Agency of Japan, *Keizai hakusho* (*Economic White Paper*) (Tokyo: EPA, 1982), p. 630.

39 See Akio Torii and Richard Caves, "Technical Efficiency in Japanese and U.S. Manufacturing Industries" in Richard Caves (ed.), *Industrial Efficiency in Six Nations* (Cambridge, Mass.: MIT Press, 1992), pp. 453–4.

40 Mark Fruin, *The Japanese Enterprise System: Competitive Strategies and Cooperative Structures* (Oxford: Oxford University Press, 1992).

41 Sakurai Masao, *Tōshi masatsu* (*Investment Friction*) (Tokyo: Tōyō Keizai Shinpōsha, 1988), p. 104.

42 Rajan R. Kamath and Jeffrey K. Liker, "A Second Look at Japanese Product Development," *Harvard Business Review*, November–December 1994, p. 156.

43 Aoki Satoshi, *Toyota, sono jitsuzō* (*Toyota, the Reality*) (Tokyo: Sekibunsha, 1982), p. 78.

44 David Friedman, *The Misunderstood Miracle: Industrial Development and Political Change in Japan* (Ithaca: Cornell University Press, 1988), pp. 146–61.

45 See Small and Medium Enterprises Agency, *Chūshō kigyō hakusho* (*White Paper on Small and Medium-sized Enterprises*) (Tokyo: MOF Printing Office, 1988), pp. 42–3.

46 Ministry of Labor, *Rōdō hakusho* (*White Paper on Labor*) (Tokyo: Daiichi Hoki Shuppan, 1992), p. 344; Keizai Koho Center, *Japan: 1995* (Tokyo: Taiheisha Ltd, 1995), p. 67.

47 See "Kyūgeki na endaka de shitauke ijime" ("The Harsh Treatment of Subcontractors due to the Sudden Appreciation of the Yen"), *Nihon keizai shinbun*, 19 May 1986.

48 Japanese newspapers during this period carried numerous stories about small firms subjected to *shiwayose* (squeezing). One example: "Shukkō ukeire, shiwayose haiten" ("Accepting Transfer, Shiwayose Rotation"), *Asahi shinbun*, 6 December 1994, p. 2.

49 *New York Times*, 23 October 1994, p. 1 of section 3.

50 In the mid-1980s, Ishida Hideto, a former official of the JFTC, called these

distribution *keiretsu* "unparalleled in strength and breadth." See Ishida Hideto, "Anticompetitive Practices in the Distribution of Goods and Services in Japan: The Problem of Distribution *Keiretsu,*" *Journal of Japanese Studies,* Vol. 9, No. 2 (Summer 1983), p. 324.

51 *Asahi shinbun,* 30 November 1994, p. 11.

52 *Japan Economic Journal,* 25 November 1989.

53 These trends are discussed in "Ryūtsū gekihen" ("Dramatic Changes in Distribution"), *Nihon keizai shinbun,* 16 March 1995, p. 1

54 *Asahi shinbun,* 19 July 1994, p. 1.

55 *Asahi shinbun,* 4 March 1995, p. 13.

56 Gerlach, *Alliance Capitalism,* pp. 71–9.

57 ibid., p. 6.

58 Aoki, *Information, Incentives and Bargaining,* p. 101.

59 ibid., p. 165.

60 Ronald Dore, *British Factory – Japanese Factory: The Origin of National Diversity in Industrial Relations* (Berkeley: University of California Press, 1973), p. 364.

61 Masahiko Aoki, "The Japanese Firm in Transition" in Yamamura and Yasuba (eds), *The Political Economy of Japan, Vol. 1,* pp. 270–2.

62 This "system" really covers only an estimated one-third of Japan's labor force. As we have stressed already, it does not cover workers in small or medium-sized firms that use relatively unsophisticated technology. See Kazuo Koike, "Human Resource Development and Labor-Management Relations" in Yamamura and Yasuba (eds), *The Political Economy of Japan, Vol. 1,* p. 329.

63 ibid.

64 Robert E. Cole, *Japanese Blue Collar: The Changing Tradition* (Berkeley: University of California Press, 1971), p. 204.

65 The economic recession of the mid 1970s presented perhaps the most severe challenge to this practice of providing quasi-permanent tenure to employees of large firms. See Thomas P. Rohlen, "Permanent Employment Faces Recession, Slow Growth and an Aging Population," *Journal of Japanese Studies,* Vol. 5, No. 2 (Summer 1979), pp. 235–72.

66 *Nikkei Weekly,* 11 July 1992.

67 *New York Times,* 28 November 1993. Mazda engaged in a similar job-juggling act in the mid 1970s, when an oil embargo destroyed the profitability of its gas-guzzling rotary engine.

68 Murakami and Rohlen argue that Japan's government has used administrative guidance to promote cartels and other exclusionary alliances. "Recognizing the importance of limiting membership for the purpose of establishing consensus, the ministries have explored every means to restrict entry or at least to screen entrants into such major industries as steel, automobiles, synthetic fibers, petrochemicals and various financial activities." Murakami and Rohlen, "Social Exchange Aspects of the Japanese Political Economy," p. 94.

69 In an interview, Nakatani Iwao, one of Japan's leading economists, said that "much of Japan's business strength comes through the corporate networking and labor–management relations that serve as community bonds, joining everyone in a common fate." *Nikkei Weekly,* 11 July 1992.

70 Okumura Hiroshi, "The Closed Nature of Japanese Intercorporate Relations," *Japan Echo,* Vol. IX, No. 3 (1982), p. 57.

71 These costs include exorbitant retail prices. A team of Japanese economists has estimated that developmentalist policies and practices designed to benefit domestic producers robbed Japanese consumers of as much as ¥15 trillion

($110 billion, using the prevailing exchange rate of ¥138 = $1) in 1989 alone. Yoko Sazanami, Shujiro Urata, and Hiroki Kawai, *Measuring the Costs of Protection in Japan* (Washington: Institute for International Economics, 1995), p. 31.

72 Quoted in Bernard Wysocki, "Guiding Hand," *Wall Street Journal*, 20 August 1990, p. A1.

5 The Political Economy of Asia

1 Daniel Okimoto, "The Asian Perimeter, Moving Front and Center" in "Facing the Future: American Strategy in the 1990s," an Aspen Strategy Group report, published by the Aspen Strategy Group and University Press of America, the Aspen Institute for Humanist Studies, 1991, p. 145.

2 ibid.

3 See Anne Krueger, *Trade and Employment in Developing Countries: Synthesis and Conclusions* (Chicago: University of Chicago Press, 1982); Bela Belassa, *The Newly Industrializing Countries in the World Economy* (New York: Pergamon Press, 1981), and "The Lessons of East Asian Development," *Economic Development and Cultural Change*, Vol. 36, No. 3 (April 1988); Jagdish N. Bhagwati, "Rethinking Trade Strategy" in John P. Lewis and Valeriana Kallab (eds), *Development Strategies Reconsidered* (New Brunswick: Transaction Books, 1986); and William James, Seiji Naya, and Gerald Meier, *Asian Development: Economic Success and Policy Lessons* (Madison: University of Wisconsin Press, 1989).

4 See Stephen Haggard, *Pathways from the Periphery* (Ithaca: Cornell University Press, 1990); and Robert Wade, "The Role of Government" in Helen Hughes (ed.), *Achieving Industrialization in East Asia* (Cambridge: Cambridge University Press, 1988).

5 Roy Hofheinz, Jr and Kent Calder, *The Eastasia Edge* (New York: Basic Books, 1982); William J. O'Malley, "Culture and Industrialization" in Hughes (ed.), *Achieving Industrialization in East Asia*; and Ezra F. Vogel, *The Four Little Dragons: The Spread of Industrialization in East Asia* (Cambridge, Mass.: Harvard University Press, 1991).

6 Paul Krugman, in "The Myth of Asia's Miracle," *Foreign Affairs*, Vol. 73, No. 6 (November/December 1994), pp. 62–78, says Western observers are making the same mistake about East Asia that they once made about the former Soviet Union. That is, they are confusing economic growth caused by increased inputs, which is not sustainable, with economic growth caused by increased efficiency, which *is* sustainable. Krugman's analysis is based on a method of growth accounting pioneered by economists such as Simon Kuznets, Robert Solow, and Edward Dennison. A good example of this work is Edward Dennison, *Trends in American Economic Growth, 1929–1982* (Washington: Brookings Institution, 1985).

7 Orthodox dependency theory is typified by the work of Andre Gunder Frank. See, for example, Andre Gunder Frank, *Capitalism and Underdevelopment* (New York: Monthly Review Press, 1969). Faced with the reality of economic growth in some parts of the Third World, a new breed of *dependencistas* has attempted to improve upon this theory. See, for example, Fernando Henrique Cardoso, "Associated Dependent Development: Theoretical and Practical Implications" in Alfred Stepan (ed.), *Authoritarian Brazil: Origins, Policies, and Future* (New Haven: Yale University Press, 1973); and Peter Evans, *Dependent Development: The Alliance of Multinational, State and*

Local Capital in Brazil (Princeton: Princeton University Press, 1979). Evans argues that a "triple alliance" of multinational corporations, local capital, and the state is able to produce economic growth in a Third World country, but only at the expense of the mass of people in that country.

8 See Albert O. Hirschman, *National Power and the Structure of Foreign Trade* (Berkeley: University of California Press, 1945).

9 Fukuyama argues that Japan, unlike most Asian nations, has an abundant supply of "social capital," which fosters the sort of cooperation we have described. We choose not to use this trendy term because it is excessively vague. See Francis Fukuyama, "Social Capital and the Global Economy," *Foreign Affairs*, Vol. 74, No. 5 (September–October 1995).

10 This is a term used by Frederic C. Deyo, "Coalitions, Institutions and Linkage Sequencing" in Deyo (ed.), *The Political Economy of the New Asian Industrialism* (Ithaca: Cornell University Press, 1987), pp. 232–5.

11 Readers will notice quickly that we do not discuss Hong Kong in this chapter. The reason is simple: it is not a sovereign state.

12 Interview, 16 July 1992, Bangkok.

13 Yoshihara Kunio, *The Rise of Ersatz Capitalism in Southeast Asia* (Singapore: Oxford University Press, 1988), p. 112.

14 In Thailand, for example, patrimonialism continues to inform the state's economic planning efforts. This argument is made forcefully in Harvey Demaine, "*Kanpatthana*: Thai Views of Development" in Mark Hobart and Robert H. Taylor (eds), *Context, Meaning and Power in Southeast Asia* (Ithaca: Cornell University Press, 1986).

15 We are not subscribing here to the teleological assumptions of the "modernization" school of the 1950s and 1960s, perhaps best represented by Daniel Lerner, *The Passing of Traditional Society* (New York: Free Press, 1958). Using the West as their model of successful development, Lerner and his colleagues argued that all societies follow a simple, unilinear process of social evolution by which they progressively abandon "tradition" and become ever more complex, secular, differentiated, and, of course, "modern." This approach was debunked by Samuel Huntington in *Political Order in Changing Societies* (New Haven: Yale University Press, 1968), who argued that modernization was in fact a tumultuous, socially disruptive process that, without stable political institutions, could engulf developing societies. We have been influenced by Huntington and one of his students, Joel Migdal, *Strong States and Weak Societies: State-Society Relations and State Capabilities in the Third World* (Princeton: Princeton University Press, 1988). Migdal notes that developing societies can become stuck in a vicious cycle of accommodation between local "strongmen" and state leaders.

16 Mark Turner, "The Political Economy of the Philippines: Critical Perspectives," *Pacific Affairs*, Vol. 57, No. 3 (Fall 1984), p. 467.

17 Gary Hawes, "Theories of Peasant Revolution: A Critique and Contribution from the Philippines," *World Politics*, Vol. XLII, No. 2 (January 1990), p. 296.

18 "Hungry for Land," *Economist*, 5 March 1994.

19 See, for example, Donald K. Emmerson, "The Bureaucracy in Political Context: Weakness in Strength" in Karl D. Jackson and Lucien W. Pye (eds), *Political Power and Communication in Indonesia* (Berkeley: University of California Press, 1978); and Carol Warren, "Indonesian Development Policy and Community Organization in Bali," *Contemporary Southeast Asia*, Vol. 18, No. 3 (December 1986), pp. 213–30.

20 David Brown, *The State and Ethnic Politics in Southeast Asia* (London: Routledge, 1994), p. 118.

21 Sources for this history include Yoshihara, *Rise of Ersatz Capitalism*; Victor Purcell, *The Chinese in Southeast Asia* (London: Oxford University Press, 1965); G. William Skinner, "Chinese Assimilation and Thai Politics," *Journal of Asian Studies*, Vol. 16 (February 1957); and Leo Suryadinata, *Pribumi Indonesians, The Chinese Minority and China: A Study of Perceptions and Policies* (Kuala Lumpur: Heinemann Educational Books, 1978).

22 The rent-seeking relationship between local capitalists and state bureaucrats in Southeast Asia largely explains why the ASEAN-4 were slower to abandon import substitution policies than the more authoritarian regimes in the more homogeneous societies of Northeast Asia (South Korea, Taiwan, and Singapore).

23 Steven Schlossstein, *Asia's New Little Dragons: The Dynamic Emergence of Indonesia, Thailand, and Malaysia* (Chicago: Contemporary Books, 1991), p. 241.

24 *U.S. News and World Report*, 21 December 1992, p. 73.

25 Exporters and importers reported an immediate improvement – at least until 1992, when Indonesian officials began to reclaim authority: "Indonesia: The Long March," *Economist*, 17 April 1993, p. 7.

26 ibid., p. 8. Although he was not charged by authorities, Tommy Suharto, the president's youngest son, was a central figure in a recent case that fixed attention on Indonesia's cozy financial world. Indonesian prosecutors say Golden Key, a chemical and manufacturing group based in Jakarta, fraudulently obtained a $430 million line of credit from Bapindo, a state-owned bank. Tommy Suharto allegedly was the go-between who introduced the head of Golden Key to officials at Bapindo. See *FEER*, 23 June 1994, pp. 25–6.

27 Harold Crouch, *Domestic Political Structures and Regional Economic Cooperation* (Singapore: Institute of Southeast Asian Studies, 1984), p. 82.

28 *FEER*, 27 September 1990.

29 *Bangkok Bank Monthly Review*, Vol. 32 (November 1991), p. 424.

30 United Nations Development Programme (UNDP), *Human Development Report 1994* (New York: Oxford University Press, 1994).

31 Aoki Takeshi, "Mareishia: gaishi no kyuryunyu to nettowāku no keisei" ("Malaysia: A Rapid Inflow of Foreign Capital and the Formation of Networks") in Yanagihara Toru (ed.), *Ajia taiheiyō no keizai hatten to chiiki kyōryoku* (*Asia-Pacific Economic Development and Regional Cooperation*) (Tokyo: Ajia Keizai Kenkyūsho, 1992), p. 182.

32 UNDP, *Human Development Report 1994*.

33 Interview, 17 July 1992, Bangkok.

34 Interview, 13 July 1992, Bangkok.

35 Gunnar Myrdal, in *The Challenge of World Poverty: A World Anti-Poverty Program in Outline* (New York: Random House, 1970), may have been the first to distinguish between "hard" and "soft" states. Unfortunately, though, he never really defined such terms. He only offered a description of the "soft state" as undisciplined, and thus characterized by lax enforcement of laws and rules, and by collusion between public officials and powerful private interests.

36 Chong-Yah Lim, *Policy Options for the Singapore Economy* (Singapore: McGraw-Hill, 1988).

37 Economic Development Board of Singapore ("Investment Commitments by Country of Origin, 1985–1992"), data provided to authors.

38 Noeleen Heyzer, "International Production and Social Change" in Peter Chen (ed.), *Singapore: Development Policies and Trends* (Singapore: Oxford University Press, 1983); Frederic Deyo, "State and Labor in East Asia" in

Deyo (ed.), *The Political Economy of the New Asian Industrialism* (Ithaca: Cornell University Press, 1987), pp. 189–90.

39 Quoted in James Clad, *Behind the Myth: Business, Money and Power in Southeast Asia* (London: Unwin Hyman, 1989), p. 129.

40 Garry Rodan, *The Political Economy of Singapore's Industrialization* (New York: St Martin's Press, 1989), p. 180.

41 Chong Li Choy, "Singapore's Development: Harnessing the Multinationals," *Contemporary Southeast Asia*, Vol. 8, No. 1 (June 1986), p. 62.

42 Ian Chalmers, "International and Regional Integration: The Political Economy of the Electronics Industry in ASEAN," *ASEAN Economic Bulletin*, Vol. 8, No. 2 (November 1991).

43 Chng Meng Kng et al., *Technology and Skills in Singapore* (Singapore: Institute of Southeast Asian Studies, 1986), p. 79.

44 Interview, 27 April 1993, Singapore.

45 *FEER*, 16 July 1987, p. 60.

46 See Jung-en Woo, *Race to the Swift: State and Finance in Korean Industrialization* (New York: Columbia University Press, 1991), p. 107.

47 The bribes, which also financed the ruling junta's political party and secret police, are detailed in a special CIA report: "The Future of Korea–Japanese Relations," 18 March 1966, Country File, Box 251, NSF, LBJ Library.

48 Dal Joong Chang, "Japanese Corporations and the Political Economy of South Korean–Japanese Relations, 1965–1979" (PhD diss., University of California, Berkeley, 1982).

49 See Woo, *Race to the Swift*, pp. 159–75.

50 Byung-Nak Song, *The Rise of the Korean Economy* (Hong Kong: Oxford University Press, 1990).

51 ibid., p. 111.

52 Kenji Tahara-Domoto and Hirohisa Kohama, "Machinery Industry Development in Korea: Intra-Industry Trade Between Japan and Korea" in IDCJ Working Paper Series No. 43 (Tokyo: International Development Center of Japan, 1989).

53 Interview, 29 July 1992, Seoul.

54 See Song, *The Rise of the Korean Economy*, pp. 195–200; and You Jon-Il, "Capital–Labor Relations of the Newly Industrializing Regime in South Korea: Past, Present and Future," unpublished paper, April 1989, quoted in Walden Bello and Christine Rosenfeld, *Dragons in Distress: Asia's Miracle Economies in Crisis* (San Francisco: Institute for Food and Development Policy, 1990), p. 29.

55 Interview, 31 July 1992, Seoul.

56 *FEER*, 19 April 1990, pp. 74–5.

57 George E. Ogle, *South Korea: Dissent within the Economic Miracle* (London: Zed Books, 1990), pp. 122–4.

58 Alice Amsden, *Asia's Next Giant: South Korea and Late Industrialization* (New York: Oxford University Press, 1989).

59 *Electronic News*, 5 September 1994. Samsung's big announcement came about a year after a less publicized report by four Japanese manufacturers claiming that *they* had just developed the 256 MB DRAM chip. See *Journal of Electronic Engineering*, Vol. 30, No. 323 (November 1993), pp. 30–1.

60 Sohn Jie-Ae, "Korea–Japan Rivalry: A Different Kind of War," *Business Korea*, February 1995, pp. 18–20.

61 *Nikkei Weekly*, 4 October 1993.

62 Interview, 31 July 1992, Seoul.

63 Shuet-Ying Ho, *Taiwan, After a Long Silence* (Hong Kong: Asia Monitor Research Center, 1990), p. 63.
64 "Labor Disputes Create Major Problems for Country," Central News Agency, 2 February 1989, reproduced in FBIS: China, 2 February 1989, p. 76.
65 In 1991, the Economist Intelligence Unit estimated that wages in Taiwan were rising twice as fast as productivity: see *Economist*, 16 November 1991, pp. 12–13. However, in early 1995 it estimated that wages and productivity were rising at almost the same rate: see Economist Intelligence Unit, *Country Report: Taiwan* (London: EIU, 1995).
66 Bello and Rosenfeld, *Dragons in Distress*, p. 241.
67 Denis Fred Simon, "External Incorporation and Internal Reform" in Edwin A. Winckler and Susan Greenhalgh (eds), *Contending Approaches to the Political Economy of Taiwan* (Armonk, New York: M. E. Sharpe Inc., 1988), p. 147.
68 For a solid history of this period, see Samuel P. S. Ho, *Economic Development of Taiwan, 1860–1970* (New Haven: Yale University Press, 1978).
69 The KMT's Leninist structure seems less surprising when we recall that, in the early days, before they finally split from the Chinese Communist Party, KMT leaders received advice from Bolshevik organizers.
70 *Tian xia zazhi* (*Commonwealth Magazine*, Taipei), 10 June 1994, p. 99.
71 Thomas B. Gold, *State and Society in the Taiwan Miracle* (Armonk, New York: M. E. Sharpe Inc., 1986); Bing Su, *Taiwan's 400 Year History: The Origins and Continuing Development of the Taiwanese Society and People* (Washington: Taiwan Cultural Grassroots Association, 1986).
72 Bello and Rosenfeld, *Dragons in Distress*, p. 237.
73 Ichiro Namazaki, "Networks of Taiwanese Big Business: A Preliminary Analysis," *Modern China*, Vol. 12, No. 4 (October 1986), p. 515.
74 Gold, *State and Society in the Taiwan Miracle*, p. 108.
75 *Economist*, 20 April 1991, pp. 83–4, and 16 November 1991, p. 15; also *Business Week*, 29 November 1993, p. 104.
76 Rob Steven, *Japan's New Imperialism* (Armonk, New York: M. E. Sharpe, 1990), p. 121.
77 Thomas B. Gold, "Entrepreneurs, Multinationals and the State" in Winckler and Greenhalgh (eds), *Contending Approaches*, p. 190.
78 Huang Chi, "The State and Foreign Capital: A Case Study of Taiwan" (PhD diss., Indiana University, 1986), p. 189; Denis Simon, "Taiwan, Technology Transfer and Transnationals: The Political Management of Dependency" (PhD diss., University of California, Berkeley, 1980), p. 350.
79 *Economist*, 16 November 1991.
80 *FEER*, 23 February 1995, p. 50.
81 *Wall Street Journal*, 23 August 1994, p. A10.
82 *Asahi Evening News*, 1 August 1994.
83 The government uses a two-track pricing policy that is designed to compensate these industries for artificially low output prices by offering them inputs at below-market prices. This does little good, because the regulated industries still have to buy most of their inputs on the free (and unregulated) market. Instead, it encourages rent-seeking. State enterprises gain large, but illegal, profits by storing and later reselling in the free market the inputs they receive from the government at below-market prices. See Edward K.Y. Chen and Po-Wah Wong, "Recent Developments in the Chinese Economy with Special Reference to Industrial Issues," a paper presented at the third joint research conference on Asia-Pacific Relations sponsored by FAIR, Malaysia, July 1992, pp. 205–41.

84 Roy Grow, "Japanese and American Firms in China: Lessons of a New Market," *Columbia Journal of World Business*, Spring 1986, p. 54.
85 *FEER*, 7 July 1994, p. 60. For a more in-depth analysis of this dilemma, see Gordon White, *Riding the Tiger: The Politics of Economic Reform in Post-Mao China* (Stanford: Stanford University Press, 1993).
86 *Fortune*, 5 October 1992, p. 125.
87 ibid., p. 126.
88 ibid., pp. 120–2.
89 ibid., pp. 121–2; and *Economist* ("A Survey of China"), 18 March 1995.
90 *Business Week*, 29 November 1993, p. 103.
91 *Nikkei Weekly*, 13 April 1995, p. 20.
92 *Boston Globe*, 5 December 1993.
93 *Economist* ("A Survey of China"), 18 March 1995.
94 See *Seattle Times* (with an article by *Baltimore Sun* reporter Ian Johnson), 25 September 1994, p. A15, and *Seattle Times* (with an article by *Chicago Tribune* reporter Uli Schmetzer), 8 May 1994, p. A16.
95 *Seattle Times*, 25 September 1994, p. A15.
96 *Fortune*, 5 October 1992; John Kao, "The Worldwide Web of Chinese Business," *Harvard Business Review*, March/April 1993, p. 24.
97 *Business Week*, 29 November 1993.
98 "Where Tigers Breed," *Economist*, 16 November 1991, p. 6.
99 Similar descriptions of overseas Chinese capital can be found in Watanabe Toshio (ed.), *Kajin keizai no nettowāku (The Networks of [Overseas] Chinese)* (Tokyo: Jitsugyō no Nihonsha, 1994).

6 Holding Technology

1 Thomas S. Arrison, C. Fred Bergsten, Edward M. Graham and Martha Caldwell Harris, "Japan's Growing Technological Capability and Implications for the U.S. Economy" in Thomas S. Arrison, C. Fred Bergsten, Edward M. Graham, and Martha Caldwell Harris (eds), *Japan's Growing Technological Capability: Implications for the U.S. Economy* (Washington: National Academy Press, 1992), p. 3.
2 National Science Board, *Science and Engineering Indicators: 1993* (Washington: US Government Printing Office, 1993), pp. 177–85.
3 Science and Technology Agency, *Kagaku gijutsu hakusho (White Paper on Science and Technology)*, cited by Shigetaka Seki, "What Can we Learn from Technology Assessment?" in Arrison et al. (eds), *Japan's Growing Technological Capability*, pp. 51–2.
4 US R&D expenditures in 1993 represented 2.6 percent of GNP. If we exclude spending on defense-related research and development, however, the US proportion falls to only 1.9 percent. Figures for both Japan and the United States are included in US Bureau of the Census, *The Statistical Abstract of the United States: 1994*, 114th edn (Washington: US Printing Office, 1994), p. 610.
5 "More Funds for Japan Research," Associated Press, 29 November 1994.
6 Kosai Yutaka, president of the Japan Center for Economic Research (JCER), is even more sanguine. Technology transfer via FDI is "disrupting the pattern of 'flying geese'" in Asia and "widening the changes for success of a 'leapfrog' development strategy." Kosai, "APEC Summit in Osaka in 1995," *JCER Report*, Vol. 7, No. 1 (January 1995), p. 2. Kosai ignores the reality we hope to expose in this chapter – that technology transfer from Japan is a painfully slow, relatively controlled process.

7 See *FEER*, 8 June 1989, p. 73.
8 Ajia Keizai Kenkyūjo, *Minkan keizai kyōryoku chōsa kenkyū hōkokusho* (*A Research Report Examining Private Economic Cooperation*) (Tokyo: MITI, March 1992), p. 320.
9 Interview, 28 July 1992, Seoul.
10 Peter Chow and Mitchell Kellman, *Trade: The Engine of Growth in East Asia* (New York: Oxford University Press, 1993), p. 61.
11 The similarity index measures the degree of export-vector overlap. If two countries exported mutually exclusive categories of products with no product overlap, the index would be 0. If they exported identical product categories, the index would equal 1. See J. Finger and M. Kerinin, "A Measure of 'Export Similarity' and Its Possible Use," *Economic Journal*, Vol. 89 (1979), pp. 905–12.
12 Chow and Kellman, *Trade*, p. 49.
13 ibid., p. 42.
14 Tatsuo Tanaka, "Technology-based Trade Pattern of Japan and Korea," a research paper, International University of Japan, Summer 1994, pp. 15–16. In this study, Tanaka assumes that capital moves freely; if new technology becomes available, Korea would be able to increase the capital–labor ratio necessary to adopt it. By "trade pattern" he means "specialization index" (SI) calculated as the ratio of [export–input] divided by [export + input]. His finding that Korea's trade pattern changed around 1980 is based on the Chow test he performed on the pooled data for the 1973–80 and 1980–89 periods. The form of the multiple regression equation is $SI = a + bKL + cYL$ where KL is the capital–labor ratio and YL is the output–labor ratio.
15 ibid., p. 21.
16 Jong-Il Kim and Lawrence J. Lau, "The Sources of Economic Growth of the East Asian Newly Industrializing Countries," Stanford University, September 1993, pp. 34–41. Their study uses what is known as the transcendental logarithmic production function, first introduced by L. R. Christensen, D. W. Jorgensen, and L. J. Lau in "Transcendental Logarithmic Production Frontiers," *Review of Economics and Statistics*, Vol. 55 (1973), pp. 28–45.
17 ibid., p. 35. Young has reached much the same conclusion. See Alwyn Young, "The Tyranny of Numbers: Confronting the Statistical Realities of the East Asian Growth Experience," NBER Working Paper No. 4680, March 1994.
18 *FEER*, 8 June 1989, p. 73.
19 In an analysis of the technological challenges facing Korean automakers, Green makes a similar point. "The Koreans, unlike the Japanese of twenty years ago, are chasing a target that is moving away from them at an ever increasing rate." Andrew E. Green, "South Korea's Automobile Industry," *Asian Survey*, Vol. 32, No. 5 (May 1992), p. 427.
20 See Yasusuke Murakami, "Technology in Transition: Two Perspectives on Industrial Policy" in Hugh Patrick (ed.), *Japan's High Technology Industries: Lessons and Limitations of Industrial Policy* (Seattle: University of Washington Press, 1986).
21 John Cantwell, "Japan's Industrial Competitiveness and the Technological Capabilities of the Leading Japanese Firms" in Arrison et al. (eds), *Japan's Growing Technological Capability*, p. 184.
22 Christopher Freeman, *Technology Policy and Economic Performance: Lessons from Japan* (London: Pinter Publishers, 1987), pp. 31–54. Also see Richard Samuels, *"Rich Nation Strong Army": National Security and the Technological Transformation of Japan* (Ithaca: Cornell University Press, 1994), which

argues that Japan pursues a policy of indigenizing, diffusing, and nurturing technology in its own long-term national interest.

23 See Allen L. Brown and Gregory A. Daneke, "The Rising Electric Sun: Japan's Photovoltaics Industry," *Issues in Science and Technology*, Vol. III, No. 3 (Spring 1987), p. 70. The authors conclude that Japanese firms have "done a better job than U.S. firms of seeing the broad-scale potential of photovoltaics."

24 D. J. Teece, G. Pisano, and A. Shuen, "Dynamic Capabilities and Strategic Management," working paper, Center for Strategic Management, University of California, Berkeley, 1990.

25 B. Bowonder, T. Miyake, and H. A. Linstone, "Japanese Institutional Mechanisms for Industrial Growth: A Systems Perspective – Part I," *Technological Forecasting and Social Change*, Vol. 47, No. 2 (October 1994).

26 Michael Borrus, "Reorganizing Asia: Japan's New Development Trajectory and the Regional Division of Labor," working paper 53, Berkeley Roundtable on the International Economy, March 1992, p. 24.

27 Ken-ichi Imai, "Globalization and Cross-border Networks of Japanese Firms," SJC-R Working Papers Series No. 1, Stanford–Japan Center-Research, September 1991, p. 22.

28 Gary Hamel, "Competition for Competence and Inter-partner Learning within International Strategic Alliances," *Strategic Management Journal*, Vol. 12 (1991), p. 94.

29 ibid., p. 93.

30 Charles Lindsey, "Transfer of Technology to the ASEAN Region by U.S. Transnational Corporations," paper presented at the Conference on ASEAN–US Economic Relations, Institute of Southeast Asian Studies, Singapore, 22–24 April 1985.

31 Park Woo-hee, "Japan's Role in the Structural Adjustment of the Asian-Pacific Economies," *Journal of International Economic Studies*, No. 6 (March 1992).

32 Interview, 23 April 1993, Kuala Lumpur.

33 Dan Biers, "Matsushita Pioneers Effort to Localize," *Asian Wall Street Journal*, 9 August 1994, p. 4.

34 Chia Siow Yue, "Japanese Overseas Direct Investment in ASEAN and Asian NIES," a research monograph, VRF Series No. 187, Institute of Developing Economies, Tokyo, February 1991, p. 64.

35 Chng Meng Kng et al., *Technology and Skills in Singapore* (Singapore: Institute of Southeast Asian Studies, 1986), pp. 98, 100.

36 *Asahi shinbun*, 25 March 1995, p. 11.

37 Nigel Campbell, "Japanese Business Strategy in China," *Long-range Planning*, Vol. 20, No. 5 (1987), p. 71.

38 *Wall Street Journal*, 7 November 1994.

39 Korea–Japan Economic Cooperation Association, "Hanilgan sanŏp mit kisul hyŏmnyŏk hyŏnhwang" ("The current condition of technological cooperation between Korean and Japanese Industries"), research findings based on a questionnaire, Seoul, 1992, p. 15.

40 *FEER*, 8 June 1989, p. 73; *Electronic Business*, 6 February 1989, p. 28.

41 *Business Korea*, February 1992, p. 24.

42 Lee Wong-Young and Kim Jae-Hyung, "Kisul toip taegga ŭi kyŏlchong" ("Determinants of the Royalty Payment in Technology Licensing), *Han'guk kaebal yŏn'gu* (*Korea Development Review*), Korea Development Institute, Vol. 9, No. 1 (Spring 1987). An abbreviated, English version of the article is available through KDI. The authors attribute the larger monopoly rent

earned by Japanese technology suppliers to the oligopolistic structure of Japan's high-tech industries. US firms supplying technology to Korea often are, in contrast, small companies that lack the capacity to engage in mass production. As a result, they are only too eager to license their innovations.

43 Anuwar Ali, "Japan's Role in Technology Transfer to Malaysia," a paper for a conference on Japan's Role in the Transfer of Technology to ASEAN Countries, organized by Thammasat University, Bangkok, 26–27 June 1992, pp. 6-22–6-23.

44 Interview, 22 April 1993, Kuala Lumpur.

45 Richard F. Doner, *Driving a Bargain: Automobile Industrialization and Japanese Firms in Southeast Asia* (Berkeley: University of California Press, 1991), p. 119.

46 *Nikkei Weekly*, 2 May 1992, p. 1.

47 Walden Bello and Christine Rosenfeld, *Dragons in Distress: Asia's Miracle Economies in Crisis* (San Francisco: Institute for Food and Development Policy, 1990), pp. 148–9.

48 *Nikkei Weekly*, 2 May 1992, p. 1.

49 *New York Times*, 13 April 1993, pp. C1–C2.

50 C. Y. Ng, R. Hirono, and Robert Y. Siy, *Technology and Skills in ASEAN: An Overview* (Singapore: Institute of Southeast Asian Studies, 1986), p. 45; United Nations, *Costs and Conditions of Technology Transfer Through Transnational Corporations* (Bangkok: Economic and Social Commission for Asia and the Pacific, ESCAP/UNCTC Joint Unit on Transnational Corporations, 1984), pp. 193–226; Mingsarn Santikarn Kaosa-ard, "Comparative Analysis of Direct Foreign Investment in Thailand," a paper for a conference at the Hoover Institution, Stanford University, on Japan and the Regionalization of Asia, March 1993, p. 15.

51 Anuwar, "Japan's Role in Technology Transfer," pp. 6-20–6-21.

52 See *FEER*, 3 May 1990, p. 54; Denis Fred Simon, "Technology Transfer and National Autonomy" in Edwin A. Winckler and Susan Greenhalgh (eds), *Contending Approaches to the Political Economy of Taiwan* (Armonk, New York: M. E. Sharpe Inc., 1988), pp. 213–14; and *Business Korea*, July 1990, p. 77.

53 Sakong Mok, "Han-Il sanŏp hyŏmnyŏk ŭi hyŏnhwang kwa hyanghu ch'ujin panghyang" ("Korean-Japan Industrial Cooperation: Current Conditions and Future Directions"), *Segye kyongje tonghyang* (*Trends in the Global Economy*), December 1991, p. 98.

54 *Electronics Korea*, February 1989, pp. 31–2.

55 T. Tsuneishi, "Tai-Nikkei kigyō shūdo ni yoru gijutsu iten" ("Japanese Affiliates in Thailand Playing the Leading Role in Technology Transfer") in Taniura Takao (ed.), *Ajia no kōgyōka to gijutsu iten* (*Asian Industrialization and Technology Transfer*) (Tokyo: Ajia Keizai Shuppankai, 1990); Charles T. Stewart and Yasumitsu Nihei, *Technology Transfer and Human Factors: A Comparative Study of American and Japanese Contributions to Indonesia and Thailand* (Washington: George Washington University, 1986).

56 See Yoshihara Kunio, *The Rise of Ersatz Capitalism in Southeast Asia* (Singapore: Oxford University Press, 1988).

57 See E. K. Y. Chen, *Multinational Corporations, Technology and Employment* (London: Macmillan, 1983); and Seiji Naya and Eric Ramstetter, "Policy Interactions and Direct Foreign Investment in East and Southeast Asia," *Journal of World Trade*, Vol. 22, No. 2 (April 1988).

58 Tran Van Tho, "Status of Technology Transfer in the ASEAN Region," a paper for a conference on Japan's Role in the Transfer of Technology to

ASEAN Countries, organized by Thammasat University, Bangkok, 26–27 June 1992, p. 1–3.

59 Robert E. Lipsey, "Direct Foreign Investment and Structural Change in Developing Asia, Japan and the United States" in Eric Ramstetter (ed.), *Direct Foreign Investment in Asia's Developing Economies and Structural Change in the Asia-Pacific Region* (Boulder: Westview Press, 1991), p. 290; Bunluasak Pussarungsri, "Effect of Foreign Direct Investment," Thailand Development Research Institute, April 1993.

60 Dieter Ernst, "Carriers of Regionalization: The East Asian Production Networks of Japanese Electronics Firms," working paper 73, Berkeley Roundtable on the International Economy, November 1994, p. 26.

61 Stewart notes that Japanese affiliates in Thailand and Indonesia experience far less turnover than US affiliates in those countries. See Charles Stewart, Jr, "Comparing Japanese and U.S. Technology Transfer to Less Developed Countries," *Journal of Northeast Asian Studies*, Vol. 4 (Spring 1985), p. 13.

62 ibid., pp. 14–15.

63 This distinction is made by Mun De Yang, "Gijutsu no torihiki to seisan" ("Production and technology trade") in Taniura (ed.), *Ajia no kōgyōka to gijutsu iten*, p. 53.

64 See Shōichi Yamashita, "Economic Development of the ASEAN Countries of the Role of Japanese Direct Investment" in Yamashita (ed.), *Transfer of Japanese Technology and Management to the ASEAN Countries* (Tokyo: University of Tokyo Press, 1991), pp. 17, 201.

65 *Wall Street Journal*, 20 August 1990, p. A4.

66 Takao Kiba and Fumio Kodama, "Measurement and Analysis of the Progress of International Technology Transfer: Case Study of Direct Investment in East Asian Countries by Japanese Companies," NISTEP Report No. 18, National Institute of Science and Technology Policy, Science and Technology Agency of Japan, April 1991, p. 33.

67 Mirza has called this phenomenon "peripheral intermediation," which he defines as "the production of goods and services in a given country, *predominantly* utilizing inputs from *abroad* for the *principal* purpose of *export* to other countries." See Hafiz Mirza, *Multinationals and the Growth of the Singapore Economy* (London: Croom Helm, 1986), p. 195.

68 Dennis Normile, "Japan Holds on Tight to Cutting-edge Technology," *Science*, Vol. 262 (15 October 1993), p. 352.

69 Tessa Morris-Suzuki, "Japanese Technology and the new International Division of Knowledge in Asia" in Shojiro Tokunaga (ed.), *Japan's Foreign Investment and Asian Economic Interdependence: Production, Trade and Financial Systems* (Tokyo: University of Tokyo Press, 1992), p. 149.

70 Anuwar, "Japan's Role in Technology Transfer," pp. 6-27–6-29.

71 Kodama and Kiba make this same point in a research monograph. Fumio Kodama and Takao Kiba, "The Emerging Trajectory of International Technology," Asia-Pacific Research Center, Stanford University, 1994, p. 22.

72 Rob Steven, *Japan's New Imperialism* (Armonk, New York: M. E. Sharpe Inc., 1990), p. 202.

73 Interview with Kamimoto Tadashi, director of R&D for the Matsushita air conditioning group, 23 April 1993, Shah Alam, Malaysia.

74 Ng et al. (eds), *Technology and Skills in ASEAN*, pp. 56–7.

75 Japan Machinery Exporters Association, "Wagakuni kikai sangyō no Ajia ni okeru seisan bungyō jittai ni tsuite" ("The Actual State of Production and Division of Labor by Japanese Machine Industries Operating in Asia"), a survey, June 1994, p. 20. Multiple responses were possible to this question.

76 Ernst, "Carriers of Regionalization," p. 19.
77 Mark McQuillan, "An Imposing, 'Invisible' Presence," *Japan Economic Journal*, "The Rising Tide: Japan in Asia," special supplement, Winter 1990, p. 26.
78 The same conclusion is reached by Anupup Tiralap of the Thailand Development Research Institute in "Japan's Role in Technology Transfer in Thailand," a paper for a conference on Japan's Role in the Transfer of Technology in ASEAN Countries, organized by Thammasat University, Bangkok, 26–27 June 1992, pp. 8–15.
79 Imano Kōichiro, "Nihon kigyō no chokusetsu tōshi to gijutsu iten" ("Direct Investment and Technology Transfer by Japanese Firms") in Taniura (ed.), *Ajia no kōgyōka to gijutsu iten*, p. 71.
80 Shujiro Urata, "Changing Patterns of Direct Investment and the Implications for Trade and Development" in C. Fred Bergsten and Marcus Noland (eds), *Pacific Dynamism and the International Economic System* (Washington: Institute for International Economics, 1993), pp. 288–9.
81 Kinbara Tatsuo, "Possibilities and Conditions of Japanese Management," a paper presented at the Hiroshima Conference on "Beyond Japanese-style Management in ASEAN Countries," October 1989, cited in Chia Siow Yue, "Japanese Overseas Direct Investment in ASEAN and Asian NIEs," Visiting Research Fellow Series No. 187, Institute of Developing Economies, Tokyo, February 1991, pp. 64–5.
82 Samart Chiasakul and Prasert Silapipat, "Case of Thailand" in Institute of Developing Economies, *The Role of Japanese Direct Investment in Developing Countries* (Tokyo: IDE, 1992), pp. 317–19.
83 Interview, 17 July 1992, Bangkok.
84 Karatsu Hajime, "Kaku ni naru gijutsu o osaereba kūdō-ka wa kowaku nai" ("If We Control the Core Technology, We Need Not Fear 'Hollowing Out'"), *Ekonomisuto*, 11 November 1994, p. 33.

7 The Visible Handshake

1 The anti-Japanese demonstrations are discussed in detail in Raul Manglapus, *Japan in Southeast Asia: A Collision Course* (New York: Carnegie Endowment for International Peace, 1976). In part, demonstrators – especially those in Indonesia – used the event (a visit by Tanaka Kakuei) as a pretext to register opposition to military-bureaucratic elites in their own countries. But many also felt genuine resentment over Japan's large and growing commercial presence in the region.
2 Interview with Pradup Pibulsonggram, deputy director general of the department of economic affairs in Thailand's foreign ministry, 17 July 1992, Bangkok.
3 For a review of this literature, see Gregory W. Noble, "The Japanese Industrial Policy Debate" in Stephen Haggard and Chung-in Moon (eds), *Pacific Dynamics* (Boulder: Westview Press, 1989).
4 Michio Muramatsu and Ellis Krauss, "Bureaucrats and Politicians in Policy-making: The Case of Japan," *American Political Science Review*, Vol. 78, No. 1 (March 1984).
5 Chalmers Johnson, "MITI, MPT and the Telecom Wars: How Japan Makes Policy for High Technology" in Chalmers Johnson, Laura D'Andrea Tyson, and John Zysman (eds), *Politics and Productivity: The Real Story of Why Japan Works* (Cambridge, Mass.: Ballinger, 1989).
6 Van Wolferen, a Dutch journalist, expresses the new orthodoxy most passionately. "The frustration of many a foreign negotiator, meeting the

umpteenth mediator sent his way, can be summed up in the single cry, 'Take me to your leader.' Japan does not have one. It is pushed, or pulled, or kept afloat, but not actually led, by many power-holders in what I call the System." Karel van Wolferen, *The Enigma of Japanese Power: People and Politics in a Stateless Nation* (New York: Vintage Books, 1990), p. 43.

7 See, for example, Inoguchi Takashi, "Japan's Response to the Gulf Crisis: An Analytic Overview," *Journal of Japanese Studies*, Vol. 17, No. 2 (Summer 1991); and Yamaguchi Jirō, "The Gulf War and the Transformation of Japanese Constitutional Politics," *Journal of Japanese Studies*, Vol. 18, No. 1 (Winter 1992).

8 T. J. Pempel, "The Unbundling of 'Japan Inc.': The Changing Dynamics of Japanese Policy Formation," *Journal of Japanese Studies*, Vol. 13, No. 2 (Summer 1987), pp. 287–8.

9 We could refer to this network as a "bureaucratic-industrial complex." While Japan's politicians have the final say on "redistribution" policies affecting special interests, such as agriculture and small business, bureaucrats more often than not get their way on larger or more long-run issues perceived to be in the national interest, such as foreign policy and economic planning. See, for example, Yamaguchi Jirō, "Kanryōsei no minshuka o dō susumeru ka" ("How Do We Promote the Democratization of the Bureaucratic System?"), *Ekonomisuto*, 24 August 1993. The political instability of the late 1980s and early 1990s, when a new prime minister seemed to arrive every year, served to reinforce this pattern. See, for example, Ikuta Tadao, "Jimintō seiken hōkai de tōrai shita `kanryō dokusai'" ("'Bureaucratic Dictatorship' in the Wake of the Collapse of the LDP"), *Foresight*, August 1993.

10 See Richard J. Samuels, *The Business of the Japanese State: Energy Markets in Comparative and Historical Perspective* (Ithaca: Cornell University Press, 1987), p. 9.

11 Consider the title of MITI's 1986 white paper on economic cooperation: *Toward a New International Division of Labor: Promoting Aid, Trade, and Investment as One in International Cooperation.*

12 David Arase, "Japanese Foreign Aid: The State, the Polity and the International System" (PhD diss., University of California, Berkeley, 1989), p. 130.

13 Nobutoshi Akao (ed.), *Japan's Economic Security* (New York: St Martin's Press, 1983).

14 *Straits Times*, 13 December 1977.

15 MITI, *Nihon no sentaku: Nyū gurōbarizumu e no kōken to "shin sangyō bunka kokka" no sentaku (Japan's Choices: Options for a Nation with a New Corporate Culture and Contributions Toward a New Globalism)* (Tokyo: Tsūshō Chōsakai, 1988), quoted in Masataka Kosaka (ed.), *Japan's Choices: New Globalism and Cultural Orientations in an Industrial State* (New York: Pinter Publishers, 1989), p. 6.

16 Foundation for Advanced Information and Research (FAIR), *Interim Report of the Committee for Asia-Pacific Economic Research* (Singapore: Look Publishing, 1989), p. v.

17 MITI, *Tsūshō hakusho (White Paper on Trade)* (Tokyo: Ministry of Finance Printing Bureau, 1989), pp. 237–8.

18 We discuss Vernon's product cycle theory in chapter one and Akamatsu's flying geese theory in chapter two.

19 Kitamura Kayoko, "Developments and the Status of Direct Investment in Asia," a paper presented at the second Asia-Pacific conference sponsored by FAIR, Tokyo, 9–10 May 1991, p. I–454.

20 Japan Research Institute, *Kokusai keizai kankyō gekihenka ni okeru sōgōteki keizai kyōryoku suishin chōsa hōkokusho: Ajia nettowāku no kōchiku ni mukete* (*Promoting Comprehensive Economic Cooperation in an International Economic Environment Undergoing Dramatic Change: Toward the Construction of an Asian Network*) (Tokyo: Economic Planning Agency, 1988), pp. 126–7, as quoted in Arase, "Japanese Foreign Aid," p. 374.

21 Arase, "Japanese Foreign Aid," p. 376.

22 *Kore kara no ASEAN kyōryoku* (*Future Cooperation with ASEAN*) in *The OECF Research Quarterly*, special edn, 1987, as quoted in Daniel Unger, "Japanese Manufacturing Investment and Export-Processing Industrialization in Thailand," USJP Occasional Papers 90-15, Harvard University, 1990, p. 27.

23 Interview, 9 July 1992, Tokyo.

24 Susumu Yamakage, "From Investment to Integration: The Political Economy of Foreign Direct Investment of Japanese Enterprises in the ASEAN Region," a paper presented at the first conference on Asia-Pacific relations sponsored by FAIR, Tokyo, 20–22 April 1988, p. II–193.

25 Mingsarn Santikarn Kaosa-ard, "Comparative Analysis of Direct Foreign Investment in Thailand," a paper for a conference sponsored by the Hoover Institution, Stanford University, on Japan and the Regionalization of Asia, March 1993, p. 24.

26 "Seifu shusshi gōben: Chūgoku no Dairen kōgyō danchi kaihatsu" ("Joint Venture with Government Investment: Development of an Industrial Park in China's Dalian"), *Nihon keizai shinbun*, 26 September 1991, p. 1; "Dairen kōgyō danchi ni 51-oku en o shutsuyūshi" ("Investing ¥5.1 billion in Dalian Industrial Park"), *Nihon keizai shinbun*, 18 April 1992, p. 5; "Kita no Honkon e Dairen no chōsen" ("Dalian's Challenge to Hong Kong in the North"), *Nihon keizai shinbun*, 20 June 1991, p. 9.

27 MITI, *Background Information: Japan's Economic Cooperation, 1993* (Tokyo: MITI, Economic Cooperation Division, 1993), p. 179.

28 MITI, *Dai-san-kai, kaigai jigyō katsudō kihon chōsa* (*The Third Basic Survey on Overseas Investment*) (Tokyo: MOF Printing Bureau, 1986), p. 71; MITI, *Dai-ni-kai, kaigai jigyō katsudō kihon chōsa* (*The Second Basic Survey on Overseas Investment*) (Tokyo: MOF Printing Bureau, 1983), p. 65.

29 *FEER*, 2 May 1991, p. 47.

30 Thee Kian Wie, "Interactions of Japanese Aid and Direct Investment in Indonesia," *ASEAN Economic Bulletin*, Vol. 11, No. 1 (July 1994), p. 31.

31 Shojiro Tokunaga (ed.), *Japan's Foreign Investment and Asian Economic Interdependence* (Tokyo: University of Tokyo Press, 1992), pp. 21–4. Also see MITI, *Background Information: Japan's Economic Cooperation, 1993*, p. 182.

32 *Mainichi shinbun*, 11 May 1987, p. 23. The newspaper revealed confidential records of a JETRO workshop (Wairo no susume, or The Promotion of Bribery) at which officials of general trading companies lectured on the topic of bribing foreign officials to win construction contracts.

33 "MITI Urges Electronics Firms to Produce Abroad," *Nikkei Weekly*, 13 June 1992, p. 1.

34 *Asahi Evening News*, 9 August 1994.

35 "Beyond the Trade Game," *Time*, 21 February 1994, p. 19.

36 Interview with Isoyama Katsuhiko, representative of JFS in Kuala Lumpur, 26 April 1993.

37 "Ajia shokoku ni sangyō ritchi shidō" ("Local Guidance for Industry in Asian Countries"), *Nihon keizai shinbun*, 20 September 1990, p. 5.

38 "Gathering of the Clan," *FEER*, 28 March 1991, p. 52.

39 "Guide to AOTS, 1989," informational brochure.

40 MFA, *Wagakuni no seifu kaihatsu enjo no jissho jōkyō* (*Annual Report on the Status of Japanese ODA*) (Tokyo: MFA, research and planning section of the Economic Cooperation Bureau, 1994), p. 73. These numbers come from Alexander R. Love, *Development Cooperation: Efforts and Policies of the Members of the Development Assistance Committee (1993 Report)* (Paris: OECD, 1994).

41 JETRO, *Sekai to Nihon no kaigai chokusetsu toshi* (*Foreign Direct Investment of the World and Japan*) (Tokyo: JETRO, 1992), pp. 175–220. Also see "Jam Tomorrow: Japan Warns on Malaysian Infrastructure," *FEER*, 5 April 1990, pp. 46–7.

42 Peter J. Katzenstein and Martin Rouse, "Japan as a Regional Power in Asia" in Jeffrey A. Frankel and Miles Kahler (eds), *Regionalism and Rivalry: Japan and the United States in Pacific Asia* (Chicago: University of Chicago Press: 1993), p. 232. In the same volume, Islam attacks this logic as "misleading." He notes that bridges, roads, and ports are "public goods" that benefit all firms using them, not just Japanese multinationals: Shafiqul Islam, "Foreign Aid and Burdensharing: Is Japan Freeriding to a Coprosperity Sphere in Pacific Asia?", p. 355. This is true. But it does not undermine our argument that Japanese ODA promotes Japanese investment.

43 Yen loans accounted for more than 43 percent of Japan's bilateral aid in 1993, 55 percent in 1992, and 62 percent in 1991. On average, loans accounted for only 21 percent of the bilateral ODA given by all of the world's major donors in 1992. See MFA, *Wagakuni no seifu kaihatsu enjo no jissho jōkyō*, pp. 40, 68, and *Japan's ODA: Annual Report, 1993* (Tokyo: Association for the Promotion of International Cooperation, 1994), p. 45. Alan Rix offers a historical analysis of this issue in his essay, "Japan's Foreign Aid Policy: A Capacity for Leadership?", *Pacific Affairs*, Vol. 62, No. 4 (Winter 1989–1990), pp. 464–5.

44 Love, *Development Cooperation*, p. 119. We cannot help but wonder whether Japan will continue to make much progress toward increasing the quality of its aid. In November 1993, an advisory panel to MOF called for a reduction in the grant portion of Japan's ODA. It cited budget constraints. See "Government Panel Agrees to Limit ODA Budget," Kyōdō Economic News Wire, 2 November 1993.

45 Japan's grant ratio was only 42.6 percent in 1991–92 and 38.6 percent in 1990–91. The DAC average was 77.5 percent and 85.1 percent in those two periods. Japan's average grant element was 77.6 percent in 1991–92 and 75.1 percent in 1990–91. The DAC average was 89.9 percent and 85.1 percent. See MFA, *Wagakuni no seifu kaihatsu enjo no jissho jōkyō*, p. 70.

46 See the comments by Hayashi Azusa, head of aid policy in MFA, and Yasuda Osamu, former deputy director general of the EPA's Economic Research Institute, in Yūichiro Yamagata, "The Role of Japan's Aid in Asia's Development," *Economic Eye*, Summer 1992, p. 26.

47 *Japan Times*, 2 January 1994, p. 10.

48 Robert M. Orr, Jr, "Japanese Foreign Aid in a New Global Era," *SAIS Review*, Summer/Fall 1991, pp. 136–7.

49 Interview with Miyagi Kenichi, assistant manager, International OEM Manufacturing, Fujitsu, 23 July 1992, Tokyo.

50 Japan, like most countries, continues to attach strings to its grants.

51 See Robert M. Orr, Jr, "Collaboration or Conflict: Foreign Aid and U.S.–Japan Relations," *Pacific Affairs*, Vol. 62, No. 4 (Winter 1989–90), p. 484.

52 Interviews, July and August 1994, Tokyo.

53 Robert M. Orr, Jr, *The Emergence of Japan's Foreign Aid Power* (New York: Columbia University Press, 1990), p. 68.

54 Interview, 24 April 1993, Kuala Lumpur.

55 Margee Ensign, *Doing Good or Doing Well? Japan's Foreign Aid Program* (New York: Columbia University Press, 1992), p. 59. There is an overwhelming amount of anecdotal evidence buttressing Ensign's conclusion. From the Kedung Ombo Dam in Indonesia, an Ex-Im Bank project carried out by Nichimen, a Japanese trading company, and Hazama-gumi, a Japanese construction firm, to the Philippine General Hospital in Manila, an OECF project built by Kumagai-gumi, a Japanese contractor, and filled with state-of-the-art but little-used medical equipment from Japan, projects financed by Japanese aid seem to benefit Japanese interests as much as anyone. A good but somewhat polemical source of information on such projects is Sumi Kazuo (ed.), *No moa ODA baramaki enjo* (*No More Scattering of ODA Assistance*) (Tokyo: Sokosha K.K., 1992).

56 MFA, *Japan's ODA: Annual Report, 1993*, p. 14.

57 Interview, 21 July 1992, Tokyo.

58 Arase, "Japanese Foreign Aid," p. 183.

59 Orr, "Japanese Foreign Aid in a New Global Era," pp. 139–41.

60 David Potter, "Meeting the Need? Japan's Foreign Aid to Thailand," a paper presented at the Association for Asian Studies annual meeting in Washington, 4 April 1992.

61 *New York Times*, 5 August 1991, p. D8.

62 "Keizai kyōryoku hakusho: kunibetsu enjo shikin o teian" ("ODA White Paper: Proposals on Guiding Country-by-country Assistance"), *Nihon keizai shinbun*, 14 June 1991, p. 5.

63 Interview, 21 July 1992, Tokyo.

64 *Christian Science Monitor*, 28 January 1991.

65 *Time*, 15 February 1993, p. 44.

66 *Japan Times*, 19 November 1991.

67 *Economist*, 24 April 1993, p. 34.

68 Pete Carey and Lewis M. Simons, "Philippine Project is a Model of Japan's Development Plan," *San Jose Mercury News*, 20 April 1992, p. 6A.

69 *Yomiuri Daily News*, 7 June 1994; *Japan Times*, 27 May 1994, p. 1.

70 *Look Japan*, April 1992, pp. 4–11.

71 Interview, 24 April 1993, Kuala Lumpur.

72 Nagai Raitaro, "Win Win Games," unpublished essay for the Institute for Strategic and International Studies, Kuala Lumpur, April 1993, p. 3.

73 MFA, *Diplomatic Bluebook 1991: Japan's Diplomatic Activities* (Tokyo: MFA, 1992), p. 426.

74 MFA, *Wagakuni no seifu kaihatsu enjo no jissho jōkyō*, p. 42. To calculate the regional distribution of its ODA, the Japanese government defines "Asia" to include South Asia (which includes countries such as India and Pakistan) and non-ASEAN members in Southeast Asia (such as Myanmar, Vietnam, and Cambodia). Using our narrower definition of this region, we find that Japan donated at least 44.2 percent of its total bilateral aid to Asia in 1993. See ibid., p. 50.

75 ibid., p. 42. We must note again that the Japanese government's definition of Asia is different from ours. At least 75.6 percent of Japan's soft loans went to the nine countries of Asia, as we define this region.

76 ibid., p. 50; MFA, *Japan's ODA: Annual Report, 1993*, p. 45.

77 *Japan Times*, 1 January 1994, p. 10.

78 *New Straits Times*, 20 March 1993, p. 6.

79 Although it helped establish JAIC, the Japanese government no longer helps to finance it.

80 Interview, Ishi Makoto, chief representative, JAIC-Thailand, 10 July 1995, Bangkok.

81 Yufu Shinichi, "Kigyōka seishi o hakkishi kaigai toshi ni charenji" ("Exhibit Entrepreneurial Spirit and [Rise to] the Challenge of Overseas Investment") in Tōyō Keizai Shinpōsha, *Kaigai shinshutsu kigyō sōran, 1994* (*A Comprehensive Survey of Firms Expanding Overseas, 1994*) (Tokyo: Tōyō Keizai Shinpōsha, 1994), p. 21.

82 "Nitchū ga gappei de sofutouea-sha" ("A Joint Sino-Japanese Software Company"), *Nihon keizai shinbun*, 17 July 1991, p. 9.

8 Vertical Veins of Humanity

1 Kavi Chongkittavorn, "Looking for Japan's Political Clout," *Nation* (Bangkok), 11 December 1991.

2 Ministry of Foreign Affairs (MFA), *Wagakuni no seifu kaihatsu enjo no jisshō jōkyō* (*Annual Report on the Status of Japanese ODA*) (Tokyo: MFA, research and planning section of the Economic Cooperation Bureau, June 1994), p. 42. As we noted in chapter seven, MFA's definition of Asia is broader than ours, including Southwest Asian countries as well.

3 *Business Week*, 10 April 1995, p. 112.

4 Robert M. Orr, Jr, "The Rising Sum: What Makes Japan Give?", *International Economy*, September–October 1989, p. 83.

5 MFA, *Wagakuni no seifu kaihatsu enjo no jisshō jōkyō*, pp. 50–1.

6 Ford S. Worthy, "Japan's Spreading Regional Power," *Fortune*, Vol. 122 (Fall 1990), No. 8, p. 96.

7 *FEER*, 27 September 1990.

8 Oda Toshio, "Practical Business Approach to Vietnam and the International Synergy," remarks at a roundtable on investment opportunities in Vietnam sponsored by the American Chamber of Commerce in Japan, China–Asia business committee, 15 November 1993, Tokyo.

9 Interview, 26 July 1994, Tokyo.

10 Masashi Nishihara, *The Japanese and Sukarno's Indonesia: Tokyo–Jakarta Relations, 1951–1966* (Honolulu: University Press of Hawaii, 1976).

11 Rob Steven, *Japan's New Imperialism* (Armonk, New York: M. E. Sharpe Inc., 1990), p. 235.

12 *FEER*, 2 May 1991, pp. 45–6.

13 Steven, *Japan's New Imperialism*, p. 235.

14 Mamoru Tsuda, *Preliminary Study of Japanese-Filipino Joint Ventures* (Quezon City: Foundation for Nationalist Studies, 1978), pp. iii, 140–52.

15 Yoshihara Kunio, *The Rise of Ersatz Capitalism in Southeast Asia* (Singapore: Oxford University Press, 1988), p. 70.

16 "Indonesia: The Long March," a survey, *Economist*, 17 April 1993, pp. 7–8.

17 Steven Schlossstein, *Asia's New Little Dragons: The Dynamic Emergence of Indonesia, Thailand and Malaysia* (Chicago: Contemporary Books, 1991), pp. 149–50.

18 We are indebted here to Daniel Okimoto and an early draft of a paper he contributed to a 1993 conference organized by Stanford's Hoover Institution, on Japan's role in Asia.

19 *Nikkei Weekly*, 20 June 1994, p. 24.

20 Interview, 23 April 1993, Kuala Lumpur.

21 *FEER*, 28 March 1991, p. 51.

22 Interview, 21 April 1993, Bangkok.

23 Anny Wong, "Japan's National Security and Cultivation of ASEAN Elites," *Contemporary Southeast Asia*, Vol. 12, No. 4 (March 1991), pp. 316–17.

24 MFA, *Japan's ODA: Annual Report, 1993* (Tokyo: Association for the Promotion of International Cooperation, 1994), pp. 121, 123.

25 *Nikkei Weekly*, 25 July 1994, p. 2. This training program is part of MITI's Asia Supporting Industry Action (ASIA) program.

26 Ajiken, *Ajia Keizai Kenkyūjo no goannai, 1993/1994* (*Introduction to the Institute for Research on Asian Economies*) (Tokyo: Ajiken, 1994), pp. 12–13.

27 *NIRA News*, June 1989, p. 4.

28 Tokyo Club Foundation for Global Studies, *Asia Club Papers No. 1* (Tokyo: Tokyo Club Foundation for Global Studies, June 1990).

29 Dennis Normile, "Japanese Universities Become Magnets for Asian Students," *Science*, Vol. 262 (15 October 1993), p. 351.

30 *Nikkei Weekly*, 20 June 1994, p. 24. In our interviews with government officials throughout the region, we found surprisingly little concern about the possible use of "transfer pricing" by Japanese MNCs. Although they certainly did not invent this practice, Japanese multinationals may – by virtue of their network structure – be particularly well positioned to engage in it. By paying artificially high prices for inputs purchased from related firms and charging artificially low prices for outputs sold to related firms, they can reduce the reportable and thus taxable earnings of their affiliates.

31 Interview with Nakajima Daisuke, manager of administration for Fujitsu Thailand Co., 20 April 1993, Bangkok.

32 *Bangkok Post*, 16 June 1992, p. 16. In many cases, the benefits of Japanese network-building are merely symbolic. Minebea, for example, can boast that it is the only company in Thailand that is allowed to own and operate a private helicopter. It also has its own waiting room for company VIPs at Bangkok's Dong Muang airport. *Los Angeles Times*, 21 May 1991, p. H6.

33 Zhao Quansheng, "Japan's Aid Diplomacy with China" in Bruce Koppel and Robert Orr, Jr (eds), *Japan's Foreign Aid: Power and Policy in a New Era* (Boulder: Westview Press, 1993), pp. 175–7.

34 Mitsubishi Corp., Motor Vehicle Department C, "Master Plan for the Automobile Industry in the Socialist Republic of Vietnam," June 1992. This is an internal company document.

35 Interview with Trinh Nguyen Xuan, deputy director, State Committee for Cooperation and Investment, 19 November 1994, Victoria, BC, Canada.

36 *Japan Times*, 14 May 1994.

37 Interview, 5 August 1994, Tokyo.

38 Richard F. Doner, *Driving a Bargain: Automobile Industrialization and Japanese Firms in Southeast Asia* (Berkeley: University of California Press, 1991), pp. 80–1.

39 *San Jose Mercury News*, 20 April 1992, p. 1.

40 Franklin Weinstein, *Indonesian Foreign Policy and the Dilemma of Dependence* (Ithaca: Cornell University Press, 1976), p. 284.

41 *San Jose Mercury News*, 19 April 1992, p. 1.

42 Interview in Bangkok, 17 July 1992.

43 MITI, "IDJ Interview: Ajia kōgyōka seisaku ni sofuto-men shutai de kyōryoku" ("Cooperating in Asian Industrial Policies by Focusing on Soft Aspects"), *Kaihatsu jānaru* (*Development Journal*), July 1987, pp. 30–1. This is an interview with Okabe Takenao, an architect of the MITI plan.

44 MITI, "New Aid Plan," a two-page summary provided by the ministry, 1992.

45 "Philippine Project is a Model of Japan's Development Plan," *San Jose Mercury News*, 20 April 1992, p. A6.

46 Sumitomo Business Consulting in collaboration with JETRO, JICA, and the Malaysian Industrial Development Authority, "The Study on Selected Industrial Product Development in Malaysia: Computers and Computer Peripherals," undated.

47 MITI, "Shin-Ajia kōgyōka sōgō kyōryoku puran" ("The New AID Plan"), *Kaihatsu jānaru (Development Journal)*, July 1988, p. 55.

48 See Robert J. Orr, Jr, *The Emergence of Japan's Foreign Aid Power* (New York: Columbia University Press, 1990), p. 38.

49 MITI, *Background Information: Japan's Economic Cooperation, 1993* (Tokyo: MITI, economic cooperation division, 1993), p. 178.

50 Satō Hideo, assistant manager, division of development cooperation, Bureau of Economic Cooperation, MFA. Interview on 23 July 1992, Tokyo.

51 Interview with Munakata Naoko, deputy director of Asia-Pacific affairs in MITI's economic cooperation division, 9 July 1992, Tokyo.

52 *Asahi shinbun*, 3 November 1990, p. 9.

53 *Nihon keizai shinbun*, 29 June 1993, p. 5.

54 Peter J. Katzenstein and Martin Rouse, "Japan as a Regional Power in Asia" in Jeffrey A. Frankel and Miles Kahler (eds), *Regionalism and Rivalry: Japan and the United States in Pacific Asia* (Chicago: University of Chicago Press, 1993), p. 237.

55 *Yomiuri Daily News*, 8 April 1994, p. 8.

56 Interview, 9 July 1992, Tokyo.

57 David Arase, "Japanese Foreign Aid: The State, the Polity and the International System" (PhD diss., University of California, Berkeley, 1989), pp. 183–4.

58 JODC, "Technical Guidance and Performance," an informational booklet, March 1992, p. 5.

59 *Nikkei Weekly*, 25 July 1994, p. 2.

60 Interview with Isoyama Katsuhiko, JFS representative, 26 April 1993, Kuala Lumpur.

61 Jusmaliani, "Japan's Role in the Technology Transfer to Indonesia," a paper for an international seminar on Japan's Role in the Transfer of Technology in ASEAN Countries, 26–27 June 1992, Bangkok, pp. 5–6.

62 Thee Kian Wie, "Interactions of Japanese Aid and Direct Investment in Indonesia," *ASEAN Economic Bulletin*, Vol. 11, No. 1 (July 1994), p. 33.

63 "Japanese Experts Help KL Plan Development Projects," *Straits Times*, 18 October 1992, p. 6.

64 Interview, 24 April 1993, Kuala Lumpur.

65 Interview with Cholchineepan Chiranond, deputy-director, department of East Asian affairs, MFA (Thailand), 17 July 1992, Bangkok.

66 Interview with Munakata Naoko, 9 July 1992, Tokyo.

67 Daniel Unger, "Japanese Manufacturing Investment and Export Processing Industrialization in Thailand," occasional paper no. 90-15, Program on US–Japan Relations, Harvard University, 1990, pp. 23–4.

68 Interview, 19 April 1993, Bangkok.

69 Interviews with Thai and Japanese officials, July 1992 and April 1993, Bangkok. Doner says Japanese ODA has been conditioned on the creation of such public–private linkages in Thailand. See Richard F. Doner, "Japanese Foreign Investment and the Creation of a Pacific Asian Region" in Frankel and Kahler (eds), *Regionalism and Rivalry*, pp. 192–3.

70 JICA, "A Study on Industrial Sector Development in the Kingdom of Thailand," Bangkok, 1989, p. A-III-26, cited in ibid., p. 193.
71 This is less true in Taiwan and South Korea, which have created relatively stronger economies and thus have acquired more bargaining power with the Japanese. Taiwan, for example, still maintains stiff trade barriers to Japanese automobiles. In exchange for removing or lowering such barriers, it has asked Japan to "voluntarily" limit its automobile exports to Taiwan. See Takaaki Sasaki and Yoshie Shimane, "The New Dynamics of the Asian Economy," *Japan Research Quarterly*, Vol. 3, No. 3 (Summer 1994), p. 81.
72 *Asahi shinbun*, 20 October 1994, p. 10.
73 These incentives included "pioneer" status, a 50 percent reinvestment allowance, and an exemption on some customs duties. See Malaysian Industrial Development Authority, *Malaysia: Investment in the Manufacturing Sector; Policies, Incentives and Facilities*, a manual, 1993, pp. 16–17. Japanese business leaders cheered this policy change, calling it a "win–win" outcome for Malaysia and Japan. See *New Straits Times*, 17 April 1993. The trade-off was simple: Japan would be able to transplant some of its home-grown *keiretsu*, while Malaysia would be able to strengthen its industrial base and curb its growing trade deficit with Japan.
74 Interview with Omar Yusuf, 26 April 1993, Kuala Lumpur.
75 Interviews (cited above) with Omar Yusuf and Sutin Leepiyachart.
76 15 July 1994 correspondence from Miwa Naomi, manager, research and planning division, economic analysis department, OECF.
77 *FEER*, 28 March 1991, p. 51.
78 Cholchineepan Chiranond, deputy director general, department of East Asian affairs, MFA (Thailand). Interview, 17 July.1992, Bangkok. Japan is also hoping to help Thailand improve its air, rail, and road systems leading into China, Myanmar, and Indochina. See *Straits Times*, 4 January 1993, p. 11.
79 Dan Biers, "A New Japanese Co-Prosperity Captivates East Asia," *Seattle Post-Intelligencer*, 25 November 1991, p. B4.
80 Schlossstein, *Asia's New Little Dragons*, p. 218.
81 The BOI initially rejected Guardian's permit application, but then changed its mind after the US government intervened. "Some U.S. Concerns Grasp New Opportunities in Asia," *Asian Wall Street Journal*, 13 January 1992, pp. 4, 6.
82 Arase, "Japanese Foreign Aid," p. 319.
83 *Bangkok Post*, 13 January 1984, p. 18.
84 ibid., 26 January 1984, p. 1.
85 ibid., 27 January 1984, p. 1.
86 See Prasert Chittiwatanapong, "Japan's Role in the Asia-Pacific Region: Political Dimension," a paper delivered at the Japan Institute of International Affairs conference in Tokyo, 3–4 March 1988.
87 Stephen Krasner, "Comment" on Shafiqul Islam, "Foreign Aid and Burdensharing" in Frankel and Kahler (eds), *Regionalism and Rivalry*, p. 373.
88 *FEER*, 3 May 1990, p. 50.

9 The Labor Network

1 Karatsu Hajime, "Kaku ni naru gijitsu o osaereba kūdōka wa kowaku nai" ("Control the Core Technology, Fear Not Hollowing"), *Ekonomisuto*, 11 November 1994, pp. 30–3.

2 Hiroshi Kumon, "Multinationalization of the Toyota Motor Corporation," *Journal of International Economic Studies*, No. 6 (March 1992), p. 94.

3 Yoshihara Hideki, "Nihon-teki seisan shisutemu no kaigai iten" ("The Overseas Transfer of the Japanese Production System") in Yoshihara Hideki, Hayashi Kiichirō, and Yasumuro Ken-ichi (eds), *Nihon kigyō no gurōbaru keizai* (*The Global Economy of Japanese Firms*) (Tokyo: Tōyō Keizai Shinpōsha, 1988).

4 Arthur Zich, "Japan's Sun Rises Over the Pacific," *National Geographic*, November 1991, p. 65.

5 See Hazama Hiroshi, *Nihonteki keiei no keifu* (*The Origins of Japanese-style Management*) (Tokyo: Nōritsu Kyōkai, 1963). A solid, comparative economic analysis of this system is M. Hashimoto and J. Raisian, "Employment Tenure and Earnings Profiles in Japan and the United States," *American Economic Review*, Vol. 75 (1985), pp. 721–35.

6 For more on OJT, see Shoichi Yamashita, "Economic Development of the ASEAN Countries and the Role of Japanese Direct Investment" in Yamashita (ed.), *Transfer of Japanese Technology and Management to the ASEAN Countries* (Tokyo: University of Tokyo Press, 1991), p. 17; Jōzen Takeuchi, "'Technology Transfer' and Japan-Thai Relations" in ibid., pp. 201–4; and Samart Chiasakul and Prasert Silapipat, "Case of Thailand" in Institute of Developing Economies (ed.), *The Role of Japanese Direct Investment in Developing Countries* (Tokyo: IDE, March 1992), p. 265.

7 Interview, 22 April 1993, Kuala Lumpur.

8 Interview with Imai Hiroshi, senior managing director, 21 April 1993, Bangkok.

9 Interview, 17 July 1992, Bangkok.

10 Mingsarn Santikarn Kaosa-ard, "Comparative Analysis of Direct Foreign Investment in Thailand," a paper for a conference sponsored by the Hoover Institution, Stanford University, on Japan and the Regionalization of Asia, March 1993, p. 18.

11 *FEER*, 3 May 1990, p. 55.

12 C. Y. Ng, R. Hirono, and Robert Y. Siy, *Technology and Skills in ASEAN: An Overview* (Singapore: Institute of Southeast Asian Studies, 1986), p. 95.

13 Yukio Shōtoku, "Factors of Success of Matsushita in Malaysia," a paper for Industrial Management Seminar III organized by Persatuan Pelajar Kejuruteraan Jentera, University of Technology, Malaysia, 5 September 1992, p. 17.

14 Hideki Imaoka, "Japanese Corporate Employment and Personnel Systems and Their Transfer to Japanese Affiliates in Asia," *Developing Economies*, Vol. 27, No. 4 (December 1989), pp. 407–25.

15 This "delinking" phenomenon was mentioned by numerous Japanese managers we interviewed in Asia.

16 Interview with Kozuki Yasutsugu, secretary general of the Japanese Chamber of Commerce and Industry (Singapore), 27 April 1993, Singapore.

17 Imaoka reports that job rotation was practiced by 32 percent of the affiliates surveyed in Singapore and 30 percent in Taiwan, but only 17 percent in Malaysia, 15 percent in the Philippines, and 16 percent in Indonesia and Thailand. Meanwhile, 53 percent of the parent firms in Japan indicated they used job rotation as a method of training workers. Imaoka, "Japanese Corporate Employment and Personnel Systems," p. 424.

18 Consensus decision-making was found to be a "management policy target" at 83 percent of the firms surveyed in Japan, but only 17 percent of the Japanese affiliates surveyed in Malaysia, 20 percent in Hong Kong,

Singapore, and Thailand, 25 percent in Indonesia, 33 percent in the Philippines, 43 percent in Taiwan, and 65 percent in South Korea. ibid., p. 424.

19 Ide Takashi, in an interview with *FEER*, 28 March 1991, p. 50.

20 Sanoh Industries, a Japanese auto parts manufacturer, owns 25 percent of a UI member company.

21 Interview, 24 April 1993, Klang, Malaysia.

22 Interview, 20 April 1993, Bangkok.

23 Interview with Supong Chayutsahakij, deputy general manager, TPL, 17 July 1992, Bangkok.

24 Hugh Williamson, *Coping with the Miracle: Japan's Unions Explore New International Relations* (London: Pluto Press, 1994), p. 101.

25 ibid., p. 214.

26 Interview, 28 July 1992, Chungnam, South Korea.

27 ibid.

28 JETRO Kuala Lumpur, "NIES, ASEAN ni okeru Nikkei seizōgyō no katsudō jōkyō (Mareishia)" ("Japanese Manufacturing Industry Activities in the NIEs and ASEAN [Malaysia]"), unpublished report, 1992.

29 Fumihiko Adachi, "Small and Medium-sized Firms in Japan's Foreign Direct Investment" in Tran Van Tho (ed.), *Japan's Direct Investment in Thailand: Patterns and Issues* (Tokyo: Japan Center for Economic Research, 1991), p. 63.

30 *New Straits Times*, Malaysia, 16 April 1993, p. 41.

31 *FEER*, 28 March 1991, p. 52.

32 Interview, 22 April 1991, Penang.

33 Interview, 24 April 1993, Shah Alam, Malaysia.

34 Nakajima Daisuke, who represents Fujitsu at the meetings. Interview, 20 April 1993, Bangkok.

35 This was attributed, in part, to "differences in recruitment practices, in training, and in attitudes toward turnover:" Charles T. Stewart, Jr, "Comparing Japanese and U.S. Technology Transfer to Less-Developed Countries," *Journal of Northeast Asian Studies*, Vol. 4 (Spring 1985), p. 13.

36 In interview after interview, Japanese managers in Asia told us that blue-collar workers (as opposed to white-collar employees) were relatively content. We believe this assertion is plausible given the higher than average wages and benefits provided to shopfloor workers at Japanese affiliates in the region.

37 "The Rising Tide: Japan in Asia," a special supplement, *Japan Economic Journal*, Winter 1990, p. 18.

38 Nobuo Kawabe, "Problems of and Perspectives on Japanese Management in Malaysia" in Yamashita (ed.), *Transfer of Japanese Technology and Management*, p. 262.

39 ibid., p. 260.

40 Interview, 15 April 1993, Penang.

41 Japanese nationals occupy an unusually large number of management positions not only in the Asian affiliates of Japanese MNCs, but in almost all overseas affiliates. In a comparison of management practices used around the world by Matsushita and 3M, Bartlett and Yoshihara found that 2 percent of the Japanese firm's overseas managers were Japanese, while only 0.3 percent of the American firm's managers were American. Christopher Bartlett and Yoshihara Hideki, "New Challenges for Japanese Multi-nationals: Is Organizational Adaptation Their Achilles Heel?" in Vladimir

Pucik, Noel Tichy, and Carole Barnett (ed.), *Globalizing Management: Creating and Leading the Competitive Organization* (New York: Wiley, 1992), p. 282.

42 See Helen Hughes and You Poh Seng, *Foreign Investment and Industrialization in Singapore* (Canberra: Australian National University Press, 1969); and Somsak Tambunlertchai, *Japanese and American Investments in Thailand's Manufacturing Industries: An Assessment of Their Relative Contributions to the Host Economy* (Tokyo: Institute of Developing Economies, 1977).

43 Ng et al., *Technology and Skills in ASEAN*, pp. 38–9.

44 Yoshimitsu Nihei, Makoto Ōtsu, and David A. Levin, "A Comparative Study of Management Practices and Workers in an American and Japanese Firm in Hong Kong" in Ng Sek Hong and David A. Levin (eds), *Contemporary Issues in Hong Kong Labour Relations* (Hong Kong: University of Hong Kong, 1983).

45 Stewart, "Comparing Japanese and U.S. Technology Transfer," pp. 13–14. As a partial explanation, Stewart concludes that "it is difficult to integrate non-Japanese into the Japanese management system."

46 *Straits Times*, 20 June 1992, p. 18. Mokhzani Abdul Rahman's criticism was sparked by a Majeca survey of 846 Japanese MNCs in Malaysia, none of which had a Malaysian in a senior management position.

47 *Asian Wall Street Journal*, 13 January 1992, p. 6.

48 *FEER*, 20 June 1991, p. 92. We should add that, in 1994, Seiko Instruments Singapore joined this very short list of Japanese affiliates led by local Singaporeans. See *Asian Wall Street Journal*, 9 August 1994, p. 4.

49 *FEER*, 27 September 1990, p. 59.

50 Izumi Hara, "Development of the Asia-Pacific Region and the Outlook for Loan and Investment Activities of Japanese Companies," a report presented at the second Asia-Pacific conference sponsored by FAIR, 9–10 May 1991, Tokyo, p. I-524.

51 Kawabe, "Problems of and Perspectives on Japanese Management," p. 266; Yamashita, "Economic Development of the ASEAN Countries," p. 18.

52 Interview with Abdul Karim Nor, executive director, Matsushita Air Conditioning Group (Malaysia), 23 April 1993, Kuala Lumpur. We were shown, but not allowed to keep, a copy of Matsushita's organizational chart. The company has pledged to put a Malaysian in the managing director's chair by 2000.

53 *FEER*, 3 May 1990, p. 54.

54 Schon Beechler, "International Management Control in Multinational Corporations: The Case of Japanese Consumer Electronics Firms in Asia," *ASEAN Economic Bulletin*, November 1992, p. 163.

55 JETRO Bangkok, "Nikkei kigyō no jittai chōsa" ("Survey on the Actual Situation of Japanese-affiliated Enterprises"), report no. 197 of the economic research group, Bangkok, December 1990, p. 18.

56 Interview, Imai Hiroshi, senior managing director, 21 April 1993, Bangkok.

57 See Tran Van Tho, "Japan's Technology Transfer in ASEAN: Some Issues on the Effective Transfer and Management Style," p. 1–18; and Anuwar Ali, "Japan's Role in Technology Transfer in Malaysia," p. 6–24, two papers presented to an international seminar on Japan's Role in the Transfer of Technology in ASEAN Countries, organized by the Institute of East Asian Studies, Thammasat University, Bangkok, June 1992.

58 MITI, *Kaigai tōshi tōkei sōran* (*Comprehensive Statistics on Japanese Foreign Investment*), No. 5 (1994), pp. 34–5, and No. 4 (1991), pp. 34–5.

59 Interview, Supong Chayutsahakij, 17 July 1992, Bangkok.

60 Tran, "Japan's Technology Transfer in ASEAN," pp. 1–18, 1–19; Kawabe, "Problems of and Perspectives on Japanese Management," p. 263.

61 Bernard Wysocki, "Guiding Hand: In Asia, the Japanese Hope to 'Coordinate' What Nations Produce," *Wall Street Journal*, 20 August 1990, p. A4.

62 Sony is not alone in using this "big brother" style of cooperative but unequal management. Jusmaliani presents the case of a Japanese joint venture in Indonesia that did exactly the same. "It seems, from the Japanese view, that training/learning through guidance is much better than learning by mistakes," the author writes. See Jusmaliani, "Japan's Role in Technology Transfer in Indonesia," a paper presented to the international seminar on Japan's Role in the Transfer of Technology in ASEAN Countries, p. 5-24.

63 Interview, 16 April 1993, Penang.

64 Interview, 18 July 1992, Bangkok.

10 The Supply Network

1 MITI, Small and Medium Enterprises Agency, *Chūshō kigyō hakusho* (*White Paper on Small and Medium-sized Enterprises*) (Tokyo: Ministry of Finance Printing Office, 1988), p. 148.

2 Young-Kwan Yoon, "The Political Economy of Transition: Japanese Foreign Direct Investments in the 1980s," *World Politics*, Vol. 43 (October 1990), p. 19.

3 Edward M. Graham and Paul R. Krugman, *Foreign Direct Investment in the United States* (Washington: Institute for International Economics, 1991), p. 60.

4 We should consider rival hypotheses to try to explain the fact that Japanese manufacturers in Asia, compared to those in North America and Europe, import a smaller share of their parts and materials from Japan. One might be that Japanese high-tech manufacturers simply *cannot*, despite their proximity to the home country, import goods more cheaply. There is something to this. As a general rule, Asian nations have erected taller trade barriers against manufactured imports than North American and European nations have. This hypothesis, however, cannot fully withstand the weight of evidence showing that these barriers have fallen steadily over the past 15 years (partly due to policy initiatives to attract export-oriented FDI), while imports from Japan, as a percentage of total procurements by Japanese affiliates in Asia, have not increased. Another possible explanation is that Japanese affiliates in the West are manufacturing more technology-intensive products that require precise specifications laid out by the parent firm in Japan. This is a related explanation, but not a sufficient one.

5 Interview with David Wong, general manager of Tan Chong Motors, 22 April 1992, Kuala Lumpur.

6 *FEER*, 27 September 1990, p. 59. Although the local procurement rate is low in Indonesia, the Philippines, and China, it may be increasing rapidly. This was one of the conclusions of a recent survey by the Japan Machinery Exporters Association. "Wagakuni kikai sangyō no Ajia ni okeru seisan bungyō jittai ni tsuite" ("The Actual State of Production and Division of Labor by Japanese Machine Industries Operating in Asia"), a survey, June 1994, p. 17.

7 We test this hypothesis more carefully in chapter eleven.

8 MITI, *Wagakuni kigyō no kaigai jigyō katsudō* (*Overseas Business Activities of Japanese Firms*), various years; and MITI, *Dai-go-kai, kaigai jigyō katsudō kihon chōsa* (*Basic Survey on Overseas Business Activities*), 5th edn (Tokyo: MOF Printing Office, 1994).

9 ibid.
10 *Asian Wall Street Journal*, 9 August 1994, p. 4.
11 Interview with Kurahashi Masayuki, TMT purchasing manager, 21 April 1993, Bangkok.
12 Interview with Koiso Shigeru, 22 July 1992, Tokyo.
13 Interview with Shibata Naoaki, general manager of planning for Sony Mechatronic Products, 16 April 1993, Penang.
14 Matsushita handout, undated.
15 Interview, 18 July 1992, Bangkok.
16 Keizai Doyūkai, "A Survey of the Attitude of Japanese Companies in ASEAN Regarding Management Towards 1990," conducted in anticipation of the 16th Japan–ASEAN Businessmen's Meeting held in Fukuoka, Japan, November 1990. Cited by Hiroyasu Higuchi and Yuhanis Kamil, "Trends in Japanese Direct Foreign Investment and Implications for Southeast Asian Countries" in Institute of Strategic and International Studies, *JASA: Towards an Economically Resilient Southeast Asia* (Kuala Lumpur: ISIS, 1991), p. 191.
17 See, for example, Pasuk Phongpaichit, *The New Wave of Japanese Investment in ASEAN* (Singapore: Institute of Southeast Asian Studies, 1990), pp. 55–9; and Chia Siow Yue, *Japanese Overseas Direct Investment in ASEAN and Asian NIEs* (Tokyo: Ajiken, 1991), pp. 65–6.
18 Sree Kumar and Ng Chee Yuen, "Japanese Manufacturing Investments in Singapore: Linkages with Small and Medium Enterprises" in Institute of Developing Economies, *The Role of Japanese Direct Investment in Developing Countries* (Tokyo: IDE, 1992), p. 31.
19 Export-Import Bank of Japan, "Wagakuni denshi denki sangyō no Ajia ni okeru kokusai bungyō no tenkai" ("The Rise of an International Division of Labor in Japan's Electric and Electronic Industries), *Kaigai tōshi kenkyūjōhō* (*Report of the Institute on Overseas Investment*), February 1988.
20 Takeshi Aoki, "Foreign Investment and Network Formation" in Shojiro Tokunaga (ed.), *Japan's Foreign Investment and Asian Economic Interdependence* (Tokyo: University of Tokyo Press, 1992), p. 82.
21 Takao Kiba and Fumio Kodama, "Measurement and Analysis of the Progress of International Technology Transfer: Case Study of Direct Investment in East Asian Countries," NISTEP Report No. 18 (Tokyo: National Institute of Science and Technology Policy, Science and Technology Agency, April 1991), pp. 27, 30.
22 ibid., p. 30.
23 Quoted in *Japan Times*, 5 January 1993, p. 1.
24 Chiu Lin Fee, "The Effects of Tax Incentives on Foreign Investments in Singapore," Department of Business Administration, National University of Singapore, 1978/79, p. 117; cited in Sueo Sekiguchi (ed.), *ASEAN-Japan Relations: Investment* (Singapore: Institute of Southeast Asian Studies, 1983), p. 155.
25 Bunluasak pans the local content rules used in Thailand, saying they "fail to promote the development of technology capability of Thai suppliers." Bunluasak Pussarungsri, "Effect of Foreign Direct Investment," Thailand Development Research Institute, April 1993, ch. 5, p. 9.
26 All but five of the 68 Japanese auto parts producers investing in the ASEAN-4 nations between 1964 and 1983 did so after 1970, when host governments began to implement local content rules. See Richard F. Doner, *Driving a Bargain: Automobile Industrialization and Japanese Firms in Southeast Asia* (Berkeley: University of California Press, 1991), p. 291, note 40.
27 This statement is quoted by Mingsarn Santikarn Kaosa-ard, "TNC

Involvement in the Thai Auto Industry" in TDRI (Thailand Development Research Institute) *Report*, Vol. 8, No. 1 (1993), p. 12.

28 See Hiroshi Kumon, "Multinationalization of Toyota Motor Corporation," *Journal of International Economic Studies*, No. 6 (March 1992), p. 95. A Nissan official claims his firm used a gentler approach: "We took the time to meet with each and every member of the Takarakai [Nissan's *keiretsu*] to detail our plans and outline the projected capacity for our plants in Asia. We strongly encouraged them to make the move and promised to do what we could to help." Interview with Takase Hiroyuki, 24 July 1992, Tokyo.

29 Edward W. Desmond, "Beyond the Trade Game," *Time*, 21 February 1994, p. 18.

30 Interview, 24 April 1993, Shah Alam, Malaysia.

31 MITI, Small and Medium Enterprises Agency, *Chushō kigyō hakusho* (*White Paper on Small and Medium-sized Enterprises*) (Tokyo: MOF Printing Office, 1989), pp. 54–5. Quoted in Fumihiko Adachi, "Small and Medium-sized Firms in Japan's Foreign Direct Investment" in Tran Van Tho (ed.), *Japan's Direct Investment in Thailand: Patterns and Issues* (research report no. 2) (Tokyo: Japan Center for Economic Research, August 1991), p. 54.

32 *FEER*, 9 June 1994, p. 45. This article refers to Toshiba, which lured its principal suppliers to a new industrial park in China's Hanzhou City, guaranteeing the electronics manufacturer "a similar level of support as available at its main plant in Kawasaki."

33 Sucha Chubayt, as quoted in Nihon Zaigai Kigyō Kyōkai (Association of Overseas Japanese Firms), *Tai-ASEAN toshi masatsu* (*Investment Friction in ASEAN*) (Tokyo: Association of Overseas Japanese Firms, May 1989), p. 85.

34 *FEER*, 30 May 1991, p. 64.

35 Management and Coordination Agency of Japan, *Kagaku gijutsu kenkyū chōsa hōkoku, 1994* (*1994 Research Report on Science and Technology*) (Tokyo: Management and Coordination Agency, 1994), p. 168. The dollar amount is based on ¥115 = $1.

36 Interview with Kurahashi Masayuki, Toyota Motor Thailand, 21 April 1993, Bangkok; Toyota, "TCC: A History of the First Ten Years," an anniversary report issued in 1992.

37 Interview, 21 April 1993, Bangkok.

38 Interview, 16 July 1992, Bangkok.

39 *Nikkei Weekly*, 20 June 1994, p. 24.

40 *Asahi shinbun*, 4 January 1995, p. 9.

41 JETRO, "NIES, ASEAN ni okeru nikkei seizōgyō no katsudō jōkyō – Mareishia" ("Japanese Manufacturing Industry Activities in the NIEs and ASEAN – Malaysia") (Tokyo: JETRO, 1991).

42 Interview, 16 April 1993, Penang.

43 Tokunaga (ed.), *Japan's Foreign Investment*, p. 74.

44 Japanese MNCs, especially the GTCs, played a big part in turning Singapore into the world's busiest container port. From 1986 to 1990, they invested $512 million in transportation services in Singapore – about 12 percent of all Japanese FDI in that country in that period. Kume Gorōta, Research Institute for Overseas Investment (an arm of Japan's Export-Import Bank), "Trends and Prospects for Japanese Direct Investment in Asia," a paper delivered at a workshop on investment relations between developed nations and the developing nations of Asia, 26–27 March 1992, Bangkok, p. 15.

45 Interview with Shōtoku Yukio, former managing director, Matsushita air conditioning group in Malaysia, 23 April 1993, Kuala Lumpur.

46 Interview with Tony Ng, project controller, UI Group, 24 April 1993, Klang, Malaysia.
47 Interview, 23 April 1993, Puchong, Malaysia.
48 Sree and Ng, "Japanese Manufacturing Investments in Singapore," p. 23.
49 Samart Chiasakul and Prasert Silapipat, "The Case of Thailand" in IDE, *The Role of Japanese Investment in Developing Countries*, p. 225.
50 ibid., pp. 233–4.
51 Interview, 23 April 1993, Kuala Lumpur.
52 Sree and Ng, "Japanese Manufacturing Investment in Singapore," p. 36.
53 Interview, 24 April 1993, Kuala Lumpur.
54 Interview, 24 April 1993, Klang, Malaysia.
55 Interview, 19 April 1993, Bangkok.
56 Imran Lim, "Direct Foreign Investments in Malaysia," a paper presented at the first conference on Asia-Pacific relations, sponsored by FAIR, 20–22 April 1988, Tokyo, p. I-289.
57 Interview with Miyagi Kenichi, assistant manager, international OEM Manufacturing, Fujitsu, 5 April 1993, Tokyo.
58 Interview with Kurahashi Masayuki, Toyota, 21 April 1993, Bangkok; interview with Nishina Akira, Mitsubishi Electric, 21 July 1992, Tokyo.
59 Interview, 26 April 1993, Kuala Lumpur.
60 Interview, Fujii Noboru, 18 July 1992, Bangkok.
61 Doner, *Driving a Bargain*, pp. 85–6.
62 Interview with Lim Chin Ewe, 16 April 1993, Penang.
63 "Where Tigers Breed," a special survey of Asia's emerging economies, *Economist*, 16 November 1991, p. 8.
64 Interview with Shuzui Takeo, director of operations for Asia, Oceania, and the Middle East, Matsushita Electric, 9 April 1993, Osaka.
65 *FEER*, 20 August 1992, pp. 52–3.
66 *Asahi shinbun*, 21 April 1993.
67 "MITI Plan to Help SMIs Supply Industrial Parts," *New Straits Times*, 21 April 1993, p. 16.
68 Interview, 20 April 1993, Bangkok.
69 Fumio Kodama and Takao Kiba, "Emerging Trajectory of International Technology," Asia/Pacific Research Center, Stanford University, 1994, p. 7.
70 "Honda World Purchasing: Establishing Relationships," p. 12.
71 *Asahi shinbun*, 30 December 1994, p. 7.
72 *Asian Wall Street Journal*, 13 January 1992, p. 4.

11 The Ties that Bind

1 Proponents of this view include Ippei Yamazawa, "Gearing the Japanese Economy to International Harmony," *The Developing Economies*, Vol. 28, No. 4 (March 1990); and Derek Healey, *Japanese Capital Exports and Asian Economic Development* (Paris: OECD, 1992). The Foundation for Advanced Information and Research, a Japanese think tank controlled by the Ministry of Finance, also engages in such happy talk. See, for example, the report by FAIR's International Economic Structure Research Group in FAIR, *Interim Report of Asia-Pacific Economic Research* (Singapore: Look Japan Publishing, 1989), pp. 78–96.
2 Japan was to become, in other words, a *bōeki rikkoku*, a nation built on trade. See Odaka Konosuke, "Seichō no kiseki (2)" ("The Path of Growth [2]") in Yasuba Yasukichi and Inoki Takenori (eds), *Kōdo seichō (Rapid Growth)*,

Vol. 8 of *Nihon keizaishi* (*The Economic History of Japan*) (Tokyo: Iwanami Shoten, 1989), p. 154.

3 International Monetary Fund, *Direction of Trade Statistics* (Washington: IMF, various years).

4 The commission, appointed by then prime minister Nakasone, was named after its chairman, Maekawa Haruo, former president of the Bank of Japan. Known in Japan as Kokusai Kyōchō no Tame no Keizai Kōzō Chōsei Kenkyūkai (Study Group on Adjustments in the Economic Structure for International Cooperation), it released its strongly worded report on 7 April 1986.

5 Two important holdouts are Komiya and Irie. See Ryūtaro Komiya and Kazutomo Irie, "The U.S.–Japan Trade Problem: A Japanese Perspective" in Kozo Yamamura (ed.), *Japan's Economic Structure: Should it Change?* (Seattle: Society for Japanese Studies, 1990).

6 *Nihon keizai shinbun*, 6 February 1995; *Japan Digest*, 6 February 1995, p. 2.

7 Paul Summerville, Jardine Fleming in Tokyo, quoted in *FEER*, 25 July 1991, p. 53.

8 Yoo Jung-ho, "The Trilateral Trade Relation among the Asian NIEs, the U.S. and Japan," KDI Working paper No. 9005, Korea Development Institute, April 1990, pp. 30–3, 45.

9 MITI, *Tsūshō hakusho* (*White Paper on Trade*) (Tokyo: JETRO, 1992), pp. 146–7.

10 ibid.

11 James Sterngold, *New York Times*, 13 April 1993, pp. C1–2.

12 *Electronics Korea*, March 1990, p. 101; *Asiaweek*, 11 August 1989, p. 56; *Business Korea*, November 1986, p. 39.

13 Terry Ursacki and Ilan Vertinsky, "Long-Term Changes in Korea's International Trade and Investment," *Pacific Affairs*, Vol. 67, No. 3 (Fall 1994), p. 402.

14 Hanazaki Masaharu, "Deepening Economic Linkages in the Pacific Basin Region: Trade, Foreign Direct Investment and Technology," Japan Development Bank Research Report, September 1990, pp. 69–73.

15 Management and Coordination Agency, computer tables prepared for "Kagaku gijutsu kenkyū chōsa" ("The Study of Science and Technology"), 1994. Based on 1993 exchange rate of ¥115 = $1.

16 Denis Fred Simon, "Technology Transfer and National Autonomy" in Edwin A. Winckler and Susan Greenhalgh (eds), *Contending Approaches to the Political Economy of Taiwan* (Armonk, New York: M. E. Sharpe Inc., 1988), p. 213.

17 *Wall Street Journal*, 12–13 March 1993, pp. 1, 8.

18 MITI, *White Paper on International Trade*, 1995 (Tokyo: JETRO, 1995), p. 99.

19 *Wall Street Journal*, 12–13 March 1993, p. 8.

20 MITI, *White Paper on International Trade*, 1995, pp. 100, 218.

21 MITI, *White Paper on Trade*, 1992.

22 Asian Development Bank, *Asian Development Outlook 1994* (Hong Kong: Oxford University Press, 1994), p. 234.

23 Japan's status as an absorber of Asia's *total* exports has actually faded in recent years. In 1993, it received only 12.5 percent of the region's combined exports. A little more than a decade earlier, in 1980, it had received 22.2 percent of Asia's exports: IMF, *Direction of Trade Statistics*. Of course, this reduction is partly linked to Japan's diminished appetite for imported raw materials from Southeast Asia.

24 Peter Chow and Mitchell Kellman, *Trade: The Engine of Growth in East Asia* (New York: Oxford University Press, 1993), pp. 161–2.

25 We have computed these figures based on forecasts published in ibid., pp. 158–9, 164–5.

26 Indeed, during that period, Japanese imports of manufactured goods from Asia increased, on average, 50 percent a year. In fact, the region accounted for 41 percent of the increase in Japan's volume of imported manufactured goods. Shujiro Urata, "Export Increase of Developing Countries in Asia and Japanese Imports," a paper presented at the third joint research conference on Asia-Pacific relations sponsored by FAIR, Kuala Lumpur, 5–7 July 1992, p. 342. But while Japan increased such imports from $6.1 billion in 1980 to $30.7 billion in 1990, it actually began to import a smaller share from Asia in the early 1990s (see Table 11.2).

27 Reuters, "Japan Opening its Wallet to Other Asian-made Goods," *Seattle Times*, 31 May 1988, p. C7; William K. Tabb, *The Japanese Political Economy* (New York: Oxford University Press, 1994).

28 *FEER*, "No Longer a Bargain: Japan Cools toward Cheap NIC Electronics Goods," 5 July 1990, p. 53.

29 Mitchell Bernard and John Ravenhill, "Beyond Product Cycles and Flying Geese: Regionalization, Hierarchy and the Industrialization of East Asia," *World Politics*, Vol. 47, No. 2 (January 1995), p. 188.

30 Urata, "Export Increase of Developing Countries in Asia," p. 343.

31 Richard Cronin, in "Japan's Expanding Role and Influence in the Asia-Pacific Region: Implications for U.S. Interests and Policy," Congressional Research Service, 7 September 1990, pp. 26–7, came to the same conclusion: "Indigenous producers themselves are still finding it very hard to crack the Japanese market."

32 Kosai, president of the Japan Center for Economic Research, concludes that much of the increased volume of manufactured goods imported by Japan comes from Japanese transplants in Asia. See Kosai Yutaka, "APEC Summit in 1995 in Osaka," *JCER Report*, Vol. 7, No. 1 (January 1995), p. 2.

33 *FEER*, 5 July 1990, p. 54.

34 "Japan and Asian NICS: A Deepening Relationship," *Mitsubishi Bank Review*, Vol. 19, No. 7 (July 1988), p. 1108.

35 Japanese Chamber of Commerce and Industry, Bangkok, "Nikkei kigyō no jittai kōkendo chōsa" ("An Analysis of the Actual Contribution of Japanese Related Firms"), December 1990, p. 13.

36 Kenji Takeuchi, "Does Japanese Direct Foreign Investment Promote Japanese Imports from Developing Countries?", Working Paper Series 458, International Economics Department, World Bank (June 1990), p. 34.

37 Interview, 16 July 1992, Bangkok.

38 One such exception was Narongchai Akrasanee's complaint, made in an interview with an *Asahi* reporter, that Japan has "created too many enemies" by pursuing economic development in a "self-centered" way. See *Asahi shinbun*, 14 January 1995.

39 Kyodo News Service, "ASEAN Group Calls Japanese Market 'Inscrutable,'" Japan Economic Newswire, 16 February 1993.

40 MITI, *White Paper on International Trade*, 1995.

41 Interview, 1 August 1992, Seoul.

42 Japanese officials press this point in defending their imbalanced relationship with Asian trading partners. "In the long run, we shouldn't view trade relations on a bilateral basis," says Mizutani Shiro, president of JETRO Bangkok (interview, 16 July 1992). "We should consider them globally. A bilateral approach will only lead to a reduction in overall trade relations."

43 "Trade Pact Worries Asia Nations," *Los Angeles Times*, 23 August 1992, p. C2.

44 Okita Saburo, *Japan in the World Economy of the 1980s* (Tokyo: University of Tokyo Press, 1989), p. 210.

45 See, for example, Iwata Kazumasa, "Changes of Economic and Trade Structure" in FAIR, *Interim Report of Asia-Pacific Economic Research*, p. 48; and Sakurai Makoto, "Japanese Direct Foreign Investment and Asia," Mitsui Marine Research Institute, Discussion Paper No. 12, September 1991, p. 6.

46 MITI, *Tsūshō hakusho (White Paper on Trade)* (Tokyo: MOF Printing Office, 1992), pp. 132–5.

47 Tomisawa Konomi, "Development and Future Outlook for an International Division of Labor in the Automobile Industries of the Asian NICs," a briefing paper for the First Policy Forum of the International Motor Vehicle Program, Cambridge, Massachusetts, 5 May 1987, p. 17.

48 Shujiro Urata, "The Rapid Increase of Direct Investment Abroad and Structural Change in Japan" in Eric D. Ramstetter (ed.), *Direct Foreign Investment in Asia's Developing Economies and Structural Change in the Asia-Pacific Region* (Boulder: Westview Press, 1991), p. 196.

49 MITI, *Dai-go-kai, Kaigai jigyō katsudō kihon chōsa (Basic Survey of Overseas Business Activities)*, 5th edn (Tokyo: MOF Printing Office, 1994), pp. 219, 213. See Appendix I.

50 We are not alone in calling for this kind of data. Kazumasa Iwata, for example, has encouraged the Japanese government to broaden its definition of intrafirm trade to include transactions within "alliance relationships." See Iwata, "Changes of Economic and Trade Structure," p. 60. For a while, we believed we had discovered a source for such data. Every three years, MITI publishes its *Kaigai jigyō katsudō kihon chōsa (Basic Survey of Overseas Business Activities)*, which includes an entry called "Dōitsu kigyō guruupu nai torihiki" ("Transactions within the Same Enterprise Group"). It turns out, however, that MITI leaves it up to each survey respondent to define an "enterprise group." We suspect, with good reason, that most firms define "enterprise group" to mean fully integrated corporate group, rather than *keiretsu* or even corporate network. Japanese scholars seem to have the same suspicion, and thus use these MITI statistics only to talk about intrafirm trade.

51 MITI, *Kaigai jigyō katsudō kihon chōsa*.

52 US affiliates in Asia also rely heavily on their parent firms for sales to and purchases from America. In 1992, the parents of these affiliates were on the receiving end of 91 percent of their high-tech exports to the United States, and on the sending end of 86 percent of their high-tech imports from America: US Department of Commerce, *U.S. Direct Investment Abroad, Preliminary 1992 Estimates* (Washington: US Government Printing Office, 1994). Unfortunately, the US government does not collect data on intrafirm trade between American affiliates in Asia, or between American affiliates in Asia and those in Japan. This may be due to the fact that American affiliates in Asia, unlike their Japanese counterparts, focus almost exclusively on the host and home country (rather than third country) markets. See Dennis Encarnation, *Rivals Beyond Trade: America Versus Japan in Global Competition* (Ithaca: Cornell University Press, 1992). This in turn is probably related to the fact that American MNCs, unlike their Japanese counterparts, have not built strategic networks in the region.

53 FAIR, *Interim Report of Asia-Pacific Economic Research*, p. 163.

54 MITI, *Wagakuni kigyō no kaigai jigyō katsudō (Overseas Business Activities of Japanese Firms)*, No. 24 (Tokyo: MITI, 1995), pp. 90–1, 100–1. Impressed by such statistics, Alburo, Bautista, and Gochoco exaggerated

only a little by concluding that Japanese FDI in this region "is not a means primarily to serve the needs of the domestic Asian markets, although this was true in the 1960s and 70s. Instead, the Asian region serves primarily as a low-cost export base." F. A. Alburo, C. C. Bautista, and M. S. H. Gochoco, "Pacific Direct Investment Flows into ASEAN," *ASEAN Economic Bulletin*, March 1992, p. 287.

55 Japanese manufacturers of electrical machinery in Asia exported 62.1 percent of their output from 1990 to 1993 while manufacturers of precision machinery exported 68.4 percent. Japanese automakers in Asia, which exported less than 10 percent in the 1980s, exported 21.8 percent in 1993. MITI, *Kaigai jigyō katsudō kihon chōsa* (various years), and *Wagakuni kigyō no kaigai jigyō katsudo* (various years).

56 "Japanese Boosting Investment in Indonesia," *Ward's Automotive International*, January 1991, p. 1; "Backyard Boom," *Automotive News*, 9 July 1990, p. 26.

57 The value of such reverse imports in 1993 was $7.94 billion (or ¥913.4 billion, using ¥115 = $1 as the exchange rate then in effect). That represented 37 percent of all exports by Japanese manufacturing affiliates in Asia. MITI, *Wagakuni kigyō no kaigai jigyō katsudō*, No. 24 (1995), pp. 90–1.

58 For a good example of the analysis presented in this special section, see Sadao Fujiwara, "Kyūshinten suru Nihon kigyō no gurōbaru-ka" ("The Rapid Growth of Globalization by Japanese Firms"), *Ekonomisuto*, 29 June 1993, p. 51.

59 *FEER*, 9 June 1994, p. 42. Small color TVs have been a favorite reimport item. In 1992, Sharp planned to import 100,000 units from its affiliate in Malaysia. Hitachi planned to import 150,000 units from its affiliate in Taiwan. And Matsushita, a giant TV manufacturer, planned to import at least 400,000 units from its affiliate in Malaysia. *Nikkei Weekly*, 11 July 1992.

60 *Asahi shinbun*, 3 February 1995, p. 11. The newspaper noted that MITI hopes to capitalize on *kūdōka* phobia by reclaiming its role as a "cradle" supporting sunrise industries.

61 EPA, *Economic Survey of Japan (1993–1994): A Challenge to New Frontiers beyond the Severe Adjustment Process* (Tokyo: EPA, 26 July 1994), p. 37.

62 MITI, *Wagakuni kigyō no kaigai jigyō katsudō*, No. 24 (1995), p. 12.

63 *Shipping and Trade News*, 26 March 1993.

64 *JEI Report*, No. 39 A, 22 October 1993, p. 4.

65 "By retaining in the home country the capacity for innovation in critical parts, Japan avoids the 'hollowing out' phenomenon," argue Fumio Kodama and Takao Kiba, in "The Emerging Trajectory of International Technology," Asia-Pacific Research Center, Stanford University, 1994, p. 22. We discussed this issue in chapter six.

66 Elaine Kurtenback, AP, "Japan Looks to Asian Markets to Boost Trade," *Seattle Post-Intelligencer*, 7 September 1993, p. B9.

67 Industrial Structure Deliberation Council, MITI, *Sangyō kōzō no chōki bijon* (*A Long-range View of Industrial Structure*) (Tokyo: Sangyō Kōzō Shingikai, 1974), quoted in Jonathan Morris (ed.), *Japan and the Global Economy: Issues and Trends in the 1990s* (London: Routledge, 1991).

68 EPA, *Keizai hakusho 1989: Heisei keizai no kadode to Nihon keizai no atarashii chōryū* (*Economic White Paper, 1989: The Launching of the Heisei-era Economy and New Currents in the Japanese Economy*) (Tokyo: MOF Printing Office, 1989), pp. 124–6.

69 *Nikkei Weekly*, 4 October 1993, p. 1.

70 Japanese electrical and electronics manufacturers in Asia sold 23.3 percent of their output to Japan from 1990 to 1993. See MITI, *Wagakuni kigyō no*

kaigai jigyō katsudō, and MITI, *Dai-go-kai, Kaigai jigyō katsudō kihon chōsa*. Also see Encarnation, *Rivals beyond Trade*, p. 181.

71 ibid. Japanese electrical machine makers sold 9.7 percent of their output ($1.86 billion, using ¥115 = $1 to North America in 1993, 4.9 percent in 1992, 13.5 percent ($2.08 billion, using ¥133 = $1) in 1991, and 10.3 percent ($1.35 billion, using ¥141 = $1) in 1990.

72 See Iwata, "Changes of Economic and Trade Structure," p. 58.

73 Tejima Shigeki, "Sekkyoku shisei ni tenjita Nihon no kaigai tōshi" ("Japanese Overseas Investment Turns Active") in Shūkan Tōyō Keizai, Tōyō Keizai Shinpōsha, *Kaigai shinshutsu kigyō sōran, 1994 (A Comprehensive Survey of Firms Expanding Overseas)* (Tokyo: Tōyō Keizai Shinpōsha, 1994), p. 13.

74 Japan Machinery Exporters Association, "Wagakuni kikai sangyō no Ajia ni okeru seisan bungyō jittai ni tsuite" ("The Actual State of Production and Division of Labor by Japanese Machine Industries Operating in Asia), a survey, June 1994, pp. 11–12. Multiple responses were allowed.

75 Interviews with Sony officials, *Asian Wall Street Journal*, 19 March 1993, p. 1.

76 *Economic Eye*, Summer 1992, p. 19.

77 *Japan Times*, 6 January 1993.

78 *Asian Wall Street Journal*, 19 March 1993.

79 Rob Steven, *Japan's New Imperialism* (Armonk, New York: M. E. Sharpe Inc., 1990), p. 201. Accused of dumping, Sharp announced in 1993 that it would begin producing color TVs in Europe, rather than export them from plants in Asia. *Nihon keizai shinbun*, 26 April 1993.

80 *U.S. News and World Report*, 17 May 1993, p. 61.

81 *Japan Digest*, 6 October 1994.

82 United Nations, *Commodity Trade Statistics*.

83 Paitoon Wiboonchutikula, "Thailand's Trade in Manufactured Goods in the Asia-Pacific Region," Thailand Development Research Institute, February 1993, p. 43.

84 Jacob Schlesinger, "Hidden Surplus: Asian Factories Complicate Japan's U.S. Trade Position," *Wall Street Journal*, 19–20 March 1993, p. 1.

85 ibid.

86 IMF, *Direction of Trade Statistics*.

87 Joseph Romm, "Japan's Flying Geese," *Forbes*, 23 November 1992, p. 109.

88 *Asahi shinbun*, 2 June 1993, p. 11.

89 Bernard Wysocki, "Guiding Hand: In Asia, the Japanese Hope to 'Co-ordinate' What Nations Produce," *Wall Street Journal*, 20 August 1990, p. A4.

90 *Business Asia*, 30 June 1986, p. 202; *Nikkei Weekly*, 13 June 1992, p. 1.

91 *FEER*, 20 August 1992, pp. 52–3.

92 JETRO, "The Study on Selected Industrial Product Development in Malaysia: Computers and Computer Peripherals," undated, p. 56.

93 Takeshi Isayama, "Implications of Long-term Trends for Japan's Interaction with Asia," an outline of a paper for a conference sponsored by the Hoover Institution, Stanford University, Japan and the Regionalization of Asia, March 1993.

12 Loosening the Knot

1 This estimate was made by the Mitsubishi Research Institute and cited by Steven Wong in a paper ("The Pacific's Role in Moderating U.S.–Japan Economic Conflicts," p. 45) he wrote for a conference, Preparing for a

Pacific Century, sponsored by the Commission on US–Japan Relations for the 21st Century, November 1991.

2 Some Asian nations are skeptical about any regional organization, such as APEC, that includes the United States. Malaysia has been openly hostile to the concept.

3 Japan exports about as much as Germany, but imports far less (only $1,900 per person in Japan in 1993, compared with $4,100 per person in Germany). Japanese imports actually fell from 11 percent of GDP in 1983 to 6 percent in 1993. See *Asahi shinbun*, 2 January 1995, p. 7. Japan's track record in attracting and supporting inward FDI is equally poor. Local affiliates of foreign firms accounted for about 18 percent of total sales in Germany in 1986, but only 1 percent in Japan. See Laura D'Andrea Tyson, *Who's Bashing Whom? Trade Conflict in High Technology Industries* (Washington: Institute for International Economics, 1992), p. 8.

4 Steven Schlossstein, *Asia's New Little Dragons: The Dynamic Emergence of Indonesia, Thailand and Malaysia* (Chicago: Contemporary Books, 1991), p. 306.

5 For example, US firms could join forces with local firms to build a regional information superhighway. As the architects of such high-technology infra-structure, these firms would become indispensable partners in the region's future development.

6 See Edward M. Graham, "Multinationals and Competition Policy," *International Economic Insights*, Vol. 4, No. 4 (July/August 1993), pp. 26–8.

7 Michael Oksenberg and Hong Ying Wang, "America and Post-Cold War Asia," a paper for a conference sponsored by the Hoover Institution, Stanford University, on Japan and the Regionalization of Asia, March 1993, p. 2.

8 Chalmers Johnson made a similar point in a column ("The Empowerment of Asia: America's Need for 'the Vision Thing'") he wrote for *Japan Digest Forum*, 10 June 1994.

9 *New York Times*, 9 November 1992. Under pressure from the government of the Philippines, the United States has already shut down two military bases in that country. The Pentagon has hinted that further retrenchment might be in the offing.

10 *Seattle Post-Intelligencer*, 6 May 1994, p. A1.

11 Dornbusch, an MIT economist, made the correct diagnosis but recom-mended the wrong cure when he called for a similar proposal – a series of bilateral free trade agreements with developing countries in Asia. "Japan," he wrote, "is emphasizing a new division of labor that encompasses Asian locations as cost-effective parts of a Japanese manufacturing strategy. A free trade agreement with the Pacific Rim is therefore all the more important because it offers a check on Japan's attempt to build a coprosperity area of its own." See Rudiger W. Dornbusch, "Policy Options for Freer Trade: The Case of Bilateralism" in Robert Z. Lawrence and Charles L. Schultze (eds), *An American Trade Strategy: Options for the 1990s* (Washington: Brookings Institution, 1990), pp. 130–1.

12 This idea was first presented by the Economic Strategy Institute in its study of NAFTA. See Clyde V. Prestowitz, Jr and Robert B. Cohen, *The New North American Order: A Win–Win Strategy for U.S.–Mexico Trade* (Washington: Economic Strategy Institute, 1991). US multinationals operating in Asia might try harder to export to third countries if they did not have such a strong incentive to reimport back to the United States. Under current US

law, an affiliate assembling parts from its parent firm in the United States can ship finished goods back home and avoid paying an import duty on anything but the value created overseas. This law should be changed.

13 Richard Cronin, "Japan's Expanding Role and Influence in the Asia-Pacific Region: Implications for U.S. Interests," Congressional Research Report, 7 September 1990, p. 69, calls this a strategy of "fighting fire with fire." But under current budget constraints, there is no way the US government can match the Japanese government's ability to arm its own manufacturers.

14 *Asahi shinbun*, 7 November 1994, p. 5.

15 In 1990, for example, Japan resumed aid to China, even though all the other member-states in G-7 continued to impose sanctions on that government for its brutal suppression of China's prodemocracy movement. In addition, Japan opted to resume aid to Vietnam in 1992, 15 months before the United States lifted its trade embargo against that country. And finally, Japan strayed from the US fold in 1994, when it softened its hard-line policy toward the military junta in Myanmar.

16 Kobayashi Yōtarō, president of Fuji Xerox, has called on his fellow Japanese to undergo a "re-Asianization." See his essay, "Nihon: Sai-Ajia-ka" ("The Re-Asianization of Japan"), *Foresight*, April 1991, p. 44. In a similar way, Ogura Kazuo, director general of the economic affairs bureau of the Ministry of Foreign Affairs, has called on Japan to reclaim its "Asian spirit." See his essay, "'Ajia no fukken' no tame ni" ("Toward an 'Asian Restoration'"), *Chūō kōron*, July 1993, pp. 60–73.

17 EPA, *Ajia taiheiyō chiiki, han'ei no tetsugaku: sōgō kokuryoku no kanten kara mita Nihon no yakuwari (The Philosophy of Prosperity in the Asia-Pacific Region: Japan's Role as Viewed from the Perspective of its Comprehensive National Capability)* (Tokyo: MOF Printing Bureau, 1989), p. 17.

18 Nukazawa Kazuo, managing director, Keidanren, "Regional Economic Development and the Roles of Korea and Japan," a paper presented to the Tenth Korea–Japan Intellectual Exchange Conference, 12–13 June 1992, Seoul.

19 In an interview with *Time* (20 November 1989, p. 82), Ishihara states bluntly that "Japan's franchise is Asia." Japan, he argues, "should assume greater responsibility than the U.S. or Europe in the development of the Asian region."

20 *Tōyō keizai*, 18 July 1987, pp. 4–17.

21 Interview, 3 July 1992, Tokyo.

22 Ishiyama Yoshihide, "Regional Routes to a New World Order," *Japan Echo*, Vol. XIX, No. 1 (Spring 1992), p. 22.

23 Nakatani Iwao, "Nihon keizai no tsuyosa wa hon mono da" ("The Strength of the Japanese Economy is for Real"), *Chūō kōron*, November 1988, p. 129.

24 Despite its diplomatic bravado, Japan is actually quite leery of NIC exports. The editor of this volume, John Ravenhill, informs us that in December 1994 Taiwanese authorities were complaining about Japanese pressure to get them to "voluntarily" restrict their export of bicycles to Japan – even though Japan enjoys a sizeable trade surplus with Taiwan.

25 *New York Times*, 7 June 1993. In 1994, the Clinton administration moderated its results-oriented policy.

26 Yuichiro Nagatomi, "Asia-Pacific Rim Cooperation and U.S.–Japan Rela-tions," a speech to the Jackson School of International Studies, University of Washington, 18 November 1993, p. 11.

27 Interview, Sakakibara Eisuke, 3 July 1992, Tokyo.

28 See Dieter Ernst, "Carriers of Regionalization: The East Asian Production Networks of Japanese Electronics Firms," working paper no. 73, Berkeley Roundtable on the International Economy, University of California at Berkeley, November 1994.

29 ibid., p. 52.

30 Bunluasak Pussarungsri, "Effect of Foreign Direct Investment," Thailand Development Research Institute, April 1993, p. 9.

31 F. A. Alburo, C. C. Bautista, and M. S. H. Gochoco, "Pacific Direct Investment Flows into ASEAN," *ASEAN Economic Bulletin*, March 1992, p. 307.

32 Quoted in Chalmers Johnson, "The Problem of Japan in an Era of Structural Change," Research Report 89-04, Graduate School of International Relations and Pacific Studies, University of California at San Diego, June 1989, p. 19.

33 In 1978, Singapore launched a "Learn from Japan" campaign to encourage the nation's labor force to work as hard and be as productive as Japan's. And in 1982, Malaysian prime minister Mahathir called on his country to "Look East" to Japan. See Lee Poh-ping, "Japan and the Asia-Pacific Region," a paper presented at the Woodrow Wilson Center's Japan and the World conference, 27–28 January 1992.

34 Noordin Sopiee, "Political Issues Associated with Economic Cooperation in East Asia," a paper presented at the third joint research conference on Asia-Pacific relations, sponsored by FAIR, Kuala Lumpur, 5–7 July 1992, p. 70.

35 *Asian Wall Street Journal*, 25 October 1993.

36 Japan Economic Institute, *JEI Report*, No. 12 A (27 March 1992), p. 6.

37 *National Geographic*, November 1991, p. 57.

Select Bibliography

Adachi Fumihiko. "Small and Medium-sized Firms in Japan's Foreign Direct Investment." In *Japan's Direct Investment in Thailand: Patterns and Issues*, ed. Tran Van Tho. Tokyo: Japan Center for Economic Research, August 1991.

Ajia Keizai Kenkyūjo. *Minkan keizai kyōryoku chōsa kenkyū hōkokusho (A Research Report Examining Private Economic Cooperation)*. Tokyo: MITI, March 1992.

Akamatsu Kaname. "A Historical Pattern of Economic Growth in Developing Countries." *The Developing Economies*, No. 1 (March–August 1962).

Amsden, Alice. *Asia's Next Giant: South Korea and Late Industrialization*. New York: Oxford University Press, 1989.

Anchordoguy, Marie. "Mastering the Market: Japanese Government Targeting of the Computer Industry." *International Organization*, Vol. 42, No. 3 (Summer 1988).

Aoki Masahiko. *The Cooperative Game Theory of the Firm*. London: Oxford University Press, 1984.

Aoki Masahiko. *The Economic Analysis of the Firm*. Amsterdam: North-Holland, 1984.

Aoki Masahiko. *Information, Incentives and Bargaining in the Japanese Economy*. Cambridge: Cambridge University Press, 1988.

Aoki Satoshi. *Toyota, sono jitsuzō (Toyota, the Reality)*. Tokyo: Sekibunsha, 1982.

Aoki Takeshi. "Foreign Investment and Network Formation." In *Japan's Foreign Investment and Asian Economic Interdependence*, ed. Shojiro Tokunaga. Tokyo: University of Tokyo Press, 1992.

Aoki Takeshi. "Japanese FDI and the Forming of Networks in the Asia-Pacific Region: Experience in Malaysia and its Implications." In *Japan's Foreign Investment and Asian Interdependence: Production, Trade and Financial Systems*, ed. Shojiro Tokunaga. Tokyo: University of Tokyo Press, 1992.

Aoki Takeshi. "Mareishia: gaishi no kyuryunyu to nettowāku no keisei" ("Malaysia: A Rapid Inflow of Foreign Capital and the Formation of Networks"). In *Ajia taiheiyō no keizai hatten to chiiki kyōryoku (Asia-Pacific*

Economic Development and Regional Cooperation), ed. Yanagihara Toru. Tokyo: Ajia Keizai Kenkyūsho, 1992.

Arase, David M. "Japanese Foreign Aid: The State, the Polity and the International System." PhD diss., University of California, Berkeley, 1989.

Arrison, Thomas S., C. Fred Bergsten, Edward M. Graham, and Martha Caldwell Harris. "Japan's Growing Technological Capability and Implications for the U.S. Economy." In *Japan's Growing Technological Capability: Implications for the U.S. Economy*, ed. Thomas S. Arrison, C. Fred Bergsten, Edward M. Graham, and Martha Caldwell Harris. Washington: National Academy Press, 1992.

Arrow, Kenneth J. "The Economic Implication of Learning by Doing." *Review of Economic Studies*, Vol. 29 (1969).

Axelrod, Robert. *The Evolution of Cooperation*. New York: Basic Books, 1984.

Bartlett, Christopher A. and Sumantra Ghoshal. "Organizing for Worldwide Effectiveness: The Transnational Solution." *California Management Review*, Vol. 31, No. 1 (Fall 1988).

Bartlett, Christopher and Yoshihara Hideki. "New Challenges for Japanese Multinationals: Is Organizational Adaptation Their Achilles Heel?" In *Globalizing Management: Creating and Leading the Competitive Organization*, ed. Vladimir Pucik, Noel Tichy, and Carole Barnett. New York: Wiley, 1992.

Basu, K., E. Jones, and E. Schlicht. "The Growth and Decay of Custom: The Role of New Institutional Economics and Economic History." *Explorations in Economic History*, Vol. 24 (1987).

Beechler, Schon. "International Management Control in Multinational Corporations: The Case of Japanese Consumer Electronics Firms in Asia." *ASEAN Economic Bulletin*, November 1992.

Belassa, Bela. *The Newly Industrializing Countries in the World Economy*. New York: Pergamon Press, 1981.

Belassa, Bela. "The Lessons of East Asian Development." *Economic Development and Cultural Change*, Vol. 36, No. 3 (April 1988).

Bello, Walden and Christine Rosenfeld. *Dragons in Distress: Asia's Miracle Economies in Crisis*. San Francisco: Institute for Food and Development Policy, 1990.

Bergsten, C. Fred and Marcus Noland. *Reconcilable Differences? The United States-Japan Economic Conflict*. Washington: Institute for International Economics, 1993.

Bernard, Mitchell and John Ravenhill. "Beyond Product Cycles and Flying Geese: Regionalization, Hierarchy and the Industrialization of East Asia." *World Politics*, Vol. 47, No. 2 (January 1995).

Borrus, Michael. "Reorganizing Asia: Japan's New Development Trajectory and the Regional Division of Labor." Working paper 53, Berkeley Roundtable on the International Economy, March 1992.

Bowonder, B., T. Miyake, and H. A. Linstone. "Japanese Institutional Mechanisms for Industrial Growth: A Systems Perspective – Part I." *Technological Forecasting and Social Change*, Vol. 47, No. 2 (October 1994).

Broad, Robin, John Cavanagh, and Walden Bello. "Development: The Market is not Enough." In *International Political Economy: Perspectives on Global Power and Wealth*, Jeffrey A. Frieden and David A. Lake. New York: St Martin's Press, 1995.

Brown, Allen L. and Gregory A. Daneke. "The Rising Electric Sun: Japan's Photovoltaics Industry." *Issues in Science and Technology*, Vol. III, No. 3 (Spring 1987).

Buckley, P. J. and R. D. Pearce. "Overseas Production and Exporting by the World's Largest Enterprises." *Journal of International Business Studies*, Vol. 10 (1979).

Buckley, Peter J. and Mark Casson. "A Theory of Cooperation in International Business." In *Cooperative Strategies in International Business*, Farok J. Contractor and Peter Lorange. Lexington, Mass.: D. C. Heath & Co., 1988.

Calder, Kent. *Strategic Capitalism: Private Business and Public Purpose in Japanese Industrial Finance*. Princeton: Princeton University Press, 1993.

Campbell, Nigel. "Japanese Business Strategy in China." *Long-Range Planning*, Vol. 20, No. 5 (1987).

Cantwell, John. "Japan's Industrial Competitiveness and the Technological Capabilities of the Leading Japanese Firms." In *Japan's Growing Technological Capability*, ed. Arrison et al.

Cardoso, Fernando Henrique. "Associated Dependent Development: Theoretical and Practical Implications." In *Authoritarian Brazil: Origins, Policies, and Future*, ed. Alfred Stepan. New Haven: Yale University Press, 1973.

Casson, Mark. *Firm and the Market*. Cambridge, Mass.: MIT Press, 1987.

Chen, E. K. Y. *Multinational Corporations, Technology and Employment*. London: Macmillan, 1983.

Chen, Edward K. Y. "The Electronics Industry." In *Technological Challenge in the Asia-Pacific Economy*, ed. Hadi Soesastro and Mari Pangetsu. Sydney: Allen & Unwin, 1990.

Chia Siow Yue. *Japanese Overseas Direct Investment in ASEAN and Asian NIEs*. Tokyo: Ajiken, 1991.

Chng Meng Kng et al. *Technology and Skills in Singapore*. Singapore: Institute of Southeast Asian Studies, 1986.

Chong Li Choy. "Singapore's Development: Harnessing the Multinationals." *Contemporary Southeast Asia*, Vol. 8, No. 1 (June 1986).

Chou Tien-Chen. "American and Japanese Direct Foreign Investment in Taiwan: A Comparative Study." *Hitotsubashi Journal of Economics*, Vol. 29 (1988).

Chow, Peter and Mitchell Kellman. *Trade: The Engine of Growth in East Asia*. New York: Oxford University Press, 1993.

Christensen, L. R., D. W. Jorgensen, and L. J. Lau. "Transcendental Logarithmic Production Frontiers." *Review of Economics and Statistics*, Vol. 55 (1973).

Chuta Thianthai. "Japanese Management in Thailand." In *Thai Perceptions of Japanese Management*, ed. Kunio Yoshihara. Kuala Lumpur: Falcon Press, 1989.

Clad, James. *Behind the Myth: Business, Money and Power in Southeast Asia*. London: Unwin Hyman, 1989.

Clark, Kim B. and Takahiro Fujimoto. *Product Development Performance*. Boston: Harvard Business School Press, 1991.

Coase, Ronald H. "1991 Nobel Lecture: The Institutional Structure of Production." In *The Nature of the Firm: Origins, Evolution and Development*, ed. Oliver E. Williamson and Sidney G. Winter. New York: Oxford University Press, 1993.

Contractor, Farok J. and Peter Lorange. *Cooperative Strategies in International Business*. Lexington, Mass.: D. C. Heath & Co., 1988.

Crouch, Harold. *Domestic Political Structures and Regional Economic Cooperation*. Singapore: Institute of Southeast Asian Studies, 1984.

Cumings, Bruce. "The Origin and Development of the Northeast Asian Political Economy." *International Organization*, Vol. 38, No. 1 (Winter 1984).

Demaine, Harvey. "*Kanpatthana*: Thai Views of Development." In *Context, Meaning and Power in Southeast Asia*, ed. Mark Hobart and Robert H. Taylor. Ithaca: Cornell University Press, 1986.

Demsetz, Harold. "The Theory of the Firm Revisited." In *The Nature of the Firm: Origins, Evolution and Development*, ed. Oliver E. Williamson and Sidney G. Winter. New York: Oxford University Press, 1993.

Dennison, Edward. *Trends in American Economic Growth, 1929–1982.* Washington: Brookings Institution, 1985.

Deyo, Frederic C. "Coalitions, Institutions and Linkage Sequencing." In *The Political Economy of the New Asian Industrialism,* ed. Frederic C. Deyo. Ithaca: Cornell University Press, 1987.

Deyo, Frederic C. "State and Labor in East Asia." In *The Political Economy of the New Asian Industrialism,* ed. Frederic C. Deyo. Ithaca: Cornell University Press, 1987.

Doner, Richard F. *Driving a Bargain: Automobile Industrialization and Japanese Firms in Southeast Asia.* Berkeley: University of California Press, 1991.

Doner, Richard F. "Japanese Foreign Investment and the Creation of a Pacific Asian Region." In *Regionalism and Rivalry: Japan and the U.S. in Pacific Asia,* ed. Jeffrey Frankel and Miles Kahler. Chicago: University of Chicago Press, 1993.

Dore, Ronald. *British Factory – Japanese Factory: The Origin of National Diversity in Industrial Relations.* Berkeley: University of California Press, 1973.

Dosi, Giovanni, Laura D'Andrea Tyson, and John Zysman. "Trade, Technologies and Development: A Framework for Discussing Japan." In *Politics and Productivity: The Real Story of Why Japan Works,* ed. Chalmers Johnson, Laura D'Andrea Tyson, and John Zysman. Cambridge, Mass.: Ballinger, 1989.

Dunning, John. "Toward an Eclectic Theory of International Production: Some Empirical Tests." *Journal of International Business Studies,* Vol. 11 (Spring/Summer, 1980).

Dyer, Jeffrey H. "Dedicated Assets: Japan's Manufacturing Edge." *Harvard Business Review,* November–December 1994.

Eads, George C. and Kozo Yamamura. "The Future of Industrial Policy." In *The Political Economy of Japan, Volume 1: The Domestic Transformation,* ed. Kozo Yamamura and Yasukichi Yasuba. Stanford: Stanford University Press, 1987.

Economic Planning Agency of Japan. *Economic Survey of Japan (1993-1994): A Challenge to New Frontiers Beyond the Severe Adjustment Process.* Tokyo: EPA, 1994.

Economist Intelligence Unit. *The ASEAN Motor Industry.* London: Economist, 1985.

Eggertsson, Thrainn. *Economic Behavior and Institutions.* Cambridge: Cambridge University Press, 1990.

Emmerson, Donald K. "The Bureaucracy in Political Context: Weakness in Strength." In *Political Power and Communication in Indonesia,* ed. Karl D. Jackson and Lucien W. Pye. Berkeley: University of California Press, 1978.

Encarnation, Dennis. *Rivals beyond Trade: America versus Japan in Global Competition.* Ithaca: Cornell University Press, 1992.

Enos, J. L. and W. H. Park. *The Adoption and Diffusion of Imported Technology: The Case of Korea.* New York: Croom Helm, 1988.

Ensign, Margee. *Doing Good or Doing Well? Japan's Foreign Aid Program.* New York: Columbia University Press, 1992.

Ernst, Dieter. "Carriers of Regionalization: The East Asian Production Networks of Japanese Electronics Firms." Working paper 73, Berkeley Roundtable on the International Economy, November 1994.

Evans, Peter. *Dependent Development: The Alliance of Multinational, State and Local Capital in Brazil.* Princeton: Princeton University Press, 1979.

Frankel, Jeffrey. "Is a Yen Bloc Forming in Pacific Asia?" In *Finance and the International Economy: The AMEX Bank Review Prize Essays,* ed. Richard O'Brien. Oxford: Oxford University Press, 1991.

Frankel, Jeffrey. "Is Japan Creating a Yen Bloc in East Asia and the Pacific?" In *Regionalism and Rivalry: Japan and the U.S. in Pacific Asia*, ed. Jeffrey Frankel and Miles Kahler. Chicago: University of Chicago Press, 1993.

Frankel, Jeffrey and Miles Kahler (eds), *Regionalism and Rivalry: Japan and the U.S. in Pacific Asia*. Chicago: University of Chicago Press, 1993.

Freeman, Christopher. *Technology Policy and Economic Performance: Lessons from Japan*. London: Pinter Publishers, 1987.

Friedman, David. *The Misunderstood Miracle: Industrial Development and Political Change in Japan*. Ithaca: Cornell University Press, 1988.

Fruin, Mark. *The Japanese Enterprise System: Competitive Strategies and Cooperative Structures*. Oxford: Oxford University Press, 1992.

Gerlach, Michael. *Alliance Capitalism: The Social Organization of Japanese Business*. Berkeley: University of California Press, 1992.

Gerlach, Michael. "Twilight of the Keiretsu? A Critical Assessment." *Journal of Japanese Studies*, Vol. 18, No. 1 (Winter 1992).

Gold, Thomas B. *State and Society in the Taiwan Miracle*. Armonk, New York: M. E. Sharpe Inc., 1986.

Gold, Thomas B. "Entrepreneurs, Multinationals and the State." In *Contending Approaches to the Political Economy of Taiwan*, ed. Edwin A. Winckler and Susan Greenhalgh. Armonk, New York: M. E. Sharpe Inc., 1988.

Graham, Edward M. and Naoko T. Anzai. "The Myth of a De Facto Asian Economic Bloc: Japan's Foreign Direct Investment in East Asia." *Columbia Journal of World Business*, Vol. 24, No. 3 (Autumn 1994).

Graham, Edward M. and Paul R. Krugman. *Foreign Direct Investment in the United States*. Washington: Institute for International Economics, 1989.

Graham, Edward M. and Paul R. Krugman. *Foreign Direct Investment in the United States*, 2nd edn. Washington: Institute for International Economics, 1991.

Green, Andrew E. "South Korea's Automobile Industry." *Asian Survey*, Vol. 32, No. 5 (May 1992).

Greenhalgh, Susan. "Families and Networks in Taiwan's Economic Development." In *Contending Approaches to the Political Economy of Taiwan*, ed. Edwin A. Winckler and Susan Greenhalgh. Armonk, New York: M. E. Sharpe, 1988.

Grow, Roy. "Japanese and American Firms in China: Lessons of a New Market." *Columbia Journal of World Business*, Spring 1986.

Guy, John. *The Motor Industry of South East Asia*. London: Economist Intelligence Unit, 1991.

Haggard, Stephen. *Pathways from the Periphery*. Ithaca: Cornell University Press, 1990.

Hamel, Gary. "Competition for Competence and Inter-partner Learning within International Strategic Alliances." *Strategic Management Journal*, Vol. 12 (1991).

Hawes, Gary. "Theories of Peasant Revolution: A Critique and Contribution from the Philippines." *World Politics*, Vol. XLII, No. 2 (January 1990).

Healey, Derek. *Japanese Capital Exports and Asian Economic Development*. Paris: Development Centre of the Organization for Economic Cooperation and Development, 1991.

Helpman, Elhanen and Paul Krugman. *Market Structure and Foreign Trade: Increasing Returns, Imperfect Competition and International Economy*. Cambridge, Mass.: MIT Press, 1985.

Heyzer, Noeleen. "International Production and Social Change." In *Singapore: Development Policies and Trends*, ed. Peter Chen. Singapore: Oxford University Press, 1983.

Hirschman, Albert O. *National Power and the Structure of Foreign Trade.* Berkeley: University of California Press, 1945.

Ho Shuet-Ying. *Taiwan, After a Long Silence.* Hong Kong: Asia Monitor Research Center, 1990.

Hughes, Helen and You Poh Seng. *Foreign Investment and Industrialization in Singapore.* Canberra: Australian National University Press, 1969.

Hymer, Stephen. *The International Operations of National Firms: A Study of Direct Foreign Investment.* Cambridge, Mass.: MIT Press, 1976.

Imai Ken-ichi. "The Japanese Pattern of Innovation and its Evolution." In *Technology and the Wealth of Nations,* ed. Nathan Rosenberg, Ralph Landau, and David Mowery. Stanford: Stanford University Press, 1992.

Imai Ken-ichi and Kaneko Ikuyo. *Nettowāku soshiki ron (Theory of the Network System).* Tokyo: Iwanami Shoten, 1988.

Imaoka Hideki. "Japanese Corporate Employment and Personnel Systems and Their Transfer to Japanese Affiliates in Asia." *Developing Economies,* Vol. 27, No. 4 (December 1989).

Ishiyama Yoshihide. "Regional Routes to a New World Order." *Japan Echo,* Vol. XIX, No. 1 (Spring 1992).

Islam, Shafiqul. "Foreign Aid and Burdensharing: Is Japan Freeriding to a Coprosperity Sphere in Pacific Asia?" In *Regionalism and Rivalry: Japan and the U.S. in Pacific Asia,* ed. Jeffrey Frankel and Miles Kahler. Chicago: University of Chicago Press, 1993.

Itami Takayuki. "Nihon kigyō no jinponshugi shisutemu" ("The Employee-first-ism of the Japanese Enterprise System). In *Nihon no kigyō (Japanese Business),* ed. Komiya Ryūtarō and Imai Ken-ichi. Tokyo: University of Tokyo Press, 1989.

James, William, Seiji Naya, and Gerald Meier. *Asian Development: Economic Success and Policy Lessons.* Madison: University of Wisconsin Press, 1989.

Johnson, Chalmers. *MITI and the Japanese Miracle.* Stanford: Stanford University Press, 1982.

Johnson, Chalmers. "MITI, MPT and the Telecom Wars: How Japan Makes Policy for High Technology." In *Politics and Productivity: The Real Story of Why Japan Works,* ed. Chalmers Johnson, Laura D'Andrea Tyson, and John Zysman. Cambridge, Mass.: Ballinger, 1989.

Jones, G. and C. Hill. "Transaction Cost Analysis of Strategy-Structure Choice." *Strategic Management Journal,* Vol. 9, 1989.

Kamath, Rajan R. and Jeffrey K. Liker. "A Second Look at Japanese Product Development." *Harvard Business Review,* November–December 1994.

Kao, John. "The Worldwide Web of Chinese Business." *Harvard Business Review,* March–April, 1993.

Katzenstein, Peter J. and Martin Rouse. "Japan as a Regional Power in Asia." In *Regionalism and Rivalry: Japan and the United States in Pacific Asia,* ed. Jeffrey A. Frankel and Miles Kahler. Chicago: University of Chicago Press, 1993.

Kawabe Nobuo. "Problems of and Perspectives on Japanese Management in Malaysia." In *Transfer of Japanese Technology and Management,* ed. Shoichi Yamashita. Tokyo: University of Tokyo Press, 1991.

Kenney, Martin and Richard Florida. *Beyond Mass Production: The Japanese System and its Transfer to the U.S.* New York: Oxford University Press, 1993.

Kim Jong-Il and Lawrence J. Lau. "The Sources of Economic Growth of the East Asian Newly Industrializing Countries." Asia/Pacific Research Center, Stanford University, September 1993.

Kodama Fumio and Takao Kiba. "Emerging Trajectory of International Technology." Asia/Pacific Research Center, Stanford University, 1994.

Koike Kazuo. "Human Resource Development and Labor–Management Relations." In *The Political Economy of Japan, Volume. 1: The Domestic Transformation*, ed. Kozo Yamamura and Yasukichi Yasuba. Stanford: Stanford University Press, 1987.

Kojima Kiyoshi. "Transfer of Technology to Developing Countries – Japanese Type versus American Type." *Hitotsubashi Journal of Economics*, Vol. 17 (February 1977).

Kojima Kiyoshi. *Direct Foreign Investment: A Japanese Model of Multinational Business Operations*. London: Croom Helm, 1978.

Kojima Kiyoshi. "Japanese and American Direct Investment in Asia: A Comparative Analysis." *Hitotsubashi Journal of Economics*, Vol. 26 (June 1985).

Komiya Ryūtarō and Kazutomo Irie. "The U.S.–Japan Trade Problem: An Economic Analysis from a Japanese Viewpoint." In *Japan's Economic Structure: Should it Change?* ed. Kozo Yamamura. Seattle: Society for Japanese Studies, 1990.

Kreinin, Mordechai. "How Closed is Japan's Market? Additional Evidence." *World Economy*, Vol. 11, No. 4 (1988).

Krugman, Paul. "Is Free Trade Passe?" *Journal of Economic Perspectives*, Vol. 1 (Fall 1987).

Krugman, Paul. *Rethinking International Trade*. Cambridge, Mass.: MIT Press, 1990.

Krugman, Paul. "The Myth of Asia's Miracle." *Foreign Affairs*, Vol. 73, No. 6 (November/December 1994).

Kumon Hiroshi. "Multinationalization of Toyota Motor Corporation." *Journal of International Economic Studies*, No. 6 (March 1992).

Lawrence, Robert Z. "Japan's Different Trade Regime: An Analysis with Particular Reference to *Keiretsu*." *Journal of Economic Perspectives*, Vol. 7, No. 3 (Summer 1993).

Lee Wong-Young and Kim Jae-Hyung. "Kisul toip taegga ŭi kyŏlchong" ("Determinants of the Royalty Payment in Technology Licencing"). *Han'guk kaebal yŏn'gu* (*Korea Development Review*), Korea Development Institute, Vol. 9, No. 1 (Spring 1987).

Lim Chee Peng and P. P. Lee. *Japanese Direct Investment in Malaysia*. Tokyo: Institute of Developing Economies, 1979.

Lim Chong-Yah. *Policy Options for the Singapore Economy*. Singaore: McGraw-Hill, 1988.

Lincoln, Edward. *Japan's New Global Role*. Washington: Brookings Institution, 1993.

Liu, Linda Y. C. *The New Ascendance of Chinese Business in Southeast Asia: Political, Cultural, Economic and Business Implications*. Ann Arbor: University of Michigan, 1991.

Love, Alexander R. *Development Cooperation: Efforts and Policies of the Members of the Development Assistance Committee (1993 Report)*. Paris: Organization for Economic Cooperation and Development, 1994.

Machado, Kit. "Japanese Transnational Corporations in Malaysia's State Sponsored Heavy Industrialization Drive: The HICOM Automobile and Steels Projects." *Pacific Affairs*, Vol. 62, No. 4 (Winter 1989–90).

Management and Coordination Agency of Japan. *Kagaku gijutsu kenkyū chōsa hōkoku, 1993* (*1993 Research Report on Science and Technology*). Tokyo: Management and Coordination Agency, 1993.

Marston, Richard C. "Price Behavior in Japanese and U.S. Manufacturing." In *Trade with Japan: Has the Door Opened Wider?* ed. Paul Krugman. Chicago: University of Chicago Press, 1991.

Masataka Kosaka (ed.) *Japan's Choices: New Globalism and Cultural Orientations in an Industrial State.* New York: Pinter Publishers, 1989.

McQuillan, Mark. "An Imposing, 'Invisible' Presence." *Japan Economic Journal,* "The Rising Tide: Japan in Asia," a special supplement, Winter 1990.

Migdal, Joel. *Strong States and Weak Societies: State-Society Relations and State Capabilities in the Third World.* Princeton: Princeton University Press, 1988.

Mingsarn Santikarn Kaosa-ard. "Comparative Analysis of Direct Foreign Investment in Thailand." Paper for a conference sponsored by the Hoover Institution, Stanford University, on Japan and the Regionalization of Asia, March 1993.

Mingsarn Santikarn Kaosa-ard. "TNC Involvement in the Thai Auto Industry." In *TDRI* (Thailand Development Research Institute) *Report,* Vol. 8, No. 1 (1993).

Ministry of Finance. *Taigai chokusetsu tōshi no kyoka todokede jisseki (Statistics on the Approval/Notification of Overseas Direct Investment).* Tokyo: MOF Printing Bureau, various years.

Ministry of Foreign Affairs. *Japan's ODA: Annual Report, 1993.* Tokyo: Association for the Promotion of International Cooperation, March 1994.

Ministry of Foreign Affairs. *Wagakuni no seifu kaihatsu enjo no jissho jōkyō (Annual Report on the Status of Japanese ODA).* Tokyo: MFA, research and planning section of the Economic Cooperation Bureau, June 1994.

Ministry of International Trade and Industry. *Kaigai tōshi tōkei sōran (Comprehensive Statistics on Japanese Foreign Investment),* various years.

Ministry of International Trade and Industry. *Tsūshō hakusho (White Paper on Trade).* Tokyo: MOF Printing Bureau, various years.

Ministry of International Trade and Industry. *Wagakuni kigyō no kaigai jigyō katsudō (Overseas Business Activities of Japanese Firms).* Tokyo: MITI, various years.

Ministry of International Trade and Industry. *Nihon no sentaku: Nyū gurōbarizumu e no kōken to "shin sangyō bunka kokka" no sentaku (Japan's Choices: Options for a Nation with a New Corporate Culture and Contributions toward a New Globalism)* (Tokyo: Tsūshō Chōsakai, 1988).

Ministry of International Trade and Industry. "Shin-Ajia kōgyōka sōgō kyōryoku puran" ("The new AID plan"). *Kaihatsu jānaru (Development Journal),* July 1988.

Mirza, Hafiz. *Multinationals and the Growth of the Singapore Economy.* London: Croom Helm, 1986.

Montgomery, Cynthia A. and Michael E. Porter (eds). *Strategy: Seeking and Securing Competitive Advantage.* Cambridge, Mass.: Harvard Business Review, 1991.

Morris, Jonathan (ed.). *Japan and the Global Economy: Issues and Trends in the 1990s.* London: Routledge, 1991.

Morris-Suzuki, Tessa. "Japanese Technology and the new International Division of Knowledge in Asia." In *Japan's Foreign Investment and Asian Economic Interdependence: Production, Trade and Financial Systems,* ed. Shojiro Tokunaga. Tokyo: University of Tokyo Press, 1992.

Murakami Yasusuke. *An Anticlassical Political-Economic Analysis: A Vision for the Next Century.* Stanford: Stanford University Press, 1996.

Murakami Yasusuke and Thomas P. Rohlen. "Social Exchange Aspects of the Japanese Political Economy: Culture, Efficiency and Change." In *The Political Economy of Japan, Volume 3: Cultural and Social Dynamics,* ed. Shumpei Kumon and Henry Rosovsky. Stanford: Stanford University Press, 1992.

Murakami Yasusuke and Kozo Yamamura. "A Technical Note on Japanese Firm Behavior." In *Policy and Trade Issues of the Japanese Economy*, ed. Kozo Yamamura. Seattle: University of Washington Press, 1982.

Mytelka, Lynn Krieger (ed.). *Strategic Partnerships: States, Firms and International Cooperation*. Rutherford: Fairleigh Dickinson University Press, 1991.

Nakakita Tōru. "The Globalization of Japanese Firms and Its Influence on Japan's Trade with Developing Nations." *Developing Economies*, Vol. 26, No. 4 (December 1988).

Nakatani Iwao. "The Economic Role of Financial Corporate Groupings." In *The Economic Analysis of the Japanese Firm*, ed. Masahiko Aoki. Amsterdam: North-Holland, 1984.

Namazaki Ichiro. "Networks of Taiwanese Big Business: A Preliminary Analysis." *Modern China*, Vol. 12, No. 4 (October 1986).

Naya Seiji and Eric Ramstetter. "Policy Interactions and Direct Foreign Investment in East and Southeast Asia." *Journal of World Trade*, Vol. 22, No. 2 (April 1988).

Nelson, Richard and Sidney Winter. *An Evolutionary Theory of Economic Change*. Cambridge, Mass.: Harvard University Press, 1982.

Ng, C.Y., R. Hirono, and Robert Y. Siy. *Technology and Skills in ASEAN: An Overview*. Singapore: Institute of Southeast Asian Studies, 1986.

Nihon Zaigai Kigyō Kyōkai (Association of Overseas Japanese Firms). *Tai-ASEAN toshi masatsu (Investment Friction in ASEAN)*. Tokyo: Association of Overseas Japanese Firms, May 1989.

Nishihara Masashi. *The Japanese and Sukarno's Indonesia: Tokyo-Jakarta Relations, 1951–1966*. Honolulu: University Press of Hawaii, 1976.

Noble, Gregory W. "The Japanese Industrial Policy Debate." In *Pacific Dynamics*, ed. Stephen Haggard and Chung-in Moon. Boulder: Westview Press, 1989.

Noguchi Yukio. "The 'Bubble' and Economic Policies in the 1980s." *Journal of Japanese Studies*, Vol. 20, No. 2 (Summer 1994).

Noguchi Yukio. "The Role of the Fiscal Investment and Loan Program in Postwar Japanese Economic Growth." In *The Japanese Civil Service and Economic Development*, ed. Hyung-Ki Kim et al. Oxford: Oxford University Press, 1995.

Normile, Dennis. "Japan Holds on Tight to Cutting-edge Technology." *Science*, Vol. 262 (15 October 1993).

Normile, Dennis. "Japanese Universities Become Magnets for Asian Students." *Science*, Vol. 262 (15 October 1993).

North, Douglass. *Institutions, Institutional Change and Economic Performance*. Cambridge: Cambridge University Press, 1990.

Ogle, George E. *South Korea: Dissent Within the Economic Miracle*. London: Zed Books, 1990.

Ohkawa Kazushi and Katsuo Otsuka. *Technology Diffusion, Productivity, Employment and Phase Shifts in Developing Economies*. Tokyo: University of Tokyo Press, 1994.

Okada Yoshitaka. "The Dilemma of Indonesian Dependency on Foreign Direct Investments." *Development and Change*, Vol. 14 (1983).

Okada Yoshitaka. "Indigenization Policies and Structural Cooptation by Multinational Corporations." *Development and Change*, Vol. 16 (1985).

Okazaki Hisahiko. "New Strategies toward a 'Super Asian Bloc.'" *This Is* (Tokyo), August 1992.

Okimoto, Daniel. *Between MITI and the Market: Japanese Industrial Policy for High Technology*. Stanford: Stanford University Press, 1989.

Okimoto, Daniel. "The Asian Perimeter, Moving Front and Center." In "Facing the Future: American Strategy in the 1990s," an Aspen Strategy Group report. Aspen Strategy Group and University Press of America, the Aspen Institute for Humanist Studies, 1991.

Okuno-Fujiwara Masahiro. "Industrial Policy in Japan: A Political Economy View." In *Trade With Japan: Has the Door Opened Wider?* ed. Paul Krugman. Chicago: University of Chicago Press, 1991.

Orr, Robert M., Jr. *The Emergence of Japan's Foreign Aid Power*. New York: Columbia University Press, 1990.

Orr, Robert M., Jr. "Japanese Foreign Aid in a New Global Era." *SAIS Review*, Summer/Fall 1991.

Panglaykim, J. *Japanese Direct Investment in ASEAN: The Indonesian Experience*. Singapore: Maruzen Asia, 1983.

Park Woo-hee. "Japan's Role in the Structural Adjustment of the Asian-Pacific Economies." *Journal of International Economic Studies*, No. 6 (March 1992).

Pascale, Richard and Thomas P. Rohlen. "The Mazda Turnaround." *Journal of Japanese Studies*, Vol. 9, No. 2 (Summer 1983).

Pasuk Phongpaichit. *The New Wave of Japanese Investment in ASEAN*. Singapore: Institute of Southeast Asian Studies, 1990.

Pempel, T. J. (ed.). *Policymaking in Contemporary Japan*. Ithaca: Cornell University Press, 1977.

Pempel, T. J. "The Unbundling of 'Japan Inc.': The Changing Dynamics of Japanese Policy Formation." *Journal of Japanese Studies*, Vol. 13, No. 2 (Summer 1987).

Prasert Chittiwatanapong. "Japanese ODA to Thailand and Thai Management of Japanese ODA." In *Japan's Foreign Aid: Power and Policy in a New Era*, ed. Bruce Koppel and Robert Orr. Boulder: Westview Press, 1993.

Preyaluk Donavanik. "Thai Electronics – Not Just a Production Base." *Bangkok Bank Monthly Review*, Vol. 31 (October 1990).

Purcell, Victor. *The Chinese in Southeast Asia*. London: Oxford University Press, 1965.

Rix, Alan. "Japan's Foreign Aid Policy: A Capacity for Leadership?" *Pacific Affairs*, Vol. 62, No. 4 (Winter 1989–90).

Rodan, Garry. *The Political Economy of Singapore's Industrialization*. New York: St Martin's Press, 1989.

Roemer, John E. *U.S.–Japanese Competition in International Markets: A Study of the Trade-Investment Cycle in Modern Capitalism*. Research Series No. 22. Berkeley: Institute of International Studies, University of California, 1975.

Romer, Paul M. "Increasing Returns and Long-Run Growth." *Journal of Political Economy*, Vol. 94, No. 51 (1986).

Sakamoto Yoshikazu. "Korea in Japan's Foreign Policy-Making." *Korean Journal for Japanese Studies*, Vol. 5 (1986).

Sakong Mok. "Han-Il sanŏp hyŏmnyŏk ŭi hyŏnhwang kwa hyanghu ch'ujin panghyang" ("Korean-Japan Industrial Cooperation: Current Conditions and Future Directions"). *Segye kyongje tonghyang* (*Trends in the Global Economy*), December 1991.

Sakurai Masao. *Tōshi masatsu* (*Investment Friction*). Tokyo: Tōyō Keizai Shinpōsha, 1988.

Samart Chiasakul and Prasert Silapipat. "Case of Thailand." In *The Role of Japanese Direct Investment in Developing Countries*, ed. Institute of Developing Economies. Tokyo: Institute of Developing Economies, March 1992.

Samuels, Richard J. *The Business of the Japanese State: Energy Markets in Comparative and Historical Perspective*. Ithaca: Cornell University Press, 1987.

Samuels, Richard J. *"Rich Nation Strong Army": National Security and the Technological Transformation of Japan*. Ithaca: Cornell University Press, 1994.

Sasaki Takaaki and Yoshie Shimane. "The New Dynamics of the Asian Economy." *Japan Research Quarterly*, Vol. 3, No. 3 (Summer 1994).

Sato Ichiro. "Localization Policy for Automobile Production." Bangkok: Japanese Chamber of Commerce and Industry, Bangkok, 1982. Cited by Richard Doner. *Driving a Bargain: Automobile Industrialization and Japanese Firms in Southeast Asia*. Berkeley: University of California Press, 1991.

Saxonhouse, Gary. "Pricing Strategies and Trading Blocs in East Asia." In *Regionalism and Rivalry: Japan and the U.S. in Pacific Asia*, ed. Jeffrey Frankel and Miles Kahler. Chicago: University of Chicago Press, 1993.

Sazanami Yoko, Shujiro Urata, and Hiroki Kawai. *Measuring the Costs of Protection in Japan*. Washington: Institute for International Economics, 1995.

Schlossstein, Steven. *Asia's New Little Dragons: The Dynamic Emergence of Indonesia, Thailand, and Malaysia*. Chicago: Contemporary Books, 1991.

Schmalensee, Richard. "Industrial Economics: An Overview." *Economic Journal*, Vol. 98 (September 1988).

Seki Shigetaka. "What Can We Learn from Technology Assessment?" In *Japan's Growing Technological Capability*, ed. Thomas S. Arrison, C. Fred Bergsten, Edward M. Graham, and Martha Caldwell Harris. Washington: National Academy Press, 1992.

Shigeki Tejima et al. "The Recent Trends of Japanese Foreign Direct Investment and Prospects in the 1990s Based on the Japanese Ex-Im Bank's Survey Implemented in FY 1993." *EXIM Review*, Research Institute for Overseas Investment, 1994.

Shūkan Tōyō Keizai, Tōyō Keizai Shinpōsha. *Kaigai shinshutsu kigyō sōran, 1994 (A Comprehensive Survey of Firms Expanding Overseas)*. Tokyo: Tōyō Keizai Shinpōsha, 1994.

Simon, Denis Fred. "External Incorporation and Internal Reform." In *Contending Approaches to the Political Economy of Taiwan*, ed. Edwin A. Winckler and Susan Greenhalgh. Armonk, New York: M. E. Sharpe, Inc., 1988.

Simon, Denis Fred. "Technology Transfer and National Autonomy." In *Contending Approaches to the Political Economy of Taiwan*, ed. Edwin A. Winckler and Susan Greenhalgh. Armonk, New York: M. E. Sharpe Inc., 1988.

Simon, Denis Fred (ed.). *The Emerging Technological Trajectory of the Pacific Rim*. Armonk, New York: M. E. Sharpe, 1995.

Somsak Tambunlertchai. *Japanese and American Investments in Thailand's Manufacturing Industries: An Assessment of Their Relative Contributions to the Host Economy*. Tokyo: Institute of Developing Economies, 1977.

Song Byung-Nak. *The Rise of the Korean Economy*. Hong Kong: Oxford University Press, 1990.

Spencer, Barbara J. and James A. Brander. "International R&D Rivalry and Industrial Strategy." *Review of Economic Studies*, Vol. 50 (October 1983).

Steven, Rob. *Japan's New Imperialism*. Armonk, New York: M. E. Sharpe, 1990.

Stewart, Charles T., Jr. "Comparing Japanese and U.S. Technology Transfer to Less Developed Countries." *Journal of Northeast Asian Studies*, Vol. 4 (Spring 1985).

Stewart, Charles T. and Yasumitsu Nihei. *Technology Transfer and Human Factors: A Comparative Study of American and Japanese Contributions to Indonesia and Thailand*. Washington: George Washington University, 1986.

Su Bing. *Taiwan's 400 Year History: The Origins and Continuing Development of the Taiwanese Society and People*. Washington: Taiwan Cultural Grassroots Association, 1986.

Sumi Kazuo (ed.). *No moa ODA baramaki enjo* (*No More Scattering of ODA Assistance*). Tokyo: Sokosha K.K., 1992.

Suryadinata, Leo. *Pribumi Indonesians, The Chinese Minority and China: A Study of Perceptions and Policies*. Kuala Lumpur: Heinemann Educational Books, 1978.

Tabb, William K. *The Japanese Political Economy*. New York: Oxford University Press, 1994.

Takeuchi Jōzen. "'Technology Transfer' and Japan–Thai Relations." In *Transfer of Japanese Technology and Management to the ASEAN Countries*, ed. Shoichi Yamashita. Tokyo: University of Tokyo Press, 1991.

Tanaka Tatsuo. "Technology-based Trade Pattern of Japan and Korea." Research paper, International University of Japan, Summer 1994.

Teece, D.J., G. Pisano, and A. Shuen. "Dynamic Capabilities and Strategic Management." Working paper, Center for Strategic Management, University of California, Berkeley, 1990.

Tejima Shigeki. "Sekkyoku shisei ni tenjita Nihon no kaigai tōshi" ("Japanese Overseas Investment Turns Active"). In *Kaigai shinshutsu kigyō sōran, 1994* (*A Comprehensive Survey of Firms Expanding Overseas*), Shūkan Tōyō Keizai, Tōyō Keizai Shinpōsha. Tokyo: Tōyō Keizai Shinpōsha, 1994.

Thee Kian Wie. "Interactions of Japanese Aid and Direct Investment in Indonesia." *ASEAN Economic Bulletin*, Vol. 11, No. 1 (July 1994).

Tokunaga Shojiro (ed.). *Japan's Foreign Investment and Asian Economic Interdependence: Production, Trade and Financial Systems*. Tokyo: University of Tokyo Press, 1992.

Torii Akio and Richard Caves. "Technical Efficiency in Japanese and U.S. Manufacturing Industries." In *Industrial Efficiency in Six Nations*, ed. Richard Caves. Cambridge, Mass.: MIT Press, 1992.

Tsuneishi T. "Tai-Nikkei kigyō shūdo ni yoru gijutsu iten" ("Japanese Affiliates in Thailand Playing the Leading Role in Technology Transfer"). In *Ajia no kōgyōka to gijutsu iten* (*Asian Industrialization and Technology Transfer*), ed. Taniura Takao. Tokyo: Ajia Keizai Shuppankai, 1990.

United Nations. *Costs and Conditions of Technology Transfer through Transnational Corporations*. Bangkok: Economic and Social Commission for Asia and the Pacific, ESCAP/UNCTC Joint Unit on Transnational Corporations, 1984.

Urata Shujiro. "The Rapid Increase of Direct Investment Abroad and Structural Change in Japan." In *Direct Foreign Investment in Asia's Developing Economies and Structural Change in the Asia-Pacific Region*, ed. Eric D. Ramstetter. Boulder: Westview Press, 1991.

Urata Shujiro. "Changing Patterns of Direct Investment and Implications for Trade and Investment." In *Pacific Dynamism and the International Economic System*, ed. C. Fred Bergsten and Marcus Noland. Washington: Institute for International Economics, 1993.

Ursacki, Terry and Ilan Vertinsky. "Long-term Changes in Korea's International Trade and Investment." *Pacific Affairs*, Vol. 67, No. 3 (Fall 1994).

US International Trade Commission. "East Asia: Regional Economic Integration and Implications for the United States." USITC Publication 2621 (1993).

Wade, Robert. "The Role of Government." In *Achieving Industrialization in East Asia*, ed. Helen Hughes. Cambridge: Cambridge University Press, 1988.

Watanabe Toshio. *Seichō no Ajia, teitai no Ajia* (*Growth and Stagnation in Asia*). Tokyo: Tōyō Keizai Shinpōsha, 1986.

Watanabe Toshio (ed.). *Kajin keizai no nettowāku* (*The Networks of [Overseas] Chinese*). Tokyo: Jitsugyō no Nihonsha, 1994.

Weinstein, Franklin. *Indonesian Foreign Policy and the Dilemma of Dependence.* Ithaca: Cornell University Press, 1976.

Weinstein, Franklin. "Multinational Corporations and the Third World: The Case of Japan and Southeast Asia." *International Organization,* Vol. 30 (1976).

White, Gordon. *Riding the Tiger: The Politics of Economic Reform in Post-Mao China.* Stanford: Stanford University Press, 1993.

Williamson, Hugh. *Coping with the Miracle: Japan's Unions Explore New International Relations.* London: Pluto Press, 1994.

Williamson, Oliver E. *Markets and Hierarchies.* New York: Free Press, 1975.

Williamson, Oliver E. "Introduction." In *The Nature of the Firm,* ed. Oliver E. Williamson and Sidney G. Winter. New York: Oxford University Press, 1993.

Wolff, Alan. "U.S.–Japan Relations and the Rule of Law: The Nature of the Trade Conflict and the American Response." In *Japan's Economic Structure: Should It Change?* ed. Kozo Yamamura. Seattle: Society for Japanese Studies, 1990.

Wong, Anny. "Japan's National Security and Cultivation of ASEAN Elites." *Contemporary Southeast Asia,* Vol. 12, No. 4 (March 1991).

Woo Jung-en. *Race to the Swift: State and Finance in Korean Industrialization.* New York: Columbia University Press, 1991.

Yamaguchi Jirō. "Kanryōsei no minshuka o dō susumeru ka" ("How do We Promote the Democratization of the Bureaucratic System?). *Ekonomisuto,* 24 August 1993.

Yamamura Kozo. "Success Illgotten? The Role of Meiji Militarism in Japan's Technological Progress." *Journal of Economic History,* Vol. 37, No. 1 (March 1977).

Yamamura Kozo. "Success that Soured: Administrative Guidance and Cartels in Japan." In *Policy and Trade Issues of the Japanese Economy: American and Japanese Perspectives,* ed. Kozo Yamamura. Seattle: University of Washington Press, 1982.

Yamamura Kozo. "Will Japan's Economic Structure Change?" In *Japan's Economic Structure: Should It Change?* ed. Kozo Yamamura. Seattle: Society for Japanese Studies, 1990.

Yamamura Kozo and Yasukichi Yasuba (eds). *The Political Economy of Japan, Volume 1: The Domestic Transformation.* Stanford: Stanford University Press, 1987.

Yamashita Shoichi. "Economic Development of the ASEAN Countries and the Role of Japanese Direct Investment." In *Transfer of Japanese Technology and Management to the ASEAN Countries,* ed. Shoichi Yamashita. Tokyo: University of Tokyo Press, 1991.

Yamazawa Ippei. "Gearing the Japanese Economy to International Harmony." *Developing Economies,* Vol. 28, No. 4 (March 1990).

Yoda Kaoru. *Nihon no kyo-ninka-seido no subete* (*All about Japan's Permit and Licensing System*). Tokyo: Nihon Jitsugyo Shuppansha, 1993.

Yoshihara Hideki. "Nihon-teki seisan shisutemu no kaigai iten" ("The Overseas Transfer of the Japanese Production System"). In *Nihon kigyō no gurōbaru keizai* (*The Global Economy of Japanese Firms*), ed. Yoshihara Hideki, Hayashi Kiichirō, and Yasumuro Ken-ichi. Tokyo: Tōyō Keizai Shinpōsha, 1988.

Yoshihara Kunio. *Japanese Investment in Southeast Asia.* Honolulu: University Press of Hawaii, 1978.

Yoshihara Kunio. *The Rise of Ersatz Capitalism in Southeast Asia.* Singapore: Oxford University Press, 1988.

Yoshimitsu Nihei, Makoto Ōtsu, and David A. Levin. "A Comparative Study of Management Practices and Workers in an American and Japanese Firm in Hong Kong." In *Contemporary Issues in Hong Kong Labour Relations*, ed. Ng Sek Hong and David A. Levin. Hong Kong: University of Hong Kong, 1983.

You Jon-Il. "Capital–Labor Relations of the Newly Industrializing Regime in South Korea: Past, Present and Future." Unpublished paper, April 1989, quoted in Walden Bello and Christine Rosenfeld, *Dragons in Distress: Asia's Miracle Economies in Crisis*. San Francisco: Institute for Food and Development Policy, 1990.

Young, Alwyn. "The Tyranny of Numbers: Confronting the Statistical Realities of the East Asian Growth Experience." NBER working paper No. 4680, March 1994.

Young Kwan Yoon. "The Political Economy of Transition: Japanese Foreign Direct Investments in the 1980s." *World Politics*, Vol. 43 (October 1990).

Zhao Quansheng. "Japan's Aid Diplomacy with China." In *Japan's Foreign Aid: Power and Policy in a New Era*, ed. Bruce Koppel and Robert Orr, Jr. Boulder: Westview Press, 1993.

Index

Administrative guidance, 4, 65–67, 75, 122–23, 226 n.68; New AID plan, a vehicle of, 139; role in developmentalism, 53, 67, 193; window guidance, 64
Africa, 40, 128, 130
Agency for Industrial Science & Technology, 67
Ajia Keizai Kenkyujo (Ajiken), 15, 134–35
Amakudari (descent from Heaven), 141
ASEAN, xii; ASEAN Free Trade Area (AFTA), 35, 186; ASEAN Industrial Projects (AIP), 35; ASEAN–Japan Development Fund, 129; ASEAN–Japan Economic Council, 183; division of labor, 23, 184; economic development, 30, 77, 192, 201; education, 84; ethnic Chinese in, 84; exports to, 180, 183, 189–90; in flying geese theory, 28; in regional production alliance, 9, 27, 31, 178; Japanese investment in, 6, 22; Japanese ODA in, 128; labor, 152; political economy, 79–84, 101; regional cooperation, 3, 40, 119
Asia Pacific Economic Cooperation (APEC), 192, 198, 199
Asian Brain, 119–20
Asianism, 199–200
Asset specificity, 47–48, 58, 194
Association for Overseas Technical Scholarships (AOTS), 123, 134
Association for the Promotion of International Cooperation (APIC), 128
Audio and visual equipment industry, 10, 25, 29, 38, 60, 136, 161, 165–66, 182

Authoritarian regimes, 77, 85, 89, 91, 133, 151, 197, 203
Automobile industry, 22, 34–37, 61, 70–71, 80, 119, 136–37, 142, 159, 162, 179, 184, 186; auto manufacturers, 10, 17–18, 23, 26, 31, 33–35, 37, 47, 52, 60–61, 71, 75, 89, 106, 110, 140, 159, 163–65, 168–70, 196; auto parts, viii, 9, 18, 26, 35, 37, 47, 59, 71, 74, 88, 143, 164, 196

Banking, xii, 8, 21, 64–65, 68, 69, 81, 92, 93, 95, 122
Batamindo Industrial Park (BIP), 35–36
Brand to brand complementation (BBC), 35, 186
"Bubble" economy, 21, 29, 68, 86, 181, 212 n.6
Bumiputra, 82, 143
Bureaucracy: China, 94–95; Indonesia, 83; Japan, 9, 27, 63, 65–67, 69, 116, 121, 138–39, 193; Korea, 87–89; Malaysia, 134, 166; Taiwan, 93; Thailand, 130

Calbarzon project, 127, 138
Cambodia, 37
Capital, 12, 38, 68–70, 72, 83, 124, 192; capital-intensive industries, 14, 20, 99, 109, 188; dependence on Japanese capital, xi, 80, 203; ethnic Chinese, 81–83, 96; exports, 28, 30, 118, 198–99; foreign, 32, 81, 85, 91, 93, 107, 195; goods, 60, 176–77, 180, 183; human, 16, 49, 58, 73, 74, 107, 148, 186, 194; in economic theory, 44–53 passim; in joint ventures, 33, 83; investment, 29–30, 35, 65, 95, 143,

Capital *cont.*
167; local, 85–87, 94, 107, 144, 195–96; "local capital umbrellas," 23–25; role in Japanese foreign investment, ix–xii, 4, 6, 9–11, 22, 30, 33, 56–58, 78, 92, 100, 117, 126, 129, 156, 160, 182, 189–90, 193–94, 200; markets, 21, 62, 64, 88; small and medium-sized enterprises, 9, 21
Capitalism: "Asian" styles versus "Western" styles, 199–200; ersatz, 80
"Captive development," 31, 195
Cartel, 53, 65, 66; wage, 123, 153
Chaebol, 32, 37, 87, 88, 89, 90, 132
Chemical industry, 20, 52, 64, 67, 85, 123, 132, 145, 181
Cheng-bao system, 94
Chiang Kai-shek, 92
China, xii; Dalian, 121–22; division of labor, 23, 29, 184, 188; economic growth, 30, 180, 192; exports, 189–90; foreign investment in, 6, 10–11, 25, 28, 182, 259 n.15; Guangdong Province, 95; in regional production alliance, 9, 27, 31, 40, 203; Japanese ODA in, 127–29; joint ventures, 140; Kyongsang, 90; political economy, 94–96; technology transfer, 60, 104; Tiananmen Square, 136; Western automakers in, 37. *See also* Chinese, ethnic
Chinese commonwealth, 96
Comparative advantage, ix, 14; changes in, 99; in labor-intensive manufacturing, 93, 99; Japan's, 119; loss of, 27, 175–76; theory of, 45, 209 n.49
Cooperation, 12, 25, 40, 54, 63–64, 69, 72, 75–76, 138, 165, 184, 203; economic, 115, 117–21, 129, 139, 193, 195; business and business, 15–16, 67–72, 75, 90, 91, 94, 137; government and business, 15, 64–67, 75, 123, 138, 193; government and business, business and business, management and labor, x, xiii, 19, 21, 50, 56, 101, 192–93; international strategic, 56; management and labor, 16, 54, 72–76, 90, 91, 147, 151; triangle of, 78–79
Corruption, 54, 63, 76, 193; bribery, 50, 55, 82, 83, 95, 122; *ochadai,* 137; US Foreign Corrupt Political Practices Act of 1976, 137
Credit rationing, 64

Democratic Liberal Party (Korea), 87
Dependency theory, 78, 227–28 n.7
Deregulation, 55, 63, 139, 223 n.5

Development Assistance Committee (DAC), 124, 125, 129
Developmentalism: costs of, 54, 193–94; defined, xiii, 220–21 n.34; in domestic political economy, 62–65, 76, 96, 176, 193, 203; model for catch-up industrialization, 53–54; regionalization of, 27, 55–56, 59, 62–63, 76, 78–79, 98, 111, 178, 191, 192, 201, 177; system of cooperation, 21, 78, 151, 158, 198; theory, 43, 53–54; vehicle for achieving DTE, xiii. *See also* Dynamic technological efficiency, Flying geese theory, Regionalization
Division of labor: international, 119; intrafirm, 159, 186–87; regional, 3, 22–23, 27, 29, 35, 86, 93, 108, 119, 138; vertical versus horizontal, 28–29, 98, 121, 184
Doi moi (renovation), 127
Domestic dumping, 53, 65
DRAM, *see* Dynamic random access memory
DTE, *see* Dynamic technological efficiency
Dual economic structure, 73, 194
Dynamic random access memory (DRAM) chips, 29, 90, 100, 104, 188
Dynamic technological efficiency (DTE): defined, xii–xiii, 21, 31, 53, 61, 64, 79, 193–94; lack of, in developing Asian nations, 78, 96; slowdown of, 31; total factor productivity, 78. *See also* Developmentalism

East Asian Economic Caucus, 40, 201
Eastern Europe, 40, 200
Eastern Seaboard Development (ESD) Program (Thailand), 144–45
Economic Planning Agency (EPA), 27, 119–20, 121, 187, 199
Economies of networking, 3–4, 22, 108
Economies of scale, 3, 12, 13, 22, 35, 51, 65, 108, 136, 167, 177, 108, 187
Economies of scope, 3, 22, 108, 187
Education, 82, 83–84, 202
Electronics industry, viii, 3–4, 10, 18, 23, 29, 31–32, 60–61, 71, 86, 88, 98, 106–10, 118–19, 123, 125, 138, 147, 153–57, 159–60, 163–65, 168, 171, 182, 184, 188–90, 195–96; consumer electronics industry, 18, 24, 25, 29, 38, 123, 161–62, 181, 182
Embraced development, 30–31, 78
Employment system, Japanese: enterprise union, 73–74, 75, 147–48, 151; familism, 74, 146–48; in Korea, 89;

in Taiwan, 91; job-hopping, 152–53; labor-management relations, 16, 73–74, 147–48, 151; quality control circles, 74, 147; quasi-permanent employment, 73, 75, 104, 108, 147–48; seniority-based pay, 16, 73, 147–48, 156

Endaka, 21, 24, 28, 29, 63, 118, 124, 129, 143, 163, 182, 190

England, 34

Entrepreneurs, 15, 31–32, 72, 80, 83, 101–2; Chinese, 81–82; Ethnic Chinese, 81–84, 96, 132; Korean, 88; Taiwanese 92

Europe: auto industry, 37; European Community/Union, 39, 175, 184, 196; European MNCs, xi, 15, 16, 17, 38, 85, 153–55, 185, 196; exports to, 9, 28, 36, 60, 86, 139, 177–78, 183, 188–91; foreign aid, 40; foreign investment in, 6, 10–11, 22; independent firms, 193; Japanese firms in, 158–59; joint ventures with local interests, 133; labor-management relations, 63; political goals, 196; protectionism, 135; technology transfer, 103, 107

"Excessive competition, " 4, 53. *See also* Domestic dumping

Exchange rates, 60, 176, 178, 212 n.4

Export-Import Bank of Japan, 15, 65, 122, 161, 188

Fiscal Investment and Loan Program (FILP), 64–65, 124, 128

"Flying geese" theory, 27–28, 60, 98, 119, 176, 203; pattern in Taiwan, 29; relation to sub-regional zones, 35

Foreign direct investment (FDI): by small and medium-sized enterprises, 122; developmentalism, 78, 158, 193; European, 6; flying geese theory, 27, 29; in Asia, 7, 10, 11, 22, 117, 207 n.13, 208 n.30, n.38; in China, 11, 127; in developing versus developed regions, 6; in Indonesia, 141–42; in Korea, 9; in Thailand, 10; Japanese versus American, 5–6, 13–16, 38, 187; Japanese, ix, 175–76; New AID plan, 121; old wave versus new wave, 20; promotion of, 123–24, 129, 138, 143, 202; Taiwanese, 30; technology transfer, 104, 107–8, 110; theory of, 12–13

Forward pricing, 60, 178, 189

Foundation for Advanced Information & Research (FAIR), 40, 201

France, 20, 38

Fukuda Doctrine, 118

Game theory, 56

General trading company (GTC), 16, 33, 34, 36, 69, 93, 122, 125–26, 131–32, 134, 136–37, 138, 157, 163, 166

Generalized System of Preferences, 201

Germany, 20, 106, 258 n.3

Globalization, 22, 185; of economic activity, 118; of financial markets, 62–63; of industry, 21, 158; risks involved in, 19, 54

Gravity model, ix, 52

Great Britain, 20

Greater East Asia Co-Prosperity Sphere, ix, 40, 115, 132, 203

Gyosei shido, *see* Administrative guidance

Heavy Industries Corporation of Malaysia (HICOM), 33

Heckscher-Ohlin-Samuelson theory, *see* Theory of international trade

High-technology industries, 7, 38, 61, 86, 100, 104, 140, 143, 162, 188, 193; computer industry, 24, 25, 30, 38, 66–67, 138–40, 179–80, 188–89, 191; computer software industry, 123, 129; economy, 21; goods, x, 36, 60, 97, 140, 165, 177–79, 180, 181, 185, 190, 194, 198; Japanese firms, xi, 4, 9–11, 22, 23, 28, 29, 31, 56, 61, 98, 102, 104, 106, 108, 135, 158, 159, 160, 163, 185, 188–89; semiconductors, 22, 25, 26, 38, 67, 84, 90, 97, 100, 104–5, 119, 140, 180, 188; Western firms, 36, 195, 201, 204

Hollowing out, 19, 109, 118–19, 187–88

Hong Kong, 8, 38, 86, 95, 96, 99, 100, 132, 154, 181; considered an NIC, xii, 85, 182; deficit with Japan, 30; export pattern, 99; Hsinchu Science Park, 110; imports into, 178; investment in China, 28, 161

Import substitution, 85, 136

India, 28, 128–29, 139

Indigenization, 154–56

Indochina, 117, 144

Indonesia, xii; corruption, 83, 137; division of labor, 29; economic development, 77; ersatz capitalism, 80; ethnic Chinese in, 81–82; exports, 189; foreign investment in, 28, 122, 138, 180, 182; in regional production alliance, 25–26, 36–37, 159; indigenization, 154–55; Industrial Bank of Japan, 35, 155; Japanese advisors in, 141; Japanese ODA in, 127–29, 130–31; joint ventures, 35–36,

Indonesia *cont.*
83, 133; patrimonialism, 81;
promotion of FDI, 143; US
manufacturers in, 38
Industrial policy, 59, 137; administrative
guidance, a tool of, 65; change in, 67;
credit rationing, a tool of, 64;
effectiveness of, 54; FILP, a tool of,
124; flying geese theory, 27; in Asian
countries, 91, 144; in rapid growth
period, 66; JAIDO, a tool of, 129;
ODA, a tool of, 128
Industrialization: catch-up, 45, 54, 69, 75;
cooperation, a legacy of, 73, 89;
export-oriented, 85, 93; flying geese
pattern of, 28, 214 n.34; stages of, 147;
"technologyless, " 80; Infrastructure,
46, 65, 78, 127, 145; bureaucratic-
industrial, 54, 139; financed by FDI,
15; financed by FILP, 125; financed by
ODA, 123; hard and soft, 138; in
China, 95, 122
Innovation, 13, 18, 19, 31, 50–52, 54, 97,
101, 103, 110, 111; innovating firms,
66, 73, 74, 101, 148, 176; innovating
industries and manufacturers, 53, 100,
121, 147; innovative capacity, 109, 177;
risks involved in, 54, 69, 101; stifling
of, 61, 109
Institute of Strategic and International
Studies, Kuala Lumpur, 125, 128, 141,
168, 203
Internationalization, 18
ISO 9000, 169

Japan Chamber of Commerce and
Industry, 18–19, 117, 134, 160, 182
Japan Development Bank, 65
Japan External Trade Organization
(JETRO), 15, 23, 122, 123, 142, 152,
163, 165, 191
Japan Finance Corporation for Small
Business (JFS), 122, 123, 141, 169
Japan Inc., 116
Japan International Cooperation Agency
(JICA), 125, 134, 136, 141–42, 169
Japan International Development
Organization (JAIDO), 129
Japan Overseas Development Corp.
(JODC), 15, 122, 140–41, 169
Japan–Asia Investment Co. (JAIC), 129
Japan's Fair Trade Commission (JFTC), 63,
68
Jinmyaku (networks of personal ties), 132,
135, 137
Job-hopping, *see* Employment system,
Japanese

Joint ventures, xii, 13–14, 23–25, 37, 56,
133, 157, 163, 169; disadvantages of,
31–33, 168; in China, 11, 104, 140,
129; in Indonesia, 83; in Malaysia, 166;
in the Philippines, 122; in Thailand,
155, 164; in Vietnam, 136; promotion
of, 129, 136, 139. *See also* Local capital
umbrellas
Just-in-time (JIT) system, 70, 141, 164,
165–166, 168

Kaizen (product improvement), 147, 150
Kanban system, *see* Just-in-time system
Keidanren, 12, 129, 199
Keiretsu (enterprise groupings), x, xii, 4, 5,
9, 33, 34, 48, 62–64, 67–68, 73, 75,
110, 125, 164, 176, 178, 193–94, 225
n.34; distribution, 71–72; horizontal,
xii, 64, 69–70, 129, 140; *keiretsu*-like
networks, 4, 9, 58, 76, 102, 165, 196;
keiretsu subcontractors, 16; *keiretsu*
suppliers, 31, 162, 177, 195; vertical,
xi, 30, 56–61, 70–71, 140, 163
Keizai Doyukai (Association of Corporate
Executives), 18, 129, 160
Kodoka (upgrading of technological
capacity), 187–88
Korea, xii, 85, 87–90; capitalism, 199–200;
economic development, 77, 100, 180;
education, 84; employment system,
89, 149; foreign investment in, 9, 161,
182; government business
cooperation, 32, 79, 132, 203; imports
from Japan, 178–79, 183; in regional
production alliance, 25, 37, 203;
investment in Asia, 6; Japan's imports
from, 181–82; joint ventures, 24; labor
movement, 91, 151–52; technology
transfer, 98–100, 105–7; US
manufacturers in, 38
Kudoka, see Hollowing out

Labor, 12, 29, 36, 47, 53, 85, 100, 184, 186,
201; cheap, 13, 22, 85, 86, 91, 148,
187; disputes and strikes 73, 79, 89,
91, 135, 142, 144, 152; labor-intensive
firms and industries, 11, 13, 14, 20, 61,
85–86, 91, 106, 186–88, 194; market,
75, 123, 147, 149, 152; movements, 85,
91; productivity, 70, 99; relations with
management, 54, 63, 73, 79, 89, 90;
relations, 24, 147, 151; shortage, 84,
148, 152; skilled, 31, 46, 83, 84, 148,
149, 152–53; "total development
programs," 148; unions, 89–90, 91,
127, 135
Laos, 28, 37, 144, 192

Latin America, 40, 78, 128, 130, 196, 201
Liberal Democratic Party (LDP), 63, 87, 116
Liberalization: of capital markets, 21; of distribution system, 62; of domestic economy, 139; of financial markets, 65
Local capital umbrellas, 23–24. See also Joint ventures
Local content rules, 142, 161–62, 165
Local suppliers, 25, 31, 57, 87–89, 107–8, 160–61, 164–65, 167–70, 196, 202. See also Parts suppliers
Localization: of foreign firms in Japan, 17, 103; of Japanese firms in Asia, x, 33, 162; of Japanese firms in the US, 18; technology transfer, 103

Machinery industry, viii, x, 7, 10, 14, 30, 57, 64, 119, 123, 138, 143, 155, 159, 178–81, 182, 185–86, 188, 189, 190, 208 n.21, 256 n.55, 257 n.71
Macroeconomic theory, 49; conditions, 178, 186; policy, 77, 199, 200
Maekawa Commission, 177
Malaysia, xii; division of labor, 3, 23, 29; economic development, 77; education, 83–84; employment system, 153; ersatz capitalism, 80; ethnic Chinese in, 81; exports, 139, 189, 191; foreign investment in, 6, 10, 28, 30, 86, 138, 160–61, 180, 182; government business cooperation, 32, 128, 134–35; in regional production alliance, 25–26, 37, 159; indigenization, 154–55; Japanese advisors in, 141; Japanese ODA in, 125, 128–29, 130–31; joint ventures, 33, 133, 168; labor movement, 85, 147, 152; localization, 165, 202; Penang, 38, 154, 157, 160, 165, 166; promotion of FDI, 143; recession, 33; technology transfer, 106, 109, 170; US manufacturers in, 38
Manufacturing industries, 6, 8, 19, 61, 88, 91, 94, 99, 156, 178, 179, 181; export-oriented, 25, 30, 88, 121, 127, 138, 143, 191; labor-intensive, 28, 29, 82, 85–86, 91, 93, 99, 106, 118, 187–88; role of foreign capital in, 81
Market share maximizing strategy, 73
Market sharing agreements, 167, 196
Metal industry, 123, 163
Mexico, 11, 40, 198
Microeconomic theory, 12–13, 44–46; conditions, 170, 186
Middle East, 196, 200
Ministry of Finance (MOF), 40, 64–65, 66, 69, 118, 119, 121, 124, 126, 200, 201

Ministry of Foreign Affairs (MFA), 40, 76, 126–28, 134
Ministry of International Trade and Industry (MITI), 5, 11, 15, 17, 23, 27, 65, 66, 67, 97, 116, 118, 119, 120, 121, 128, 134, 138–39, 140, 141, 156, 169, 184, 187, 191
Ministry of Posts and Telecommunications (MPT), 123
Multiple sourcing, see Market sharing agreements

National Economic and Social Development Board (NESDB) (Thailand), 40, 142
Nemawashi (consensus building), 149
Neoclassical economic theory, 12, 43, 44–48, 52–55, 62, 70, 72, 74, 77, 175–76, 177, 194–95, 206 n.6. See also Theory of the firm, Theory of international trade
Neoinstitutional economic theory, 43, 49–50, 54, 81, 219 n.24, 220 n.25
Network: cluster, hub, and web, 23–28; distribution, 165–66; government-business, 55, 116–19, 121, 128–29, 132, 133–34, 135, 137, 138–40, 143, 193–94, 199, 201; production, 4, 11, 18, 23, 28, 31–36, 58–60, 86, 107–9, 128, 136, 157, 177, 194, 195, 198, 201–2; supply, 159, 164
New Asian Industries Development (AID) plan, 120–21, 128, 129, 138–40
New Economic Policy (NEP) (Malaysia), 82
"New Series" Project, 67
Newly industrializing countries (NICs), xii, 22, 99, 101, 119, 182, 185, 201, 206 n.11; division of labor, 23, 184; economic growth, 30, 77, 192, 201; exports, 181, 189–90; in regional production alliance, 9, 27, 31, 119, 178; Japanese investment in, 6, 22, 28, 180, 182; regional cooperation, 40; technology transfer, 60, 99–101, 104
Nokyo (agricultural cooperatives), 116
Nongovernmental organizations (NGOs), 127–28, 201
North America: exports to, 9, 30, 86, 188–89, 163, 257 n.71; Japanese firms in, 158–59
North American Free Trade Agreement (NAFTA), 11, 40, 198, 201

Official development assistance (ODA): biased, 39, 122, 127, 132, 137; developmentalism, 193–94;

Official development assistance (ODA)
cont.
  distribution of, 128–29, 131; in forms
    of credit, 124, 130, 240 n.43; relation
    to investment, 117, 126; role of host
    nations, 59, 130–31; role of JICA, 134;
    uses of, 122, 23, 138–40, 151
On-the-job training (OJT), 5, 74, 108, 148,
  150, 170
Organization for Economic Cooperation
  and Development (OECD), 124, 129
Original equipment manufacturing
  (OEM), 15, 57
Overseas Economic Cooperation Fund
  (OECF), 122, 125–26, 127, 129,
  130–31, 143–44, 145

Parts suppliers, 9, 18, 60, 70, 136, 138, 141,
  161. See also Local suppliers
Path-dependence, 50, 64
Patrimonialism: in Southeast Asia, 80–81;
  of authoritarian regimes, 133
"Pax Nipponica, " 203
Philippines, the, xii; corruption, 137;
  ersatz capitalism, 80; ethnic Chinese
  in, 81; exports, 189; foreign
  investment, 28; foreign investment in,
  10, 122, 127, 138, 180; in regional
  production alliance, 26, 34, 37, 76;
  indigenization, 154; Japanese ODA in,
  128–29, 130; joint ventures, 24, 133;
  patrimonialism, 81; US manufacturers
  in, 38
Plaza Accord of 1985, 20–21, 71, 182
Product cycle, 13, 19, 27, 28, 105, 119, 101,
  106
Production alliance, x–xi, 4, 6, 8, 16, 19,
  27, 31, 32, 35, 36, 38, 63, 78, 94, 96,
  98, 111, 118, 138, 159, 178, 190,
  193–95, 202–4. See also Soft
  cooperation network
Protectionism, 135, 139, 211 n.73

Quasi-integration, x, xi, 98, 108, 163, 177,
  191, 193–96; vertical, 56–57, 59,
  60–61, 102, 201

R&D, see Research and development
Recession, 6, 9–10, 12, 62, 66, 68, 71, 75,
  98, 199; global, 86; Malaysian, 33
Regionalization: of developmentalism, 34,
  55, 56, 59, 61, 63, 76, 111, 121, 176,
  177, 178, 191, 192, 199; of domestic
  production alliance, xi, 27; of
  economy, 28; of political economy, 10,
  121; of vertical keiretsu, 163
Rent-seeking, 50, 82, 83, 93, 96

Research and development, 22, 45, 51, 56,
  98, 110; diversification of, 109; in
  ASEAN-4, 84; in Taiwan, 93;
  internalization by MNCs, 13, 23, 61;
  joint efforts in, 66–67; localization of,
  103
Research Institute on Overseas Investment,
  10, 161, 188

Sanmi-ittai (trinity of economic
  cooperation), 117, 120
Shipbuilding industry, 64, 85, 89
Shukko (secondment), 125–26, 140
Similarity index, 99, 233 n.11
Singapore, xii; division of labor, 3, 23;
  economic development, 100;
  education, 83–84; employment
  system, 149, 153; exports, 189; foreign
  investment in, 10, 86, 160–61; GTCs,
  166; imports from Japan, 178; in
  regional production alliance, 25–26;
  indigenization, 154; investment in
  Asia, 6; Japan's imports from, 181–82;
  joint ventures, 35–36; labor
  movement, 147; localization, 167, 202;
  political economy, 85–87; Singapore-
  Johore-Riau Growth Triangle, 35–36;
  technology transfer, 170; US
  manufacturers in, 38
Small and medium-sized enterprises, 6, 15,
  21, 71, 129, 138, 141, 143; American,
  198; in Dalian project, 122; in joint
  ventures, 13; in Taiwan, 93; role in
  keiretsu, 30; Small and Medium
  Enterprises Agency (Japan), 158;
  supported by MITI, 187
Soft cooperation network, 5. See also
  Production alliance
Soviet Union, 200
State-owned enterprises: China, 94–95;
  Malaysia, 106; Singapore, 85; Taiwan,
  92
Steel industry, 20, 52, 64, 71, 85, 92, 97,
  184
Subcontracting: associations, 165; avenue
  of technology diffusion, 108; in home-
  based keiretsu, xi, 74, 143, 158; in
  Korea, 87–89; in regional keiretsu-like
  alliance, 9, 30, 71, 93, 122, 194; in
  Taiwan, 91; relations with parent
  companies, 22, 70, 167; transplanted
  from Japan, 16, 25, 38, 161–64, 166,
  168
Sub-regional zones, 35

Taiwan, xii, 85; division of labor, 184;
  economic development, 77, 100;

ethnic Chinese in, 132; foreign investment, 28–30; foreign investment in, 110, 161, 182; government business cooperation, 132, 203; imports from Japan, 178–80; in regional production alliance, 25–26, 37, 96; indigenization, 154; investment in Asia, 6; Japan's imports from, 181–82; Kuomintang (KMT) government, 91–92; labor movement, 147, 152; political economy, 91–94; US manufacturers in, 38

Technological Promotion Association, Thailand, 84, 110

Technology: gap with Japan, 48, 90, 98–101, 176; licensing agreements, 8, 25, 32, 37, 56, 57, 100, 104, 107, 110, 136, 164, 167, 179, 183, 185, 193, 202; technological dependence, xi, 34, 78, 88, 109, 110, 179–80, 195; transfer, ix–x, xii, 8, 13, 14, 18, 28, 31, 60, 98, 102–8, 110, 147, 155, 170, 179, 194, 196, 202

Textiles, 20, 84, 89, 92, 118, 123, 142

Thai Board of Investment, 142, 162

Thailand, xii; corruption, 137; division of labor, 3, 23, 29, 188; economic development, 77, 83, 142; education, 84; employment system, 150; ersatz capitalism, 80; ethnic Chinese in, 81–82; exports, 189; foreign investment, 28; foreign investment in, 6, 10, 30, 121, 138, 160–61, 163–64, 180, 182; government business cooperation, 135; GTCs, 126; in regional production alliance, 25–26, 34, 36–37, 140; indigenization, 154–56; Japanese advisors in, 141–42; Japanese ODA in, 125, 145, 128–29, 130; joint ventures, 24–25, 133; labor movement, 153; localization, 167, 202; promotion of FDI, 142–43; technology transfer, 98, 109–10, 170; US manufacturers in, 38

Thailand Development Research Institute, 14–15, 142, 145, 170

Theory of comparative advantage, *see* Theory of international trade

Theory of international trade: neoclassical, 43, 45, 51, 55; new, 51–52

Theory of the firm: neoclassical, 43, 55; new, 46–50

Trade, 13, 14, 75, 90, 179, 184, 175, 187; barriers, 20, 178, 186, 198, 200; deficit, 9, 21, 30, 175–76, 179, 183, 190, 195; free, 35, 38, 51–52, 67, 76, 138, 139, 144, 200, 258 n.11; friction, 54, 55, 176, 191; intrafirm/ intranetwork, 185–86, 255 n.50; intra-industry, 28, 185; managed, 52; policy, 51, 117, 138, 183, 198, 201; surplus, 9, 21, 36, 60, 117, 126, 175–76, 177, 180, 182, 183, 190, 191; trading bloc, ix–x, 115; triangular, 190–91, 198; unfair practices, 89, 177

Transaction costs, 19, 44–50, 54, 56, 64, 75, 108, 163

Transfer pricing, 31, 33, 243 n.30

Transportation industries, 14, 159

United Malay Nationalist Organization (UMNO), 133

United States, 29, 63, 69, 73, 89, 97–98, 100–1, 137, 147; American MNCs, xi, 16, 17, 38, 85, 93, 109, 153, 154–55, 185, 196; auto industry, 18, 37; exports to, 28, 36, 60, 139, 177–78, 181, 183, 188–91, 212 n.5; firms, 20, 72, 165, 188, 193; foreign aid, 40, 91, 123; foreign investment in, 5–7, 10–11, 13–15, 22, 187, 203–4; Japanese firms in, 158; joint ventures with local interests, 133; labor-management relations, 63; mistakes of, 19, 118, 187, 199; political pressure, 65, 92, 116, 125, 176, 196; protectionism, 135; role in Asia, 197–200; technology transfer, 103–7, 179; trade deficit, 175, 190

Vietnam, xii; American automakers in, 37, 196; economic growth, 192; foreign investment in, 28, 30, 127, 144; government business cooperation, 132; Mitsubishi's plan for auto industry, 34–35, 136–37; regional cooperation, 40; technology transfer, 60

World Bank, 145, 182

World Trade Organization (WTO), 196

World War II, ix, 40, 69, 73, 81, 92, 115, 132, 193, 199, 203

Yuchaku, 88

Zaibatsu (large financial cliques), xii, 69, 73. *See also* Horizontal *keiretsu*

Zoku (policy tribes), 116